THE

PUBLICATIONS

OF THE

SURTEES SOCIETY.

ESTABLISHED IN THE YEAR

M.DCCC.XXXIV.

VOL. XLVI.

FOR THE YEAR M.DCCC.LXIV.

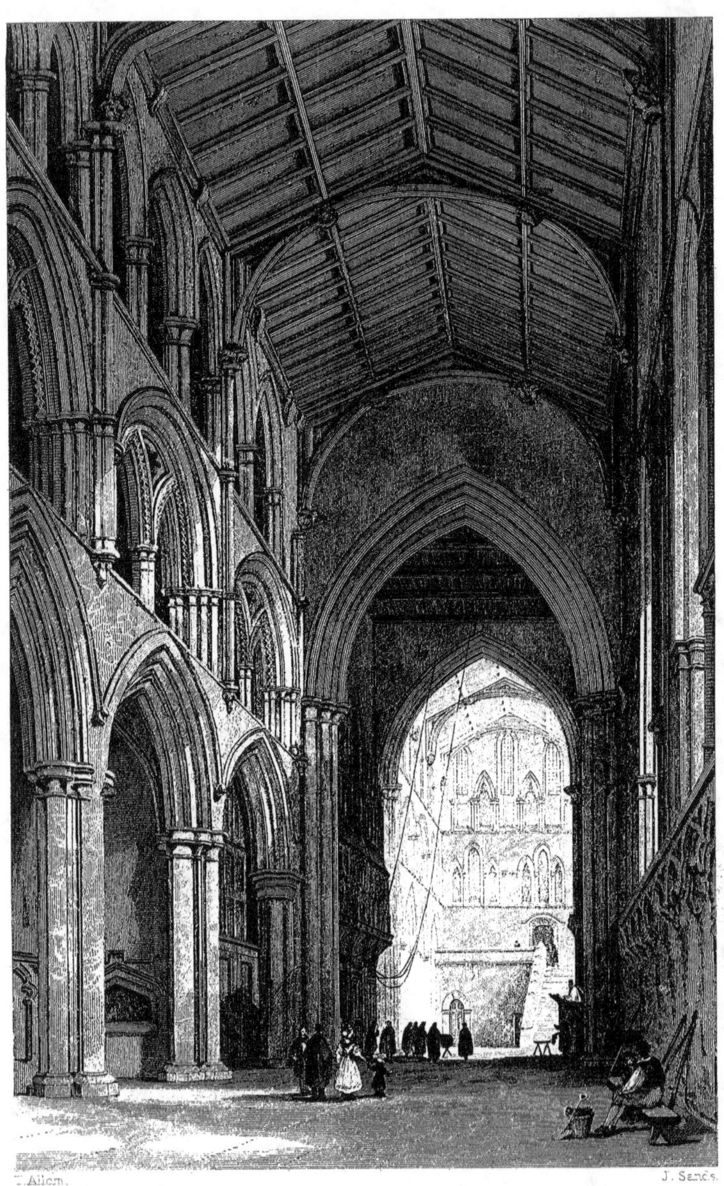

T. Allom. J. Sands.

HEXHAM CHURCH, NORTHUMBERLAND.

THE

PRIORY OF HEXHAM,

ITS

TITLE DEEDS, BLACK BOOK,

ETC.

VOL. II.

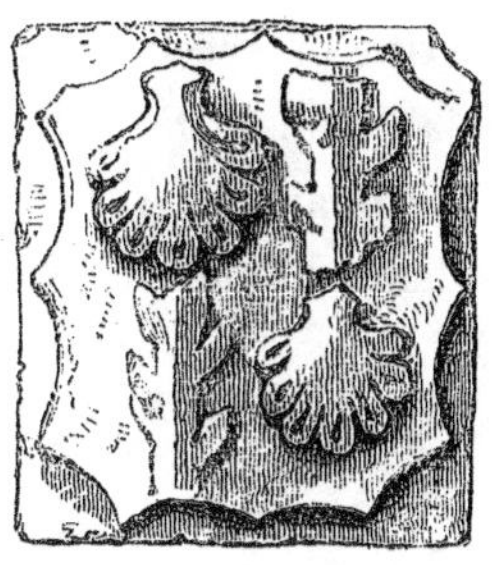

Published for the Society
BY ANDREWS AND CO., DURHAM;
WHITTAKER AND CO., 13 AVE MARIA LANE; T. AND W. BOONE,
29 NEW BOND STREET; BERNARD QUARITCH, 15 PICCADILLY;
MRS. NUTT, 277 STRAND (Foreign Agent), LONDON;
BLACKWOOD AND SONS, EDINBURGH.

1865.

At a Meeting of the Council of the SURTEES SOCIETY, held in the Castle of Durham, on Friday, the 14th of March, 1862, JOHN HODGSON HINDE, Esq., being in the chair; it was ordered "that a volume relating to Hexham should form one of the publications of the Society for 1863, and that the Secretary should be the editor."

At a General Meeting of the SURTEES SOCIETY, held in the same place, on Monday, the 15th of June, 1863, Sir WILLIAM LAWSON, Bart., in the chair, it was ordered "that the forthcoming work on Hexham should be divided into two parts."

JAMES RAINE,
Secretary.

LONDON:
MITCHELL AND HUGHES, PRINTERS, 24 WARDOUR STREET, LONDON, W.

THE PREFACE.

PART I.

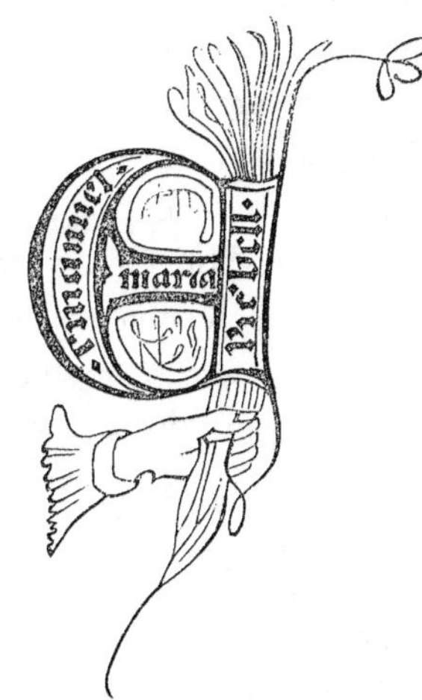

RE we proceed to the documents in this volume, some prefatorial remarks upon them may be of use and interest. The Liber Niger, or, as it is commonly called, the Black Book of Hexham, derives its name merely from the colour of the cover which it wears, like the Blue Books of the present day which are familiar to every one. Similar appellations were common enough in old times. We have the Black and Red Books of the English Exchequer, the White Register of York, the Red Book of Durham, and the Black and Red Books of Hexham. The Black Book of Hexham is a carefully drawn up rental of the possessions of the Priory. The Red Book is mentioned in the twelfth century, when we hear of some jurors taking an oath upon it.[a] It seems to have been a copy of the Gospels, a relic, perhaps, of some of the early prelates of the place; and it probably perished during some inroad of the Scots in the thirteenth century, as it is never spoken of afterwards.[b] The Red Book of Durham, which the student in history longs so ardently to discover, contained the annals of the see in Saxon times.[c]

[a] See note to p. 85. [b] Vol. I., Appendix, xxv.

[c] Hist. Dunelm. Scr. Tres, appendix, ccccxxii-v.

It is probable enough that some similar chronicle was incorporated in the Liber Ruber of Hexham.

The Black Book of Hexham is a rental of all the lands and possessions of the Prior and Convent of that place, wherever they might be. According to the title, it dates from the feast of Pentecost, 1479, but from internal evidence it is plain that the materials for the survey were being gathered together at an earlier period. In two places it is stated that a certain rent would become due for the first time at Pentecost, 1477,[d] so that this portion of the document is at all events prior to that year. The canons of Hexham had lands in places very widely apart, and some time would elapse before all the portions of the rent-roll could be prepared on anything like a regular and systematic plan. The work, probably, was going on for several years, and was not completed until 1479. The document itself is not by any means one of an unusual character, as every religious house had a similar rental. The Black Book merely took the place of an earlier document. We find in it a mention of the Old Roll.[e]

These surveys were usually compiled from the rolls of the bailiffs of each particular manor or estate, who were probably desired to be more than ordinarily exact and minute in a stated year: the rolls would be examined as they were sent in, and the information they contained would be arranged by the terrarer. It will be observed that there are now and then in the document inequalities of description. Of some places there is a fuller account than of others. This is easily explained by my supposition that the survey is merely a codification of the various bailiffs' rolls, which were drawn up with more or less care. The terrarer made the best he could of them.

The estates of the Priory of Hexham may be divided into two parts; the lands attached to the prebend of Salton, and those bestowed upon the canons in other places, and by various benefactors.

[d] pp. 8, 10. [e] p. 72.

The prebend of Salton in the cathedral church of York was annexed to the Priorate of Hexham by archbishop Thurstan in the twelfth century, and it was not only the most honourable possession of the Priory, but it was also one of the most lucrative of the estates belonging to it. The Prior of Hexham could generally rely upon the regular payment of his Yorkshire rents, as there were no Scots or thieves in that county to make his lands unprofitable. The *corpus* of the prebend consisted of the manor of Salton, and of property in Edston, Great and Little Barugh in the parish of Kirkby-Misperton, Flaxton in the parish of Bossall, Millington, and, perhaps, at Givendale. All these places, save the two last mentioned, are in the North Riding of Yorkshire.

Salton lies among the hills, about five miles from Kirkby Moorside, and almost midway between Helmsley and Malton. The Prior of Hexham had two residences there, one in the village, and another at the north end of the manor where there was a guest-hall with a *camera*, and divers other buildings attached to it. In the village itself there was a hall, with three chambers and a chapel, of which many remnants are in existence. We have some interesting materials for the history of the place. The hall seems to have been reserved for the use of the Prior and his officers, but the guest-hall was let in 1479, with the exception of a portion of the great barn, which was needed for the tithes belonging to the Prior. The Prior selected a steward or bailiff for the manor, who sent in an annual account roll,[f] and he chose besides ale-grieves, water-grieves, four jurors, and a stock-keeper. The tenants, in addition to their rents, were to contribute towards the purchase of a palfrey for every new Prior, to give to aids, to carry victuals for their lord and his suite when travelling in Yorkshire, to supply beds for his guests at Salton, to attend to the mill, and to carry stone, flint, and all kinds of timber for the repairs of the manor-

[f] Vol. I., Appendix, xxii., xxxix.

house.[g] The other constituent parts of the prebend were to make themselves similarly useful according to the extent of their land. As prebendary of Salton the Prior of Hexham had a house in York appropriated to his stall. This was let in 1457 to the parsons of the Minster; and the college of St. William, I believe, occupies its site.[h] The Prior would be very rarely in the archiepiscopal city, and would gladly be free from the incumbrance of an official residence, which he was bound to keep in repair, although he could not use it. I must leave the history of Salton to the Yorkshire topographer, and turn northwards.

Before I enter upon the general question of the estates of the Priory of Hexham, it will be well to clear the way a little by enumerating what may be called its ecclesiastical property, and to state the number of livings that it possessed. There are many documents relating to these livings in this volume, and the following list will be of some service to the reader. I have spoken elsewhere of the wretched system that prevailed of making no formal endowments for vicarages, which was exceedingly short-sighted and reprehensible.

HEXHAM. The Priory itself was the church of the parish, and a portion of it would be specially devoted to the use of the inhabitants. Every monastery, I believe, was in itself a parish. Subordinated to the parish church of Hexham were the chapels of SS. Mary and Peter in the town,[i] and those of St. John Lee, St. Oswald's, Bingfield, and Alwenton. In 1286 archbishop Romanus ordered the parishioners of Hexham to keep the chapels in repair, save the chancels, which the Prior and canons were to attend to. They were also to find a missal and a chalice for each.[j] In 1294 the same prelate cited the Prior and Convent that they might shew cause why vicars were not properly instituted at Hexham and Alwenton.[k] In the beginning of the

[g] See pp. 72-6, also pp. 83-4, 154-5.

[h] pp. 152-3.

[i] Vol. I., pp. 14-15; II., p. 123.

[j] See pp. 102-3.

[k] Ibid., 106-7.

next century archbishop Greenfield again took up the question of the vicars, but he was stopped by the production of a bull of Alexander IV., releasing the Prior and Convent from the duty of creating them.[l]

ALSTON, a Northumbrian rectory. The advowson was given to Hexham by Ivo de Veteri-Ponte, together with the chapel of Gerard's Gill.[m] It was recovered from the Prior and Convent in a suit at law by Edward I., but was restored to them towards the close of his reign.[n] In 1335 they begged Edward III. for leave to have the revenues of the living appropriated to them.[o] This did not take place until 1378, when it was done by Thomas Hatfield, bishop of Durham. A proper endowment of the vicarage was not made until the year 1420.[p]

WARDEN. This church belonged to the Priory by the gift of Adam de Tindale.[q] A pension of twenty marks per annum out of it was reserved to the bishops of Durham, and this was granted by King John in the sixteenth year of his reign to Robert Morell.[r] In 1243 there was a re-ordination of the vicarage, and the stipend of the vicar was fixed at thirty-six marks per annum.[s] As Warden was so near to Hexham, it was frequently held by a canon. According to the Augustinian rule, no canon could live out of his monastery, unless he had a brother with him. In 1337 this rule was disregarded, and its observance was ordered by archbishop Melton.[t] Dependent on the church of Warden in 1297 were the chapels of Stancroft, Hayden, and Langley.[u]

CHOLLERTON. This living, together with its chapels of Birtley, Chipchase, Gunnerton, East Swinburn, Little Heton,

[l] Ibid., 121, etc. [m] Hodgson's Northumberland, iii., part ii., 36.

[n] See p. 119. [o] Rot. Parl., ii., 77.

[p] Hodgson's Northumberland, ii., part iii., 82-6, where these documents are printed.

[q] See p. 110. [r] See p. 91.

[s] Hodgson's Northumberland, ii., part iii., 160, etc.; iii., part ii., 408.

[t] Vol. I., Appendix, xxxix., xl. [u] See p. 110.

and Colwell, was given to Hexham by Odonel d'Umfreville.[v] The deed of gift and the ordination of the vicarage are lost, and there is but one document in existence relating to the place in connection with the Priory, and that refers to the chapel at Chipchase.[w]

STAMFORDHAM. In 1245 Nicholas, bishop of Durham, appropriated to Hexham the tithes of East Matfen, Nesbit, Ulkeston, Hawkwell, and Bitchfield, a payment of fifty marks per annum to be made out of them to the bishops of Durham.[x] In the 33rd of Edward I. the king granted the advowson to the Priory, having recovered it in a court of law against the bishop of Durham, and Edward II. confirmed his father's gift.[y] In 1340 bishop Bury, in a time of emergency, reduced the annual payment to himself out of the living from fifty to forty marks.[z] Stamfordham was a vicarage usually held by a canon of Hexham, and the same order was made about it in 1311 and 1337 as was made about Warden.[a]

SLALEY. This chapel was given to Hexham in the time of Henry III. by Gilbert de Slaley.[b]

OVINGHAM. This living, which, like those already named, is in Northumberland, was appropriated to Hexham in 1378 by bishop Hatfield, the presentation having been previously given by Henry Percy, earl of Northumberland. Gilbert d'Umfreville, earl of Angus, was the originator of Earl Percy's gift, and the three canons and the vicar who were placed at Ovingham were bound to pray for the two earls and Richard II. Ovingham was thus made a cell of Hexham.[c]

THE HOSPITAL OF ST. GILES AT HEXHAM. This place, as the name of the Saint betokens, was built for the reception of

[v] See p. 111. [w] See pp. 98-9.

[x] Ibid., pp. 115-116. Hodgson's Northumberland, ii., part iii., 105-7.

[y] See p. 118. [z] Ibid., 136-7.

[a] Vol. I., Appendix, xxxix, xlix. [b] See p. 112.

[c] Vol. I., Preface, c-ci. Hodgson's Northumberland, ii., part iii., 97-101. I have not reprinted the deed of appropriation, as Mr. Hodgson gives it with sufficient fulness.

lepers. The founder was one of the early archbishops of York, probably Thomas II. or Thurstan. There is a deed preserved, by which, on Feb. 16th, 1200-1, King John allowed the lepers to be exempt in all that they buy or sell from the payment of the tolls of pontage and passage on the royal lands in Yorkshire and Northumberland.[d] In 1320 an enquiry was made into the condition of the hospital, which tells us much about its history. The name of its founder was lost, for the muniments of the place had been carried away by a brother, who fled from the Scots. They caught and killed him, and his freight perished. The estates of the hospital were literally nothing. All its arable land could easily be cultivated by a single plough. An annual rent-charge of 11s. 2d. on property in Hexham, Fallowfield, and Portgate produced nothing, as the places were waste. Before the war the brethren received daily from the Priory four loaves of black bread and four *lagenæ* of secondary beer or ale, and a *lagena* when any one brewed on the Prior's land in Hexham: now, they got nothing save six black loaves and two *lagenæ* of secondary beer a week. We learn, also, that the hospital was founded for poor sick husbandmen, born within the liberty, who were lepers. Each archbishop and each prior could appoint two of his own tenants, and no more. Thus there could not be more than four brethren of their nomination in the hospital at one time, but any one might be admitted by the leave of the master on paying a sufficient sum for his maintenance. In 1320 the property of the hospital was barely sufficient for three brothers, and, to live in it, they were obliged to work hard. Formerly there were seven or eight inmates; now, in their present poverty, none could be admitted without paying. They have but four *affri* and four oxen for their plough, two of each being lent; and their corn is scarcely sufficient for the year's sowing.[e]

One or two orders from the archbishops for the admission of

[d] See p. 89. [e] See pp. 130-2.

brothers have been preserved.[f] The following is a list of the wardens or masters of the hospital, as far as I have been able to make it out. It seems probable that the office was occasionally vacant.

1274, August 20. Dan Walter de Scrapetoft, collated by the archbishop during his stay at Hexham.[g]

1313, June 11. Robert le Porter collated.[h]

1318, April 26. Robert de Whelpington, Prior of Hexham, coll.[i]

1331, July 4. Dan William, son of Walter, the fuller, of Hexham, priest, coll.[j]

1334, July 14. Dan Robert de Ferghan, of Corbridge, chaplain, coll.[k]

1343-4, Feb. 2. Dan Robert de Ferghan, of Corbridge, chaplain, apparently re-appointed.[l]

1354, May 5. Roger de Clone, domestic chaplain of the archbishop.[m]

1354, July 20. Mr. William de Fenton collated on Clone's resignation.[n]

1359, August 6. John, son of William de Ridshawe, sen., coll. He resigned in 1377-8.[o]

When Ridshawe resigned, a great change took place in the condition of the hospital. It was so poor that it scarcely contained any inmates, and few, if any, cared to be master. Archbishop Neville, therefore, made it over to the Prior and canons, obliging them to maintain two poor men either within the hospital or their priory, and to find a chaplain to perform service

[f] See p. 129. On March 8, 1345-6, the corrody held by Robert de Aldencrawe during his life in the hospital of Hexham was granted to John de Fossceton (Reg. archiep. Zouche, 292 *b*).

1336, April 17. Breve nov. disseis., Mr. et Fratres hosp. *v.* Prior. et Conv. de Hexham. Lib. ten. in Hexham (Reg. Melton, 437 *a*).

[g] Reg. archiep. Giffard, 112.

[h] Reg. Greenfield, ii., 40 *b*. He is appointed to provide fitting sustenance for the brothers and *sisters*.

[i] Reg. Melton, 400 *b*.

[j] Ibid., 430 *a*.

[k] Ibid., 434 *a*.

[l] Reg Zouche, 291 *b*.

[m] Reg. Thoresby, 26 *b*.

[n] Reg. Thoresby, 26 *b*.

[o] Ibid., 302 *b*. Reg. Neville, i., 90 *b*.

in the chapel of the hospital once a week.[p] This arrangement seems only to have been a temporary one, as I find several masters appointed subsequently.

1398, July 18. John Martyn, the archbishop's domestic chaplain.[q]

Thomas Parker.

1409, June 28. Nicholas Tydd, clerk, collated, exchanging for it with Parker a stall in St. Sepulchre's chapel at York.[r]

1409, July 24. Mr. John Storthwayte collated.[s]

The hospital, however, seems to have reverted to the Priory, and was in its possession at the Dissolution, when it was said to be worth 13s. 4d. a year; it comprised the house and thirty-two acres of arable land attached to it.[t] It then fell into lay hands, and is now the residence of the family of Kirsopp, bearing the name of the Spital. There are some fragments of old walls still preserved, and a figure carved in oak, supposed to commemorate St. Giles.

Renwick in Cumberland. This living and the next belonged to Hexham certainly in the thirteenth century. The Prior and canons made out their title to them before the bishop of Carlisle in 1359.[u]

Isell, in the same county.

Salton, in the North Riding of Yorkshire. This living, attached to the prebend, belonged to Hexham from the time of archbishop Thurstan. There was an ordination of it made in 1312.[v] In 1344 it was retaxed on account of the injuries done to it by the Scots.[w] The records of the visitations of the church and parish in 1473, 1481, and 1519 have been preserved.[x]

Edston, in the same district, was granted to Hexham in the twelfth century. The donor is stated in one place to have been archbishop Roger,[y] in another Hugo de Twithe.[z] In 1310 there was an ordination of the vicarage, great irregularities

[p] See pp. 145-7. [q] Reg. Scrope, 106 *a*. [r] Reg. Bowet, i., 271 *a*.
[s] Ibid. [t] See p. 159. [u] Ibid., pp. 142-3. [v] Ibid., p. 128.
[w] Ibid., p. 138. [x] Ibid., pp. 155-7. [y] Ibid., p. 86.
[z] Coll. Top. et Geneal., vi., 39.

having existed previously.[a] There is an inscription in Saxon characters on a sun-dial above the church porch.

Ilkley, in the West Riding of Yorkshire. The canons had the right of presenting to this living by the gift of Henry Percy, earl of Northumberland. In 1378 archbishop Neville at their urgent request appropriated the living to them, and made an ordination of a vicarage.[b]

We now come to the landed estates of the Prior and Convent of Hexham, which were situated in four of the Northern counties, Yorkshire, Durham, Northumberland, and Cumberland. With regard to three of these counties it will be unnecessary to say much. Passing by the manor of Salton and its appendages, the Yorkshire property of the Priory of Hexham was only in four places, Great and Little Broughton, the extinct parish of Kirkby in Cleveland and Ingleby. This, which was of no great annual value, was given to the canons by various persons in the twelfth and thirteenth centuries. They had at one time a house in Goodramgate in York of the gift of Sunnulphus the priest;[c] unless we are to suppose, perhaps, that this was the official residence of the prebendary of Salton. In the county of Durham there was property belonging to Hexham at Green Heley near Muggleswick, Fenhall and Maidenstanhall in the parish of Lanchester, Kimblesworth near Durham, Stainton le Street, a house or two in Hartlepool, and some valuable lands in Silksworth and its vicinity, which were given by the Fitz Marmadukes.[d] In Cumberland some lands in the parishes of Isell

[a] See pp. 125-8. [b] Ibid., pp. 147-151. [c] Vol. I., 59.

[d] Among the evidences of the Dean and Chapter of Durham, iii., 7, Specialium, is the following deed, which is preserved there because the Prior and Convent of that place had lands in Silksworth:—"Hæc indentura testatur quod Ricardus filius Johannis filii Marmaduci remisit—Priori et Conventui de Hextildesham totum jus et clamium quod habuit—in omnibus terris et tenementis quæ prædicti Prior et Conventus habuit—de dono et concessione antecessorum suorum in Silksworth. Remisit etiam—totum jus et clamium quod habuit—in redditu cujusdam paris botarum—una cum multura et secta molendini sui in Silkesworth. Data Dunelmiæ iiij die mensis Aprilis, anno Domini mcccxij°." (Small oval seal of the Priorate of Hexham, engraved in Vol. I. Preface, cxl.)

and Renwick belonged to them, which had probably been given by Waldeve and Alan his son. They had also, at one time, a herring-fishery somewhere on the coast of Allerdale, which cannot be traced. In Carlisle they had one or two plots of ground with a house or two upon them of the gift of David king of Scotland and Henry his son.[e]

But it was in Northumberland that the Priory of Hexham had the bulk of its property, and it was very large indeed. It was chiefly in Tindale ward, and it is not too much to say that from the borders of Cumberland to Newcastle-on-Tyne there was no parish in which the Prior and canons had not a large interest. They could not have had less than twenty thousand acres of land in Northumberland. To know how all these came to the Priory we must look at the great *Inspeximus* of 1297, in which, immediately after a Scottish invasion in which the muniments of the canons had been consumed, their possessions were formally settled and assured to them by the verdict of a jury. We thus have not only a list of their Northumbrian estates, but the names of the persons who gave them. The greater part of these benefactions seems to have been made in the twelfth century or soon after it. Passing by the archbishops of York and their numerous gifts, we find among the donors many of the great potentates and barons of Northumberland. First and foremost is David king of Scotland, with his son and grandson prince Henry and William the Lion. Superior to his royal masters in munificence was Adam de Tindale, who bestowed upon the Prior and canons the manor and church of Warden with its numerous chapelries, and his lands at Byres. The illustrious family of Umfreville had many claims upon the gratitude of the house of Hexham, and the canons at Ovingham, when they prayed for the soul of Gilbert Umfreville, the last earl of Angus of that line, would call to mind a noble ancestor of their benefactor who bore both his names, together with Odonel and

[e] Ibid., ii., 14.

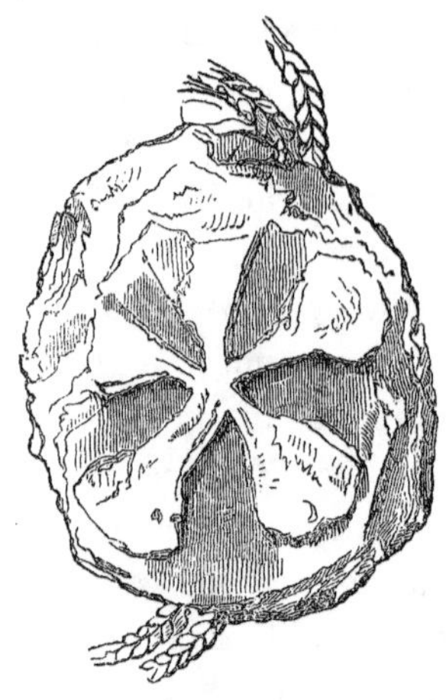

Richard Umfreville,[f] who were barons of renown in the days of Henry II. and his ill-fated sons. Richard Cumin, who with Hextilda his lady gave to the Priory the hamlet of Carraw, and other lands at Stonecroft and elsewhere, was a person of great note as well in himself as in his posterity. The bede-roll of the Priory contained the great names of Balliol, Merley, Bertram, Vipont, and Bolbeck; and, beneath them, was a goodly undergrowth of ancient gentlemen and knights, the L'Isles, the Thirlwalls, the Delavals, the Fenwicks, and the Fetherstanhaughs.

Subsequent to the great Inquisition of 1297, very few estates seem to have been acquired by the Priory. The extreme poverty in which the numerous invasions of the Scots had plunged it evoked an occasional gift, but land at that time was of little value in Northumberland, and the stringent law of mortmain was a great bar to its being acquired. Some estates indeed did accrue to the canons, and their ecclesiastical property

[f] This seal, representing the rude cinquefoil of the Umfrevilles, is on white wax, and is appended to its deed by green silk strings. The document is among the vast and priceless stores of the Dean and Chapter of Durham, and runs as follows. The number is i., 3, Specialium :—"Sciant præsentes et futuri quod ego, Ricardus de Humfranvilla concessi, et dedi, et hac præsenti carta confirmavi Willelmo filio Pagani, pro homagio et servitio suo, sexdecim acras terræ et dimidiam in campo de Prudhou, quas Ricardus Helle tenuit, cum communi pastura, et omnibus aliis aysiamentis ad prædictam villam pertinentibus. Præterea concessi et dedi prædicto Willelmo octo acras terræ de vasto meo, ex orientali parte terræ quam dedi Nicholao filio Huctredi. Tenendum ——— reddendo inde annuatim mihi et hæredibus meis unam libram piperis—pro omni servitio, excepto forinseco servitio, quantum pertinet ad tantam terram in eadem villa. Molet etiam ad molendinum meum sine multura danda, et quietus erit de pannagio propriorum porcorum suorum.—Hiis testibus Gaufrido filio Gaufridi, Gaufrido de Luci, Otuero de Insula, Roberto filio Roberti, Od' de Buruchdene,

became more extended, but we may fairly assume that the Black Book contains nearly the whole of their possessions. It is, therefore, especially to the Northumbrian antiquary, a document of exceeding value. The remarks that I shall now make upon it are merely suggestive of farther enquiry, and must necessarily be brief.

In the first place it is evident that the rent-roll of the Priory was decreasing. Places are mentioned as lying waste which were at one time in cultivation and productive, and the receipts, generally, were lower than they had been.[g] This no doubt was caused in the first instance by the misery which followed the incursions of the Scots, and these inroads were succeeded by a complete disorganization of society in Tindale. Thieves and marauders were plentiful on both sides of the Borders, but Hexhamshire seems to have been their stronghold. The farmers and tenants must have been poor men. They only held a few acres of land, and of these acres the produce was precarious. Oftentimes the sleeper was aroused by the crackling of the flames in the roof of his straw-thatched cottage or his barn. Oftentimes the steer or cow, which was left at night in the little toft or croft, would, ere the morrow's sun, be threading the passes of Redesdale, on its way to a Scottish market. Losses made the tenant careless, and carelessness made his scanty rent a burden to him. It sank lower and lower, for the canons found it better to get a smaller rent than none at all. The inmates of religious houses in general were easy landlords, and that on the highest grounds: live and let live was their principle, and they considered that their tenants had an interest in their lands as well as themselves. In this manner the proverbial hospitality of

Waltero Batail, Roberto de Fenwic, Petro de Insula, Willelmo de Suetope, Hugone de Hele, Johanne de Herle, Thoma Danenli, Henrico de Alemannia, Willelmo de Haweltun, et multis aliis."

[g] The same falling off is observable in the Rental of the Priory of Durham made in 1446 (Hist. Dunelm. Scr. Tres, appendix, cclxxxix, *et seqq.*). It was produced, probably, by the same causes.

Hexham was exemplified on every estate that it possessed. A lenient landlord, however, was not the person to have such tenants as were to be found in Tindale. The rents fell, and, although small, were often unpaid. Land was neglected, and then passed out of cultivation. Houses became ruins; the very sites of villages were ploughed up; and the population would gradually decrease. It is said that, a century ago, there was but little tillage land in Tindale. The Black Book will shew that even in the dark days of the canons of Hexham a very different state of things prevailed. If this evidence were wanting, the lay-riggs, as they are called, which the rich sward of untold years has been unable to obliterate, still shew decisively that in days long gone by the ploughman and the sower have been there.

To form some idea of the manner in which the Prior and Convent of Hexham wished to arrange and manage their estates, it will be well to take as an example one or two places which were contiguous to their abode, and consequently under their own eye. It is reasonable to suppose that these would be regarded as model farms or estates.[h] Take, for instance, the system that prevailed at Anwick, Kirk-heaton, Dalton, and Nesbit. In all these places the land is divided out between three kinds of tenants, whom we may call farmers, husbandmen, and cottagers. It is most observable, that every person seems to have had some portion of land, and there was no better way in Tindale to make the land productive and its cultivators honest and industrious.

1. The farmers at Anwick were the canons themselves: at the other places they were persons who held the lands either by homage, or by lease. They were the chief persons in the villages, and had the largest share of land.

[h] The older divisions of land were dying out. In 1297 the carucate was common enough, as we learn by the Inspeximus. It is only mentioned twice in the Black Book in connection with Northumberland. See pp. 38-9. At Whalton a carucate is said to have consisted of 105 acres. We find carucates and oxgangs retained on the Yorkshire estates.

2. Husbands or husbandmen. A husband-land was a stated quantity varying according to the landlord's will, and scarcely the same in any two places. In Anwick there were twelve husband-lands, each of sixteen acres of arable and meadow land. In Dalton there were nineteen husband-lands, eleven of twenty-three acres and eight of sixteen. In Nesbit there were nineteen husband-lands, each of twenty-five acres. In Sandhoe and Bingfield a husband-land consisted of twenty-four acres. In Kirk-heaton it was as much as thirty-four. As the number of acres was larger, the rent per acre was lower, thus shewing that the best land was let in the smallest quantities. In Presdale, near Alston, a husband-land contained twenty-four acres, or two oxgangs.

3. Cottagers. In Anwick there were nineteen cottagers to twelve husbandmen, each cottager having his cottage and a portion of land. One has as much as nine acres, but most of the others have less than five. In Dalton there were but seven cottagers, all of whom save one had a cottage and three acres of land. In Nesbit there were four cottagers, each with a cottage and three acres of land. In Sandhoe there were twelve cottagers, each having a house and an acre of land or less. In Bingfield there were twelve cottagers, most of whom had six acres of land. In Kirk-heaton there were eight cottagers, each having between three and seven acres of land. One has as much as thirteen acres, but it was waste. Originally each cottager in this place had seven acres of ground. Occasionally a garden appertains to a cottage.

The annual rent of these lands, and of all the other meadow and arable ground in Northumberland belonging to the Priory, ran from sixpence to a shilling an acre, and the rent of a cottage seems to have been eighteenpence or two shillings. In addition to this there were various services and duties for which the tenants were responsible, and which varied slightly in different places—a few days' works at the mill or at hedging, and the gift of a cock or a hen to the landlord—but in no cases were they burdensome; and the addition to the rent which they caused would in no case exceed twopence per acre. We have thus a pretty good idea of the sums which accrued to the canons of Hexham from their best land, and of the way in which that land was portioned out.

Another class of persons peeps out now and then, for it still existed, and that is the serfs. In Eachwick they held certain portions of land called *bondagia* (there were seven of them), each *bondagium* consisting of twenty-four acres of arable land and meadow.[i] The serfs also appear here and there throughout the whole rental under the title of *nativi domini.* It is evident that, whatever their social position was, they could hold land, and they are generally to be found among the cottagers. And yet in the eye of the law they were really slaves, and belonged to their lords as much as the negro did to the planter. At an earlier period I have discovered several documents in which an archbishop of York sells a *nativus* and his wife and children, bag and baggage. Such transactions were common enough.

As a general rule, the Prior and canons let all their lands in a particular place to one person or set of persons. The lessees had their own sub-tenants and cottagers, but that was a matter in which the canons of Hexham had no interest, and such matters are not mentioned in their Rental. They content themselves with making a most minute description of the various lands that belonged to them in every place. We see also that, like other monastic bodies, the Prior and canons appropriated estates to the use of various offices within their house. Several belonged to the bursar and the sacrist. The cellarer of the kitchen had, very properly, a large share, and the spicery of the convent was not forgotten.

It is very difficult to understand how, with all their care, the canons, or any other landowners in the North, were able to understand what lands were really their own. Even that part of the country which was under cultivation was very often

[i] See p. 45.

unenclosed. This accounts for the very careful way in which the boundaries of so many of the estates of Hexham are stated in the Black Book. If the owners of land had now and then as a limit one of the few hedges that existed (there were no stone walls), or, better than that, the course of a brook or burn, they were most fortunate; very often there was a syke or ditch that separated them from a neighbour, but frequently there seems merely to have been some imaginary line pointing to a saugh or willow, or some standing stone, as it was called, the relic of a still wilder age. Meres or boundary stones were common enough upon the moors. More puzzling than anything else seems to have been the possession of half-acres, or roods, or perches in the middle of a field. It seems probable that several landowners combined occasionally to assart or rid a piece of moor or woodland, and that they divided it among themselves in small portions, one adjoining to or overlapping the other, like the allotments in the common garden of a village, although far more difficult to distinguish.[j] To ascertain the rights of the several landlords, it was customary to take the verdict of a jury.[k] The canons seem to have had no idea of uniting their property, as they might have done, by exchange or otherwise. Probably they had no desire to part with even a fragment of land which had been made solemnly over to them; and they held it on, as its donor wished, often with little or no profit and at much inconvenience. It is singular that when their lands were in this condition, and their ancient muniments lost, we find so few attempts made to wrest any of their possessions from the canons: but many others were in the same plight.

The Prior and Convent had many wild moors within their territories, and on them it was even more difficult to say what

[j] This system was necessary to allow to each tenant his portion of each kind of land, just as in modern enclosures of commons a man often gets a piece of the more and a piece of the less improvable kind.—W. H. D. L.

[k] See pp. 41, 50.

really belonged to them. The meres were insecure boundaries, and it was for the most part necessary to have an understanding with the adjacent proprietors, by which their cattle could either have their rake together, or, if they transgressed, that no mischief should ensue. There is little said of the native woods with which the country must have abounded, filled with oaks and ashes, and with a goodly undergrowth of hazel and holly, yew and ivy. We find little allusion to the game, which must have been plentiful everywhere. The canons had two fisheries for salmon at Newburn, but the vicar of that place had his nets, and paid well for his sport.[l] Above that place no fisheries on the Tyne are recorded, although that river was open to the canons wherever their own and the archbishop's lands adjoined it,[m] so that it is probable that the lock at Bywell was in existence, which checked the run of the salmon. The canons, however, had enclosed parks of their own, and by an early grant of Edward I. they had the right of free warren on several of their estates.[n] The visitations of their house shew that they were only too ready to join in the chase.[o] They would look with some envy upon Master Peter de Insula, who, with his brother, Sir John, had a wider range than themselves, and could follow the chase over the whole of the archbishop's lands in Hexhamshire.[p]

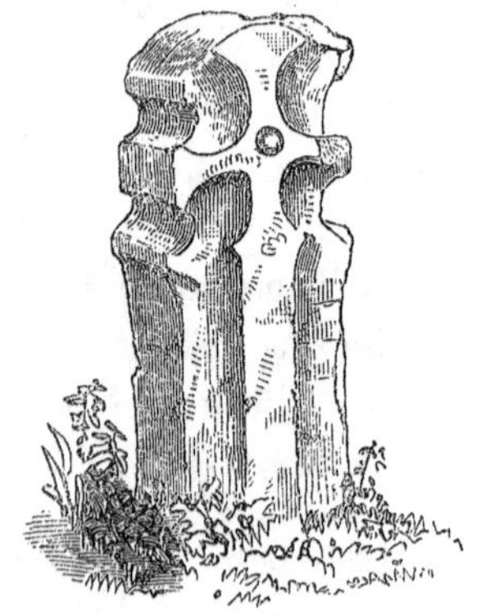

Several objects are mentioned in the Black Book which served now and then as landmarks, and to these a peculiar interest still attaches itself. A wayside cross occurs here and there, and seems to have occupied the place in which we so often erect a milestone. The accompanying engraving shews one that remains in a garden at Warden, to which it has

[l] See p. 56. [m] See pp. 104-5. [n] See pp. 103-4.
[o] Vol. I., xix, xxxviii. [p] Reg. archiep. Greenfield, ii., 54 *a*.

been removed from its old position. The standing-stones are memorials of early British or Celtic tribes, and some of them still exist to remind us painfully how entirely ignorant we are of the history of the earliest inhabitants of our island.[q] The Roman wall is mentioned once or twice, and the Prior of Hexham, from his tower at Carraw, could look out upon an extensive reach of that magnificent barrier, out of which, no doubt, his fortalice was constructed. The occasional occurrence of the word Chester appended to a place makes us think that we have the site of some mile-castle or camp in connection either with the wall or the Watling-street.[r] That singular word Deer-street is several times used for the Watling-street.[s] It occurs also in Symeon's History of St. Cuthbert,[t] and in a deed connected with the abbey of Melrose. Does it mean the road to or from Deira? or the Forest Road? That ancient and mysterious boundary the Black-dyke is also mentioned, and we have the Maiden-gate, and the Carlisle-gate,[u] which is the great Roman road between Carlisle and Newcastle.

The Black Book contains but few notices of unusual services and tenures. Some of the tenants in Durham and Yorkshire were bound to provide lodging, hay, straw, fuel, and candles for the Prior when he paid them a visit. No races of ginger, nor grains of pepper, nor a rose in the proper season of the year, are mentioned: an occasional cock or hen for the Prior's larder is, perhaps, the only addition to the almost universal money-payment. The Prioress of Lambley, in return for some privileges at Byres, supplied a decent towel or board-cloth annually for the Prior's table.[v] One curious custom must not be forgotten. The wife of the lord of Dissington was bound to

[q] These stones are generally plain, but at Rischeles (p. 17) there was a cross-standing stone.

[r] See pp. 7, 31, 37, 48-9. [s] See pp. 5, 7, 9.

[t] Apud Twysden, coll. 70, 74. Mr. Longstaffe informs me that the name occurs in Sykes's Local Records under the year 1716.

[u] See pp. 7, 15, 17, 22, 23. [v] See p. 22.

present at the high altar of Hexham on St. Andrew's day two corporax cloths, to free the Prior's tenants at Eachwick from any charge for moulter. For the same reason the husband of the lady was to rise whenever the Prior of Hexham met him and to offer him his seat, unless his ecclesiastical superior condescended to bid him retain his place.[w] May not this custom have been some kind of a perpetuation of an acknowledgment of the offence of Edgar, son of Earl Cospatric, and Robert and Uctred Fitz Meldred, who assaulted the suite of the Prior at Dissington in the twelfth century, and slew three of his servants?[x]

The names assigned to the different fields and portions of estates in Tyndale will attract the attention of the philologist. The ingenuity of successive landowners must have been often taxed to create so many appellations, and it would be interesting to know whether, as a general rule, they are still used. Occasionally most suggestive names are found. At Colden there was a curiously-shaped rock called Colden Kirk, and in the same place there was a Trow-hill and a Trow-burn, a trow being a fairy.[y] In Presdale, near Alston, there was a Fiends'-fell,[z] which carries us at once to a less gentle influence that that of the good people. Dedmansyke[a] makes the lover of good Border ballads, even though they are occasionally spurious, think of the Deadman's shaw, at which one of the Fetherstonhaughs is said to have been killed. Ravenstan-more[b] tells us of a resting-place of a bird which was at one time a regular inhabitant of many parts of the county. But ravens and red deer, and many of the birds and beasts which were once so common in Tindale, are no longer to be found there.

The Black Book must now be left to the reader. To throw more light on the subject of which it treats, I have appended to it all the deeds connected with the Priory of Hexham and its estates that have occurred to me. It will be seen that they have been derived from many sources, and that they are by no

[w] See p. 43. [x] Vol. I., p. 95. [y] See p. 34.
[z] Ibid., p. 20. [a] Ibid., p. 43. [b] Ibid., p. 50.

means numerous. No trouble, however, has been spared in gathering them together. The greatest number is to be found in the registers of the archbishops and the dean and chapter of York. When Dodsworth, the antiquary, visited Hexham in 1638, he made notes of some deeds which he discovered in the possession of Sir John Fenwick, the then lord of the manor. A most careful search after these documents has been altogether fruitless. They are not in Mr. Beaumont's muniment-box, nor are they in the possession either of Sir Walter Calverley Trevelyan or Sir Edward Blackett, the representatives of the two lines of the family of Blackett. I have also been unable to find them at Castle Howard among the papers belonging to the famous Sir John Fenwick, which came into the possession of his brother-in-law, the earl of Carlisle. It is probable that these charters have been destroyed long ago. There is no chartulary of Hexham in existence. I must, however, make an exception in favour of a fragment of a charter-book formerly belonging to Ralph Thoresby, of Leeds, and now in the possession of Mr. John Gough Nichols, one of the treasurers of this Society. A pretty full abstract of this is printed in the Collectanea Topographica.[c] It consists merely of fourteen folios of a small quarto size, and it relates exclusively to the Yorkshire property of the Priory. I should have liked to have given this manuscript entire, but its owner has unfortunately mislaid it.

The registers at York contain many documents relating to the archbishop's regality of Hexham and his officers. These will probably be given on some other occasion by themselves. It would be perplexing to mix them up in this volume with the papers which relate exclusively to the Priory.

[c] Vol. vi., pp. 38-46.

THE PREFACE.

PART II.

THE ARCHITECTURE OF HEXHAM PRIORY.

THE chief entrance to the close was formerly through a gate-house on the north side of the conventual church, now partially ruined. It appears to have been built about the close of the twelfth century, and was divided inside into three bays, the archways at each end being semi-circular. The first bay from the north formed an open vestibule or porch, crossed, at its eastern extremity, by a thick wall, now removed; in which, when Mr. Hutchinson wrote his View of Northumberland in 1778, was "a large gateway for horsemen and carriages, and a narrow one for foot passengers."[d] A walled-up doorway on the west side communicated with the porter's lodge, of which no other traces remain. The vaulting has been removed within memory, but Mr. Hutchinson describes it as "of ribbed arching, meeting in the centre; the interstices filled with thin stones or bricks, such as are seen in Roman works." Mr. Pennant says that "this gate is of the old Saxon architecture, and perhaps part of the labours of the great Wilfrid." In a fence wall, built after the Reformation, and leading from the east side of this gate-house towards the church, are many large stones which evidently have formed part of a Saxon building. Similar stones may be also seen in the western boundary of the churchyard.

The earliest church at Hexham was begun by Wilfrid in 674. The most intelligible description of it has been given us

[d] Vol. i., p. 106.

by Prior Richard in his History of the Church of Hexham, although many most desirable particulars are omitted. He says that it was an edifice of immense length and height, and divided into three stories, in which we recognize an arcade, and consequently aisles, a triforium and a clerestory. The capitals of the columns and the "*arcus sanctuarii*" were enriched with sculptures and painting. The nave was surrounded (he does not say whether continuously or not) "*appentitiis et porticibus,*" which may have been a series of chapels placed at right angles with the nave, and on each side open to it. In these appendages or porticoes, which must have been chambered,—since some of them retained so much elevation as to appear like fortresses and towers in Prior Richard's day,—Wilfrid instituted, both above and below, altars in honour of the Virgin Mary, St. Michael the Archangel, St. John Baptist, and other holy Apostles, Martyrs, Confessors, and Virgins. The church had also "*cochleæ,*" or lofty round towers, probably placed at the west end, in a similar position as the "*cochleæ*" represented in a plan of the monastery of St. Gall, which will be found in the fifth volume of the Archæological Journal. This monastery was begun in the year 829, and its arrangements may form suggestive illustrations of Prior Richard's description of the church of Hexham. The founder also surrounded the *atrium*, or site of the church, with a wall of great substance and strength, and conducted water through the town in a stone channel to the offices of the monastery. Not many years ago, some earthenware pipes were found fitted neatly into each other *in situ* in the vicinity of the Manor office, which are supposed to have formed part of this aqueduct; but the peculiar mode in which the centre or core has been screened out of the tube resembles that found in Roman examples,[e] which, however, Wilfrid may have copied. When our author wrote, the extensive foundations of many other of Wilfrid's buildings were apparent, which

[e] Three of these tubes are now in the possession of Mr. Fairless.

had been devastated and ruined during the lapse of nearly five hundred years.

The building of which Wilfrid was the founder seems to have been completed by Acca, his friend and successor. It continued uninjured until the year 875, when every part of the monastery, except the stone-work, was destroyed in an invasion of the Danes. It is possible that some attempts at restoration may have been soon made, but they did not succeed. Some years after the Conquest, Eilaf, the priest of Hexham, was the first person to renovate his ruined church. He put new roofs on the old walls, and did his best to make things seemly and decent. This brings the architectural history of Hexham down to the time of Prior Richard in the middle of the twelfth century. It is evident from his description that the stone-work of the Priory in his day was the same that Wilfrid had erected in the seventh century.

I shall now speak more minutely about the remains of Saxon work at Hexham. This is a point of the very deepest interest, because at no other place in England do we find Christian architecture brought into closer contact with the handiwork of Roman builders, native as well as foreign. Wilfrid, we are expressly told, had a number of Italian and French masons in his employ, and I think that some of their work may still be recognized. At Ripon, when any excavation is made on the site of Wilfrid's monastery, a number of small white tesseræ are discovered such as are only found in this country in or near Roman camps. In the chapel of St. Mary Magdalene, close to the same town, before the altar, lies a coloured tesselated pavement which cannot but be traced to the same source, and which has evidently been constructed to fill a position such as it at present occupies. At Hexham Wilfrid and his band of artizans found on the spot, and in its immediate vicinity, the remains of Roman buildings of considerable grandeur and importance, and his workmen would recognize with pleasure the workmanship of kindred hands. There are a few sculptured

W.H.D. Longstaffe, del^t. J.H. Le Keux, sc.

CROSS AT THE SPITAL, NEAR HEXHAM.

stones at Hexham, which will be alluded to hereafter, which it is difficult to appropriate with certainty either to Christian or Pagan hands. With regard to the church that Wilfrid built at Hexham, we are told plainly that in this country it was unsurpassed; and that in sculpture, painting, and architecture in general, there was nothing like it on this side of the Alps. It owed nothing, in fact, to Pictish or Irish taste, nor was it intended that it should owe anything, for it was obviously Wilfrid's wish to assimilate English architecture to the French and Italian, just as he had united those countries in ecclesiastical uses and observances. Hexham was the first church that he built in Bernicia, and at Hexham, therefore, we may expect to find some traces of French or Italian art. The principal remains that we have of Saxon sculpture are fragments of crosses, and at Hexham we observe on them that peculiar use of the vine which is so often seen in the earliest churches on the Continent. This is shewn by the crosses which are engraved in the first volume of this work, and by one which is still preserved at the Spital. In the case of the cross which may possibly have commemorated Acca, there is a beauty of execution and design which suggests at once its foreign origin. The same thing may be said of the sculptures represented on the following page, which are now in the possession of Mr. Fairless. The larger of the two was used for steps on the site of St. Mary's church. There is a classic severity of style in the treatment which is at once observable. The same influence may be traced on the banks of the Tyne, where the religious houses were, through Benedict Biscop, connected immediately with Rome. The sculptures at Jarrow bear strong testimony to this. There is one in particular representing two doves seated on the tendrils of a vine,—a design which is seen frequently in Italy and France.

That it was the design of Wilfrid to bring a new character of architecture into England, and that he did so to a great extent successfully, is evident, I think, from the similarity between

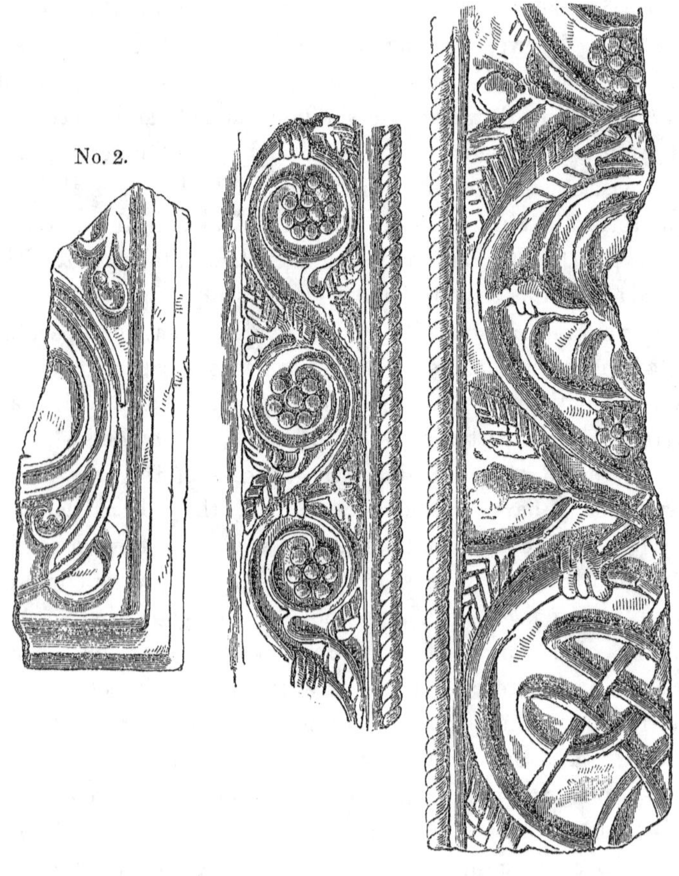
No. 1.
No. 2.

the greater part of the Saxon sculptured remains that have been discovered in the tract of country which was ruled over by the bishop or archbishop of York and his suffragans. That tract comprised at one time the whole of the Lowlands of Scotland up to the Frith of Forth. Beyond that barrier, the stones, covered with mysterious symbols, are found in great abundance: on this side a very different class at once begins; and at Abercorn itself, the seat of a bishop for a very short period, we have on a cross a vine represented in the same remarkable way in which it is treated at Hexham. The same pattern may be seen at Bewcastle and at Ilkley; and I may say, generally, that the crosses from the Frith of Forth southwards, throughout Northumberland, Durham, and Yorkshire, bear evident traces of having been created by the same school of art. The influence of the monks of Iona upon the old kingdom of Northumbria lasted for too short a time to enable them to make such a school; nor is it likely that plain simple men, as they were, should have Wilfrid's magnificent spirit, or any wish to make architecture a direct means of nursing devotion. It seems to me that Wilfrid was the originator of the beautiful forms that appear at Hexham and other places, and which overran Northumbria. I do not say for one moment that sculptured crosses had not been in use in that country before his time; far from it. They had come into it perhaps with Paulinus, perhaps from Ireland; but in the hands of Wilfrid's foreign masons they appeared in a new character, with foreign designs and ornamentation. The lessons of taste which these men gave must have been soon lost, as the crosses in Northumbria are often somewhat rude. There is little of that marvellous beauty which characterizes the sculptured memorials in the north and east of Scotland, and which, although derived perhaps more immediately from Ireland, is at the same time of an Eastern character. I am not speaking now of the strange symbols which the zeal and intelligence of the Scottish antiquaries will, I trust, be soon able to explain.

No. 1.

No. 2.

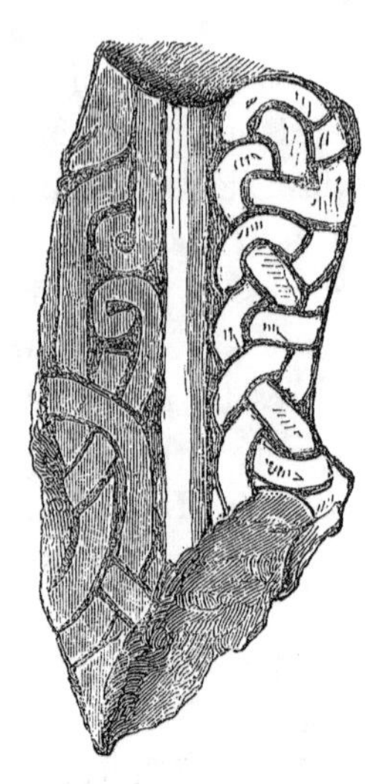

No. 3.

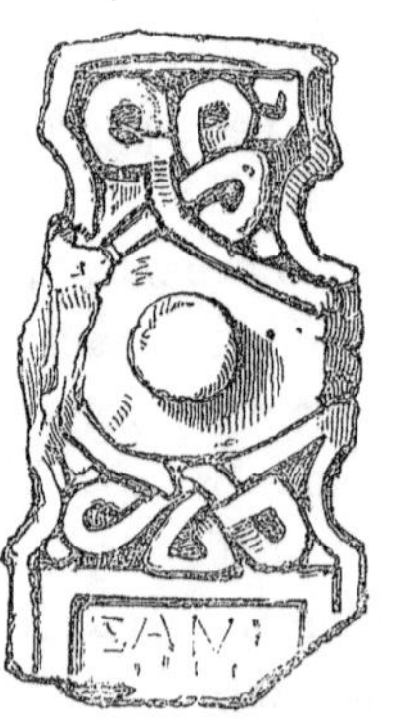

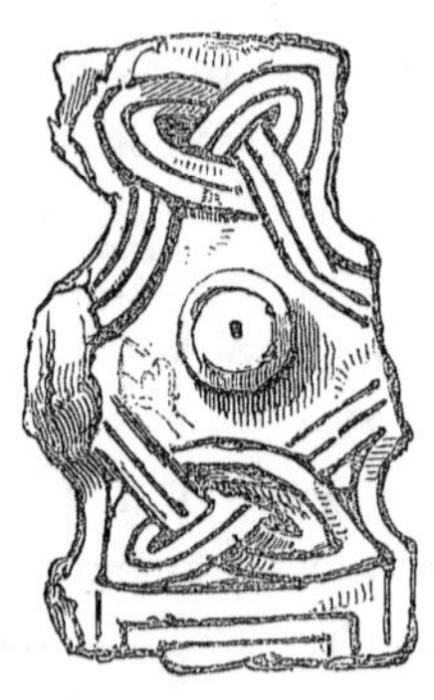

CROSSES, ETC., AT HEXHAM.

The cut, which is given below, represents a stone in the churchyard at Warden, which has evidently been at one time a Roman altar or sepulchral memorial. The surface has been cut away, and it has been changed with little difficulty into a Saxon monument.

It is not easy to say what the stone, No. 2, has been. It is now in the possession of Mr. Fairless.

No. 2.

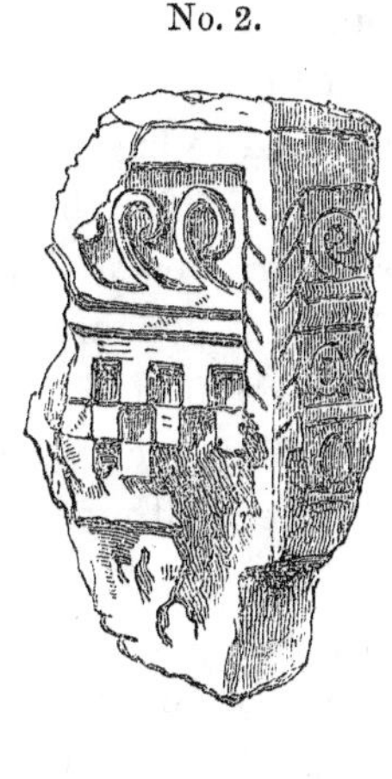

The pieces of baluster work which occur below are apparently of Saxon character, but are rather unusually treated.

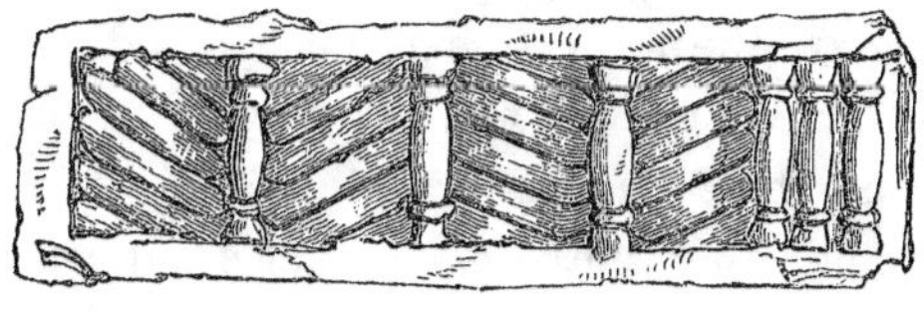

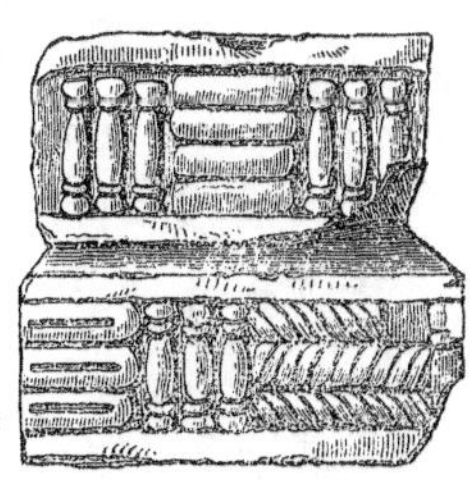

The most remarkable and distinctive specimen of Saxon architecture at Hexham is undoubtedly the crypt; though a question may be raised whether a portion of the extreme western angles of the choir, where it joins the north and south wings of the transept, may not be of this early date. The contiguous piers of the tower are not bonded into these walls behind them. Indeed, if the church which the Early English builders of the choir began to reconstruct had a central tower in the position of that which now remains of subsequent date, they could not have removed this portion of the previous choir without damaging its eastern superstructure. The width of the space between these angles, greater than that which might be supposed to have occurred in a Saxon fabric, does not affect the question; for the church which Wilfrid built, and which probably was repaired and not altered materially in plan after the Norman conquest, was of unusual dimensions; and in the present church of Stowe, in Lincolnshire—"the only example now remaining of what a Saxon church of the largest class was"—the width of the choir, as determined by the Saxon piers of the central tower, is twenty-four feet.[f] Moreover, it will be remembered that the capacious centre tower of York Minster rests on piers containing in their cores similar angles of Norman work, which could not safely be removed when the adjacent parts of the fabric were reconstructed.

If this supposition be correct, Wilfrid's church—or, at all events, one which required rebuilding at the end of the twelfth century—must have covered a considerable portion of the space occupied by the Early English structure, the central square of each being of the same dimensions; and this idea may derive some confirmation from the relative position of the older and the present choir and the crypt; for if a line be drawn eastward through the centre of the latter, it will fall midway of the tower and these presumed angles of the Saxon choir. It is improbable, also, that Wilfrid's crypt was originally placed in any other than in its present relative position, for

[f] Associated Arch. Soc. Reports, vol. i., p. 315.

had it been introduced under the eastern end of his church, as found in churches of subsequent date, the Early English rebuilders must have rejected westward, beyond their walls, a considerable portion of a hallowed site which had far more than ordinary claims on their veneration and assiduous protection.

Both Eddi and Prior Richard seem to have been especially struck with the apartments which Wilfrid constructed deep down below this church, and it may have been that he first introduced such features in English churches. Eddi, speaking of the church, says:—"Cujus profunditatem in terra cum domibus mirifice politis lapidibus fundatam," etc. Richard speaks more explicitly of crypts, underground oratories, and winding passages. Of these, with their appurtenant passages, only one is now known, and that so recently discovered as the year 1726, although, most probably, it will be found at a future day to communicate with another. Whatever position it may have occupied with reference to its original superstructure, it was left by the early English rebuilders at the eastern extremity of their nave. That portion of the church is now destroyed, and the crypt is therefore now entered from the churchyard. There is no object of similar character in the kingdom, except one in the cathedral church of Ripon, which unquestionably owes its origin to St. Wilfrid. The annexed plans[g] will describe better than words in what respects they resemble each other; but it must be remembered that the approach to the crypt of Ripon was altered when the central tower was erected above it. As to other points of difference in detail, the chapel of the crypt at Hexham is rather larger than that of Ripon, measuring 13 feet 4 inches by 8 feet, against 11 feet 3 inches by 7 feet 9 inches. It is also placed much deeper in the ground, and is constructed almost entirely of stones brought from a Roman

[g] My readers must be referred to the general plan of the church for a ground-plan of the crypt at Hexham.

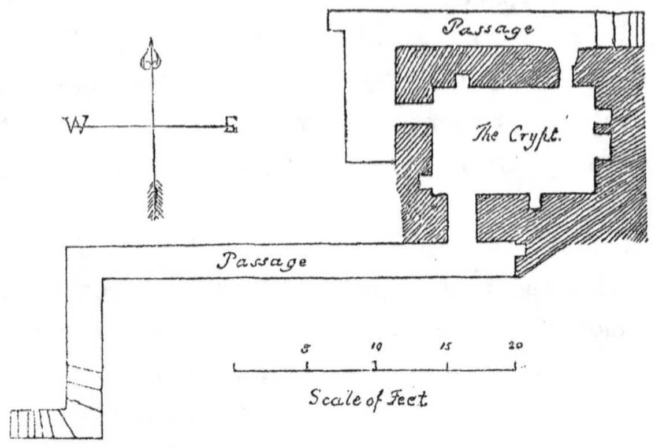

CRYPT AT RIPON.

building, whereas the other is formed of the grit stone of the country. In the one, the cells at the west end of the flanking passages have triangular roofs; in the other, the cells are not defined from the passages by arches, and are covered with flat stones. At Hexham the anti-chapel has a barrel vault, at Ripon a semi-vault only. In the one, two passages lead eastward and one southward; the other has but one outlet towards the choir. In this crypt the heads of the niches are flat, and there are none in the eastern wall; in the other, they have semi-circular heads, and there is one on the north side of the space once occupied by the altar, and a larger one above that space, in the middle of the wall. But both the crypts have obviously proceeded from a common type, although the idea is more elaborated at Hexham than at Ripon. Both chapels have their entrances in the same positions. In both, the semi-circular heads of the doorways, which are of the same height—6 feet 3 inches—are cut out of horizontal slabs. The passages in each agree in width within an inch. Both have funnel-like apertures in the heads of the niches, and deep round basins in the bases. In both, the north-east niche is pierced through to the passage behind. Both have a small rectangular opening in the roof of the anti-chapel, which may have been connected by a flue with the floor of the church above, and both have been plastered throughout.

Irrespective of the general interest which must attach to this crypt as one of the earliest and most curious of the Saxon structures that we possess, it is remarkable from having been built almost entirely of stones which have been used in an earlier work. Two of these bear Roman inscriptions, and the rest are presumed to have had the same origin. Evidently they have been used here as the most eligible materials which Wilfrid could command, and, as is shewn by their positions, not for the sake of ornament or enriching the character of his design. The lesser inscription contains fragments of five lines, which have been so injured by insertion in its present position as to be unintelligible. The other is on a stone, which forms the cover of the south-east angle of the passage which flanks the crypt on the north. It is engraved in Horsley's Britannia Romana, together with a Roman altar, dedicated to Quintus Calpurnius Concessinus, apparently a prefect of a troop of Corionototari, which was observed also by Stukely and Gale, when they visited the crypt in the year in which it was discovered, but which cannot now be found.

Of the sculptured and incised stones which are to be observed on all sides in the crypt there are two pieces of a Roman cornice in the southern passage, of which an example is engraved in the Archæological Journal,[h] together with two patterns, of which Mr. Hudson Turner there says :—"Though some doubt may be entertained, we are inclined to consider them relics of that debased style of art which marked the works of the Roman legionaries in Britain." I cannot enter into his doubtfulness, being unable to conceive from what Saxon building they could have been brought, or what builder could have produced such works between the departure of the Romans and the advent of Wilfrid. Within the last few

[h] Vol. i., p. 240.

years many more incised stones have been denuded of the plaster with which they were covered, and singular devices exposed, best expressed by the graver, by which they most certainly should be perpetuated.

This crypt was discovered in the year 1726, in digging for a buttress to support the west side of the tower. When Hutchinson[i] visited it in 1776 he says it had "for several years past been used as a private burial-place, and the entrance is covered with a table of marble of prodigious size, which is not usually moved but at the denunciation of mortality. The massive *claustrum* was heaved from the mouth of the vault by iron crows and rollers, at which the ground trembled over the arches." This covering is removed, but immediate access to the crypt is only obtained now, as it was then, by descending eighteen feet by a ladder, in a pit or shaft, 2 feet 7 inches wide,

[i] Vol. i., p. 102.

sunk above the foot of the original entrance from the west, several of the steps of which, prolonged to their *former* length in the plan, may still be seen. After passing through a narrow doorway or opening in the wall with a semi-circular head, devoid even of the accompaniment of a chamfer, the visitor enters the anti-chapel, a chamber with a barrel vault 9 feet 2 inches long, 5 feet 7 inches wide, and 9 feet in extreme height. Nearly in the centre of the vault, which shews some stones of the characteristic Saxon dressing, are traces of a small rectangular opening, like one in a similar position in the crypt at Ripon; but for what purpose it has been used (the coincidence inclining me to think it is not merely accidental) it is not easy to conjecture. In the south wall is a small recess or niche, with a flat head in front, but hollow like a funnel behind, and with a deep circular cavity or basin in the base. This niche, which resembles all the rest in the crypt, is also perfectly unornamented. From this chamber we pass by a doorway opposite to that by which we entered, and of similar size and character, into the chapel or main body of the crypt. It is vaulted, like the anti-chapel, and to the same height, the length being 13 feet 4 inches, and the width 8 feet. There is a niche in the west wall, on the right hand as we enter. The only member on the north side is a niche towards the east end, in all respects like the rest; but with this additional peculiarity, which appears not to have been noticed by previous writers on the crypt, that, like the celebrated "St. Wilfrid's Needle," exactly in the same position in the crypt at Ripon, it is voided to the passage on the other side of the wall. For what purpose these peculiar openings may have been originally used it is, perhaps, now useless to inquire. Certain only it is that, in this case, the niche has never been applied to the purpose for which that at Ripon was *enlarged* and became famous, as the wall behind is not cut away so as to allow a person to be drawn through the orifice.[j] There are no

[j] See sections of the "Needle" and the other niches in the crypt at Ripon, etc., in Arch. Inst. Proc. at York, 1846.

remains of the altar, but on the north side of its site a plain semi-octagonal bracket is inserted in the wall, above which, the disposition of some drilled holes, one retaining a piece of solder, suggests that a crucifix had once been placed there. On the south side of the chapel, a doorway, like those before mentioned, with a niche in the wall a little to the left, opens into a cell 5 feet 4 inches long, by 3 feet 6 inches wide, and roofed with large flat stones, inclining like the sides of a triangle, the apex of which is 8 feet from the floor. Hence we pass eastward, through an archway, into a passage 2 feet 6 inches broad, and covered with large stones placed horizontally, leading in the same direction for the space of 8 feet 6 inches, with a gentle ascent. At this point it turns southward, and further progress was until recently arrested by a dry wall, probably placed there, like one in the passage on the opposite side of the crypt, when the western piers of the tower of the church were strengthened by the superincumbent buttresses. We can, however, now see that the western side of it continues in the same southern direction for the space of ten feet and more, and that near the point of divergence another passage has gone forward towards the east; but the unprotected state of the earth and stones overhead prevents further investigations from this side, though the southern passage might probably be traced by an excavation opposite the doorway which formerly led from the south transept to the cloister court. Returning now to the anti-chapel, we pass through a doorway, like those we have seen previously, into a cell 6 feet long by 3 feet 6 wide, with a triangular roof, similar to that of the little chamber on the south side of the chapel. Hence a passage, covered with flat stones, leading east, rises so considerably, that, behind the voided niche in the chapel, the floor is level with its base, as occurs in the crypt at Ripon. At this point, too, it turns northward and rises four steps, the roof becoming semi-circular and sloping, parallel to the graduation of the stairs. After four more steps eastward, further access is closed, but so little of the passage remains unexplored that a person stationed in it can distinctly hear words spoken in the transept of the church. It is very desirable that this outlet should be restored, for many persons might thereby be enabled to visit the crypt who cannot use the present very inconvenient mode of entrance.

After a very careful examination of the church, I have been unable to discover any traces of pure Norman architecture, or any materials that might be supposed to have been used in a building of that character. It is entirely Early English, commencing with transitional detail; but how far the ground-plan has been suggested from the previous structure, there are no facts upon which to base a definite judgment. The work of reconstruction commenced with the choir, at the very end of the twelfth century. Then followed, at respective periods, very briefly removed, the south transept, the west side and the end of the north transept, the south side of the same transept, the central tower, and the nave; but whether the latter portion was completely transformed or not we are not now able to ascertain. In surveying the building I shall proceed in the same course, describing first the external, and then the internal features.

The elevations of both the north and south sides of the choir exhibit six bays, the eastern one of each having been recently rebuilt. In the aisles they are divided by shallow flat buttresses, or pilasters, rising from a splayed base, the heads dying into the corbel table. In each is a lancet light, under a plain head supported by single cylindrical shafts, and covered by a hood moulding, which passes from light to light continuously over the buttresses, like the string course on which the windows stand. About midway is a pointed doorway walled up on a plane with the enclosing wall, but as it has neither been moulded nor splayed in the jambs or the architrave, and has no hood moulding either within or without, it may have originally been introduced for a temporary purpose. In the clerestory the divisions are made by narrower pilasters than those of the aisles, reeded at the angles, with triangular heads, each having the face relieved with a sunken trefoil. In each bay is an arcade of three pointed members supported by single cylindrical shafts, —the central and widest one enclosing a lancet light. Above, is a corbel table and plain coped parapet. The eastern façade has been recently rebuilt, but an idea of its general character may be formed from a north-east "prospect" of the church, taken about the year 1661.[k] The central compartment seems to have been flanked by two large buttresses staged only once on a level with the parapet of the clerestory, above which point they assume the shape of lofty square turrets with pyramidal heads, not unlike those which their builders may have admired in the transitional Norman work of their patron, archbishop Roger, at Ripon. On the apex of the gable was a large pinnacle with a niche in front, surmounted by a plain Latin cross having three smaller crosses at its base,—one on each side, and one in front attached to the head of the niche. How faithfully the artist has rendered the detail may be a question on which different opinions may be entertained. The same observation will apply to the great east window, which is represented in the same plate as divided into five lights under two intersecting sub-arches, the space in the head of the main arch, above the point of intersection, being filled apparently with four quatrefoils; while the rest of the tracery is formed by merely doubling the number of the mullions of the lights below. The inaccuracy which occurs in many of the plates in the Monasticon, especially in the delineation of tracery, need not indeed have raised a doubt whether such a window was inserted at the close of the fifteenth century, when the fittings of the choir appear to have been renovated, had not a window of an earlier character actually occupied its place until about thirty years ago, when another of somewhat similar design was substituted, and in its turn was superseded at the recent rebuilding of the gable. Wright, in

[k] Dugdale's Mon. Angl. Vet. ed., ii., 135.

his History of Hexham, says of the window which he saw in the year 1823, that it "is singular in this, that it is, or appears to be, broader at the spring of the arch than at the base of the columns. It is likewise distinguished by that ornament commonly called the witches' wheel. It is divided by 'slender shafts of shapely stone,' as usual: but the great ornament of such buildings, and what ought particularly to distinguish them —painted glass, is totally wanting." He then goes on to "lament the *mutilated state* in which it is," a fact which in one respect corroborates the opinion expressed to me by a competent observer who had examined it, that the tracery had remained unaltered for a much longer period than that which had elapsed since the publication of Dugdale's engraving. If a conjecture may be hazarded on an object of which we have a very imperfect description, I would suggest that the old window was inserted soon after the spoliation of the Church by the Scots in 1296, in the place probably of two tiers of lancet lights, surmounted by a wheel; and that in the enlargement of the space to obtain a lighter effect, while the walls and shafts between the lights were diminished to mullions, a semblance of the wheel was fondly retained in the disposition of the tracery by which it had been displaced. Mr. Fairless has seen a piece of pot metal glass, taken from this window, painted with a brown pattern in the style which obtained in the latter part of the thirteenth century.

As to the eastern ends of the choir aisles, their windows are obscured in Dugdale's view, but each outer angle is flanked by a large buttress which rises above the roof in the shape of a square turret with a pyramidal cap; there appears also to have been a light on each side for the use of the triforium, flanked on the outer side by a pointed blank recess.

Running along the eastern wall there was formerly a kind of eastern transept, 59 feet long by 25 in width, called the old school. It probably took the place of the sanctuary, or shrines behind the altar, in which the remains of the Saints of the church were for awhile deposited.[l] When they were removed and laid in closer proximity to the high altar, the site that they had once occupied seems to have been reserved for sacred purposes, and a school was erected there; for the Augustinian canons were ordered to pay particular attention to learning and education. It is said that this school was burned by the Scots in 1296, when the scholars were within it. This is the more probable, because, after the demolition of adjoining houses, the exterior of a building of this description was exposed, with five square-headed Decorated windows of three lights each looking towards the east, and one of four lights in the northern and southern gables, of the customary shape. Under each of these windows there was a door. It may be presumed, therefore, that this is the building which was erected in the fourteenth century, when there was a temporary rest from invasion. Like its predecessor, it was used for the purposes of education. It appears in Dugdale's view of the church in 1661. For some years the restoration of this curious adjunct to the choir was contemplated, but from want of funds the project was deferred; other counsels prevailed, and it was ultimately demolished.

On the east side of the south transept the clerestory ranges with that of the choir, and is made into bays by flat buttresses with pyramidal heads, but without a trefoil in them. The triple arcade, which in each division carries the light in the centre, is not supported by shafts hewn from a single stone, as is usually the case, and as they appear in the choir, but by semi-octagonal projections walled in courses. The corbel table, above which is a plain parapet, is continued from the choir. A peculiar appearance is imparted to the aisle by its inclusion, in the southernmost of its three bays, of a passage and chamber above, which, in most other conventual churches, are found intervening between the south transept and the chapter-house. In its lower story is a doorway with a semi-circular head, between two narrow flat-

[l] See Vol. I.

topped lights. Above is a triangular recess, and then come two windows of the same shape as those below, but of larger dimensions. The buttress which flanks this compartment on the north is semi-octagonal, rising from a rectangular base, but it has not the singular footing for the diagonal sides which appears on the east side of the north transept, nor any other peculiarity about the head, which merely sinks into a flat pilaster below the corbel table. The buttress, however, next to the choir, is triple-gabled at the stage where the octagonal changes into the flat surface. The windows are of the same character as those of the contiguous aisle of the choir, but neither the string course on which they stand, nor that which connects their hood moulding, ranges with those of that earlier portion of the structure.

In the south face of this transept the most prominent features are three plain lancet lights in the upper part, a very considerable space below having been flanked by the chapter-house and an apartment above it, the high pitched roof of which encroached on the lower portion of the central light. There are octagonal turrets at the two angles, and the gable has been lowered and corniced like that of the north wing of the transept, at the end of the fifteenth century.

The west side, which originally formed a portion of the boundary of the cloister-court, presents, in its basement, a continuous arcade of pointed members of varying width; the largest enclosing the doorway which once opened into the church, and another, of lesser size, that which leads into the passage above mentioned at the extreme end of the transept. Above, are the corbels which carried the pent-house roof of the eastern cloister. At the height of two courses of masonry work above them is a plain string course, and at the distance of seven more, another, on which, without a divisional buttress or accompaniment of any kind, stand the four lancet lights of the triforium passage in the wall. Above these, on another string course, comes the clerestory, having four sets of triplets with masonry for shafts, as on the opposite side, and a similar corbel table and coped parapet as appear there.

Of the nave nothing more remains above-ground than a fragment at the west end, which defines little more than the length of this part of the church, before it was burnt by the Scots in 1296; and the fact, otherwise obvious, that it had an aisle on the north side. Whether the absence of a corresponding member on the south side was occasioned by some arrangement of the buildings on the west and south sides of the cloister-court, which would not admit of encroachment on its space; or by some reason connected with the structure of the original Saxon nave; or by some custom which prevailed among the Augustinian canons, cannot perhaps be determined; but I may remark that in the conventual church of Bolton-in-Craven, of that order, the nave has no southern aisle; and, in that case, the adoption of the plan must have been voluntary, and not dictated by pre-existing arrangement. Be this as it may, it is obvious that this peculiarity must have produced a different design in the elevation of the northern and southern sides; and how these were detailed—if the nave *was entirely rebuilt* in the Early English period—we may form a tolerable opinion by examining those fragments of the two main walls which are now embedded in the great modern buttresses which support the central tower. On the south side, the three string courses which define the several peculiar divisions of the west side of the contiguous transept are prolonged into this remnant of the nave; suggesting the idea that, both internally and externally, the south side of the nave was of the same design as the present west wall of the south transept. Both, too, must have been similarly affected by their engagement with the cloister. Of the north side, we can only infer that the clerestory was of the same character as that of the contiguous west side of the north transept, from the continuation, as in the other case, of the string course under the windows, and also of the corbel table. The pitch of the nave roof is defined by the weather moulding on the face of the tower, and that of its aisle by the same kind of indication in the wall of the transept. There appears to have been no tower at the west end, and, most probably, the gable was flanked externally by two turrets, like those which existed formerly at the opposite extremity of the church. The wall which now stands upon the foundation of the south side of the nave, so as to form a screen and carry the cloister of the quadrangle, has been built in the fifteenth century.

The north transept is of graceful and effective character, and in several respects differs in design from the opposite wing. It rises from a bold basement, at a higher level than that of the choir, into which a dog-tooth moulding is introduced. The main front is flanked, on the west by a flat buttress, on the east by one of semi-octagonal form, which, after assuming a more slender substance below the base of the clerestory, becomes a slight flat projection, the top of which is splayed to the wall. The doorway, placed in the centre, was erected by the Mercers' Company of London, to which the patronage of the lectureship in this church belongs; but it appears from Dugdale's plate that, in the year 1661, one with a semi-circular head had occupied its place. Immediately above, and filling the intermediate space under the base of the clerestory, are three very long lancet lights under an arcade of pointed arches, the members containing the lights being the widest; but the cylindrical shafts, banded twice in their elevation, which must have added materially to the design, are all destroyed, with the exception of a nook shaft in the western angle. The clerestory has three lancet lights under an arcade rising with the inclination of the gable, the members being divided, as in instances previously noticed, not by shafts, but by semi-octagonal masonry. Towards the end of the fifteenth century the pitch of the gable was lowered, and decorated with a cornice of concave moulding, charged with quatrefoils, which rises from two plain octagonal turrets with pointed heads, but part of the Early English work.

It is remarkable that these windows, like all the rest in the transept, where a pathway crossed the sill in the interior, are walled up to about the height of six feet, not improbably after the Scottish incursion in 1296, and for the purpose of sheltering those using the passage from arrows or other missiles that might otherwise have been aimed at them by those marauders, from whom the canons must have experienced frequent annoyance. The north face of the attendant aisles is enclosed between two semi-octagonal buttresses, the head of the eastern one being adorned with a peculiar little finial. There is one light under a triple arcade, and another above, with a blank-pointed arch by its west side, which formerly lit the triforium, but is now walled up, like the whole of the clerestory lights on the east side of the transept. At what period this was done, and for what purpose, has not been ascertained.

The west side of this wing of the transept is divided by three buttresses. That which flanks the outer angle is flat, the others in a great degree resemble those on the east side; and, after rising in a semi-octagonal form from a rectangular base, diminish to a smaller substance, retaining, however, the same form, and then recede to the wall to divide, in a flat shape, the bays of the clerestory. They differ, however, from the buttresses on the east side, in the three outer faces of the upper semi-octagon ending in a triple gable. The three long lancet lights which adorn this façade are not placed under an arcade, but are surmounted merely by a hood moulding, which runs continuously from end to end, passing over the buttresses. The clerestory resembles that of the opposite wing.

The same arrangement is followed in the clerestory of the east side of the north transept, where the aisle has three semi-octagonal buttresses, on rectangular bases, banded by the string course which runs at the sills of the windows, the foot of each diagonal face being turned up with a curious ornament. The heads recede to the wall, and one of them has a small finial of foliage on a slender stem, rising like a plant out of the upper

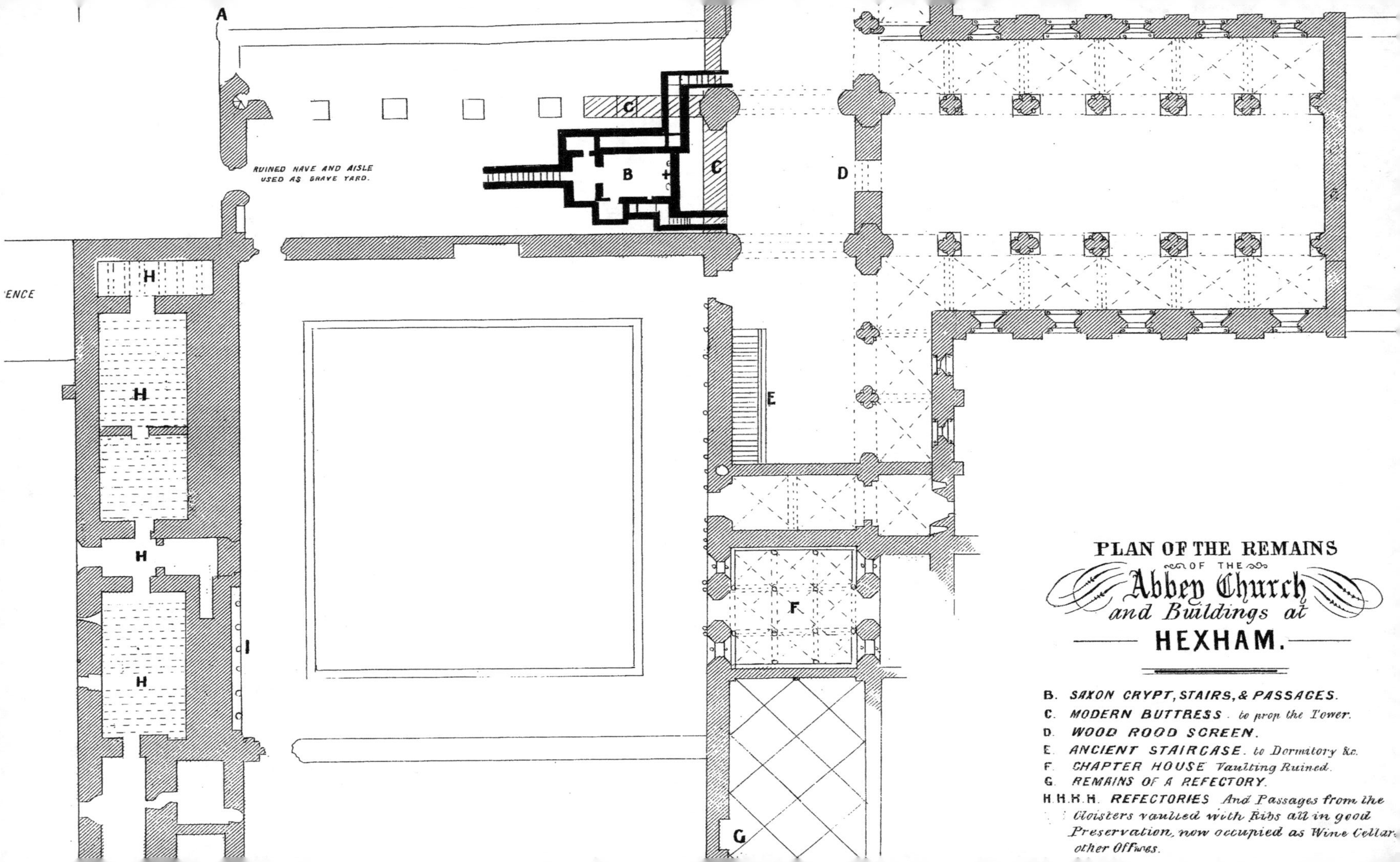
A
RUINED NAVE AND AISLE
USED AS GRAVE YARD.
B
C
C
D
E
F
G
H
H
H
H
I
ENCE
PLAN OF THE REMAINS
OF THE
Abbey Church
and Buildings at
HEXHAM.
B. SAXON CRYPT, STAIRS, & PASSAGES.
C. MODERN BUTTRESS. to prop the Tower.
D. WOOD ROOD SCREEN.
E. ANCIENT STAIRCASE. to Dormitory &c.
F. CHAPTER HOUSE Vaulting Ruined.
G. REMAINS OF A REFECTORY.
H.H.H.H. REFECTORIES And Passages from the Cloisters vaulted with Ribs all in good Preservation, now occupied as Wine Cellar, other Offices.

part, but not from the apex or extreme upper surface of the front face. The three lancet lights are each placed under an arcade of three members, the moulding which decorates the jambs and heads of the windows being continued at their bases. The corbel table, prolonged horizontally across the north face of the aisle, is of the plainest character. In Dugdale's plate, a high buttressed wall, apparently of mediæval work, runs from the north-east angle of the transept for a considerable distance, parallel with the choir.

The tower, placed at the intersection of the choir and transept, rises little higher than its square above their roofs, from which it emerges as a mere mass of plain masonry. A little above their ridges it is slightly contracted, and each face exhibits, between two flat buttresses, a pointed arcade of five members—divided by triple shafts of masonry—of which the second and fourth are larger and higher than the rest, and contain in each a pointed window, originally subdivided into two pointed lights by a mullion now destroyed. The corbel table is surmounted by an embattled parapet, enclosing a low pyramidal roof. In the plate just mentioned, the roof, which was then covered with lead, assumed the form of a spire, about as high as the width of the base of the tower. Upon this was placed a cross surmounted by a vane of considerable height. These, however, like the present battlement, must have been erected after the church was burned by the Scots.

The old bells, which have been for some time melted down, were six in number, and, according to Mr. Wright, three of them bore the date 1404. St. Mary's bell was the largest, weighing as much as 70 cwt. It was called the fray bell, and was rung specially when there was an alarm, particularly of a foray or inroad. Its last peal was at the marriage of Sir William Blackett, when it was cracked by the boisterous demonstrations of the ringers. St. Andrew's bell, the next in size, was rung at funerals, and was called the haly or holy bell.

Mr. Wright in his History of Hexham[m] gives the following inscriptions from the bells, the inaccuracies of which cannot be now corrected. Several of the legends are striking.

1.

AD PRIMOS CANTUS P(RO)VISAT NOS REX GLORIOSUS.

2.

ET CANTARE . . . . FACIET NOS VOX . . . .

3.

EST NOBIS DIGNA KATERINÆ VOX BENIGNA.

4.

OMNIBUS IN ANNIS EST VOX DEO ORATA IOHANNIS.
A. D. M CCCC IIII.

5.

ANDREA MI CARE, IOHANNI CONSOCIARE.
A. D. M CCCC IIII.

6.

EST MEA VOX ORATA DUM SIM MARIA VOCATA.
A. D. M CCCC IIII.

It may here be observed that the roofs of both the choir and transept were formerly covered with lead, and that on its being smelted, a quantity of silver was obtained from that which was taken from the choir.

INTERIOR OF THE CHURCH.—On entering the choir, we infer by comparison of the sections of mouldings, and other detail, that the south side is probably a little earlier in date than the other. The five columns which divide it from the aisles on each side all stand on rectangular bases, and are composed of eight members or shafts, not rounded, but shaped in section like the end of a lance. On the south side, all the capitals are quite plain, but on the north, foliage of an incipient character is introduced. The eastern responds, indeed, judging from the modern edition of them, must have been of transitional Norman character. "The originals are said to have been more spirited." On both sides the abacus is rectangular over those shafts of the pillars which face the cardinal points of

[m] pp. 100-3.

the compass, but, over those that intervene, it follows their pointed section. The mouldings of the archivolts, which these pillars support, are bold and well composed, but their arrangement, on the south side, differs a little from that on the north, and it has also a serrated, instead of the plain hood moulding which occurs on the opposite side.

The triforium—strongly savouring of Norman influence, both in the general design and the large space which it occupies between the arcade and the clerestory—contributes to this part of the church a dignified and powerful effect, not unheeded by the builders of the transept at an advanced period, when a modified form of it might otherwise have been introduced. It is divided, on both sides, into bays by triple shafts resting on semi-cylindrical bases, with something like three nail heads projecting from the face of each; and these again are supported by floriated brackets, the string course intervening. The mouldings of the semi-circular arches, very little inferior in span to those of the arcade below, rise from two cylindrical shafts in the splay and two in the soffit, corresponding with the two shafts, placed one behind the other, which carry the two pointed sub-arches; between which a sunken quatrefoil appears in the spandril. On the north side there is no decoration attempted, except the nail-head ornament in one member of the arch, common to both sides,—and in the last bay westward, where the angle flanking the nook shaft is ornamented with dog-tooth work; a treatment which obtains throughout the southern triforium.

Both sides of the choir are lighted alike with plain lancet lights on a nail-headed string course passing over the dividing vaulting shafts, each light appearing in the middle of an arcade of three members. It is supported by shafts tripled at the level of the head of the pathway which passes over the sill, but single from that point to the springing of the head of the window. There are consequently two sets of capitals. Below the point of springing, the jamb of the window is splayed or shouldered, so as to form a trefoil head towards the interior, and to admit more light.

The east end having been rebuilt needs no other comment than that it is of a more advanced character than the lateral walls, and appears to have been compiled from various portions of the church, without observing the different stages of development which it presents. As the modern character of the work is obvious to the most careless observer, no such misconception can arise as must be caused by the prolongation, at the same period, of the nook shafts at the west angles of the choir, which were formerly pendentive, and the introduction of the wall ornament, which occurs only in the latest portion of the church, in the north transept. The reredos behind the altar seems to have been suggested from the arcade of the aisle of that portion of the church. It is composed of seven trefoil-headed arches, supported by shafts, except the central one, which rises in a curvilinear direction from the wall, without the interposition of either capital or bracket!

The aisles of the choir have single lancet lights, enclosed within a moulded head, supported by cylindrical shafts, with capitals of transitional Norman feeling, and a rectangular abacus. They stand on a bold string course. Both aisles are vaulted with stone, supported by pendentive shafts, which vary in section on the respective sides. In the diagonal ribs of the groining a large between two smaller reeds appears; in the transverse ribs they are of equal size. The bosses are adorned with foliage. In the third bay from the east, on the south side, is a doorway inserted, in the Decorated period, but now walled up, with a trefoil-headed piscina on its west side. Each aisle, no doubt, had its altar at the east end, with the necessary appendages, but as the bay in which they would have been enclosed has been rebuilt, we find no other indication than a large locker on each side, the heads of which, however, from some whim, not to be explained, were changed in that work from the flat to the semi-circular form.

Towards the close of the fifteenth century, while Rowland Leschman and Thomas Smithson sat in the Prior's stall, the whole of the woodwork of the church seems to have been renewed, including the roofs of the choir and transept. After the Reformation, time and neglect wrought their usual effects upon it, though probably some definite idea of the general nature of the arrangements might have been still obtained had not the recent alterations swept away all that rested on the floor, except the rood-screen, and left it only for the student to examine the ruin in fragments. This screen,—certainly one of the most singular and interesting combinations of carving and painting in the kingdom,—stands between the eastern piers of the central tower, and projects or caves over, both to the east and west, for the sake of obtaining greater space in the loft; forming thus on the east side a continuous canopy for the stalls. On this side, the screen shews only a panelled front on each side of the central doorway, and appears to have been "restored." In front, over the entrance, projects a semi-octagonal jube, the panels of which and the rest of the loft, sixteen in number, are each painted with the figure of a Saint, archbishop, or bishop, but I could not distinguish their particular characteristics from the floor. Being not immediately accessible, they remain in a good state of preservation, but require cleaning to bring out the detail.[n] In the heads of the pointed doorways in the sides of the porch are two large pictures, one of the Salutation and the other of the Annunciation of the Blessed Virgin. The west side of the vertical part of the screen under the loft is divided into three bays, the central one being occupied by the doorway. The lower portion of the rest exhibit a row of sixteen panels, each containing the picture of a mitred personage,—some of them nimbed,—and about 2 feet 4 inches high. A few of their names are painted on them, but the light is seldom sufficiently powerful to

[n] In these panels there are some shields of arms; one exhibiting a coat of Neville, another a kind of vulture grasping an annulet in its claws.

enable them to be read, or the symbols connected with the figures ascertained. St. Cuthbert, however, stands obviously prominent. Above, the pointed heads of the panels between the shafts which support the fan-tracery ceiling below the loft, are filled with blank flamboyant tracery of exquisite composition, but still more charming when the back-ground retained the colours with which it was filled in.[o] The ceiling is still coloured in contrast, red and green, the face of the ribs having been originally gilded. The front of the loft stands upon a cornice, in the concavity of which are inserted, along with quatrefoils and roses, the following letters, each with contractions, or letters entwined, forming a monogram of a whole word, carved in relief upon a separate square tablet:—

> O(RATE) P(RO) A(NIMA) D(OMINI) T(HOMÆ) S(MITHSON) P(RIORIS) H(UJUS) E(CCLESIÆ) Q(UI) F(ECIT) H(OC) O(PUS).

It is decorated with a series of twenty-one niches, with the fronts of all the canopies cut away, though sufficient is left to tell how beautiful they once have been. The spaces between the niches, delicately ornamented, have been coloured also red and green. Above this arcade is a broad fillet of fine flamboyant tracery work, surmounted by a cornice enriched with quatrefoils in the hollow, together with the letters T S and another object which I could not make out. This was, originally, the termination of the work; but there has long been fixed upon it a continuous row of twenty-four panels with tracery in their square heads, containing a series of pictures, like those in the base of the screen, painted on the wood. Five of them in the central part represent as many subjects in the "Dance of Death," and are engraved in Mr. Fairless's Guide to the Church; the rest, which all appear to be single figures, are so obscured by dirt as not to be intelligible from below.

[o] This tracery presents an adaptation of the forms found in the great west window of York minster.

According to a plan of the pews taken in the year 1830, it appears that there were four stalls on each side of the west end of the choir, fourteen on the north side and sixteen on the south, but both series terminated at the same point eastward; though, on the north side, *two* stalls were included within the third intercolumniation from the west, but *three* within the same space on the opposite side. Thirteen of these stalls are now placed at the eastern extremity of each aisle of the choir, but they have no tabernacled heads or canopies; and, judging from the plain surface of the elbows or divisions between each, it does not appear that they originally had such a protection. It may have been that they had a panelled screen behind, something like the blank tracery work, with a coved ceiling of fan tracery projecting, like that on the west side of the rood-screen; but the heads of the west stalls have been so mangled that this is little more than conjecture. The misereres do not attain the general interest of that class of objects, being chiefly foliage, though one bears the figure of a bird which has been supposed to be a memorial of Edward Jay, the last Prior. The font formerly stood immediately in front of the northern groupe of the western stalls.

Of the lattices or screens which divided the main body of the choir from its aisles, not one now remains in position. Probably they exhibited such flamboyant tracery as still happily remains on the west side of the rood screen, combined with the pictured panels which have been, and with others that will be hereafter, alluded to. Some fragments of them, which are still preserved, must evoke as high an admiration of the skill and piety of those who produced them, as of the opposite feeling towards those who destroyed the works of men into whose minds they could not enter.

Before the late "restoration," the sedilia stood under the easternmost bay of the choir, on the south side. They joined the wall at the east end, and left a passage between the opposite end and the pillar, not being wide enough to fill the space.

The base under the seat was of stone, but the superstructure of wood. Of the latter a remnant is now preserved in the north transept, in the shape of a bench with a plain back, like a long-settle, divided into four seats by three open-work partitions resembling flying buttresses, each end having a similar termination. Two elbows or finials of the lower portion of these partitions remain; the one resembling a nondescript animal sitting on its haunches; the other an angel holding a shield charged with a bugle-horn, stringed, between three Roman letters, W; the armorial bearings, perhaps, of the family of Woodhorne, though the style of the work forbids their assignation, in this case, to the Prior of Hexham of that name. A piece of open crest-work, engraved at p. clxxii of the Preface of Vol. I., bearing the same shield in connexion with an eagle, was taken from the front of a gallery above the object now under description, but whether it originally formed part of it I have not ascertained. Each of the seats was originally surmounted by a semi-sexagonal canopy, divided from each other by a tall pinnacle which rose from the hinder part of the partition, and ceiled with fan tracery, now mutilated, except the bosses, in which are introduced two human faces and as many roses. Until recently, the sedilia were occupied by the churchwardens.

Considering the limited space that could be allotted to private altars, in consequence of the absence of a nave, there were probably several screens passing transversely across the aisles of the choir, leaving only a processional path between them and the wall. Two chapels indeed remained in a tolerable state of preservation until the recent period to which we are compelled so often to allude; when one was mangled and removed to another part of the church, and the other was wantonly torn in pieces and dispersed, as "old materials." I prefer, however, to describe them here in connexion with their original sites, that the reader may be in some degree enabled to recall those ancient associations of the choir which cannot now be enjoyed within its walls. The largest and most interesting of these enclosures stood on the north aisle of the choir, within the second bay from the east end, and was popularly called "Prior Richard's shrine." Whether this appellation had its origin before the Reformation, in connexion with a recorded fact or tradition that this celebrated member of the house was interred in this particular spot, or was associated otherwise with it, will probably never be ascertained. Certain only it is, from the late presence of the initials of Prior Rowland Leschman on the roof, that it was erected by him, either as a chantry chapel of his own foundation,—for which I am not aware that the requisite licence remains on the Patent Rolls,—or as a reconstruction of some previous enclosure connected with Prior Richard, which obtained, therefore, especial attention from Leschman when he renewed the woodwork of the choir, and which received his mark, like other parts of the fabric, in token that—"This made Leschman." The chapel filled the whole intercolumniation, and projected on the south side beyond the bases of the pillars, having an entrance from the choir at the east part of this front, which was stopped up within memory, when another entrance was made from the aisle, at the east end. It did not free the aisle, but a passage occurred between it and the wall. As it now stands in the aisle of the south transept, the "shrine" measures 13 feet 6 inches long on the south side, 11 feet on the north, and is 11 feet 6 inches high, and upwards of 6 feet wide; but how far the sides retain their original proportions and respective positions I am not clearly informed. I note this only, that in a plate of the shrine which may be found in Wright's History of Hexham, p. 78, the base of what is called there the *south* front is now the *north* front, with a doorway at the eastern extremity of it, of which there are no traces at present. The plate, however, in other respects, is extremely inaccurate. In an architectural point of view, the work is of a very debased character, though some portions of the flamboyant tracery of the lattices are beautifully designed. A stone basement, 4 feet 9 inches high, bounds the chapel on the sides, which differ entirely in design; that which now fronts the south being the most decorated. It is divided into three stories or stages. The lowest is but plain masonry, 1 foot 5 inches high, in front of which, at intervals of about twelve inches, as regards the first four spaces from the west,—for the rest are smaller,—sit a series of nine grotesque figures, having the effect of supporting the superstructure. The first is a grim-looking lion: the second represents a fellow with a rude smirk of satisfaction on his countenance, playing the bagpipes: the third, a fox in a pulpit, caped and hooded, preaching to four geese cleverly grouped below: the fourth, a man sitting on a low stool playing on a harp: the fifth, a rude representation of a man with three faces,—the middle one the largest,—but with little or no body, in a sitting posture, apparently on a couchant animal: the sixth, a man sitting on the ground in a crouching posture, the relative position of his head and arms to his body passing all description by the pen, but affording an excellent material embodiment of the nightmare: the seventh, a man sitting on the ground with a small animal in his hands, and wearing a long cap with a tassel at the top turned over on one side: the eighth, a woman sitting on the ground holding an unintelligible object, resembling drapery, over her head, the nude arm presented towards the spectator, exposing the shoulder, below which the dress is rolled up in the shape of a wreath or torse: the ninth, a nondescript monster, like those found in Norman work, and probably copied from such. Immediately above this curious basement is a fillet of foliage, not, as usual, interlacing or running horizontally, but every leaf, like those of the aspen poplar, rises vertically from a stem passing in a wavy direction from end to end. Above this course is the chief member of the design. It is divided into eight panels by moulded vertical projections of considerable substance resting on corbels or bases, not bevelled or splayed at the under surface, but projecting and disengaged horizontally as far as the heads of the supporting figures I have just described. The capitals of these rude shafts or ribs are formed by representations of human heads, equally prominent as the bases. The panels thus enclosed are square-headed, but not of equal width, and though their inner heads are of a trefoil shape, they are all detailed differently. The first subject, passing from the west end, represents St. George slaying the dragon: the second, a piece of Saxon knot-work, surmounted with foliage: the third, the Ancient of Days with streaming hair, crowned, holding our Blessed Saviour in a most singular posture in His lap: the fourth, a Saxon knot, enclosed within another, twisted into the form of a lozenge-shaped wreath or torse, the apex being collected into the semblance of a trefoil: the fifth, an ape sitting on a curiously shaped stool with one paw resting on his knee, and the other applied to his mouth: the sixth, the lily, with foliage symbolical of the Blessed Virgin, rising from a vase, with a single handle and spout, precisely resembling a modern pitcher: the seventh, a tonsured front-faced figure, holding an unintelligible object in his right hand: the eighth, a front-faced figure in a gown, with no particular characteristic. Above these panels is a bold embattled cornice, not less than a foot deep. The present northern basement is much plainer in character, though equally singular in its design as the one just described. Upon plain masonry, 18 inches high, is a deeply recessed arcade of eight members, excluding the half panels at each end. The dividing ribs are flat and rudely moulded with semi-circular moulded bases but rectangular capitals merely chamfered. In the head of each arcade is a compressed trefoil, enclosed unskilfully under a cinquefoil, thus giving the effect of a cornice without its projection; the lower part is filled with a trefoil-headed arch with a plain ogee canopy, the tops decorated with a series of heads of men and animals. It is to be remarked in connexion with an object shortly to be described, that the pilaster which bounds the east end of this northern basement is ornamented with a panel defined by incised lines with a semicircular head. If this side did actually face the choir when it stood in its original position, this pilaster must have formed one jamb of the doorway as depicted in Wright's plate, and the upper portion of the compartment in which the door was placed must have been destroyed at the time of the "Restoration," thus causing the present disparity in the length of the sides. Upon this basement, on each side, stands a wooden lattice or screen of more than equal height, that on the north remaining the most perfect. It is now made into six vertical divisions by panelled shafts decorated with blank tracery, resting on brackets, in the form of heads. Each of these ogee-headed spaces was divided by a mullion, enriched in the hollows with quatrefoils, into two semicircular-headed openings, not foiled; the space between and the cornice being filled with delicate flamboyant tracery. There is a flat boarded ceiling over the chapel, originally ribbed, but all the members have been destroyed, and now only one perfect centre boss remains, decorated with a red rose, with seven half bosses at the sides, and two corner bosses, all representing well designed foliage, and painted. Mr. Fairless fortunately possesses a cast of one of the centre bosses which assigns the erection of the shrine to Prior Leschman. It bears the device of an angel holding a shield, charged with the letters 𝔯 and 𝔩 in saltire, their disposition having been perhaps suggested by St. Andrew's cross.[p] The same idea may have crossed the fancy of the designer of that elegant piece of woodwork, engraved at the 176th page of the Preface to "The Priory of Hexham," where two objects, supposed to represent barbed arrows, are placed in saltire with an *R* above and an *L* below the point of intersection, not improbably allusive to some trade or occupation in life from which the surname of the Prior was derived. Mr. Wright, in his History, published in the year 1823, says that the "north side and west end of the shrine are entirely destroyed;" but, in the first instance, he can mean no more than that the wooden lattice had been much despoiled, as is now the case on the south side.

[p] This is engraved on the title of Vol. I.

At the east end of this chapel—where it was placed before its removal from the choir—is a remarkable stone altar, occupying its entire width of 5 feet 3 inches, and 4 feet 4 inches high, the cover or slab being slightly chamfered, and bearing the five crosses. On the north side of the vertical face is a square-headed opening, 1 foot 10½ inches high, and 9½ inches wide, continued through the whole substance of the altar, and probably once used as a place of deposit for the sacred utensils. On each side of the aperture is a sculptured panel, the other exposed side of the stone forming part of the inner face of the opening, having another panel of like character. That on the north side contains a most archaic-looking Saxon scroll, copied, no doubt, from one existing at the time in the Priory, facing the spectator; and, inside the recess, an ape sitting. Opposite to it is a hare squatting under foliage; and, outside, the same stone presents a pilgrim, with his staff, wearing a wallet and cap, both with the badge of the escallop shell. In "the dark ages" of English archæology, Mr. Hutchinson[q] sagely conjectured these figures to be of Roman workmanship, the ape representing Silenus and the pilgrim Jupiter: but they are obviously of the same date as the rest of the chapel, and precisely of the same character as those found on its south side.

The whole space between the altar slab and the roof of the chapel is occupied by a piece of wainscot, 7 feet high. The lower panel, filling the whole width, contains a singular painting, not to be properly viewed without artificial light, but which Mr. Wright in his History says "represented the sufferings of Christ. The Saviour in the centre, his hands crossed before him and tied, crowned with thorns, etc.; on his right hand cords and scourges are cross-tied to a tree; above are thirty pieces of silver. In the foreground a figure like a monk in the attitude of prayer (not improbably intended to represent Prior Leschman) holds a conspicuous station. On the ground are pincers, etc. On the left hand of the Saviour the garments

[q] View of Northumberland, A.D. 1776, vol. i., p. 97.

hang; here, too, are the ladder, the spear, and the sponge, tied to a reed; and so particular has the artist been, that the dice are still visible, and it is worthy of remark that *three* dice are discernible, not *two* only, as at present in use. Gilded roses are scattered over the whole piece."[r] On three upright panels above is a figure of St. Andrew, between St. Peter on one side and St. Paul on the other, but much obscured by time and neglect.

There is now placed within this chapel a low altar tomb—of the latter part of the fifteenth century—5 feet long and 2 feet 5 inches wide, which, previous to its removal at the late "restoration," stood against the wall, towards the eastern angle of the north side of the choir. The base and cornice which support the cover have simple mouldings, and there is no other feature about it, except that at the west end of the south side is an armorial shield, bearing the letters R. L. in saltire, and most probably appropriating this as the tomb of Prior Leschman. As it has neither base nor cornice on the south side, we may conclude that the end which now faces the west, at that time was turned towards the east.

Upon this tomb rests the monumental effigy traditionally said to represent "Prior Richard." In Wright's plate of "the Shrine" (History, p. 78) this figure is shewn lying in front of it, on the south side, and on a slab, which never could have been intended to represent the tomb just described; and in a plan of the pews, taken in 1830, it is introduced on the same site; but I have been told that some time after, when the choir was re-pewed, it was removed and placed upon the monument on which it now rests. When Hutchinson visited Hexham, in 1776, it would appear that both the monuments were placed as they are now. "Within the choir," he writes, "is the recumbent effigy of an ecclesiastic, hooded, on a table monument of black marble (which the present is not) in relief;

[r] Wright's Hexham, pp. 78-9. In the Preface to Vol. I. this effigy is engraved.

at the foot, a shield with uncommon arms, or rather an emblematical device to denote mortality, being the resemblance of cross bones. The people who keep the doors, say it is the tomb of Prior Richard, an historian of the twelfth century. The device on the shield, if it is presumed to be the tomb of Richard, will then appear to be the letters *r i* placed one over the other." But, whatever changes may have been made in the relative positions of these monuments, it appears evident to me, unless the work had been erected, at first, in a *most unusual* and unskilful manner, that the effigy never formed any portion of the altar tomb originally; for not only is the latter complete in all its component parts, and properly finished by the slab above the cornice, but the lower surface of the slab on which the effigy rests is disproportionately larger than the upper surface of the tomb, and has its own proper cornice and set of mouldings, of a more ornamental character, around its sides and end; whereas the altar-tomb has been originally placed against a wall, and on that side is wholly unadorned. It is to be observed that the *crenellated portion* of the moulding around the bed of the effigy appears only on the west and south sides, suggesting the idea that these were the portions of it originally the most exposed to view. Mr. Wright, speaking of this effigy, says (p. 90), in the year 1823 it stood "exactly in front of the shrine on the north side of the centre aisle of the choir. *This was not its original situation.* It now covers another tomb, on which it rests, and this impropriety of place has caused much confusion in the accounts respecting it." Unless, also, "the recumbent effigy of an ecclesiastic hooded," which Mr. Hutchinson saw, "immediately adjoining" the shrine, was one which is now destroyed,—a thing extremely improbable,—he must have seen the figure now under consideration in a detached form. For in speaking of the tomb at the west end of the north aisle of the choir, then presumed to be that of Alfwold, king of Northumberland, he says, "I measured *an effigy which lays near this tomb*, and found it answering exactly in length. *The effigy represents an ecclesiastic with his hood thrown back to his forehead,* his hands elevated, and robed to the feet; the folds of the drapery thrown into excellent order, easy and elegant." Whether Mr. Hutchinson has fallen into confusion in making the two statements I have quoted or not, he evidently had considered that the effigy last mentioned, which corresponds exactly with that now under review, was not then placed in its original position.

There stood "near the altar" in the year 1776, and until recently, an uncouth statue of a man in an erect posture, about 3 feet 8 inches high, now removed into the aisle of the north transept. He is represented as wearing a long coat, buttoned in front from the neck to the waist, having three coils or clumsy ligatures of what may have been intended for hay or straw band round his ancles; and he holds erect with both hands a staff or club as tall as himself, expanding to a large knot at the upper end. His cap is like that which appears on one of the figures on the south side of the chapel just described. The stone out of which the figure is carved is rough and undressed on its right hand side, as if that part had joined a wall or other masonry. The opposite side retains two iron hooks, the points of each bent in a different direction, and is ornamented with an incised panel with a semi-circular head of precisely similar design to that which—as previously alluded to—appears on what was once the eastern jamb of the doorway leading into this chapel; suggesting the idea that this figure may have been connected with the eastern end of that enclosure, which has been long since removed. Mr. Pennant, in his Tour in Scotland, made in the year 1772, in allusion to this statue, says, "Against a pillar is a ridiculous figure of a barefooted man with a great club: perhaps a pilgrim." Upon which Mr. Hutchinson, four years after, remarks, "It in nowise represents a pilgrim; he carries no scrip, and wears a cap or helmet;" and afterwards says, "This, I apprehend, is the figure of Pan. It is reasonable to conjecture that they,"—that is, this and the figures in front of the altar above mentioned,—"have been saved from the ruins, when the Roman remains in the vaults,"—that is to say, the Saxon crypt,—"were obtained." Mr. Wright, while perceiving the "evident identity" of the figure "with the other sculptures of the shrine," thinks it was "intended to represent an officer of justice, with his staff and plume, his feet bared and manacled, to shew that within the bounds of sanctuary he dared not move towards his design, and that there his authority availed him not. This figure is placed within a short distance of the *stool of peace.*"

Beyond the highest limit to which living memory can extend, and most probably for six centuries more, that most venerable monument of antiquity, the well-known Frith-stool of Hexham, used before the Reformation for the unassailable security of persons seeking the sanctuary of the church, occupied a position immediately in front of the last pillar, eastward, on the north side of the choir, its face being turned towards the south. Soon after the year 1830, however, when the church was re-pewed, neither the unusual local interest which attached to it, nor the fact of its being an almost unique example of its kind, could preserve it from removal into the north aisle, immediately behind the pillar in front of which it had previously stood. Hence it was again recently removed, and placed, where it now stands, in the aisle of the south transept, at the angle of its junction with the contiguous aisle of the choir. At some distance it has the appearance of a cubical block of stone, out of which a seat has been hewn; but, on closer examination, it will be found to be composed of the stone which contains the sedile, of very close grit, and three stones below of somewhat coarser material. The whole block is 2 feet 7½ inches long, 1 foot 9 inches wide, or from back to front, and 1 foot 10 inches high. The plan or section of the seat resembles the vertical elevation of an elliptically-headed arch. The upper surface, on which the elbows of a person sitting in the chair would rest, is decorated, on each side, by an

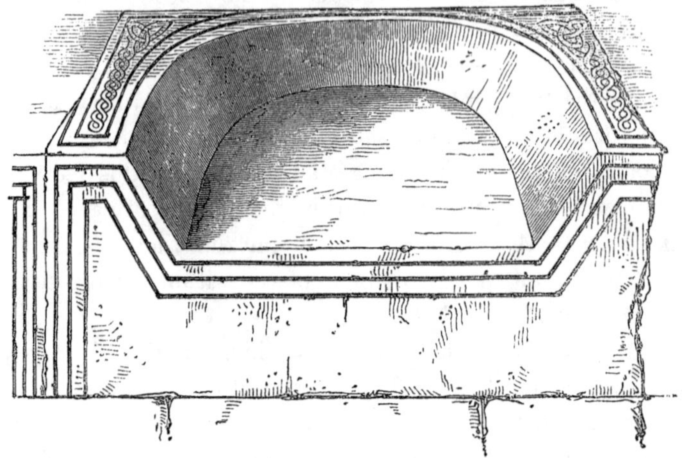

interlaced scroll, at the end of which, behind, is an interlaced Saxon knot of pointed trefoil shape. Inclosing this design, round the outer margin of the surface, and continued round that of the concavity of the seat, are incised parallel lines, giving the idea of a slightly beaded moulding; and lines of a similar kind follow the margin of the simple elevation in front. According to a plate shewing the horizontal and vertical faces of the Frith-stool, in the *Sanctuarium Dunelmense et Sanctuarium Beverlacense,* published by the Surtees Society in the year 1837, it appears that either then, or at some previous period when the drawing was made, a large concave moulding or cornice intervened between the sedile and its base, apparently of Perpendicular or Tudor character, and the base appears to have been formed of one stone. Be this as it may, I think it is questionable whether, in the original design, the lines of the ornamentation in front were not prolonged into another vertical stone below and returned at its base. I may remark here, more for the sake of future enquiry than otherwise, that on the sloping side of the elbow on the north side of the chair I fancied I could feel some incised letters, perhaps, after all, of no moment; which, in consequence of the dark situation, I was not able to observe by the eye. I have no doubt whatever that this is the cathedra of the Saxon bishops of Hexham.[s]

Until the recent "restoration," a considerable space below the third arch from the last, on the south side of the choir, was occupied by a chantry chapel, which was always known by the name of "the Lord of the Manor's pew," until the discovery of the armorial crescents of the Ogle family upon it gave it the name of "the Ogle shrine." From a drawing of it, made by Mr. Fairless, before it was ruthlessly destroyed, it appears that it was of the same Tudor style as characterized the rest of the old woodwork of the choir. The elevation on the north side remained much less perfect than on the south, but both had presented a base of six panels, merely divided by strips without tracery, upon which stood as many detached shafts with ogee heads and plain tracery in the spandrils. Above this was a cornice, returned at the west end, enriched with quatrefoils, as were the beam which divided the panelled basement from the lattices, and the outer faces of those which supported the east end. The chapel is not remembered to have retained its altar, but on stripping off the baize from the pew, before its demolition, a fine tryptich which had surmounted it was discovered; the removal of which from the church, as "old materials," was the subject of much indignant comment in the journals at the time. It is thus described in the public prints of the day:—"This interesting relic," says the writer, "is a tryptich of the fifteenth century. It has a massive frame of oak, 4 feet 3 inches by 6 feet 6 inches, of the same character of moulding and carving as the screenwork empaling the shrine. The three panels of the picture are of an uniform size—1 foot 10 inches by 3 feet 8 inches, and the subjects in each are confined within an outline of a vesica form, and enriched with diapered backgrounds. The centre compartment represents Christ in the act of rising from the tomb, the

[s] The Frith-stool at Beverley is almost identical with that of Hexham in shape, but it is entirely devoid of ornament.

lower half of the figure being concealed by the decorated side slab. The eyes are closed and head bowed down, an expression of inconceivable sorrow and compassion pervading the features. Blood streams from the crown of thorns and from the wounds. Above the crown of thorns, which is curiously raised in slight relief, is a gorgeous nimbus, which, it is evident, once blazed with gold. This ornament is in bold relief, as are two candlesticks placed on either side of the tomb. Below the tomb and behind the nimbus and in other interstices there is a diaper of gold stars. A wavy vesica of clouds confines the whole, which stands out thus cloud-encircled from a deep crimson background, diapered with hexagonal sombre-coloured rosettes, each rosette containing the letters I. H. C. painted in the same tint. The compartment to the left of this contains a full-length figure of the Virgin holding the Infant Christ on one arm, and a sceptre, announcing her sovereignty as Queen of Heaven, in the other hand. The nimbus of this figure is also in high relief, and is more elaborate in design than that upon the head of Christ. A raised nimbus surrounds the head of the Infant, and the sceptre is richly ornamented in relief. The robe of the Virgin is of a crimson colour, and has a small geometrical pattern upon it. It is fastened upon the breast with a row of embossed clasp ornaments. Over the arm, on which she holds the Child, and below her waist, falls a piece of amber-toned drapery covered with fleurs-de-lys. This figure is surrounded by a double border of golden rays following the same vesica outline, behind which the background is diapered with starry circles. The third compartment is filled with a representation of St. John. He bears in one hand a chalice, in the other a palm branch. The edge of the chalice, its stem, and its base, together with the nimbus of the Saint, are all rendered in the same character of ornament as that of the other subjects, but of different designs. The vesica outline of this painting is formed by a flowing scroll-like pattern. The diaper of the background is similar to that of the Virgin's panel. Portions of the curious raised ornament are lost, and the base of the centre panel has been used roughly." Above this tryptich was an horizontal tester-like canopy, rising higher than the lateral lattices, its concave face towards the west divided by ribs, decorated with quatrefoils; the intermediate spaces between them being boarded and painted with crescents, which, so far as I could judge from a faded specimen which I have seen, were of a white colour.

Near the site of this chapel may still be seen a marble slab in the floor with this inscription graven on a plate of brass :— "*Hic jacet Robertus Ogle, filius Elene Bertram filie Roberti Bertram militis, qui obiit in vigilia Omnium Sanctorum anno Domini m°cccc°x°, cujus anime propicietur Deus. Amen.*"[t] The corner pieces, which are known[u] to have borne the arms of Ogle and Bertram quarterly, now retain only the latter coat.

Mr. Hodgson,[v] in his description of the church of Hexham, published about the year 1809, says, "The *bishop's pew,* and *the oratory* near Prior Richard's tomb, have been ornamented with paintings, at present much defaced by time and bad usage;" these are, probably, the two chapels which have been described. He mentions also, "*The Litany desk,* at present placed on the west side of the transept." This remains there still, but I prefer to mention it here, in connexion with the other ancient furniture of the choir, from which it has at some time been dismembered. The desk itself is of polygonal form, like the jube in the rood screen, with a screen projecting laterally on each side, which, if they occupied this position originally, must have intercepted considerably a free passage in the choir. The whole is formed of fourteen oaken panels, having cinquefoiled ogee heads with plain tracery above, and divided by neatly

[t] There is much to be said about Sir Robert Ogle. He was much employed by the archbishops of York. Isabella, the widow of his grandson, Robert, first lord Ogle, desired to be buried in the monastery of Hexham in 1477-8 (MSS. Lansdowne, cccxxvi, 179 *b*).

[u] Wright, History of Hexham, p. 88.

[v] Topogr. and Hist. Description of Northumberland. Beauties of England and Wales, p. 163.

moulded styles, wreathed with labels of divers colours, but apparently without inscriptions. It is of the same date as the rest of the ancient woodwork of the choir, and has been painted throughout, like the coæval rood-screen. Each panel contains a full-length figure of a Sainted personage, about two feet high. Some of them have been designated by inscriptions, as in the unnecessary instance of St. Peter, but they are all nearly worn out, or so obscured, like the symbols which many of the figures bear, as to be illegible, without cleaning or the application of a powerful artificial light. Like the other paintings I have previously mentioned, and others about to be described, their execution is not of ruder character than might be expected from their age; but they appear to me to be of considerable value for the illustration of English art, particularly as practised in the religious houses, at the close of the fifteenth century. For although it is hardly within the verge of probability that they may not have been produced by English artists, or independent of any foreign feeling, still at least it is infinitely more probable that this should be so in the case of a large series of bulky objects of this connected character, than in that of many detached and portable pictures of a similar date, of the purpose and origin of which we can know nothing, neither whence they may have been imported. The panel in front of the desk represents our Blessed Lord holding a cross and pendent streamer, and elevating His hand in the act of benediction. The next to it, on the north, has a picture of the Virgin Mary with our Saviour in her arms. The interstices between the tracery of all the panels have been coloured alternately red and green, like similar work on the rood-screen.

At the time when Mr. Hodgson wrote, there were placed "over the Litany desk full-length portraits of the Saints Wilfrid, John of Beverley, Acca, Fridbert, Gilfrid, Alcmund, and Eata, with this inscription above their heads, '*Fundatores, hujus loci.*'" I presume Hutchinson[w] had previously alluded

[w] View of Northumberland, A.D. 1776; vol. i., p. 98.

to these pictures when he indulged in the singular observation, "There are some grim and lion-like Saints painted in the aisles, among whom stands St. John of Beverley, of hideous aspect." Mr. Wright[r] says that, in the year 1823, they were "more advantageously disposed above the screen." Recently, they have been placed—for they are in two divisions—in what we hope is only a temporary position, one reared before the other, at the west side of the north transept, where the foremost of them can only be conveniently examined, though probably they are objects unique of their kind. It is a wooden tablet between eight and nine feet square, framed of oak boards, enclosed on the sides and at the top in a frame, of which the concave moulding, inclining inwards, is enriched with quatrefoils, whilst at the front of it is a slender pinnacled buttress, to which a lower one of "flying" character is attached. The superficial surface is occupied throughout by a very curious painting, divided by pinnacled and staged buttress strips or styles into four compartments, each 4 feet 9 inches high and 1 foot 10 inches wide, and surmounted by a light and elegant semi-hexagonal ogee-headed canopy of wood, the finial of which rises to the upper cornice or frame of the tablet. The subjects below, executed in the time of King Henry VII., and in excellent state of preservation as regards design and colour, represent four full-length figures of as many bishops of Hexham. The first, mitred and nimbed, wearing the pall and holding a crosier or cross staff, may be supposed to represent St. Wilfrid. The rest are nimbed and all bear staves, but the heads are not clearly discernible through the coating of dirt. I was informed that the spandrils between the heads of the canopies contain the armorial insignia usually assigned in the middle ages to the prelates represented below, and that the name of each was inscribed below the bracket, at his feet, but the imperfect light which reaches this part of the church did not enable me to trace the one, nor the position of the tablet to see the other. These

[r] History of Hexham, p. 71.

brackets are of semi-octagonal form, and of similar width and projection as the canopies above, and perhaps, on particular occasions, may have supported lights. Behind this tablet is placed another of precisely similar design, but of three compartments only. In their original position, they do not seem to have been joined closely together, so as to form a continuous subject; for the outer transverse face of each side of the frames is ornamented with the quatrefoil moulding; a fact which also suggests that they have been placed, at first, like ordinary pictures, against the face of a wall, and not inserted between pillars or other masonry; in which case the outer margin would have been left plain, to join the stonework. Mr. Fairless was told, long ago, by an old man whose recollection extended beyond the period when Hutchinson wrote, that he remembered these pictures to have stood near the east end of the choir. It is a somewhat singular circumstance with reference to the period when they were executed, and the church where they were exhibited, that, at the very time, Huby, abbat of Fountains, in rebuilding a portion of the church which had been erected by the founder of Hexham at Ripon, introduced a series of inscriptions commemorating the sainted persons who had been monks in that monastery in Saxon times,—St. Cuthbert, St. Eata, St. Wilfrid, and St. Willebrord, two of whom are depicted in these tablets at Hexham.

The whole of the ancient sepulchral monuments in the choir, whether raised above the floor or forming a portion of it, have been either ruthlessly destroyed, or removed to another part of the church. Mr. Wallis,[y] speaking of this church in his Antiquities of Northumberland, published in 1769, observes, "The floor is mostly covered with ancient gravestones. Many have been inlaid with brass, and others with croziers. They are very entire after they have been trod underfoot for so many ages;" and Mr. Wright,[z] even so recently as the year 1823, tells us that "the floor of the church is flagged with stones, at one

[y] Vol. ii., p. 96. [z] History of Hexham, p. 83.

time nearly all monumental. Flat coffin-shaped stones laid even with the pavement, on which were simply inscribed the name and rank of the person buried, are the most ancient funeral monuments found within our churches, and these appear to have been numerous in Hexham; but what remains of them amounts to little more than nothing." The "oldest" of these, as he conjectured, was then "visible in the floor of a pew, at a short distance from the organ loft, raised a little from the common floor—long, flat, and coffin-shaped, in length 6 feet, in breadth 2½ feet, divided longitudinally by a deep cut. On the left side of this division is a cross fleury without a shield, border, or any ornament. The inscription is between two small crosses in one line along the opposite side of the division, and announces simply that + JOH'S. MALERBE JACET HIC." This stone is now placed in the aisle of the north transept. Mr. Wright goes on to say, "In the south aisle of the choir are two table monuments. From one the effigy has been removed; and on the other is the recumbent figure of a knight of the holy banner—supposed to be a member of the baronial family of Umframville." When Dr. Johnston of Pontefract visited Hexham, about two hundred years ago, he found this monument in the same aisle, so that probably this was its original position. According to Hutchinson's account, the particular spot where it stood was a little above the inlaid slab of Sir Robert Ogle. It is now laid, without any base of masonry, in the aisle of the north transept. The head of the effigy rests on two cushions, the one placed like a lozenge on a square, without supporters. The lower part of the crossed legs is broken off, and there is no trace of an animal or other object against which they may have rested; in fact the requisite space does not seem to be afforded. There is nothing peculiar about the costume, which exhibits a suite of link mail, partially covered with a sleeveless surcoat strapped round the waist. The sword is suspended from an undecorated belt, and the shield, which has a narrow guige, is charged, in relief, with a cinquefoil, surrounded by a number of crosses much battered, but it is to be remarked that one which remains uninjured is not a *cross crosslet,* as subsequently borne in the arms of Umfreville, but a *cross patee.* In Ralph Brooke's[a] Catalogue and Succession, etc., he blazons the arms of Gilbert Umfreville, earl of Angus, lord of Prudhoe, Otterburne, Harbotle, and Redesdale, whom this effigy probably commemorates, "Gueulles a une quinkfoile, & le champe croise le patee d'or;" and in a Roll of Arms, of the time of Edward the Third, "Le Conte de Angesse porte de goules ove un quintefoil d'or et croissletz d'or." The effigy rests on a slab, the chamfer of which is decorated on the south or right side with two semi-globular objects at the upper, and two at the lower end, but so much worn down as not to be positively identified with the "ball flower ornament." At the east end of it is the crouching figure of a dog; the rest of the design, if any, being lost, through a corner of the slab having been broken off. On the chamfer, at the head of the stone, are three objects, but only one, apparently a dog with something before its mouth, is tolerably well defined. In a particular light, another seems like a squirrel with a sprig of foliage. On that on the left-hand side of the figure are three animals, probably dogs or wolves—for their present situation close to the wall of the aisle forbids an accurate examination by the eye. This chamfered slab rests on another boldly embattled, but at the head, foot, and right side only, as if the figure had originally been placed against some object on the north side. It is, I think, extremely probable that these animals introduced on the chamfer may have allusion to a very peculiar tenure, by which the Umfrevilles held lands, in grand serjeanty, of the Crown. Madox in his Baronia Anglica, p. 244, says that the castle of Harbotle and the manor of Otterburne were held of the king, in capite, by Robert Umfreville, in 1428, by the service of keeping the valley of Redesdale free from wolves and robbers.

[a] Page 15.

In the Testa de Nevill, compiled from Inquisitions taken in the reigns of Henry III. and Edward I., it is said that "Ricardus de Umframvill tenet vallem de Redesdale, per servitium ut custodiat vallem a latronibus, de antiquo feoffamento;"[b] and it is elsewhere entered in the same document,[c] "G de Humframvill tenet Redesdal per regalem potestatem," but no mention is made there of wolves, neither is the serjeanty mentioned in a plea of Quo Warranto, relating to the franchise of Redesdale, held at Newcastle on the morrow of St. Hilary, 21st Edward I.[d] Mr. Hodgson,[e] however, after remarking that the printed copy of the Testa makes no mention of wolves or foxes, adds, "but a Harleian MS. of the time of Henry III., says, in one part—'Idem Henricus tenuit de rege in capite in com. Northumbriæ manerium de Laxton—per sergentiam *ad fugand. lupum cum canibus suis* per quatuor com.;' and in another part—'idem Vitali tenuit manerium de Laxton—de rege in capite per serjentiam *currendi ad lupum* ad mandatum regis.'" It may be also added, in illustration of this statement, that on the tower at Elsden in Northumberland is a sculpture—dating in the fifteenth century—of the arms of Umfreville—a cinquefoil within an orle of cross crosslets, with a cinquefoil for the crest—supported by two *wolves*.

This effigy appears originally either to have been covered with a herse, or certainly with some kind of canopy; for there still may be seen on the surface of the chamfered bed of the figure four pieces of iron soldered into it, a portion of the stone around being also cut away to form a firmer footing for the shaft which rested upon it. The two uppermost of these spikes are on a level with the bottom of the lower cushion, which supports the head of the figure; the others proportionately placed at about thirteen inches from the end of the slab in which they are inserted, one on each side of the legs. Metal

[b] Testa de Nevill, p. 392. [c] Ibid., p. 385.

[d] Placita de Quo Warr., p. 600.

[e] Topogr. and Hist. Description of Northumberland, p. 140.

also seems to have been let into a little hole, midway the slab, by the right thigh of the effigy, an opposite shaft having probably rested on the back of the middle animal in the chamfer. Besides these indications, there is a lump of solder, about 3½ inches by 1 inch, let into the lower supporting cushion for the head, in the centre of the vertical part of its west end. Gilbert de Umfreville, earl of Angus, whom this effigy may be supposed to represent, died in the year 1307, and before the 8th of November, when his son Robert was designated by that title.[f]

The vacant table near the tomb of Umfreville," mentioned by Mr. Wright, was supposed by him with great probability to have been originally occupied by an "effigy of superior workmanship, representing a lady;" which, in his time, was placed not far from "Prior Richard's shrine," but now near the tomb of Umfreville, in the north transept. The head, which rests upon a large rectangular cushion without supporters, is attired with a coverchief; the chin, neck, and shoulders being enveloped in one of those wimples or gorgets which provoked the satirical poets of the time of Edward the First. The body is enveloped in a loose mantle with tight sleeves, drawn up under the armpits, so as to throw the drapery into very effective folds. The feet rest against a mutilated animal, partly environed by the skirt of the robe. There are no data which will enable us to conjecture whom the effigy commemorates.

Another sepulchral memorial remained in the choir in the year 1823 which cannot now be identified. Mr. Wright says, "stepping out of the shrine, you tread on a stone sculptured into a cross bound with garlands. This is hidden by the pews upon it and about it."

In concluding my observations on this part of the church, I may remark that there is suspended, above the former site of the shrine, part of a helmet, which is traditionally said to have been worn by Sir John Fenwick, who was slain at Marston Moor,

[f] See a notice of him in Dugdale's Baronage, vol. i., p. 504, and Palgrave's Parl. Writs, vol. i., p. 876. Vincent upon Brooke.

and which shews an indentation said to correspond in position with a fracture on his skull, recently, and, perhaps, still, preserved at the manor-office here. It seems to be two centuries older than his time, but, no doubt, has been set up as part of a funeral achievement. Although I am not aware that it has been connected with this object, I must add that I am in possession of a curious mediæval sword, given to me by an old person, whose father said he had obtained it from Hexham church. It has a rude iron pommel, but no cross bar at the hilt, and bears on one side of the upper part of the blade this inscription, in letters inclining to Longobardic form :—

SO : IVSTICI · FLORET · SO · IST · AL · WEL · IN · DE · WERLT.

and on the other the same sentiment in old French :—

SI · IVSTICE · EST · ABONDE · TOVT · EST · BIEN · A · LE · MONDE.

Dr. Charlton, of Newcastle, has a copper chalice which was found, a few years ago, in forming the warm air flue in the choir. At the end of the Preface to the First Volume there is an engraving of a small plate of silver, now in the British Museum, which came from this church. It bears the figure of a Saint, and is of a very early date. I have reason to believe that many other relics have been discovered within the Priory which have been, most unfortunately, dispersed.

The south wing of the transept seems to have been commenced very soon after the completion of the choir. In consequence of the passage, which generally occurs in conventual churches between the outer end of the transept and the chapter house, having been included here within it, the last southern bay is occupied, in a singular fashion, by a platform over the vaulting of the passage, rising as high as the pillars of the east aisle. It is approached at the west end by a wide stone staircase of thirty-two steps, which forms a most picturesque object from the opposite extremity of the church, and is protected by a parapet wall that does not slope in the usual manner, but rises five times vertically, to form horizontal stages, and is finished by a plain coping, with a roll at the apex. Under the staircase are four recesses, or closets; the highest and largest has a semi-circular head; the next one of elliptical form; those of the lowest being flat. From the west end of the platform access is obtained to a geometrical staircase communicating with the contiguous triforium and clerestory, and, through them, with the tower. At the opposite end of it a rudely-formed doorway admits us into a chamber, measuring about twelve feet by ten feet, with a barrel-vault divided by a single transverse rib. It is lighted by two very narrow, square-headed openings, which apparently have never been filled with glass, unless it hung in in a frame upon crooks, which still remains in one of the lights. It is not known, traditionally or otherwise, to what use it was anciently applied; but it may not be a very improbable conjecture that it was used as a sanctuary chamber.

The introduction of the platform curtails the lower portion of the east side of the transept within three bays, whilst the triforium and clerestory have four. The pillars that divide it from the aisle have octagonal bases, and are formed, like those of the choir, of eight members, but have four semi-octagonal faces with as many tripled shafts intervening. The capitals are merely moulded, and the orders of the arches chamfered, without any ornament whatever. The triforium is of the same general design as that of the choir, but is a little more advanced in the development of the mouldings, and has only one pillar to support the sub-arches; while, in the arrangement of the triple arcades of the clerestory, a stilted arch in the middle supersedes that supported by shaft above shaft. The fourth bay of the triforium, surmounting the entrance to the supposed sanctuary chamber, contains only two plain lancet openings. The vaulting shafts dividing the bays, now much mutilated, have been single cylinders above the level of the capitals of the arcade of the triforium, but spring from brackets in a tripled form below. Where the string course below the triforium joins the pier of the tower, is a fragment of another with a square face, but whether of much higher antiquity, or the initiation of a work that was immediately discontinued, cannot, perhaps, be determined without the removal of the whitewash. In the latter case, however, there is no apparent reason why it should have been retained.

The aisle of this wing of the transept has two lancet lights, like those of the choir, but enriched with a convex moulding between the nook shaft and the glass. Triple shafts, with a fillet in front, resting on moulded brackets, support the vaulting, which has no bosses at the intersection of the groining ribs. The string course on which the windows stand is not prolonged from that of the contiguous aisle of the choir, but commences, as the other ends, abruptly at the angle, with a different section, and at a rather higher level. The manner in which the junction of the vaulting of this aisle with that of the choir was effected is worthy of examination. The last bay, at the south end, is now enclosed for a vestry; and, judging from the unmoulded extremities, it would seem that the lattice on the north side is in its old position. It is of Tudor date, and has nine compartments, divided by neatly panelled mullions or styles, with tall pinnacles.

Where the passage of the triforium crosses the south end of the transept it is lighted from the church by two groupes of lancet-headed openings, the middle arch being wider than that on each side and stilted. The triple supporting shafts have fillets in front, and, in the eastern groupe, the nail-head ornament appears between the reeds of the shafts. In the clerestory are three tall lancet lights, the central one higher than the rest; the intervening narrow panels, recessed for about half their height, being supported by triple shafts.

The basement-story of the west side of the transept is engaged by the staircase before mentioned, at the base of which a lofty doorway once opened into the cloister. It seems to have been the original intention of the architect to build the triforium after the same design as that of the south end, as shewn by the arch which joins it, but he afterwards changed his plan. It now presents four lancet lights, between which are three lancet-headed openings of inferior height. Like those enclosing the windows, they have a plain hood moulding, and their impost mouldings are prolonged to the jambs of the arches between which they are placed.

The clerestory is composed of four bays, each lancet light appearing in the middle of an arcade of three members, those on each side being lower and narrower, but all much stilted above the capitals of the shafts. This part of the church retains its old roof, of the same date and character as that of the choir, but the bosses are more effective, being not so flat.

Six interesting monumental slabs are now preserved in the south transept, all of them disinterred within the last few years, having been found on the south side of the church. One of them, engraved in the Journal of the Archæological Institute, vol. v., p. 257, is in as perfect condition as when it left the hand of the mason. It has an Early English moulding round the margin, and is inscribed ✠ HIC : JACET MATILDA : VXOR : PHILIPPI : MERCERARII : with a pair of shears incised after the final word. The other stones are of ruder character, but they merit perpetuation by the graver, as valuable examples of incised Longobardic letters of the thirteenth century. They taper but slightly from head to foot, and three of them have plain margins; another is beaded slightly. All the inscriptions run down the middle of the stones, enclosed within parallel lines, and are as follows:—

✠ JOH'S : DE : DALTONA.
✠ . . . V. DE WEL . . . .
✠ ROBERT' : DE KIRKEBRIDE ✠
✠ HENRICVS DE WALTONE ✠
✠ ROBERTUS : DE : BEDELINT' ✠

There is also here half of a very massive gravestone, slightly chamfered with the words RICARDVS : DE . . . ., incised between the deep grooves or channels.

In comparison with the south wing of the transept, the northern one shews much progression in style, together with some alterations in the design. On the west side, the basement,—with the exception of the space occupied by the arch, which once opened into the aisle of the nave,—is enriched by a deeply-recessed trefoil-headed arcade, of which the shafts and bases with the bench-table are destroyed, if the latter is not concealed below the modern floor. The spandrils are filled with plain recessed quatrefoils, below each of which a smaller quatrefoil of foliage is embossed. The pier of the archway, once opening into the nave aisle, which flanks this arcade, is of the same date, but the opposite one appears to be of the later date of the west side of the tower, into which it is bonded. Over this arch are three blank niches, standing on a string course. The triforium is lighted by three tall lancets, appearing under an arcade of seven members, so that the central one is flanked on each side by a double recess of little less altitude, but much less width. The shafts by which they are supported rise no higher than the ceiling of the pathway, causing, therefore, the intervention of a vertical and unmoulded space between their capitals and the imposts of the arches, of such considerable altitude that the latter can hardly come within the denomination of being "stilted." The clerestory—similar in character to that of the west side of the opposite wing, save that the mouldings are much bolder and more effective—is composed of four bays; the opening for the windows in those at the extremities being flanked only by one arch, the rest by two.

A continuation of the arcaded basement ornaments the north face of the transept. Above are three tall and narrow lancet lights, ranging with those on the west side, but divided by triple and banded shafts. They have a moulding at the angle of the jamb, and another next the glass; and the passage that traverses their sills ends abruptly, and does not pass into the triforium on the east side, which is at a much higher level, and is approached by a staircase descending from the clerestory.

These windows are surmounted by three other lancets, of similar width but lesser height; the openings much stilted in the heads, and supported by clustered shafts.

The junction of the north side of the transept with that of the east is so unskilfully managed, that we must conclude that both had not been erected as one work. The latter, however, is more ornamented than any other portion of the church, and it has an aspect which may suggest to some that either the canons had not been inattentive spectators of the works in progress at York minster, or that the influence of their illustrious patron, archbishop Walter Gray,[g] had been more directly applied. It is divided from its aisle by three columns with octagonal bases, the circular neck being adorned, on the horizontal surface, with semi-globular objects, but so worn down as not to be certainly identified with the ball-flower ornament. Each of the pillars is composed of four semi-cylindrical members, with as many triple shafts intervening. The last, towards the south, has the addition of a nail-headed moulding in the base, and the respond a semi-octagonal face like the western responds of the choir. No ornament appears on the capitals, but the archivolts are full of mouldings more perfectly developed than those of any other portion of the church, and their hood mouldings differ also, in rising from bosses of foliage. Like

[g] It is remarkable that we find at York a carpenter of the name of Gilbert de Corbridge. Archbishop Gray in the following document rewards him for his services. It is dated about 1250. We may reasonably presume that he would not be brought to York until he had made himself known and useful at Hexham: "Omnibus, etc. Noveritis nos dedisse, concessisse et præsenti carta confirmasse Gilberto de Corbrig, carpentario, pro homagio et servitio suo, duas bovatas et duas acras terræ cum pertinentiis in villa de Milford, illas videlicet quas Nicholaus filius Johannis quondam tenuit; et duodecim acras et dimidiam cum pertinentiis in Colepit-haghe de novo assarto nostro; tenendum et habendum de nobis et successoribus nostris sibi et hæredibus suis, libere, quiete, pacifice et integre jure hæreditario in perpetuum. Reddendo inde annuatim nobis et successoribus nostris xv solidos v denarios, solvendos ad duos anni terminos, videlicet medietatem ad festum Sancti Martini in hyeme, et medietatem ad Pentecosten ——" [s. d. anno xxxiij. Ex Rot. Minore Walteri Gray, in dorso].

the same member of the east side of the south transept and of the choir, the triforium exhibits four large, wide, semi-circular-headed openings, but much richer in the reduplication of the mouldings; and the two pointed sub-arches of each are enriched with dog-tooth mouldings, their shafts being tripled and finished with octagonal capitals. The vaulting shafts, also, are tripled, and spring from beautifully foliated bosses. The clerestory resembles that of the west side of the south transept, and the roof that of the opposite wing.

In the aisle, the head of the basement arcade occurs at a lower level than on the other sides. It has been highly decorated in the spandrils by sculptured foliage, and probably other subjects, much of which has been barbarously and wantonly hewn away, and the rest choked with limewash. The supporting shafts are single cylindrical columns. There are three small lancet lights towards the east, moulded at the margin of the jamb, and another towards the north, but with a trefoil head within, formed by shouldering the arch. The vaulted roof has ribs of several reeds, and bosses of foliage of slight convexity, that may have suggested the section of those on the Tudor roofs of the choir and transept; the shafts resting on beautifully designed brackets. The aisle has formerly been divided—probably soon after it was built—into three chapels, the brackets for statues still remaining. One at the south end, introduced by Prior Leschman, bears his initials disposed in the form of St. Andrew's cross, as occurs in other instances before mentioned.

Between the end of this aisle and the contiguous aisle of the choir is a tomb filling the whole space between the pier and the wall. The masonry of the base supports a slab incised with a cross, elegantly adorned with vine leaves, engraved in the first volume of this work, page 36. It is canopied by a low elliptical-headed arch of the Decorated style, with a continuous impost, having a bracket for a statue on the west side, towards the north, and one at each side of the jamb, towards the south.

The top of the tomb is coped horizontally, with a panelled projection in the centre of each diagonal face, which may have supported a figure. A century ago, as it would appear from Hutchinson's account, this was supposed to be the tomb of Elfwald, king of Northumbria, who was slain in 788, and buried—"cum magno honore"—in the church of St. Andrew of Hexham. I regard this, however, as a mere baseless conjecture. For, if the canons of Hexham, at the memorable translation of the relics of their church in the year 1154, paid no especial mark of respect—as we may infer from the silence of Aelred, who chronicled the ceremony—to the remains of King Elfwald, over the place of whose murder they were told that a "mysterious light was seen to hover and to shine," and even a church was built; it is very difficult to imagine what was the nature of the impulse which could induce their successors, or, indeed, any person, to prefer his commemoration to that of any of the sainted persons that are resting here, and to have erected such a monument after he had mouldered in his grave between five and six hundred years. Moreover, if Camden, when he made his survey in the time of Queen Elizabeth, and in earnest search of historical monuments, never noted such a supposition, while he recorded the presence of the effigy of Umfreville, and even its cross-legged position and charged shield, it is fair to infer that it has arisen in subsequent times. Dr. Johnston, also, who visited the church about two centuries ago, makes no mention of it.

At the north end of this aisle, a cross-legged effigy is now laid on the floor, which, most likely, has occupied this or an adjacent site at least for a similar period, for Dr. Johnston observes, "In the north cross of the conventuall, now the parochiall church of Hexham, lyith this effigie with a free stone," the same being identified by the armorial bearings on the shield —a fess charged with three garbs. When Mr. Hutchinson saw it in 1776, it was "in a part behind the north door;" and Mr. Wright reports it, in 1823, as being "near the north door, removed from its table." The head, which rests on a rectangular cushion without supporters, is attired in a round-topped mail hood, bound with a fillet, and overlying the surcoat. The body is vested in a suite of mail, covered with a sleeveless surcoat, fastened round the waist by a strap, which contracts the plaits below so as to appear like a row of fusils; the hands are elevated in prayer. A large shield, on which the fess is sunk so that the face of the three garbs with which it is charged is on a plane with the field, is suspended by a guige over his right shoulder. The sword belt is embossed with large round plates. One of the crossed legs is broken off, but the other, armed with a spur, rests against a couchant lion. Judging from "his shield or bearing, a fesse azure with three garbs proper," though no colour is now visible on it, Mr. Hutchinson conjectured[h] that this effigy commemorates "one of the Aydens of Ayden Castle,"—about five miles north-east of Hexham—"the arms assumed by the Edens of the north at this day being greatly similar." And he goes on to say that "the male line of the family was extinct in Edward the First's time; and Emma, the heiress and relict of that family, was by him, as a royal ward, given in marriage to Wallis." The Testa de Nevill has mention only of Geoffrey de Ayden, as tenant of a carucate of land in Whelpington, within the barony of Umfreville.[i] I do not remember to have seen any ancient roll of arms that confirms Mr. Hutchinson's assignation of the heraldic charge on the shield, but until the subject can be effectually investigated, it may be remembered that, in Somerset Glover's Roll, the baron of Tindale is said to bear the singular coat, Argent, on a fess or, three garbs sable—and that he resided at Langley Castle, above six miles west of Hexham. This barony was held by the family of Tindale until about the year 1233, when it appears from the Pipe Roll that Nicholas de Bolteby—so called from his manor near Thirsk, in Yorkshire—who had married Philippa, daughter

[h] View of Northumberland, A.D. 1776. Vol. i., p. 98.

[i] Testa de Nevill, pp. 383, 390.

and co-heiress of Adam de Tindale, paid twenty marks for his relief, and for obtaining seisin of her estates. I think that the effigy represents this Nicholas Bolteby, who died in the last year of the reign of Henry III., a period to which the costume of the figure may be assigned. Be this as it may, I need scarcely add that Mr. Wallis was obviously mistaken in supposing this effigy to represent the duke of Somerset, who was beheaded after the battle of Hexham, in 1464; although, perhaps, it had been so reported for several generations before his time; for in "A Relation of a Short Survey of Twenty-six Northern Counties,[j] made by three Norwich soldiers," in the year 1634, they said that, in this church "much defaced and decay'd, and now unseamely kept," is the monument "of a Duke that was slain in a battle against the Scotts."

In Mr. Wallis's account of this church, published in the year 1769, he says that, "near the north door on the right hand is a flat funeral stone, very ancient. It has a crozier upon it, and this inscription—Hic jacet Thomas de Devilstone."[k] Mr. Hutchinson also noticed it "in the pavement of the cross aisle," together with "another with a crozier and chalice, inscribed '*Johannes Dew*,' with the usual legendary prayer in the margin—*Orate pro anima*,"[l] etc. But both the stones were missing in 1823.[m] It is possible that both these topographers may have mistaken some other object for a crozier. At all events, there is no such person as Thomas de Devilstone on the list of the Priors of Hexham, and, if he had held that high office, it would have been recorded on his gravestone. The other stone, which, as Hutchinson tells us,[n] was "inscribed in very rude characters, *Hic jacet Johes dew*," etc., may possibly

[j] Lansdowne MS., 213.

[k] Nat. Hist. and Antiq. of Northumberland, vol. ii., p. 96.

[l] View of Northumberland, vol. i., p. 98.

[m] Wright's History of Hexham, p. 85.

[n] Tour to the Lakes, p. 310.

have covered the remains of Prior John de Walworth, who died in the year 1358.[o]

There are now preserved in the north transept several detached monuments of considerable interest which have been found within late years in or about the church. Of these the most ancient is part of the head of a Saxon cross. On one side a boss in the centre is surrounded with an interlaced scroll, on the other the scroll appears without the boss. The edge around is left plain, but a fragment of the shaft attached to the lower arm shews that it has been decorated with scroll work, and there are traces of an inscription. A delineation of this relic will be found on p. xxxi, no. 3.

Of later date is a fragment of a ridged tomb representing the roof of the *domus ultima*, the horizontal lines of the tegulation being rounded. On one side may be traced the letters ✠ EMI, and on the other SENT. Also a portion of a foot

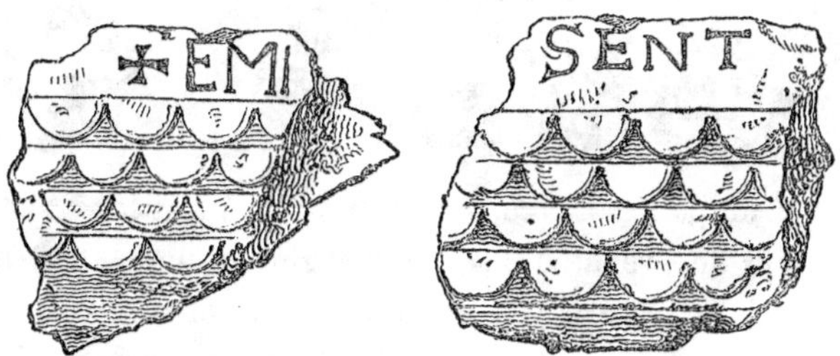

stone, one side bearing a rude cross, which heralds would describe as a cross patee fitchee, the other being rough, to face the grave.

To the Saxon era also may be referred a large sculptured stone, greater in height than width, which apparently has covered a grave. The bottom of it is unwrought, as if for fixture into the earth, but the sides and top, which has an elliptical sweep with a convex projection at each end, are covered with a very singular kind of rude ornamentation in relief, of which an adequate idea can only be conveyed by the

[o] See Vol. I., p. clxvii.

pencil. A somewhat similar stone is engraved in Mr. Cutts's volume of Incised Slabs.

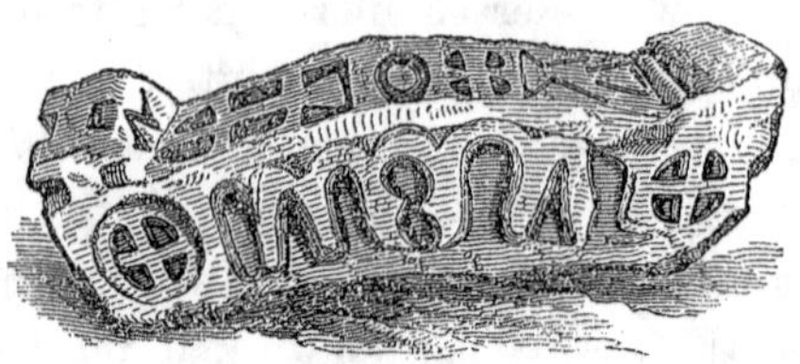

On the upper face of a semi-octagonal or ridged stone, that may have covered the grave of a Norman child, is inscribed PVEr IVRDAN'. Each sloping side bears a cross of patee form, accompanied on one face with an incised pattern of vertical and diagonal lines like the letters I and X united; on the other by an object which has been supposed to represent a sword.

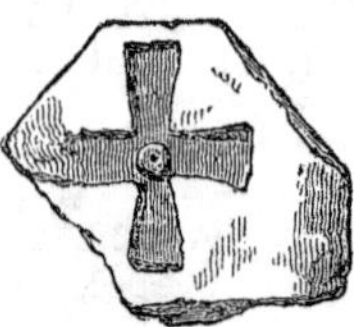

Next, in point of age, comes a slab, 5 feet long and 1 foot 7 inches wide, rebated at the margin around, that bears a deeply incised or grooved representation of a cross with its pedestal shaft and head, but without any ornamentation—containing thus the germ of the design that was so richly and tastefully developed in the thirteenth century.

There are also here two slabs incised with Early English crosses, and three massive gravestones of the same period. One to the memory of John Malerbe has been already mentioned in describing the choir, where it was formerly laid. The others have, respectively, these inscriptions incised in large Longobardic letters in a line down the middle of the stone :—

✠ HIC . JACET . RAD' . DE . TALKAN . CANO'IC'
✠ ROBERT' . DE . GISEBVRNE .

Among these sepulchral monuments is a large octagonal

stone basin like that of a font, apparently of Early English date. It has been supported by a circular shaft, and may have been used as a holy-water stoup in some part of the conventual church.

I may mention also that in the west wall of this transept, within the basement, an iron staple remains fixed, with a fetter-lock attached, but for what purpose it has been used I have not ascertained. Probably, during the confusion of the civil war of the seventeenth century, prisoners may have been sometimes kept in durance here, for a temporary period.

The central tower has been apparently erected after the completion of the choir and both wings of the transept, and on the site of one which covered the same area. Each face of its semi-piers is composed of five semi-circular shafts with plain capitals, and an abacus of the same form above the whole; the bases, like those of the pillars on the east side of the transept, being nearly buried by an elevation of the floor, which detracts much from the effect of this part of the church. On its eastern side, they appear to have been inserted, and are partly detached from the walls of the choir and transept; and from the abrupt disconnection of the base of the hood moulding above the western arch from that on the north, it may be assumed that all the sides have not been carried up at once. It will be observed also that the archivolt above the rood-screen is more richly moulded than the rest.

THE CONVENTUAL BUILDINGS.—The ruins of the conventual offices now only remain to be noticed. Of those erected by St. Wilfrid, probably no more remained after the incursion of the Danes than the foundations which Prior Richard says were visible in his day.[p] Indeed, Aelred, in his Account of the Saints of Hexham, says that his father Eilaf, at the restoration of the church, in the early part of the twelfth century, "*officina religioni convenientia, lignea tamen, propriis construxit manibus*;"[q] and these, we may infer from a passage in Prior John's

[p] Vol. I., p. 13. [q] Ibid., p. 192.

Chronicle,[r] were re-edified in stone by Prior Asketill, when archbishop Thurstan first established Augustinian canons here. All traces of these structures were, however, most probably swept away at the re-building of the conventual church in the thirteenth century, when the principal offices were ranged around such parts of the quadrangle—defined in the annexed plan—as were left unoccupied on the south side of the nave and transept. And if the portions of some of them above the basement-story were then composed of wood and plaster, like the ordinary domestic buildings of the time, we may presume that after the Scots burnt the church and town in 1296,[s] considerable renovation would be required. Although, at this time the nave is traditionally said to have been burnt down, the ruin scarcely could have been so complete as to have affected the outer walls to their foundations; and perhaps, therefore, that which protected the northern alley of the cloister may have remained until the fifteenth century, when another of sufficient height for that purpose was erected, which still remains based on the old foundation of the south side of the nave. Midway in its length it contains a large recess, covered with a four-centred arch, that may have served for keeping the books in temporary use in the carrels or studies of the canons.[t] Davies says in his Description of the Ancient Monuments of the Mo-

[r] Ibid., p. 107. [s] Ibid., Preface, p. lxxxii.

[t] I can only trace two volumes which were at Hexham.

I. A Bible, of the folio size, about 13 inches by 9, and of the writing of the twelfth century. It is in double column, and is imperfect, wanting the first pages of the books of Genesis and St. Matthew, which probably contained large illuminations. Several other initial letters have also been abstracted. Each book begins with an initial letter referring to some historical event which it contains. The other initials are blue or red, with long marginal decorations of the reverse colour. The volume is now in the parish library at the church of St. Nicholas, Newcastle-on-Tyne. The following inscriptions in it attest its history.

"LIBER SANCTI ANDREE DE HEXHAM" (manu sæc. xv.). "LIBRUM HUNC VETUSTUM ET SACRIS SCRIPTURIS REFERTUM, OLIM SANCTI ANDREÆ DE HEXHAM, NACTUS SUM EX DONO MAGISTRI JOHANNIS WELDE, CLERICI, VICESIMO DIE AUGUSTI, ANNO DOMINI 1666. RICHARDUS MATHEW APUD

nastical Church of Durham, that in "the north alley of the cloisters, opposite to the carrels in the church walls, stood great almeries of wainscot full of books;" and the same kind of arrangement existed at Fountains. At the west end of the wall, a doorway with good perpendicular mouldings has afforded an immediate passage between the quadrangle and the area of the ruined nave.

The chapter-house, though a roofless ruin, remains in better condition than might have been expected; for, after having suffered successive injuries through the unseemly purposes to which it has been applied, "to such base uses" did it "come at last," that, within memory, it was used as a butchers' slaughter-house. Fortunately, however, as yet it has escaped a projected "restoration." It is immediately adjacent to the south face of the transept, the passage which usually intervenes in conventual churches having, as before explained, been included within the church. It does not assume an octagonal form, like the chapter-houses of the canons of Bolton-in-Craven, Thornton-on-Humber, and probably of Bridlington, since we are told the latter was "coveryd with lede spere facyon;"[u] but is a parallelogram, like that in the same style which must have been among the glories of Kirkham. Until, however, the sites of many of the Augustinian Priories are relieved of the rubbish which must conceal many monuments of antiquity, it will be useless to speculate whether the octagonal form was adopted by a resolution of the Chapter-General, or otherwise. It has been erected at the same time as the south transept, the courses of

South Sheeles in com' Dunelm' oriundus, et in schola grammaticali Dunelm' per eruditos quosdam maxime honorandos educatus."

"Ex dono Thomæ Mathews filii Ricardi Mathews" (in the hand-writing of Dr. Ellison, vicar of Newcastle).

II. A copy of St. Augustine De Caritate. A plain unornamented MS. of the twelfth century, in 8vo, and written in single column. It is in the library of the dean and chapter of Durham, and constitutes MSS. Hunter, No. 57. After the preface, on the first leaf, is written "Liber Scî Andr' de Hextildesham."

[u] Chapter-house Miscell. Books. Pub. Rec. Office. Vol. A, 3, 12.

their masonry being bonded; and was approached from the eastern alley of the cloister through a lofty pointed doorway, decorated with dog-tooth work, and flanked on each side by a lancet-headed window, or rather opening, which has never contained glass. It was probably covered with drapery in the form of a curtain. The same arrangement may be seen at Kirkstall abbey, and probably once existed in many monasteries. The outer face of each of these openings—the jambs and bases of which are much fractured—was perhaps, originally, divided by a mullion into two of similar form; for that arrangement occurred in the interior, in consequence of the shaft of the arcade under the bay in which the opening was enclosed, standing in front of it. The apartment was divided into three aisles by two pillars on each side, which have been broken down, together with the vaulting which they supported. Each of the bays not occupied by the doorways was subdivided by shafts into two lancet-headed panels, the base of the arcade forming a seat. The east end, like the west, has a doorway placed between two openings, and as the wall of the transept extends beyond it on the north, and that of a contiguous building is of equal length, there has not been a glazed window in the place. I conjecture, however, that what now remains is but the vestibule to the chapter-house, though it may have served as such since the burning of the church in 1296, when, or at some subsequent period, it would appear that the eastern portion has been broken down. For, it must be observed that, not only both the exterior and the interior faces of the eastern end are arcaded and benched, but both the arcade and bench appear to have returned and extended at least as far as the end of the aisle of the transept. A few inches only of the bench table on the north side, indeed, remain; but its plinth, projecting slightly from the wall, may be traced throughout. And as the masonry above is now perfectly plain, without a trace of either panels or vaulting, though apparently not in the same condition as when originally constructed, I presume that the eastern portion of the chapter-house has never been rebuilt; and that so much of the transept wall as formed its northern side was refaced, and left as we see it now. It is evident, also, from the fractured south-east angle of the building, that the southern wall has been prolonged, but how far, the removal of a heap of rubbish alone may shew. There appears, however, to be a thick wall embedded in it, of what date is not evident, running east and west at a few yards' distance from the present termination of the ruin.

Above the present portion of the chapter-house has been a chamber, with a high-pitched roof, that encroached on the central light of the transept. It was approached from the platform at the south end of that member of the church; and some portion of it, if not the whole, may have been used as a sacristy for the preservation of the sacred vessels and the vestments, and many other purposes connected with the religious services of the convent.

On the south side of the chapter-house has been a large vaulted apartment, divided by a row of four columns, with a recess in the western wall. It has apparently had no communication with the cloister, and, perhaps, may have been used as a cellar, or for the reception of stores. The superstructure, no doubt, was the dormitory of the canons, who, had that apartment been placed elsewhere, could not, in consequence of the destruction of the nave, have descended readily to their nocturnal services in the church.

The basement-story of the modern houses, which still defines the western boundary of the cloister, has apparently served as part of the store-houses and offices of the Prior's lodgings, and to have escaped ruin, from this portion of the monastery having been chosen by the royal grantee, Sir Reginald Carnaby, for his residence in the year 1539; when, as appears from a dated panel of his arms, he made some additions to the house. The lodgings of the Prior of Bridlington and of the abbat of Sawley were in the same position; and here, as at the former place, the upper story was most likely occupied by a hall, dining-room, chapel, and sleeping chamber. Mr. Hodgson, writing in the year 1809, says of this house, then as now called the Priory, "Its cloisters and chapel were to be seen not many years since;" and adds, "Here is a finely-carved oak bedstead, around the fringe of the tester of which is this inscription in Gothic capitals, ... *Eboracensis dioseicis medit hoc opus A . . . . omini millisimo quingint* . . . . . . The imperfections were caused by an ignorant workman, who nailed the fringe to the posts of the bed without the moulding, which formerly went between them. No part of the old building remains except the manor-office, the refectory, and a small specimen of the cloisters."[v] In the year 1823, Mr. Wright observes, "A few years ago the walks of the cloister might be traced; and, within the memory of man, an elegant oratory stood on the south-east side of the garden. Its roof of stone was richly ornamented, and supported by four Ionic columns." After some unimportant remarks, he goes on to say, "the large room in the present building is supposed to have been the refectory;" and tells us that the house "was altered and repaired by Sir Walter Calverley Blackett, Bart., about 1736—burned by accident, and entirely rebuilt by T. R. Beaumont, Esq.,—again burned, and again repaired within these few years."[w]

It is to be regretted that these accounts are not given in such particular terms as might have enabled us to have inferred more clearly the condition of the house within the present century. It would have been especially interesting to have known more about the chapel, and the oratory with the ornamented roof, "supported by Ionic columns." If the latter, however, did actually exist in this form, and the volute of the capitals was not mistaken for a somewhat similar effect that occurs in Norman and transitional-Norman work, it may have been only a garden-building or summer-house, constructed, partly, by some of the

[v] Description of Northumberland, p. 166.

[w] History of Hexham, p. 185.

owners of the property out of the ruins of the Priory.[x] I apprehend that what Mr. Hodgson calls "a small specimen of the cloisters," may be a very beautiful lavatory, which still remains at the extreme southern end of what was once the wall of the western alley of the cloister, and on the right hand side of the entrance into the refectory; in which position an exquisite work of this kind may still be admired at Kirkham. The lower portion, containing the basin, has been walled up in comparatively modern times, but the head or canopy remains perfect, in the form of an arcade of seven members, all apparently in their original position, the central one being the largest. The semi-octagonal panelled shafts with spiral heads, enriched with crockets and finials, that divide the compartments, stand on short columns with beautifully sculptured capitals, which rest on fine brackets, projecting like gurgoyles, in the shape of human and animal forms. Each of these compartments is subdivided, by blank tracery, into two trefoil-headed panels with a pointed trefoil above each, the rest of the sweep of the arch being filled with a circle containing a rounded trefoil; and the whole is covered with a triangular head with crockets and finials. As it is very improbable that the canons would erect a work of this character for many years after the ravages of the Scots in 1296, when their utmost resources must have been severely taxed to provide for themselves, and more necessary works in the Church; it, perhaps, had only been just completed when the house was visited with this calamity. In 1312, the town of Hexham was burnt in a predatory incursion by Robert de Brus, and the goods of the Priory having been totally consumed or stolen, the canons were obliged to disperse, and in 1320 were still unable to return.[y] Collectors were even wandering about in the country in 1336, with the archbishop's brief, in quest of funds for the canons and their Church.[z]

[x] I have been informed by a very competent authority, that the manor house contained an interesting relic of the Priory in the shape of a painted chamber.

[y] Ibid., lix—lxv.

[z] Ibid., p. lxxv.

The refectory and kitchen of the convent probably flanked the south side of the quadrangle, but the site of the buildings is now laid level with the sward, together with that of many other offices that would be necessarily required for the domestic and agricultural purposes of the House. In consequence of probable alterations made by owners of the property after the Suppression, it is unsafe to pronounce a decided opinion on appearances that now present themselves in the contiguous portion of the Priory, but it may be noticed that the very small fragment of the south side of the cloister does not bond or course with the western wall. And, judging from the truncated form of the east shaft southward of the lavatory, it would seem that the south wall may have been erected before the other, the shaft being therefore accommodated to a projection above it. In this fragment, the jamb of a doorway of the Early Decorated period occurs, at the height of eight courses, but, for the reason just stated, it cannot be positively concluded that it was that of the refèctory. In Kirkham Priory, the refectory of the canons was entered at this point, having also a lavatory on the right hand side; and, like that of the canons of Easby, and of other houses, was placed above a basement story, occupied as cellars, the sides of the apartments also being parallel with the contiguous alley of the cloister. It is nevertheless uncertain whether, in these two cases, the declination of the ground may not have influenced the position and elevation.

For nearly the whole of this article[a] on the fabric of the Priory the Society is indebted to the able pen of one of its vice-presidents, Mr. Walbran of Ripon. The publication of this volume has been delayed for some months until this architectural description could be made after a regular survey of the church; for in these days of change and destruction, it seemed

[a] The editor is responsible for little more than the account of the Saxon sculptured stones at the beginning of the article and some notes.

to be most desirable that what remains of a place which possesses historical associations—equal certainly to those of any other church in England—should be properly noted down. It will be seen from the preceding pages that it has been cruelly dealt with. But not, the Editor must guard himself here, in an ungenerous spirit. The contributors in general, and one family in particular—the first in importance in the district—were most anxious to preserve the characteristics of a building of which the whole of Northumberland was justly proud. To secure this object large sums of money were munificently provided. It is, however, very greatly to be regretted that modern architects are so fond of trying to displace by their own work the choicest remains of Christian antiquity. They never gain by the contrast, and the word "restoration" is now, unhappily, only synonymous with destruction. In twenty years scarcely one old church will be left in the whole country.

It is much to be regretted that Hexham did not find an annalist in the late estimable and kind-hearted historian of Northumberland. Mr. Hodgson well knew the grandeur and the importance of the subject, and he was most anxious to make himself fully acquainted with all its details. In his last volume he observes in a note,—

"*The archives of the see of York have not, I apprehend, been diligently searched for materials for the history of the church and franchise of Hexham. I wish some generous antiquarian spirit would spare me that trouble.*"[b]

In the ordinary course of the History of Northumberland Hexham was the next place that Mr. Hodgson would have taken up. His mind was turned especially towards it when his health gave way. He was unwilling, however, to give up so favourite a theme without a struggle, as is shewn by the following extracts from a letter which was addressed to my father:—

"*Hexham, Sept.* 6, 1841. *I have been here a week, confined almost*

[b] History of Northumberland, iii., part ii., 405.

entirely to house or bed by indisposition and bad weather. I have seen nothing, and, till to-day, unable to say when you might expect to see me. Pray, write to me at the Post Office, Hexham, whether you could meet me here on Thursday, and at what hour, and I will be at the station to meet you. The 'Black Book' I have had, but, after I copied a part of it, I dare not collate it; doing so hurts my head."[c]

The result of this letter was that Dr. Raine went to Hexham on the Thursday, and the Editor, at that time a boy, accompanied his father, and paid his first visit to Wilfrid's cathedral. Our stay at Hexham was but a short one, as we returned to Durham in the evening; but the Editor well remembers how much he was impressed with the architectural features of the grand old church. Its "restoration" was at that time in agitation, and this was, probably, one of the reasons of Dr. Raine's journey. The following extracts from a letter addressed by Mr. Hodgson to the chairman of the committee for the "restoration," have reference to the proposed work, and shew how the sick man's fancy preserved much of its old fire and spirit, although his memory was at the time dulled, and his power of expression enfeebled. They will be read with a melancholy pleasure by those who knew the amiable writer, when they are told that Hexham was the place at which his pen dropped from his grasp, and that this was, perhaps, one of the last letters that he wrote on any topographical subject. The committee seem to have applied to him for information and advice, and, delighted with what was then before him at Hexham,[d] he urged the members to draw up a graphic account of the natural and historic glories of Hexham and its church.

"*I would remind them of the exceeding richness, as well as loveliness and strength of the situation. Its earliest history is lost in the aërial light of time; its foreground and fields still continue bright in their ancient glory, its queen-holds and poet's-see, the diadem that nature gave her, when Noah lifted the grounds out of the sea, and the two Tynes*

[c] Life of Mr. Hodgson, by Dr. Raine, ii., 425.

[d] The letter was written on Sept. 10, 1841.

joined together to build her palace, and fortify her walls; on one side the river, in broad mirrors reflecting the woods and banks that float around the skirts of her garments; and on the other has set a brook, day and night to be the song and guardian of her citadel. The Seal was the garden-place, that nature planted for solace and her joys. When the Britons began to strengthen her walls and till her fields, all traces seem to be lost: that the Romans built a station and a temple here, written monuments remain in tablets below the foundations of her first Saxon church. History now can begin to tell what poesy ceased to sing, when war began to build with stone, when nature fled from the clank of iron arms and iron tools. One Roman altar is here, and one imperial tablet, found in 1725, *besides another tablet, cut by the masons who built the crypt in its present form; and of which chapel Dr. Hunter said to Mr. Andrews, the lecturer of Hexham—'I am persuaded your church stands upon many such vaults.' Another Roman inscription Mr. Fairless shewed me in a ruinous part of the chapter-house, built in the English style—the translation of it is, 'Being present (or attendant) Flavius Hyginius the sixth legion victorious.' The inscription is probably only a fragment.—Of the Saxon church, I translated Richard of Hexham's Account in some minutes I made about your town in 'The Beauties of England and Wales,' in* 1810. *Richard's account is very curious, and deserves a very correct copy. Mr. Bird long since promised to give me a translation of John and Richard's accounts. Richard's history of the church of Hagustald, cap.* 3 *and* 4, *are the parts most interesting to you: perhaps all that can be found respecting the cathedral church in the Saxon times are those of Richard.*

"*I copied many years since in the British Museum an ancient manuscript entitled, 'Miracula Sanctorum Patrum qui in Ecclesia Hagustaldensi requiescunt.' It is in thirteen chapters, some very short, all in the original contracted Latin. The late Mr. Hedly had my copy and written to it. If I am not mistaken they are to be found translated in Cressey's History of the British Church. The remaining part of the manuscript which I copied were extracts of Bede's account of himself, writings, etc. Of the Priory church the most curious account that I have respecting it and its monks was given to me by Jasper Gibson, Esq., of Hexham, from a stamped office copy, and is entitled 'The misdemeanours of the religious persons of Hexham, in the county of Northumberland,*

28 *Sep.*, 38 *Hen. VIII.*' *It is a capital paper, and should you be not lack of room for printing it, would answer you capitally well; you will find that the brave sub-prior had brave monks to assist him, and some of the parts are very grotesque, as the commissioners 'found the gates and doors fast,' etc. And now that my letter is got into war and arms, it is time for a broken-headed man to get out of the sound he hears; and to assure the Committee and yourself how unable I am to be of any use to their very interesting undertaking.*

"*I am, dear Sir,*
"*Yours very truly,*
"JOHN HODGSON."

The Editor cannot conclude without expressing to the members of the Society his gratification at the kind reception which the first volume of this work has met with at their hands. He can only wish that the second had been issued to them long ago, as he hoped and expected it would; but all who are conversant with literary work and literary societies are well aware that punctuality, however desirable, cannot always be attained.

J. R.

YORK, FEBRUARY, 1866.

GENERAL INDEX OF CONTENTS.

A DESCRIPTIVE LIST OF THE ILLUSTRATIONS.

PREFACE.

Facing the title. A view of the interior of the Priory church looking across the transepts. From Views of Places in Durham, Northumberland, etc., by Fisher and Allom. Retouched.

On the title. The arms, for war, of Thomas lord Dacre, of the North, the archbishop's steward of the regality of Hexham. Carved in stone on a house in Hexham. Drawn by Mr. Longstaffe, and engraved by Messrs. Utting, by whom the rest of the cuts have been prepared, unless it is otherwise stated.

p. v. Initial letter from a MS. in the library of the Dean and Chapter of Durham.

p. xvi. The seal of Richard de Umfreville. From the original in the treasury of the Dean and Chapter of Durham.

pp. xxviii-ix. A cross now preserved in the garden of the Spital, near Hexham. Etched on steel by Mr. J. H. Le Keux.

p. xxx, No. 1. Portions of a large sculptured stone of Saxon workmanship in the possession of Mr. Fairless. Found among the ruins of St. Mary's church in Hexham, where it was used as a step.

p. xxx, No. 2. A fragment of Saxon sculpture in the possession of Mr. Fairless.

p. xxxii, No. 1. Saxon work discovered in 1864 in the garden of Dr. Stokoe of Hexham, at the north side of the Priory, and now in his possession.

p. xxxii, No. 2. Fragment of an early Saxon cross found in the choir of the Priory church, and now in the possession of Mr. Fairless.

p. xxxii, No. 3. A portion of the head of a cross now lying in the north transept of the Priory church.

p. xxxiii. A Saxon monument now in the churchyard of Warden, made, probably, out of a Roman altar.

p. xxxiii, No. 2. A fragment of a cross found in the nave of the Priory church, and now in the possession of Mr. Fairless. It is marked with chequers like the famous cross at Bewcastle, and it is, therefore, fairly attributable to St. Wilfrid's own time.

p. xxxiii. Two pieces of Saxon baluster work, probably string-courses, found in the Priory church, and now in the possession of Mr. Fairless.

p. xxxvi. A ground-plan of the Saxon crypt erected by St. Wilfrid at Ripon. Lent by Mr. W. Harrison, of Ripon.

p. xxxviii. A woodcut of one of the chambers in the crypt at Hexham. From Dr. Bruce's History of the Roman Wall, and lent by him.

pp. xlviii-ix. A ground-plan of the Priory church and conventual buildings at Hexham. Made by Mr. F. R. Wilson, of Alnwick, and lent by him to the Society. It is slightly altered. The scale is about 3¼ inches to the 100 feet.

p. lxvi. The frith-stool of Hexham. Now preserved in the Priory church.

p. lxxxvii. A fragment of a ridged tomb, preserved in the Priory church.

p. lxxxviii. A Saxon sculptured stone preserved at Hexham, used for covering a grave.

p. lxxxviii. The gravestone of a child, of Norman workmanship, now in Hexham church.

THE
BLACK BOOK OF HEXHAM.

RENTALE

PRIORIS ET CONVENTUS DE HEXTILDESHAME

DE FIRMIS ET REDDITIBUS OMNIUM TERRARUM ET TENEMENTORUM SUORUM INFRA HEXTILDESHAM-SCHYRE, DIOCESES KARLIOLENSEM, DUNELMENSEM ET EBORACENSEM, PRIMO TERMINO INCIPIENTE AD FESTUM PENTECOSTES, ANNO DOMINI MILLESIMO CCCCLXX. NONO.[a]

[LIBERTAS DE HEXTILDESHAM.]

[Hextildesham.] Idem Prior et Conventus habent in Hextildesham diversa tenementa et terras, quædam dimissa diversis tenentibus, ut inferius patet; et quasdam terras in propria cultura; et molendinum aquaticum de Tyna, cum secta multuræ tam tenentium domini archiepiscopi quam ipsorum Prioris et Conventus in villa de Hextildesham. Et molent grana sua ad vicesimum vas. Et si quis tenens dictæ villæ retraxerit se a dicto molendino cum grano suo, causa molendi alibi, eo ipse forisfaciet equum cum sella domino archiepiscopo, et saccum cum grano domino Priori.

[a] This is the rental of the Prior and Convent of Hexham which is known as the Black Book of Hexham. It is the property of Mr. Beaumont, who inherited it as lord of the manor and owner of the scite of the Priory of Hexham. The manuscript is a thin folio, twelve inches in length by nine in width, and is neatly written on parchment in a uniform hand, and with a wide margin. There are in it seventy-five folios. The book has sides of thick black leather (whence its name), now much faded, and the back is of wood. The sides are lined with coarse canvass. The volume is folded double, and is secured by a leathern flap. It is in a good state of preservation. The rental has been slightly used by Mr. Hodgson in his History of Northumberland, but it has never been printed entire, and it may be regarded as an unknown document. The date ascribed to it on the title is only an approximate one, as several other years are mentioned in the MS. From memoranda in the volume it appears that it has been produced in evidence on the following occasions :—" Oct. 19, 1622, Sir John Fenwick, knight, *v.* John Swinburne, esq., and John Howburne.—In Chancery, Lough, gen., *v.* Hodgson, gen., and Bird, 27 Sept., 1743 : Penrith produced.—Chanc. Thos. Coates et al. *v.* Wm. Ramsay, gen., et al."

PRESTPOFYLL. Thomas Monk tenet j tenementum in Prestpofill, et reddit per annum xviijd. Mariota Wer' tenet j tenementum, viijd. Johannes Laverok. Patricius Laverok. Thomas Monk. Thomas Barthelemew. Johannes Greene. Johannes Wanles. Archbald Dikson. Robertus Milnar. Item de eodem pro gardino. Rogerus Bischop. Johannes Hurde. Her' le Turpyn. Johannes Lee. Willelmus Whytskalez. Willelmus Chaumer. Archbald Diksun. Johannes Whyt, sutor. Johannes Whyt. Thomas Monk. Relicta Johannis Whyte. Johannes Whytskale. Johanna Nuthode.

Johanna Huton. Ric' Armstrang. Ric' Hunter. Thomas Heslihop.

PUDDYNG RAW. Johanna Gladow. Willelmus Chaumyr. Patricius Laverok. Rolland Watsun. Johannes Watsun, client'. Johannes Scot. Item est ibidem unum vastum. Johannes Leschman. Relicta Roberti Hyn.

Willelmus Spavyne. Robertus Nicolson. Robertus Stokall. Johannes Patonson. Thomas Elysun. Johannes Elysun. Alicia Hudson. Willelmus Symson. Johanna Batsun. Robertus Barkar. Johannes Lytill. Willelmus Gladow. Thomas Hyrd. Alicia Hird. Item sunt ibidem iij gardina. Willelmus Jonsun.

DOMINICÆ IN TERRITORIO DE HEXTILDESHAM. Prior et Conventus tenent in propria cultura apud le Merehak x acras. Item in territorio de Prestpofle apud Wynd-myln-stob, ex utraque parte viæ, viij acras. Item tenent ibidem j acram terræ arabilis. Item t.[b] apud Harelaw in eodem territorio v acras. Item t. in territorio de Hencotis, in loco qui dicitur Haynyng-crofte, ij acras. Item t. in Ovin-hous-gat iiij acras. Item t. le Milnflatte, cum ij acris prati ibidem, cont. in toto xij acras. Item celerarius t., juxta le miln-fleme, portionem prati quod continet di. acram. Item Johannes de Walworth t. ibidem, ex dimissione Prioris, ij acras. Item t. inter le Hall-orchard et Halywell-dene vj acras prati. Item t. quandam portionem pasturæ vocatam lez Staners, inter aquam de Tyne et le milnfleme, et continet per æstimationem xx acras. Item t. j clausuram, ex parte boriali aquæ de Tyna, voc. le Medhop, et cont. per æst. xiiij acras, quarum v acræ pertinent ad villam de Aynwyk. Item tenent ij acras terræ ad finem stagni molendini Tyne, jacentes in le Harthorn-flatte, juxta regne.[c]

[b] Where words like *tenent*, *tenet*, etc., occur frequently, I have not scrupled to abridge them in this manner. So also with *reddit* and *reddunt*, *cotagium*, *per annum*, etc.

[c] On Feb. 7, 1347-8, archbishop Zouche granted a writ to his justices at Hexham to adjudicate in a suit between John, Prior of Hexham, and John de Gosceleye, about four marks of rent in Hexham and Greenrigg (Reg. Zouche, 95 *b*).

AYNWYK.

Item t. grangiam de Aynwyk, in qua sunt diversæ domus ædificatæ et pomaria et columbaria. Item t. j barcariam, cum j gardino clauso cum muro, cont. ij acras, ex orientali parte grangiæ. Item t. in eadem grangia j gardinum clausum cum muro versus orient., et cont. j acr. Item t. in eadem ccxviij acr. et di terræ dominicæ in cultura, et l acr prati dominici jacentes in diversis locis, unde viij acræ expenduntur ad opus grangiæ, et xlij expenduntur in ab(b)athia de Hexham. Item t. ibidem xl acr. terræ dominicæ, quæ includuntur cum le Medhop. Item t. xxx acr. terræ in territorio de Corbryg, quæ vocantur le Bisschopprek, et junguntur culturæ de Aynwyk. Unde summa integra tam de terris dominicis quam de pratis—ccclxiij acræ et di.: quæ quidem acræ specificantur per parcellas et metas et suas divisas.

In primis ex australi parte magnæ grangiæ jacent j acra et di., et j barcaria, cum j gardino clauso cum muris, cont. ij acras. In le Been-garth iiij acræ. Et in le Cotis-flatt xij acræ. Et in le Pingar iiij acræ. In Ho viij acræ. Et in Henresdene cum le Toftes xvj acræ. Et sub parco de Beuanfront xiij acræ. Et super Claverige xiij acræ. Et super Hastrige xij acræ. Et super Colstan-flatt viij acræ. Et super Harbugh, cum de Wetlandes, xvj acræ. Et sub le Langsyd, juxta le Pul-medou, v acræ. Et in lez Estelys xx acræ. Et in le Thorne-bankys viiij acræ. Et in Scolebrad, ubi situm erat le connyn-garth, iiij acræ. Et super le Seven-rigges ij acræ. Et super Eden-rigge xx acræ. Et super lez Est-flores xx acræ. Et super lez West-flores xviij acræ. Et super Melmir-pul xiiij acræ. Wlwarde-thorne xiiij acræ. Et super le Rede x acræ. Et super Malabrelande iiij acræ. *Summa de terra arabili supradicta* ccxlviij acræ et di.

Specificatio terrarum. Et sunt ibidem in territorio ejusdem grangiæ diversæ acræ prati, specificatæ inferius, per certa loca; et dimissa. In primis in le Ben-garth v acræ; et in le Hol-medow, juxta le Cottis-flatt, j acra et di. Et in Hors-myres, ex utraque parte rivuli, ix acræ. Et sub lez Knolles ij acræ et di. Et in le Brad-medow, cum le Carrac-acre, ix acræ. Et in le Pul-medowe xiij acræ. Et in le Myln-medow ij acræ et di. Et in le medow sub grangia vj acræ. Et in le Counte's medow j acra et di. *Summa acrarum prati* l acræ.

Item habent j viam ab exitu villæ de Aynwyk per medium hayæ de Akwod, a barcaria de Aynwyk directe aquilonem, usque communem pasturam ultra Birkburne, quæ cont. in latitudine x perticas.

Pastura separalis. Item t. duas pasturas in seperali, quarum una vocatur le Esteles, et altera vocatur le Draknese; et cont. per æst. circiter xxx acras.

Dominicæ pertinentes villæ. Item sunt ibidem xv acræ et iij rodæ dominicæ dimissæ tenentibus villæ, et jacent inter grangiam et villam de Aynwyk; et reddunt per annum in grosso xjs. ixd. ob. qua.

Opera et consuetudines de terris husbandorum. Item sunt ibidem xij terræ husbandorum, quarum quælibet cont. xvj acras terræ arabilis et prati; et quælibet terrarum prædictarum operabitur per j diem cum j homine in stagno molendini, cum necesse fuerit; et faciet le hege-yard ubique; et dabit j gallum et j gallinam ad festum Natalis Domini; et carriabit molares molendini de Aynwyk; et faciet parietes dicti molendini, suis propriis expensis; et cooperiet molendinum propriis expensis coopertura domini. Et quælibet terra husband arabit cum aratro suo per j diem, quolibet anno, cum requisitus fuerit, in solo grangiæ prædictæ.

Terræ husband. Johannes Robinsun. Ricardus Sourbe. Johannes Reyde. Robertus Sourbe. Thomas Robsun. Alanus Kell. Johannes Greene. Willelmus Sourbe. Johannes Copden. Johannes Stodard. Thomas Robinsun. Rogerus Robinsun. Issabell Gibsun.

Opera cotagiorum. Et sunt ibidem xix cotagia, et quodlibet cotagium faciet servitium et opera ad molendinum prædictum, sicut terræ husband prædictæ. Cotagia. Thomas Stobart t. j cot. et di. acr. terræ, et reddit per ann. xxjd. Idem Thomas t. j cot. et di. acr. terræ, et reddit per ann. xxjd. Idem Thomas t. ij cot. et ij acr. et di. terræ, et r. per ann. iiijs. Willelmus Smyth t. j cot. et vij acras terræ, et r. per ann. iiijs. ixd. Johannes Couper t. j cot. et v acras terræ, et r. per ann. vjs. iiijd. Agnes de Chesburgh t. j cot. et j acr. terræ, et r. per ann. xxjd. Willelmus Oxhyrd, nativus domini, t. j cot., iij acr. et iij rodas terræ, et r. ijs. vjd. Symond Clyde t. j cot. j acram et di. terræ, et r. per ann. ijs. xd. Idem t. j cot. et iij rodas terræ, et r. per ann. ijs. vjd. Alicia Stobard t. j cot. et iij rodas terræ, et r. per ann. xxjd. Johannes Sprot t. j (cot.) et ij. acr. terræ, et r. per ann. ijs. Johannes Roger, nativus domini, t. j cot. et iiij rodas terræ, et r. per ann. ijs. vijd. Johannes filius Alani t. j cot. et v. acras terræ, et r. per ann. iijs. vjd. Alicia Stobhyrd t. j cot., et r. per ann. xviijd. Thomas Milnar t. j cot. et vij acras et di. terræ, et r. per ann. vs. iiijd. Thomas Schiphirde t. j cot. et ix acr. terræ, et r. per ann. vjs. Johannes Steele t. j cot. et v acras terræ, et r. per ann. iijs. iijd. Thomas Schiphird t. j cot. et j acr. terræ, et r.

per. ann. iijs. Idem t. ij acras terræ juxta le Schep-brig, et r. per ann. xijd. Symond Clyd t. ij acras terræ ibidem, et r. per ann. xiiijd. Johannes Alanson, nativus domini, t. j acr. prati voc. Malabrenndon, et r. per ann. xijd. Johannes Sprete t. quamdam parcellam prati voc. Petillislaw, xijd.

Terræ dominicæ. Ricardus Plummar t. iij acras sub parco de Beufront, et r. per ann. ijs. Item t. ij acr. in le Langesyde, et r. per ann. xxd.

Bracinagium. Johannes Couper t. communem bracinam villæ de Aynwyk, et r. per ann. vs.

Molendinum. Ricardus Forester de Akome t. molendinum . . . , et r. per ann. lxxiijs. iiijd.

Johannes Vaus tenet ij acras et di. . . . de Beaufront, r. ijs.

Pannagium. Tenentes de Aynwyk dabunt pannagium eodem modo sicut tenentes de Hexham, et valet communibus annis vjd.

SANDOW.

Alicia Webster t. j acr. et di. terræ in le Frerres-crofte, et r. per ann. xxd. Symon de Sandow t. j acr. terræ, et r. per ann. xijd.

Terræ dominicales. Omnes tenentes villæ t. le Cot-garth et le Cotes-flatte, quæ cont. per æst. iiij acr., et r. per ann. ijs. vjd. Et est ibidem j flatte inter Harelaw ex parte australi, et Hathorn-fur ex parte boriali, et le Der-strete ex parte orientali, et le husband-landes ex parte occidentali, quæ flatte vocatur le Baxstan-syde, et cont. per æst. xxx acr. Et est vasta in manu domini. Et est ibidem j alia flatta vasta ex occid. parte le schep-cott, quæ vocatur Horme-scheles, et cont. viij acras.

Opera et consuetudines. Sunt ibidem xiij terræ husband, quarum quælibet cont. xxiiij acras terræ arabilis et prati. Et quælibet terra faciet opera et consuetudines ad molendinum de Aynwyk, ut tenentes ejusdem villæ; et quælibet terra husband dabit j gallum et gallinam domino ad festum Natalis Domini.

(Terræ husband). Simon de Sandow, nativus domini, t. j terr. husband, et r. viijs. vd. ob. Opera ut supra. Adame del Hall t. j terram ibidem, et r. per ann. xs. vd. Willelmus del Halle t. j terram ibidem, et r. per ann. viijs. vd. ob. Adam de Halle, Willelmus de Wall, Adam del Hill t. j terram, et r. viijs. vd. ob. Adam del Hill t. j terr. ibidem, r. per ann. viijs. vd. ob. Johannes de Bywell t. j terram ibidem, et r. per ann. viijs. vd. ob. Symon de Sandow et Thomas Litilskill t. j. terr., viijs. vd. ob. Johannes de Matfen, nativus domini, t. j terr., et r. viijs. vd. ob. Thomas Litilskill t. j. terr. ibidem, et r. per

ann. viijs. vd. ob. Johannes Whytyngeham t. j terr. ibidem, et r. viijs. vd. ob. Johannes Bywell et Symon de Sandow t. inter se j. terr. ibidem, r. viijs. vd. ob. Omnes tenentes villæ t. inter se ij terras ibidem, et r. per ann. xijs. vd. *Summa* vli. vijs. vd.

Opera cotagiorum. Sunt ibidem xij cotagia, et quodlibet cotagium faciet opera ad molendinum de Aynwyk, sicut terræ husband prædictæ, unde in tenura.

Issabell de Stellyng t. j cot. et di. acr. di *(sic)* terræ, et r. per ann. xviijd., j gallum et j gallinam et opera. Willelmus de Matfen, nativus domini, t. j cot. et j acram terræ, r. xxijd. et ij gall. Johannes de Whyttingeham t. j cot. et j gardinum, et r. per ann. viijd. Symon de Sandow, nativus domini, t. j cot., et r. per ann. xijd. Alicia Webster t. j cot., et r. p. a. xiijd., ob. Alicia Schiphyrd t. iij cot., et iij rodas terræ et di.; et r. p. a. xs. xd. ob. et ij gall. Robertus de Matfen, nativus domini, t. j cot. et di. acr. terræ, et r. ijs. et. ij gall. Adam del Hall t. j cot. et di. acr. terræ, et r. p. a. viijd., ij gal(l)inas. Johannes de Matfen, nativus domini, t. j cot. iii rodas terr., et r. p. a. ijs. vjd., ij gall. Issabell de Stellyng t. j cot. et di. acr. terræ, et r. p. a. xxijd. ob. Symon de Sandow, nativus domini; t. j letch, et r. per ann. ijd. Idem t. j rodam terræ juxta le Hanyarburne, et r. p. a. iijd. Idem t ij sykes prati, et r. p. a. iiijd. Adam del Hyll t. j syk, et r. p. a. ijd.

Pannagium. Et tenentes villæ dabunt pannagium sicut tenentes de Aynwyk, communibus annis vjd.

Est ibidem j placea terræ vasta in le lonyng, versus moram, appronata de vasto domini, et solet reddere p. a. vjd.

Item dominus Petrus de Gonwarton, capellanus paroch. de Sant John Le, t. quamdam portionem terræ ibidem vocatam Kyrk-land, videlicet glebam ecclesiæ prædictæ, et continet viij acras, seperales omni tempore anni: et locatur eidem in suo stipendio per ann. xiijs. iiijd.

Item tenent terram adjacentem ecclesiæ Sancti Oswaldi, vocatam Kirk-land, et est gleba dictæ ecclesiæ; et continet per æst. iij acras terræ arabilis. Et dominus Robertus de Dissington, celebrans ibidem, r. p. ann. pro dictis iij acris viijd.

BYNGFELD.

Tenent etiam ibidem j manerium, in quo diversæ domus ædificantur, et j capella, cum tribus gardinis ex orient. parte, et j gardinum ex parte occid., cont. in toto per æst. ij acras; et est ibidem j grangia decimalis.

Et sunt ibidem in dominico xj^{xx}, xviij acræ terræ arabilis, et xvj acræ et iij rodæ prati; unde super Crawlaw, ex parte austr. juxta Erean-brig, jacent xxx acræ terræ arabilis. Et ex parte occid., juxta manarium, xxiiij acræ. Et ex parte bor., juxta Essewell medow, super le Sandilandes, v acræ. Et ex parte occid. le Linburne, super le Toftes, vj acræ. Et in le Linburn-flatt, iiij acræ. Et ex parte occid. le schip-cote, super le Ley-acre, xij acræ. Et super le Cotis-flatt et le Cote-hill, xxx acræ. Et ex parte aust. Haliden-way, super Twystes, vj acræ. Et super le Half-Furlang, juxta le Cote-lech, iiij acræ; de quibus Johannes Oxhird t. j acram cum cotagio suo. Et ex orient. parte de Linburn, super le Linburne, super le Lang-flatt, et super le ij Schort-buttes, xxiiij acræ. Et super le Brere-flatt, versus bor. partem, x acræ. Et super Warin-law-syd, versus occid., iij acræ. Et juxta rivulum de Ereane iij acræ. Et ex utraque parte viæ quæ ducit ad villam de Riell, super le Lang-lyes et le Wallaw, xviij acræ. Et ex austr. parte ejusdem viæ versus orient., super le Langthombes-flatt, vj acræ. Et ex eadem parte viæ ejusdem versus occid., super le Gos-croft, iij acræ. Et juxta le Brad-medow, super Hollchestir-bank, iiij acræ. Et ex parte aust. de Cam-medow, super Cammislaw, xij acræ. Et ex eadem parte versus or., super Halywel-flatte, inter villam de Bingfeld et Todrige, xv acræ. Et ex parte or. ejusdem villæ, juxta le Brad-medow, xv acræ. *Summa acrarum terræ arabilis* xj^{xx}, xviij acræ.

Prata dominicalia. Et quædam portio prati, vocata Whit-wel-medow, abbuttat super Craulaw, cont. vij acras. Et in le Colt-medow, prope prædictum pratum, ij acræ. Et sub lez Toftes, in le Hole-medow, ij acræ di. Et ex parte or. le Linburne, in le Ful-medow, ij acræ j roda. Et in le Brad-medow iij acræ, quarum ij acræ jacent in parte occid. in parte or. *Summa acrarum prati (blank).*

Seperalis pastura. Et sunt ibidem xvj acræ de pastura seperali inter Eryane et Craulaw, ex parte bor. et austr., et le Dere-stret ex parte occid., et le Graystanes ex parte or., inter prædictam pasturam et pasturam Rogeri de Widryngton. *Summa acrarum pasturæ* xvj acræ.

Todryge. Et est ibidem quædam portio terræ arabilis jacens inter Grotyngton et territorium villæ de Byngfelde, ex antiquo vocata Litil Grotington, modo vocata Todrige; et est seperalis domini omni tempore anni; et continetur inter has divisas; videlicet inter le Blake-dyke ex parte or.; et sic, descendendo per lez Oppots et Todryge-burn, ad le Halywell ex parte bor.; et exinde, ex parte occid., ascendendo versus or., per le Grene-lech ex parte austr., inter territorium de Boclyve et Todryge-feld usque le Blak-dyk prius nominatum.

DIMISSIO GRANGIÆ DE BYNGFELD. Robertus Colstan, Willelmus de Ledome, et Willelmus Talyor de Eryngton tenent inter se, conjunctim et divisim, totam grangiam de Byngfeld, cum omnibus terris, pratis, pasturis supradictis, et proficuis, ad terminum xiij annorum; reddendo inde de tribus primis annis, quolibet anno, vjli. Et tribus secundis annis, quolibet anno, vijli. vjs. viijd. Et per vj sequentes annos, quolibet anno, viijli., primo termino solutionis incipiente ad festum Pentecostes anno Domini m° ccc. septuagesimo septimo.

Item est ibidem quædam portio terræ, vasta, quæ vocatur le Grene-came; et jacet inter lez husband-landes ex parte occid., et Donnis-more ex parte australi, et le fote del Swete-leche, buttando super Wyne-acre-bank, ex parte or., et lez husband-landes ex parte bor.; et continet per æst. iiij acras. Et est ibidem j flatta terræ vastæ super le Gryndstan-law; et jacet inter Donnis-more ex parte occid., et le Swete-leche ex parte austr., et le Gren-syde ex parte bor.; et lez husband-landes ex parte or.; et continet per æst. xviij acras. Et sunt ibidem xvj selliones, vocatæ Anglicè rigges, jacentes super lez Schellez, juxta le Solpark ex parte aust.; et cont. per æst. xj acras et di.

Et sunt ibidem, super lez Schellis prædictas, xxv selliones; unde iiij selliones jacent ex parte bor. le Schellawe; et xxj ex parte aust. ejusdem Schellawe; et cont. per æst. xij acras et di. Et est ibidem j flatta juxta Halyden-way; et buttat super rivulum de Eriane ex parte bor.; et buttat super Warin-lau-syde ex parte austr., inter lez husband-landes ibidem; et cont. per æst., vij acras; et dimittuntur Willelmo Bewmonde pro viijli.

Item est ibidem j barcaria cum j gardino continente iiij acras; et jacet super rivulum de Eryane versus occid.; a qua barcaria de Byngfeld Prior et Conventus habent liberum introitum et exitum per territorium villæ de Colwell ad communiam pasturæ dictæ villæ de Colwell, communicand' in eadem omni tempore anni, ubique, ad quadringentas oves, et triginta boves et x vaccas, cum j tauro, ut ex[ad] in cartis.

Et sunt ibidem xij terræ husbandorum, quarum quælibet cont. xxiiij acras terræ arabilis et prati; et quælibet terra carriabit meremium et lapides molares pro portione sua; et sustentabit molendinum in muris et coopertura, suis propriis expensis, præter super le louthre; et mundabunt stagnum, et adducent aquam ad molendinum, quotiens opus fuerit; et molent blada sua ad molendinum domini: unde in tenura.

Willelmus de Ledom t. j terr. husband, et r. p. a. xjs. vjd., unde pro multura xijd. Johannes Lam t. ij terras husband,

[d] Expressa.

unde una sine multura, et r. xxxiijs. xd. ob.; pro multura vjd. Johannes, filius Johannis Thomsun, t. j terram cum multura, et r. p. a. xvjs. xd. ob.; pro multura ijs. vjd. Willelmus Leene t. j terram cum multura, et r. p. a. xvjs. xd. ob.; pro multura ijs. vjd. Adam Kempe t. j terr. sine multura, et r. p. a. xiiijs. iiijd. Walterus de Sandow, nativus domini, t. ij terras, unam sine multura, et r. xxxiiijs. vjd.; pro multura, xijd. Willelmus, filius Ricardi de Hall, t. j terr. sine multura, et r. p. a. xvijs.; pro multura ijs. vjd. Johannes Oxehird et Willelmus Trout t. ij terras sine multura, r. p. a. xxijs. vjd. Johannes Thomson t. j terr., et r. p. a. xvjs.; pro multura xijd.

Sunt ibidem xij cotagia, et quodlibet cotagium facit servitium ad molendinum modo quo terræ husband. Unde in tenura.

Opera et consuetudines. Willelmus, filius Ricardi del Hall, t. j cotagium vastum, et r. p. a. xijd. Idem t. j gard. vastum, et r. p. a. ijd. Johannes Lame t. j cotagium et vj acras terræ cum multura, iiijs. vijd. ob. Marjoria de Law t. j cotagium et vj acras terræ cum multura, et r. p. a. iiijs. vijd. ob. Johannes, filius Johannis Thomson, t. j cotagium et vj acras terræ, et r. p. a. iiijs. vijd. ob. Willelmus de Rokehope t. j cotagium et vj acras terræ cum multura, r. p. a. iiijs. vijd. ob. Johannes Thomson, lang, t. j cotagium et vj acras terræ cum multura, r. p. a. iiijs. vijd. ob. Adam Kemp t. j cotagium et vj acras terræ cum multura; r. p. a. ijs. Idem tenet ij rodas terræ, et r. p. a. iijd. Willelmus Colstane t. j cotagium et vj acras terræ cum multura, r. p. a. iiijs. vijd. ob. Johannes Oxhyrd t. j cotagium et vj acras terræ cum multura, r. p. a. iiijs. vijd. ob. Willelmus Amokson t. j cot. et vj acr. terræ cum multura, r. p. a. iiijs. vijd. ob. Johannes, filius Johannis Thomson t. j cot. vastum cum j roda terræ, r. p. a. ijd. Walter de Sandow t. j acr. terræ, et r. p. a. xd. Robertus Colstane t. j cot. vastum, r. p. a. jd. Johannes, filius Johannis Thomson, t. j cot. vastum, r. jd. Adam Kempe t. j cot. vastum, et r. p. a. jd.

Bracinagium villæ. Robertus Colstane tenet bracinam villæ pro voluntate domini, ijs.

Molendinum. Johannes Oxhird de Byngfeld t. molendinum aquaticum, r. xs.

Tenura separalis de Grotyngton. Item tenent Grotyngton, quæ includitur infra has divisas; videlicet, inter rivulum de Pont ex parte aust.; et le Dere-strete ex parte or.; le lonyng dictæ Boclive et lez Graystanes, jacentes inter prædictum Grotyngton et Codlaw-more, ex parte bor.; et quoddam fossatum antiquum inter prædictum Grotyngton et prædictam moram ex parte occid. Et Thomas Henreson t. totam prædictam Grotington, cum omnibus proficiis suis, ad terminum trium annorum, redd. inde primo anno xls., et non plus ipso anno, quia ædificabit novam domum ibidem sumptibus suis propriis; et duobus annis sequentibus, quolibet anno, ls., primo termino solutionis ad festum Pentecostes, anno Domini m° ccc septuagesimo septimo.

DOTLAND.

Item tenent parcum de Dotland, prout includitur infra ambitum murorum ejusdem, cum omnibus libertatibus et juribus parco pertinentibus, cum xxvij acris et j roda inclusis in eodem.

Consuetudines. Sunt ibidem x terræ husband, quarum quælibet cont. xv acras terræ arabilis et prati, et quælibet terra dabit j gallum et j gallinam ad festum Natalis Domini. Et molent blada sua ad molendinum de Whytley ad xiij vas.

Marmeducus filius Henrici, nativus domini, t. iij terras, r. xvs. Johannes filius Roberti t. ibidem ij terras, r. p. a. xs. et consuetudines. Johannes filius David t. ibidem iij terras, et r. p. a. xvs. Willelmus filius Henrici de Dotland, nativus domini, t. ij terras, r. xs.

Sunt ibidem x cotagia, et quodlibet eorum dabit j gallinam ad festum Natalis Domini, unde in tenura.

Johannes filius David t. j cot. et iij acras terræ, et r. p. a. ijs. Idem t. j cot. et j acram et di. terræ, et r. p. a. xviijd. Idem t. j cotagium et j acram terræ, et r. p. a. xvjd. Walterus Chamebreleyn t. j cotagium ædificatum et j acram terræ, et r. p. a. xijd., gall. Johannes filius Roberti t. j cot. ædificatum, cum j gardino cont. di. acræ terræ; r. xviijd., gall. Willelmus Breuster t. j cot. ædificatum et iij acras terræ, et r. p. a. ijs. Walterus Chambreleyn t. j cot. cum j gardino cont. di. rodæ terræ, r. vjd., gall. Willelmus filius Henrici, nativus domini, t. j cot. ædificatum, et quatuor acras terræ, r. iijs. Walterus Chambreleyn t. j cotagium ædificatum, et di. acræ terræ, et r. p. a. vjd. Idem t. j cot. ædificatum, et iiij acras terræ et di., et r. p. a. ijs. jd.

Doteland Deene. Est ibidem j locus boscosus vocatus Dotlande deene, in quo nullus tenens amputabit viride sine licentia domini et visu præpositi.

Est etiam j campus inter Dotland-feld et Dipden, versus occidentem, in quo constructus erat quondam hamelectus de eodem modo. Est etiam j locus in Knyt-lech in quo solebat esse barcaria cum j gardino, cont. per æst. iiij acras. Est etiam ibidem j locus, qui vocatur Randalphs-rydyng, et jacet inter lez croftes de Dotland ex parte bor., et communes pasturas ibidem; et cont. xv acras et di., sol. r. p. a. ijs. Item est ibidem j campus sub Dotland versus austrum, cont. in se iiij^{xx} et x acras terræ scaccarii; et jacet inter campum de Doteland ex parte occid., et campum Henrici Hunter ex parte or. Item est ibidem j campus sub Dotland versus or., cont. in se lx acras terræ scaccarii arabilis et prati, quem tenent pro emendatione molendini de Whitlye; et jacet inter campum Roberti de Wollon ex parte or.; et sic per quendam rivulum, vocatum Smalburn, ascendendo per partem bor. usque Smalburn-heued, ad campum de Dotland prædictum. Est ibidem in eodem campo quædam parcella terræ, cont. xxxiiij acras terræ scaccarii, inter prædictum rivulum ex parte austr.; et viam quæ ducit de Eward-law, inter prædictam terram et Dotland park, ad communem pasturam de Dotland more.

Yarow-ryge. Sunt ibidem vj terræ husband, quarum quælibet cont.—acras terræ arabilis et prati.

Terræ husband. Willelmus Culgath t. j terram husband, et r. p. a. vjs. Henricus filius Thomæ t. ij terras, et r. p. a. xijs. Willelmus del Abbay t. j terr., et r. p. a. vjs. Johannes de Culgath t. j terram, et r. p. a. vjs. Omnes tenentes villæ t. j terram inter se, et r. p. a. vjs.

Duæ acræ prati. Item tenent ij acras prati jacentes juxta Nobbok-scheles, pro petis ibidem ponendis et siccandis.

Item tenent ij molendina aquatica in Neulandes, videlicet, molendinum de Neubigyng et molendinum de Whytlye, cum tota secta multuræ omnium tenentium in Neulandes; quorum j est vastum et alterum dimittitur Roberto de Wollone ad firmam, pro quo r. p. a. vij marcas—celler'.

Item tenent j placeam juxta molendinum de Whytlye pro ductu aquæ usque molendinum, et vocatur le Milnels; et incipit subtus prædictum molendinum ex parte or.; ascendendo per le Smythous versus bor., usque le hege-garth de Dalton-feld; et sic per le hege-garth versus occid. usque tenuram quondam Symonis Swye; et sic, descendendo versus austr., usque le myln-fleme, et a le mylne-fleme directe ad Rouly-burn; et sic per dictum rivulum versus or. usque molendinum supradictum. Et dimittitur ad firmam Johanni Haumond, et r. p. a. vjd.

Roulye. Robertus de Ogle t. j terram husband in Roulye, et r. p. a. iiijs.

Memorandum quod dominus de Cocelye tenetur solvere Priori et Conventui iiij marcas annuatim, pro licentia habendi molendinum in dominio suo de Cocelye vel Lanhope, et pro secta multuræ ejusdem dominii.

Item tenent situm unius domus in villa de Alwenton ex or. parte ecclesiæ, prope eandem, cum j gardino et j crofto cont. di.

acræ terræ; et est gleba ecclesiæ prædictæ, et locatur capellano celebranti ibidem in stipendio suo per ann. vjs. viijd.

AKOME. Item tenent j grangiam decimalem in villa de Akome cum j gardino; et cont. in toto j rodam terræ; et dominus Petrus de Gonwarton t. gardinum prædictum, et r. p. a. xijd.

WALL. Item t. in villa de Wall j grangiam decimalem cum j gardino adjacente; et cont. in toto j rodam terræ, et r. p. a. vjd.

KEPEWYK. Item t. j grangiam decimalem in villa de Kepewyk cum j gardino adjacente, cont. j rodam terræ. Et Rogerus Underhill t. herbagium dicti gardini, r. vjd.

HALIDEN. Item t. j grangiam decimalem in villa de Halidene cum j gardino adjacente cont. j rodam terræ et plus. Et Johannes Lorimer t. herbagium dicti gardini, et sustentabit muros ejusdem, et r. p. a. vjd.

ROULY. Item t. j grangiam decimalem in villa de Rouly cum j gardino, et jacet ex parte or. villæ, et vast'.

CADDEN. Item t. j grangiam decimalem in villa de Cadden cum j gardino et vasto.

NYNBENKYS. Item t. j placeam in Nynbenkes pro j grangia decimali, cont. in toto j rodam; et jacet ad finem villæ versus occid. inter villam et molendinum. Et Johannes Bales t. prædictam placeam, et r. p. a. iiijd.

LIBERTATES INFRA HEXHAM-SCHYRE. Habent etiam infra Hextildesham-schyre socum et sacam et alias libertates, videlicet, emendas assisæ panis et cervisiæ; et servientes suos virgam portantes ad faciendum districtiones, summonitiones, et attachiamenta; et omnium emendationes transgressionum de omnibus tenentibus suis in curia Prioris.

[TERRÆ, ETC., IN CUMBRIA.]

RAVENWYKE. Tenent ibidem situm rectoris in quo ij domus ædificantur, cum iij gardinis circumjacentibus, et j domus cum parvo gardino infra dictum situm, vocata le Prest-hous. Et vj acr. terr. arabilis vocatas le Kyrk-crofte juxta Wlthwayte-feld versus bor. Et j acr. super Godrik-how, juxta fossatum quod ducit ad moram, ex parte austr. le lonyng. Et iij rodas, quæ in medio le flatte de Braythwate. Et v rodas terræ super Havirberghe. Et j acram super le Langlandes, juxta le thorne, ex occid. parte campi. Et j acr. super Mouresflat, juxta molendinum. Et ij rodas super Pete-mir-half-acre versus austr. Et j acr. super Donald-crofte versus bor. Et ij rodas super Johnshons-hous-bank. Et j acr. prati in Kilngille. Et ij rodas prati in Avenames.

SCALES. TERRÆ ARABILES. Et t. ibidem v acras juxta le Redcrosse, quarum ij jacent versus or., et iij acræ ex parte bor, prope le Crosse. Et j toftum et croftum cont. j acr. terræ, quæ in medio villæ. Et j acr. super Scharlow, ex parte bor. Et iiij acr. in diversis locis ibidem, quarum una portio jacet in medio le flatte de Der-how, et alia portio super lez Monk-toftes, et alia portio ad Kingil-heuede. Et prædictæ domus et terræ dimittuntur ad firmam Adæ Thomson de Ravenwyk ad terminum vj annorum, et r. p. a. xs.

ISALL.[e] GLEBA ECCLESIÆ CUM COTAGIIS. Tenent etiam ibidem situm rectoriæ, et omnino est vastum. Et ij acras et di. terræ arabilis de gleba ecclesiæ. Et vicarius ibidem t. j tenementum in villa et prædictas ij acras terræ et di. ad firmam, et r. p. a. iijs. vjd. Willelmus Hudson t. j ten. ibidem et di. acr. terræ, et r. p. a. xijd. Agnes Mason t. j ten. et iij acr. terræ, et r. p. a. iijs. Johannes Henreson t. j ten. et iij acr. terræ, et r. p. a. xviijd. Johannes Thomson t. ibidem j ten. et vj acras terræ j rodam, et r. p. a. iiijs. iiijd. Henricus Morland t. j acr. terræ vocatam Hoggis-crofte, et r. ixs. Idem t. j campum vocatum le Prior-feld, ad finem or. villæ, ex parte bor. aquæ de Derwent, circumfossatum per metas suas, in quo ædificantur ij domus, et r. p. a. xs.

Est ibidem j bank boscosus, vocatus le Prior-bank, ex eadem parte aquæ prædictæ, inter prædictum campum et villam; in quo nullus tenens amputabit viride sive licentia custodis ibidem.

Et est ibidem j campus jacens inter le Prior-feld prædictum et viam quæ ducit ad Sundreland, et vocatur le More-wra, et est vastus.

[e] In a more recent hand.

Habent etiam communam pasturæ in omnibus vastis et pasturis ibidem extra parcum de Isale, de novo inclusum.

Habent etiam turbariam et petariam ibidem, pro se et tenentibus suis ibidem, ad omnia sua necessaria, sive ad fossatum claudendum, sive ad commune bracinagium ibidem sustinendum; prout pertinet libero tenemento Prioris ibidem.

Et est etiam ibidem j campus ad finem orient. villæ, ex parte bor. prædictæ viæ quæ ducit ad Sondreland, et extendit usque novum parcum domini de Isale; et vocatur Aldeby; et est omnino vastus.

Tenent etiam quartam partem molendini de Plumland cum secta multuræ ad dictam partem pertinente, et valet communibus annis xvs.

Habent etiam in villa de Alneburgh j toftum vastum cum uno crofto adjacente, cont. in toto per æst. j acram terræ; et jacet ad finem or. villæ ex parte austr. ejusdem, juxta toftum Thomæ Spilgild. Habent etiam in campo ejusdem villæ per æst. xx acras terræ arabilis et prati, quarum j acra terræ arabilis et prati jacet ad finem or. cujusdam flatte vocati le Ganell: et apud le stan-brig ij acras terræ arab. et prati. Et super le Gresse-flatte, ex parte or., juxta Wilken-busk, j acram et j rodam terræ arab. Et super le Midil-holme, juxta Mat-wra, j acr. et di. terræ arab. et prati. Et super dictum Midil-holme, ex parte northwest del Hassokis, j acram: et ex parte bor. del Mat-wra j acram prati. Et super Hexham-crofte, cum le Olysyk, iij acras. Et super le See-flatte, cum quadam portione prati adjacente inter dictam flatt et rivulum de Alne, per æst. iiij acras, et r. p. a. vjs. viijd.

Et Johannes de Fausyd (et) Willelmus Parcar de Isale t. decimas garbarum parochiæ de Isale, cum omnibus terris et ten. de Isale, Plumbland, and Alneburgh prædictis, et r. hoc anno pro omnibus xxij marcas; unde cellerario coquinæ xli.

Et tenent j ten. cum j crofto in civitate Karleon. in Caldwel-gat, ex parte austr., juxta rivulum vocatum Donsbett. Et dimittitur ad firmam Roberto Goldsmyth de Karleol. ad term. xx annorum, et r. p. a. xviijd., et non plus, quia ædificavit super dictum tenementum unam novam domum sumptibus suis propriis: solebat r. p. a. iiijs. Idem Robertus r. unum annuum redditum de uno ten. ibidem juxta ten. prædictum annuatim exeuntem, pro quo solebat r. p. a. iiijs.; modo, propter debilitatem et vastationem, p. a. ijs. vjd.

LIBERTAS DE TYNDALE CUM PRESDALE ET ALDENNESTON-MORE.

Item habent unum annuum redditum xiijs. iiijd. exeuntem annuatim de molendino de Elleryngton, ex dono quondam Nicholai de Vepont, quem redditum dominus ejusdem molendini, qui pro tempore fuerit, tenetur solvere ad terminos usuales.

Item t. j toftum in villa de Stancroft, et xx acr. terræ propinquiores prædicto tofto versus le south-est; et includuntur infra has divisas. Videlicet, incipit ex parte occid. crucis stantis in Karlel-gate, vocatæ Doddis-cross, et sic directe versus bor. per quemdam limitem inter Doddis-feld et prædictam terram, usque Stancroft-burn. Et sic, descendendo per dictum burne, versus or. usque le Nonnes-feld. Et deinde per quemdam limitem inter le Nonnes-feld et dictam terram versus austr. usque Karlel-gat. Et sic, sequendo Viridem Viam, usque occid. crucis prædictæ. Et Johannes Thomson t. prædictam terram ad firmam, et r. p. a. viijs.

Item tenent apud Sadlyngstanes j toftum ad finem occid. et ex parte bor., et j acram et di. terræ arab. proximam eidem tofto, ex parte bor. Et iij acras prati juxta Fenkilles-law ad partem aquilonalem, et ad orient. duarum acrarum, quas idem *(sic)* elemosinarius prius habuerat. Et pasturam ad quatuor vaccas et xx oves: et dimittuntur ad firmam, ut patet inferius.

Item t. ibidem j toftum prope toftum supradictum, ex parte or. ejusdem tofti; et xx acras terræ arab. ibidem, quarum vj acræ jacent juxta prædictum toftum ex parte bor. Et iiij acræ jacent juxta Heppe-leche ad or.; et v acræ in Hoddes-flatte; et v acræ juxta Bere-crofte ad aquilonem. Et iiij acras prati, unde in Hauden-syde, in medio, j acra; et j acra jacet ex parte occid. lapidis vocatæ Sadlyngstane; et j acra jacet ad occid. de le Heppe-leche; et j acra jacet ex parte austr. Hoddes-flatte. Et habent pasturam ibidem ad centum oves et xxx averia et iiij equos. Et Johannes Forestar de Neuburgh t. ad firmam ten. et terr. prædictas, et r. p. a. in grosso xs.

CARRAW.

Robertus de Ogle t. ad firmam de eisdem Priore et Conventu quamdam parcellam pasturæ de Carraw, vocatam Fethre-schaue, inclusam in parte or. parci de Sewyng-shelez; et tendit a muro parci parte prædicta usque fontem de Corne-strothre; et per rivulum dicti fontis versus bor. usque le Crokid-burne; et a fonte prædicto versus austrum per j sikettum usque Sewyn-scheles moss; et sic, sequendo le moss versus or., usque murum parci in Fethres-schaw-syd positum prius nominatum; et r. p. a. viijd.

Item t. totam villam de Carraw; et est seperalis omni tempore anni per totum campum dictæ villæ, ex parte austr. muri Romanorum, infra has metas et divisas. Incipiendo ex parte or., sicut fons defluit a dicto muro in Thormer-strothre; et a rivulo fontis prædicti versus occid. per quoddam fossatum inter le Graysyd et campum de Carraw; et sic, sequendo dictum fossatum versus le south-west, inter moram de Stan-crofte et le Syde usque le Lang-strothre; et deinde per metas lapideas in le Lang-strothre positas usque fossatum de Grensyde; et exinde per rivulum occidentaliter versus bor. per lapideas metas vocatas mers, positas inter campum de Carraw et moram de Houden, usque murum supradictum; et sic per dictum murum versus or. usque dictum fontem prius nominatum.

Item t. pasturam de Carraw, et est seperalis ejusdem villæ, except' pro iiij^{xx} animalibus de Tepermore. Et minera in dicta pastura, sive carbonum aut turbarum, solummodo pertinet dictis Priori et Conventui. Et includitur infra has divisas: videlicet, infra Driden, ex parte or.; et le Crokeburne ex parte bor.; et Sewyng-scheles park ex parte occid.; et murum Romanorum ex parte austr. Et Thomas Hoggerson, Johannes Couper, Ric' de Gosden, Adam Proktorman, Willelmus Jonson t. ad firmam totam villam prædictam, et r. p. a. iiijli.

Item solebat esse ibidem molendinum aquaticum, et omnino est vastum defectu cursus aquæ.

Habent etiam communam pasturæ per totam pasturam de Syde ad omnia animalia exeuntia de Carraw omni tempore anni.

Habent j annuum redditum exeuntem de terra de Alde-scheles juxta Teket, ex dono domini Henrici Graham; unde dominus Willelmus Heron est hæres, et tenetur solvere dictum redditum, videlicet, viijs. annuatim; et est a retro xl annos.

Item t. j toftum et croftum in Teket, et decem acras terræ in cultura quæ dicitur Postulon, et jacet inter has divisas; videlicet, incipiendo ad quoddam fossatum, sicut ascendit a Fen-wyk-burne versus austr., inter dictum Postolon et campum Nicholai de Ridle, qui vocatur Kinren-howe, usque Aldscheles bog. Et exinde per dictum bogg usque quoddam siketum; et sic per dictum siketum versus bor. sicut descendit inter dictum Postolon et Ald Teket in Fenwik-burn; et sic, sequendo dictum burn, usque le fote dicti fossati prius nominati.

Item t. j rodam terræ in dominico tofto in Grendon in parte occid., et dimittitur ad firmam.

Tenent etiam in territorio de Hennishalgh, ad finem occid. villæ ibidem, quandam parcellam terræ vocatam Hamysyde, jacentem inter Hamyburn ex parte or., et le Temple-reyne ex parte occid.; et cont. ix acras et di. terræ arab. cum j acra prati, et junguntur tenuræ de Rischeles.

Ryscheles. Item t. omnia terras et ten. de Rischeles infra territorium de Hennishalghe, quæ includuntur infra has divisas; incipiendo, videlicet, ad or. partem de le Lud-yet inter Ryschels et Holmishalh-raw; et exinde usque austr. ad le Cross-standane-stan usque le south-est, per quoddam antiquum fossatum usque la More-hak, quæ stat inter campum Thomæ Hardor et dictum Rischeles; et sic a la Hac directe usque le strothre versus occid. usque le Bond-rydyng; et a le Bond-ridyng versus bor. usque le stane-gate quæ dicitur Karlel-gate; et sic per eandem viam versus occid. usque Milkrige-burn; et sic, ascendendo per le burne versus bor., usque le heued-yarde de Rischeles; et sic per le heued-yard versus or. usque or. partem de la Lid-yete prius nominatum.

Dimissiones de Henneshalgh et Ryschelez. Et Robertus Pikryng t. quamdam parcellam dictarum terrarum, et r. p. a. xiijs. iiijd. Willelmus Nicolson de Haltwesyle t. aliam parcellam earumdem terrarum, et r. p. a. vjs. Adam Smythmaugh t. tertiam parcellam earundem, et r. p. a. vijs. viijd.

THRILWALL.

Tenent ibidem quædam terras et ten. vocata Wardrew cum j clausura vocata Orbelaw-schawe, et includuntur infra has divisas: videlicet, sicut le syk ad le Freris-law-heuede discendit versus austrum usque le Burre-clough; et exinde usque le Temel-hope; et sic, sequendo le dike de le Temel-hope, versus occid. usque in aquam de Yrthin; et sic, sequendo dictam aquam, versus bor. usque le Ovir-yard-clough; et inde usque le hege-yard; et exinde versus or. usque Wardrew-hous; et deinde usque le sik ad le Frere-le-heuede prius nominatum.

Pratum de Crakdale. Tenent etiam ibidem j portionem prati inter campum Alexandri Jonson et campum de Warde-snak-colfe, vocatam Crakdale, et cont. per æst. j acram. Et Johannes Clerk et Johannes Mabson, frater ejus, tenent terras supradictas, et r. p. a. xvs. (Vide cart' pro aliis terris hic non expressis *in marg.*)

Philippus Badkok t. Wyrch-snake-colfe, sicut includitur antiqua fossatura ibidem; et t. etiam j parcellam prati jacentem ad le north-est syd de Werthmaybe, et cont. per æst. iij rodas et plus, et r. p. a. vs.

Thomas Jonson de Thrilwall t. Wyrthkeryne per homagium et fidelitatem; et debet sectam ad curiam de Aynwyk bis in anno; et r. p. a. iiijs.

Johannes de Thrilwall t. parcellam terræ ibidem vocatam le Prior-bank, jacentem ex parte bor. prope castel de Thrilwall, per homagium et fidelitatem; et r. p. a. iijs.

Habent etiam per cartas quod tenentes Prioris in Thrilwall molent blada sua ad molendinum de Thrilwall, sine multura, et omnibus consuetudinibus et demandis, ut in cartis.

Tenent etiam ibidem j locum vocatum le Welhouse, in quo est j domus de novo constructa cum j gardino ex parte bor. ejusdem, et j croftum ex parte or. ejusdem domus; et cont. per æst. di. acræ; et j acram ex parte bor. ejusdem domus vocatam le Swyn-landes; et j acr. vastam juxta prædictam acram versus occid.; et j rodam jacentem in le Crowkes juxta Wardoghe-elgarth. Et Thomas Bourdale t. prædictam domum et terram, r. xviijd.

Tenent etiam quoddam ten. vocatum Croymagh, sive Coomhoue, in quo ij domus ædificantur, et certas terras ibidem. Et omnia includuntur infra has divisas; videlicet, incipiendo ad le salgh stantem in le hege-garth ex parte occid. ejusdem domus, sic, descendendo per le hege-garth, versus or. usque le syk ex parte occid. Adæ de London; et sic directe versus bor. usque murum Romanorum. Et inde per dictum murum versus occid. usque quoddam syk inter Craymok-hill et terras de Croymagh prædictas; et sic per dictum syke versus austr. usque le salgh prius nominatum.

FLAGAN-CLOUGH.

Tenent etiam j acram et di. terræ arab. ad pedem de Flaghon-burne, qui decurrit ex parte austr. communis pasturæ dictæ tenuræ; et jacet ex utraque parte le burne. Et Johannes Mody t. prædicta terras et ten. ad terminum vitæ, et r. p. a. vjs. viijd.

WARDOG-HALL.

Tenent etiam totam quartam partem de Wardog-hall cum tofto ædificato et crofto, in boscis, planis, vastis, et assartis, pratis, pascuis, moris, et marescis, et totam quartam partem de Clesket, cum omnibus arabilibus, prout dividitur inter tenentes ibidem infra limites de Wardog-hall, ad quartam partem prædicto tofto spectantem. Quarum una portio prædictarum terrarum quartæ partis, videlicet croftum, jacet ex parte bor. domus prædicti tofti, et cont. in toto j acram; et alia portio jacet ex parte occid. juxta grangiam, di. acr. Et tertia pars jacet ex parte occid. partis proximæ antedictæ. Et alia pars jacet ex parte austr. le Wall in diversis locis super le Croke-hilles. Et alia pars in le Bergholme, j acr. Et alia pars jacet super lez Bankes in duobus locis, j acra. Et alia pars jacet in le Hole-dall, iij rodæ. Et alia portio jacet sub le Schaw, di. acræ. Et alia pars jacet in le Bradedale, j portio, di acr. Et in Wardog-hal-schaw, versus or., una portio in duobus locis, di. acra. Et, ex parte occid. ejusdem Schaw, una portio. Et super Cow-garth, de terra vasta, una portio. Et j acra prati jacet ex or. parte de Wardog-hall juxta le hege-garth ibidem. Et alia portio prati jacet sub le Schawe, juxta Poltresk-burn. Et Willelmus Henreson tenet omnia terras et ten. prædicta, p. a. xiijs. iiijd.

Pastura. Habent etiam communam pasturæ infra totum feodum de Thrilwall ad iiij^{xx} averia et totidem equas; et, si minor fuerit numerus de equabus, supleatur de aliis animalibus cum sequela duorum annorum et di., et iiij^{xx} porcos, et ad xl capras cum sequela, tam porcorum quam caprarum, unius anni.

TERRA CUM PASTURA IN KNARESDALE.

Item tenent in villa de Knaresdale totam terram cum pastura infra has divisas; scilicet, incipiendo a marchia terrarum domini de Gillisland usque in le Lanerd-sete, sicut aqua cœlestis dividit Fenen-hope et Glenden; et sic de Lanerd-fote, descendendo, usque le Mayden-gate, ubi propinquius fuit inventum. Et de le Mayden-gate versus aquilonem usque Clenden-burn; et sic, ascendendo per dictum burne, usque prædictas divisas marchiæ de Gillisland prius nominatæ.

WHYTLAW.

Willelmus de Whytlaw t. totam Whytlaw per homagium et fidelitatem; et faciet sectam ad curiam Prioris apud Aynwyke, videlicet ad duas curias capitales annuatim; et r. p. a. iiijs.

WHYTFELD.

Mattheus Whytfeld t. totam Whytfeld per homagium et fidelitatem; et faciet sectam ad curiam Prioris apud Aynwyk annuatim; et r. p. a. xvjs. viijd., unde officio sacristæ per ann. iijs. iiijd., et officio celerarii coquinæ xiijs. iiijd.

ALDENESTON.

Tenent etiam certas terras et ten. in villa de Aldeneston, ex parte or. aquæ de Tyna, per has divisas; scilicet, sicut rivulus de Natres-gille cadit in Tynam versus austrum; et ita, descendendo ex parte occid., usque ad antiquum pontem sive locum antiqui pontis; et exinde, ascendendo per antiquum fossatum, usque terram Sancti Johannis ex parte bor.; et per dictam terram directe usque longum fossatum versus or.; et sic, sequendo longum fossatum, usque rivulum de Natres-gill prius nominatum.

DIMISSIO.—

Tenent etiam in eadem villa certas terras et ten., ex parte occid. de Tyna, infra has divisas; scilicet, incipiendo ad occid. capud antiqui pontis, sive locum antiqui pontis ibidem; et sic, ascendendo per viam regiam et fossatum, usque quemdam rivulum vocatum Foule-syk, qui decurrit ex parte austr. de Crosseland; et sic, descendendo per eundem rivulum, in aquam de Tyna; et sic, descendendo per Tynam, usque locum antiqui pontis prius nominatum. Et est in tenura.

DIMISSIO.—

PASTURA. Item habent ibidem communam pasturæ pro se et tenentibus suis ad xl vaccas et x equas et centum oves, cum sequela omnium prædictorum, duorum annorum, per totum Aldeston-more, ratione terrarum dominicarum ibidem. Item habent pasturam pro se et tenentibus suis ibidem, ratione cotag', ad xxiiij vaccas et lx matrices oves., cum sequela sua trium annorum, per totum Aldeston-more. Et omnes tenentes Prioris ibidem molent ad molendinum domini de Aldenston ibidem sine multura.

GERARD-GILL.

Tenent etiam in Gerard-gill unum toftum, quod vocatur Thruswell, et pasturam ibidem ad x vaccas et duas equas cum tota sequela sua duorum annorum.

PRESDALE.

Tenent etiam totum Presdale, et est seperale omni tempore anni; et, si quis depascuerit cum bestiis aliquibus aliquo tempore infra divisas pasturæ de Presdale, debet attachiari ad curiam Prioris ibidem et justificari. Et continetur infra has divisas. Incipiendo sub Esgyl-heued, sicut aqua cœlestis dividit, usque Edestan: et inde usque Burnhop-heuyde per Hard-rode, sicut aqua dividit, usque Broun-spot-lane; et inde usque le Crokyt-burn-heued; et per dictum Crokit-burn usque in aquam de Tese; et sic ab ingressu del Crokit-burne in Tese ascendendo usque in summitatem de Fendes-fell; et exinde directe usque Wak-stan-eghe; et inde usque fontem de Kexbur-wane; et exinde usque Grosgil-heued; et inde, ex transverso mussæ, versus or. usque Ninistanes: et deinde usque Cokeley-fell; et exinde, descendendo per Ellir-burne, usque in aquam de Tyna; et sic per Tynam usque in Esk-gil-fote; et exinde, ascendendo per Esk-gille, usque Esk-gill-heuede prius nominatum.

Habent etiam liberum ingressum, transitum, et exitum per totum feodum de Aldestone ad prædictum Presdale, sine impedimento alicujus, et ad homines prædictorum Prioris et Conventus, et ad omnia genera animalium suorum: nec calumpnientur vel vexentur, sive in redeundo vel transeundo, moram faciendo die vel nocte in pastura de Aldenestone cum averiis suis extra divisas de Presdale prius nominatas. Et prædicti Prior et Conventus habent communicar' per totam pasturam de Aldeneston-more cum omnibus animalibus suis exeuntibus de Presdale, singulis diebus, pro beneplacito suo, a solis ortu usque ad occasum, absque contradictione cujuscumque.

Libertates et aysiamenta ad Presdale in Aldeneston-more. Habent etiam prædicti Prior et Conventus, et eorum homines in villa de Aldneston manentes, in boscis de Aldneston estoveria ad ædificandum, et ad domos et ad sepes suas sustinendas; et ad omnia alia necessaria, prout opus habuerint, sine contradictione cujuscumque.

Tenent etiam in villa de Chestrehope in Redesdale ij tofta et ij crofta. Quæ quidem crofta cum toftis jacent adinvicem, quia in medio villæ, ex austr. parte le ford, in le peth quod ducit ad communam pasturæ, jac. ex parte bor. dictæ peth: et duas bovatas vocatas j husband-land, cont. di. acr., ut cæteræ terræ husband in eadem villa, scilicet xxiiij acras. Et jacebant vastæ fere per xl annos: et dimittuntur omnia adinvicem in grosso ad terminum x annorum, reddendo inde annuatim xs. Et inde remittuntur Adæ de Lee, tenenti eorumdem, per Priorem, pro bono consilio suo et servitio, quolibet anno durante termino prædictorum x annorum, vjs. viijd. Et sic solvit de claro per eosdem annos iijs. iiijd.

BARONIA DE LANGLYE.

[BYERES].

Tenent ten. vocatum le Byres cum terris, boscis et pasturis; in quo est unus parcus, qui habet libertatem et omnia jura sibi, sicut cæteri parci. Et si quis depascat cum bestiis suis infra prædictas terras et pasturas absque licentia Prioris aliquo tempore anni, debet per ballivum Prioris attachiari, et pro dampnis in curia Prioris ibidem justificari; excepto quod Priorissa et Conventus de Lamblye habebunt ex concessione Prioris et Conventus pasturam pro averiis suis propriis exeuntibus de Lamblye in pasturam de Byres, vocatam le comon-pastur, videlicet ex parte austr. de Litil-blak-burn. Ita quod dictæ Moniales, vel earum servientes, nil præsumant, capiant, extrahant, vel dampnum faciant in boscis dictæ pasturæ, neque quoquo modo parcum ibidem, seu ex parte austr. dictæ burne, cum suis averiis intrent. Et dictum tenementum, cum singulis particulis suis, includitur infra has divisas: scilicet, incipiendo ad Fanen-hemp-hed per Elden-burne, sicut descendit, versus or. usque Mayden-gate; et inde per le Mayden-gate versus bor. usque Litil-blak-burne; et exinde, sequendo le Threp-garth, inter pasturam de Lamblye et dictum ten. de Byres usque Hartely-burne, ad finem or. de Carslye; et deinde, sequendo le hegge-garth, usque le Midilyale inter campum de Kellaw et campum de Ulgham; et exinde, sequendo le hegge-garth, usque Stod-hird-clogher-heuede; et deinde versus austr. usque Foul-pote, sicut decurrebat antiquo tempore usque Mikle-blak-burne; et sic, sequendo dictum Mikle-blak-burne, usque le over-noke de le Coli-close; et exinde, sequendo murum del Park, usque le Pykit-stane; et exinde, sicut aqua dividit inter Gillisland et le Byres, usque Fanen-hemp-hed prius nominatum.

Et Priorissa de Lamble prædicta solvit annuatim cameræ Prioris unum manutergium decens pro mensa dicti Prioris, et t. de dicto domino Priore per fidelitatem.

Item dicta Priorissa t. quamdam portionem pasturæ ibidem ad voluntatem Prioris, ex occid. parte le Mayden-gate, super Litil-blak-burne, inter dictam Mayden-gate et quoddam novum fossatum per dictam Priorissam constructum infra dictam pasturam; et cont. per æst. ij acras; et r. p. a. iiijd.

Tenent etiam quoddam ten. cum terr' et pastur' juxta le Byres, vocatum Ulgheham; et est seperalis omni tempore anni;

et includitur inter has divisas; scilicet, incipiendo ad le Byres-lid-yat, per le hegge-garth versus or. usque le Midil-garth inter campum de Kelloue et dictum Ulgheham. Et exinde, per le Mydil-garth, versus bor. usque Kellau-burne; et sic, ascendendo per dictum burne, usque le fote del Lanburne ubi descendit in Kellau-burne; et sic, sequendo le Lanburne versus occid., usque le hegge-garth tenur' de Langdene; et sic, sequendo le hegge-garth versus austr., usque le Bires-lyd-yete prius nominatum.

LANGDENE.

Item t. quoddam ten., cum certis terris et pasturis, seperal' omni tempore anni, juxta Ulgheham, et vocatur Langdene; et includitur infra has divisas; videlicet, incipiendo ad le fote del le Lanburne, ubi descendit in Kellau-burne; et exinde, sequendo unum syk versus bor. inter campum de Kellow et campum de Langdene (antiquo tempore vocabatur Prent-kepit-syke, modo vocatur Thude-schawe-syk) usque Carlel-gate. Et sic se dicta *(sic)* Karlel-gate versus occid. usque Prent-kepit-law; et exinde versus austr. per lez standande stanes inter Gillisland et dictum Langdene usque le heuede de Stod-hirde-highe, quod est ad finem occid. del Byres-feld; et exinde, sequendo unum hegge-garth versus or., usque le lyd-yete del Byres-feld. Et est in tenura.

Et prædictæ Ulgeham et Langdene cum omnibus pertinentiis r. p. a. in grosso xxxiijs. iiijd. Et dicta Langdene solet reddere p. a., quum ædificatum fuerit, pro quatuor ten. husband et j cot. xlijs.

Communa pasturæ de Fethrstanhalgh. Habent etiam communam pasturæ per totum feodum de Fethirstanhalgh et etiam in terris quondam de Lucye, jacentibus extra divisas del Byres, Ulgheham, et Langedene, ut ex[a] continetur in cartis.

[WHYNETLYE.]

Tenent etiam quoddam ten. in Whynetle, ædificatum, cum crofto ex parte le north-est dicti ten., ex parte bor. Lad-mannis-gate; cum certis terris et pratis ex austr. parte dicti ten., quæ includuntur infra has divisas: incipiendo, videlicet, ad orient. finem dicti ten., sicut quidam limes dividit dictas terras et quamdam parcellam terræ quam Willelmus de Redeschawe tenet libere de Priore et Conventu, vocatam Perot-land, usque in Linle-leghe. Et sic, ascendendo versus occid., per metas lapideas positas inter campum dicti Willelmi de Redeschaw et Johannis Bascenthwayt, usque ad oppositum ex parte bor. de Whynetle-law; et exinde usque bor., per metas lapideas positas inter campum dictorum Willelmi et Johannis, usque Blakhal-cloughe;

et sic, sequendo dictum cloughe, versus or. usque ad limitem ex parte or. dicti ten. prius nominati. Item t. iij acras terræ vocatas le Lang-dale adjacentes dicto ten; et jacent ex parte or. juxta parcellam liberi ten. Willelmi de Redeschaw, quod t. de Priore, ut superius dicitur.

Dimissio:—

Libera ibidem. Willelmus de Redeschawe t. quoddam ten. ibidem per fidelitatem, vocatum Holdenes-lande, et r. p. a. ijs. vjd. Idem t. aliud ten. per fidelitatem vocatum Milners-land, antiquo tempore vocatum Perotis-land, et r. p. a. xxijd.

Pastura ibidem. Habent etiam ibidem pro se et tenentibus suis ad octo boves, et ad viginti quatuor vaccas, et ad centum oves matrices, et ad quinque equas, et ad quinque sues, cum sequela omnium prædictorum unius anni.

HAYDEN.

Tenent etiam in villa de Hayden vij acras terræ et di.; quarum quatuor acræ jacent circa ecclesiam de Hayden prædicta; et ij acræ et di. jacent ad finem or. de Hayden-toun versus bor., juxta le lonyng; et j acra jacet in campo de Raton-raw, ex parte or. le lonyng ibidem, et vocatur le Cros-acre. Et Thomas Smyth t. prædictas terras, et r. p. a. iiijs. Solebat r. vjs. viijd.

Grangia decimalis. Habent etiam ibidem j grangiam decimalem ædificatam, stantem ad le north-est, juxta cimiterium ibidem; et dimittitur.

Pastura in Hayden. Habent etiam communam pasturæ ad triginta averia et centum oves cum eorum sequela, prout ex[a] [f] continetur in cartis.

MOLENDINUM DE ALLEWASSHE.

Tenent etiam molendinum de Allerwasshe cum stagno et le modir-dame ejusdem molendini, cum secta et multura cujuscumque generis bladi crescentis in Allerwasshe et Allerwasse-schelez; quorum tenentes molent bladum suum ad tertium-decimum vas; et tenentur facere, reparare, et sustinere stagnum ejusdem molendini quotiens opus fuerit, et prædictum molendinum cooperire, præter supra le louthre, et parietes, et alia necessaria dicti molendini sustinere. Et Twedye de Allerwassche t. prædictum molendinum ad firmam, et r. p. a. pro dicto molendino, et pro terris dicto molendino pertinentibus, xs.

Terra adjacens molendino de Allerwassche. Tenent etiam quasdam parcellas terræ adjacentes dicto molendino, cont.

[f] Expressa.

per æst. quinque rodas terræ; quarum una parcella jacet ex occid. parte le myln-raw ex utraque parte le myln-fleme, et vocatur le myln-dame; et j portio jacet juxta prædictum molendinum, inter quemdam rivulum vocatum le West-burne dicto molendino; et dimittitur in grosso cum prædicto molendino, ut supra.

OLMERS CUM BOSCO IBIDEM.

Tenent quoddam ten. vocatum Olmersse cum terris, boscis, pratis, et pasturis seperalibus, quæ includuntur infra has divisas; videlicet, incipiendo ad le heuede de la hegge-garth ex parte austr. de Widon-lonyng; et per dictum hegge-garth versus occid. usque le croyk; et inde per metas lapideas ibidem positas usque Colpott-flatt; et exinde directe versus occid. usque le Vepont-burn; et, sequendo dictum burne versus austr., ad quoddam antiquum fossatum ascendens de la Blak-leche; et deinde per dictum fossatum versus or. usque ad quoddam fossatum ex parte occid. de Redersdyng versus bor., usque le est ende de Pesse-flat-end; et exinde, sequendo clausuram Olmers prædicti, ad hostium aulæ ibidem; et exinde, a parte occid. dictæ aulæ, per lez hege-garth, usque ad le heued del hegge-garth ex parte austr. del Wyden-lonyng prius nominati.

LITILL OLMERS.

Tenent etiam ibidem quamdam parcellam terræ arabilis et prati vocatam Litil-Olmars, sicut includitur per quamdam fossaturam; et jacet ex parte le north-est prædicti Olmers, inter le lonyng et campum de Allerwes-scheles. Et sunt in tenura, xxiijs.

MANERIUM DE WARDON.

Tenent etiam ibidem manerium de Wardon, in quo diversæ domus sunt ædificatæ, cum terris, boscis, et pasturis: infra cujus divisas est unus parcus inclusus, vocatus Wardon-wode, qui habet libertates et jura generaliter parco pertinentia. Quod quidem manerium, cum suis quibusdam parcellis, includitur infra has divisas; incipiendo, videlicet, apud Wardon-ford; et sic, ascendendo per medium aquæ de Tyne versus occid. usque le Prior-dyk; et sic, sequendo le dyke, versus bor., quousque perveniatur ad le Westre-corner de Wardon-wod; et deinde, sequendo clausuram dictæ wod, usque perveniatur ad partem or. de Yekesyde; et exinde versus bor. per unum reygne jacens inter campum prædictæ Wardon, et quandam parcellam terræ jacentem inter dictum reygne et prædictum Yekesyd, usque perveniatur ad lez croftes-endes de Wardon Superiore; et deinde per metas lapideas inter dictos croftos et campum manerii antedicti usque quemdam locum boscosum vocatum le hotte de Ovyr-Wardon: et exinde per j reygne usque perveniatur ad viam quæ ducit ad Walwyk. Et inde, sequendo dictam viam, versus bor., quousque perveniatur ad pontem lapideum qui jacet ad introitum de Walwyk-feld. Et exinde per quemdam rivulum currentem inter campum de Walw *(sic)*, et quamdam parcellam terræ quondam vocatam Hollemarsse, modo vocatam Holmerscrofte, sicut decidit in Tynam: et exinde, sequendo medium aquæ de North-Tyne, quousque perveniatur ad Wardon-ford antedictum.

Le Cros-flatt. Tenent etiam in campo de Wardon Superiori, extra divisas prænominatas, quamdam parcellam terræ jacentem ex occid. parte de Walwyk-waye; et vocatur le Crosflatt, cont. per æst. iiij acras terræ, et adjacet manerio antedicto.

Lang acre. Tenent etiam quamdam parcellam terræ extra divisas prætactas ex parte bor.; prope le Cros-flatt prædictum, super viam prædictam; et cont. per æst. j acram terræ, et adjacet manerio antedicto.

Tenent etiam quamdam parcellam terræ ex austr. parte del South Tyne, vocatam Hardhalgh; et jacet inter quamdam parcellam de Wharnelye, vocatam Elden-halghe, ex parte occid., et Cocelye bank ex parte austr., et aquam de Tyna ex parte bor. Et cont. per æst. x acras terræ; et junguntur culturæ manerii antedicti.

Villa de Wardon. Sunt etiam ibidem in villa de Wardon — cotagia; et quodlibet cotagium metet cum j homine per quatuor dies singulis annis in autumpno, cum requisitus fuerit, excepto quod vicarius ibidem pro quadam parcella quam t. de dominicis ibidem nullum faciet servitium. Quæ quidem terra cont. xij acras et iij rodas; et jacent ex parte austr. de Yekesyde, et ex parte austr. de le reygne quæ dividit campum de Wardon Superiori et terram prædictam.

Dominus Ricardus Morlande, vicarius ibidem, t. xij acras et iij rodas terræ de dominicis, specificatas, ut supra, et continentur infra divisas prænominatas.

Idem t. j cotagium in villa ibidem ædificatum, et iij acras et j rode terræ; quarum j acra et j roda jacent ex austr. parte prædictarum xij acrarum et iij rodarum in tenura ejusdem vicarii. Et j acra terræ jacet ex austr. parte parci inter prædictum parcum et aquam de South Tyne. Et j acra jacet in Hardhalghe prænominato, et r. p. a., iiijs. et opera et consuetudines.

(Cotagia) Beatrix Wryght t. j cot. ibidem et j rodam terræ jacentis proportionaliter in locis superius in tenura vicarii specificatis; et r. p. a. iiijs. et opera. Matildis de Paris t. j cot. ædificatum et iij acras et j rodam terræ jacentes diversis locis, proportionaliter, ut supra; et r. p. a. iiijs. et opera. Johannes de Schaldfurth t. j cot. iij acras et j rodam terræ, proportionaliter, et locis, ut supra, et r. p. a. iiijs. et opera. Johannes de Ledom t. j cot. iij acras et j rodam terræ, locis, ut supra, et r. p. a. iiijs. et opera. Est ibidem j locus vocatus Clerk-place. Gilbertus Schephird t. j cot. et iij acras et j rodam terræ eidem adjacentes, ut supra, et r. p. a. iiijs. et opera. Est ibidem j cot. cum iij acris et j roda terræ eidem adjacentibus, ut supra.

Batella de Wardon. Alicia Coyk, Rob. Bacward, tenent batellam de Wardon, ad terminum x annorum, et r. p. a. xxs.

De cujus manerii antedicti fructibus et proventibus assignantur officio celerarii coquinæ singulis annis ad terminos usuales solvendi, et r. p. a. vjli. xiijs. iiijd.

PASTURA IN PASCUIS DE WALWYK.

Habent etiam pasturam communem in pascuis de Walwyke ad cc[tas] oves et sexdecem boves et x vaccas exeuntes de manerio prædicto de Wardon, cum liberis exitu et introitu ad dictam pasturam omni tempore anni communicand', ex concessione Ricardi Comyne, prout habetur ex[a] in cartis.

SCLAVELEYE.

Tenent etiam in Sclavelye diversa tenementa et di carucatam terræ, et alias certas acras, ut in cartis Conventus, et pasturas ad certas oves, ut in cartis continetur.

Johannes Forister de Corbrig t. j messuagium cum certis acris adjac., voc. Dalton-place (et jacet ex parte austr. villæ, prope finem or.), libere per fidelitatem, et r. p. a. xijd. Johannes Dobynson t. j toftum ibidem ædificatum cum j crofto, cont. in toto iij rodas; et diversas acras terræ cont. j terram husband; quarum j roda jacet ex parte occid. prope dictum croftum; et ad Wade's-crofts-endis di. acr.; et super le Parson's-lawe di. acr.; et ex parte or. juxta le Foule-well di. acr.; et super le Thorenknoll di. acr.; et ex parte bor. le Cote-garth j roda. Et in Pat-ryding, juxta le Cote-garth, j roda. Et in Pat-ryding, juxta le Cote-garth, v acræ. Et super lez Chestrez j roda. Et ad le Hollelech j acr. Et ad finem occid. del Hoghton-crofte diacr. Et occid. parte prædictæ di. acr., inter quamdam parcellam terræ Roberti de Wollowe, jac. ex parte or., et quamdam parcellam terræ dominicæ ex parte occid., ij acr. Et ad finem crofti Ricardi Gibbison, j acra. Et super le Myln-flatte, ad finem austr. de le Hoghtoncrofte, j acra. Et in le West-crofte, juxta vj acras in tenura

Ricardi Hunter, quas t. de Priore, ij acræ. Et super Schelde-schaw sunt diversæ acræ vastæ in tenura ejusdem. Et dictus Johannes t. prædicta tofta et terras ad terminum trium annorum, et r. p. a. xs.

PREST PLACE. Willelmus Wallar t. j toftum cum j crofto adjacente, et vocatur le Prest place; cont. in toto j acram et di. terræ, ad term. trium annorum; et r. p. a. ijs.

LUMBARD'S PLACE. Henricus Hanson t. toftum ædificatum cum j crofto adjacente, cont. in toto j acram, vocatam Lumbard place; et jacet ex parte occid. ecclesiæ juxta toftum prædictum, ad term. trium annorum; et r. p. a. iijs. iiijd.

TERRÆ HUSBAND. Ricardus Hunter t. j toftum vastum cum crofto, cont. in toto j acram et di.; et jacet ex parte bor. villæ ad finem occid. ejusdem; et diversas acras cont. j terram husband, quarum j acra vocatur Matfennes-acre, jacens in le west syde del North-felde. Et in le West-croftes, inter quamdam parcellam terræ dominicæ ex parte occid., et quamdam parcellam terræ Johannis de Neuton ex parte or., vj acræ. Et in le Schel-feld, ex parte or. juxta le Parrok, j acra vocata Prior-acre. Et cæteræ acræ pertinentes dictæ terræ husband jacent vastæ super Scheld-schaw. Et dominus Ricardus t. prædicta toftum et terras ad term. iij ann., et r. p. a. iijs.

Habent etiam Prior et Conventus et eorum tenentes ibidem fodere in petariis et turbariis infra communam ibidem, et capere estoveria sua, et omnia necessaria sua, etiam si dominus de Sclavelye vel ejus tenentes capere noluerunt.

BARCARIA DE SCLAVELYE. Habent etiam j barcariam ex parte bor. villæ, ad finem or. ejusdem, cum j gardino adjacente, cont. in toto j acram terræ; et communam pasturæ ad communicandum in eadem omni tempore anni. Et ad communicandum infra omnes divisas de Sclavelye temporibus congruis ad xv score oves. Et modo nil r. quia in manu domini pro bidentibus ibidem existentibus.

BARCARIA DE STELE. Habent etiam ibidem j barcariam in le Stele, prope finem occid., cum gardino adjacente ex parte bor. ejusdem, cont. in toto j acram terræ; et communam pasturæ ad xv^{xx} oves omni tempore anni; et communam infra omnes divisas del Stele, ut supra in Sclavelye. Et prædictæ oves, tam de Sclavlye quam de Stele, communicabunt utrobique, conjunctim et divisim, tam infra limites de Sclavelye quam de Stele, pro beneplacito Prioris et Conventus.

STOKYSFELD.

Willelmus Ayrike t. totam Stokesfelde per homagium et fidelitatem, et r. p. a. xiijs. viijd., videlicet ad festum Nat. Sancti Johannis Bapt. vjs. viijd., et ad festum Sancti Cuthberti in Septembre vjs. viijd.; unde ad wardum castri, xijd.

PROUDEHOWE.

Tenent etiam in Proudehowe, ex parte occid. villæ, prope finem bor., j toftum et certas acras in campo ejusdem ædificatas, cum j crofto, cont. in toto j acram et j rodam terræ: et ex parte austr. del Rayhill-syde j acram et iij rodas vocatas Hexham-land; et ex parte bor., juxta le Bradwyner, ex utraque parte le Viner'-waye, ij acras terræ; et ex parte occid. prædictarum acrarum, ex transverso viæ prædictæ, et buttantes super le Lytill Viner', ad finem austr. ejusdem, ij acras; et super le Smalrodes, buttando super le Bradwell-medoue, j rodam: et super lez Ulyrudes, buttando super terr. dominic. ibidem, j rodam; et ex parte orientali, juxta Cokrellis-well, j rodam; et ex parte occid., prope dictum well, j rodam; et ex parte or. villæ, sub gardino Roberti Hyne, di. rodæ. Et r. p. a. viijs.

De piscaria de Ovyngeham *(blank)*.

CORBRYG.

Tenent etiam in Corbryg certa ten. et redditus, unde in tenura.

Johannes Meryngton t. j burgagium liberum in Sant Maregate, ex parte occid. prope pontem, inter burgagium Johannis Fayte ex parte or. et burgagium Roberti Fayte ex parte occid.; et r. p. a. iijs. (Celerar' *in marg.*) Gilbertus Fayte t. j burg. in Syd-gate, ex parte austr. ejusdem, inter burg. Roberti Milner ex parte occid., et burg. Roberti Hudespeth ex parte or., et r. p. a. xijd. Magot Spryng t. j burg. ibidem, ex opposito le west-kyrk-style, inter burg. Willelmi de Blenkhowe ex parte austr., et burg. Thomæ Chepman ex parte bor., et r. p. a. xijd. Willelmus Hogg t. j burg. in Fischambles-gat, ex parte bor. ejusdem, quondam vocatum Mongwe-skely-place, inter burg. Johannis Fayte, et burg. domini Willelmi Heron militis ex parte or., et r. p. a. xiijs. iiijd. Johannes Forestar t. j burg. in eadem placea, inter burg. Johannis Fayte ex parte occid., et burg. Willelmi Hunter ex parte or., quod libere tenet de elemosinario, et r. p. a. iijs. Willelmus Hunter t. libere j burg. in eodem vico, inter dictum burg. Johannis Forester, et viam quæ vocatur Prent-strete, et r. p. a. ijs. vjd.; et post terminos contentos in suis indenturis, et r. p. a. vs. Adam Lauson t. libere j burg. in Narow-gate, ex parte or. ejusdem, vocatum Adam-Palmar-place, et r. p. a. iijs. Nichol Walkar t. j burg. in Thorneburgh-gate, ex parte austr. ejusdem, inter burg. *(blank)*, et r. p. a. xviijd.; et Robertus Walch t. dictum burg. (Offic. elemos' *in marg.*)

Tenent etiam j burg. in Colewell-chare, ex parte austr. ejusdem, juxta venellam quæ ducit ad Tynam, in manu domini, et solet r. iijs. Johannes Forestar de Corbrigg t. j burg., quondam in tenura Adæ de Dyghton; et solet r. p. a. iijs.

BEAUMOND.

Tenent etiam totam terram de Beaumond in territorio de Chollirton; et est seperalis omni tempore anni, et continetur inter has divisas; videlicet, incipiendo ad pontem de Eriane, ascendendo versus bor. per le Dere-strete usque Foule-brig: et deinde per j syketum vocatum Beaumond-burne usque pratum Alexandri de Swynburn, versus le south-west: et inde versus south-est per metas lapideas positas inter dictum Beaumond et pratum dicti Alexandri, usque le Sandiland-endes: et inde per j parvum siketum versus occid., inter dictum pratum et quamdam parcellam prati de Beaumond jacentem inter prædictum syketum et aquam de Eriane, usque le wythe-busk stantem ex parte or. prope le Skotis-ford. Et inde, sequendo aquam de Erian, usque pontem de Eriane antedictum. Et sciendum est quod Prior et Conventus et eorum tenentes manentes in Beaumond habebunt liberos exitus et introitus, cum omnibus suis averiis, ad communem pasturam de Chollirton, ad dictam pasturam omni tempore communicandum. Et tenentes villæ de Chollirton tenent prædictam cum suis pertinentiis ad term. trium annorum, termino primo solutionis ad festum Sancti Martini, et r. p. a. liijs. iiijd.; solebant reddere v marcas.

CHOLLIRTON.

Tenent etiam in Chollirton diversa ten. et terras; unde in tenura.

Hugo Colstane t. j ten. ex parte austr. villæ, proximum cimiterio ecclesiæ, cum j gardino cont. per æst. j acram et plus; in quo quidem gardino in fine or. stat grangia decimalis. Et idem t. xxvij acras terræ arab., pertinentes ten. prædicto; quarum ij acræ et di. acræ ex parte austr. rivulæ de Eriane, ex opposito le grangiæ decimalis, buttando super Coklau-feld. Et super le Kiln-flate, ex parte occid., di. acræ. Et super Horslaws-pule di. acr. Schot-halgh-bankys, et super Nithre di. acræ. Et super Over-schotlau-bankes di. acræ. Et super le Blaklaw, ex parte or. ejusdem, di. acræ. Et ex parte occid. ejusdem j acra. Et ex parte or. le Lons . . . ane j roda. Et ex parte or. Bronslaue-medoue j roda. Et super Bronslaw-flate, ex parte occid., di. acræ. Et ex parte bor. Bronslaw-medoue, buttando super eodem, iij rodæ. Et super le Canon-flatte, ex parte occid. le Mosse-way quæ ducit ad Swynburn, j acra et di. Et super lez buttes, juxta le dyk, ad finem bor. del Kiln-flatte, di. acræ. Et super lez heued-landes de Brouneslaw-flatte, buttando super le Canon-flatte, j roda. Et ad capud del Mayn-flatt, ex utraque parte le Messe-waye, di. acræ. Et ex parte austr. le Crosse, ex utraque parte viæ ibidem, j roda. Et super Holmers-bank, ex parte or. dictæ Crosse, di. acræ. Et in Harlaw-hop, buttando super le Messe-way, di. acræ. Et ex parte occid., juxta le Harlaw, di. acræ. Et super le Mesi-way, super eandem, j roda. Et ex parte or. le lonyng-hed j roda. Et super Ald-chestre, ex parte austr., iij rodæ. Et ex parte occid., super le Stobithorn, j roda. Et super Morelaw, ex parte or. ejusdem, buttando super leche, di. acræ. Et ex parte bor. de Dueld-rigge di. acræ. Et ex parte or. le Smythehop-side di. acræ. Et in medio Craustrige di. acræ. Et ex parte or. de Westraustrige j acra. Et super Estraustrige, ex parte occid., j roda. Et ex parte or. Fartir-mere-thorne, buttando super Crauster-merleche, j acra. Et ex parte austr. terræ prædictæ j roda. Et inter Falter-mere et lez Merl-pottes j acra. Et ex parte bor. lez Merl-pottes j roda. Et in medio Wayn-rig iij rodæ. Et ex parte or. le Brere-ryg j roda. Et ex parte or. lez Hudes-rodes j acra. Et inter lez Korn-hilles j roda. Et in medio le Miln-rig di. acræ. Et super Ful-rig iij rodæ. Et in Swynburne-feld, ex parte bor. le crosse, j acra.

Item t. di. acræ prati, ex parte austr. rivuli de Eriane, juxta ij acras et di., primo in sua tenura nominatas; et j acram ad le miln-dam-hede; et j rodam super le Prest-leche.

Item t. j cot., ex parte bor. villæ, ad finem occid. ejusdem, cum j crofto adjacente, cont. in toto per æst. di. acræ. Et pertinent ad id cotagium iij acræ terræ arab., quarum iij rodæ jacent ad Brounes-lau-medoue. Et j roda jacet ad le west-syde del Kylnes-flate. Et super Holmer-bankes di. acræ. Et ex parte bor. le crosse in Swynburn-felde j acra. Et prædictæ acræ specificatæ junguntur terris husband superius nominatis.

Item t. j cotagium ex eadem parte villæ, — tenura Alani Hoghyrd, cum j crofto adjacente, et cont. in toto j rodam et di.;

et dictus Hugo r. p. a. pro omnibus terris et tenementis prædictis xxviijs.; unde pro terris husbandorum xxvs.; et pro cot' iijs. Solebat reddere iiijs.

Alanus Hoghird t. j toftum ædificatum, cum j gardino et j crofto adjacente, inter prædicta cotagia; et cont. per æst. j acram terræ. Et xxviij acras terræ arab., quarum j roda jacet super le Kyln-flatte. Et super Hors-lawes j acra et j roda. Et in le halghe, ex parte austr. rivuli de Ereane, juxta ij acras et di. Hugonis de Colstane, ij acræ et di. Et super House-lauepole di. acræ. Et super Nethre-scot-halgh-bank di. acræ. Et ex parte bor. del Horslawe, buttando super Barens-furth-waye, iij rodæ. Et ex parte occid. ejusdem viæ di. acræ. Et super Over-schot-halgh-bank di. acræ. Et ex parte or. del Blak-lawe di. acræ. Et ex parte occid. ejusdem j acra. Et ex or. Brounslawe-medowe j roda. Et ex parte occid. Brons-lau-flatte di. acræ. Et ex parte occid. le Messe-way, quæ ducit ad Swynburn, super le Canon-flatte, j acra et di. Et super lez buttes ad le syk, ex parte bor. le Kiln-flatte, juxta le Messe-waye, di. acræ. Et super lez heued-landes de Brons-law-flatte j roda. Et sub Schothalgh-lyn j acra. Et ad capud de Mayn-flatte, ex utraque parte le Messe-way, di. acræ. Et ex parte austr. le Crosse, ex utraque parte viæ ibidem, j roda. Et in Harlaw-hop, buttando super le Messe-waye, di. acræ. Et ex parte occid., juxta le Harlawe, di. acræ. Et prope eandem terram, super le Messe-waye, j roda. Et ex parte or. le Lonyng-heuede ij rodæ. Et ex parte austr. de Agchestre iij rodæ. Et ex parte occid., super le Stob-thorne, j roda. Et ex parte or., super Mori-law, buttando super le leche, di. acræ. Et ex bor. de Dueld-rige di. acræ. Et ex parte or. de Smethop-syde di. acræ. Et in medio de Crawstrig di. acræ. Et ex parte or. de West-crawstrig j acra. Et ex parte occid. de Est-crawstrig iij rodæ. Et ex parte or. Farter-mere-thorne, buttando super Crawstrige-mere-leche, j acra. Et ex parte austr., prope terram prædictam, j roda. Et inter Farter-merethorne et lez Marl-pottes j acra. Et in medio Wayn-rige iij rodæ. Et ex parte or. le Breri-rig j roda. Et ex parte or. de Hodes-rodes j acra. Et inter lez Corn-hilles j acra. Et ex parte austr. lez Corn-hilles j acra. Et super lez Corn-hilles j roda. Et in medio de Miln-rig di. acræ. Et super Ful-rig j acra et di.

Item prædictus Alanus t. j acram, iij rodas prati, participando æqualiter, ut in tenura Hugonis Colstan, certis locis et metis specificatis.

Dimissiones. Et prædictus Alanus t. prædicta tofta et terras, et r. p. a. xxxs.

Et sciendum quod omnes terræ superiores, in tenura Hugonis et Alani specificatæ, jacent conjunctim et divisim per parcellas in locis et limitibus superius annotatis.

BAROUSFORD.

Tenent etiam in Barousford j ten. ædificatum, cum xxx acris terræ arab. et j acram prati; quod quidem ten. jacet ex parte bor. villæ prope finem or., juxta le pole, cum j gardino adjacente, cont. per æst. iij rodas terræ. Et de prædictis xxx acris terræ iiij acræ jacent in le West-egge. Et inter lez Houghes xij acræ et iij rodæ. Et in Holfurth-hegge iiij acræ. Et in Seleege-flatte ix acræ et j roda: et prædictæ acræ prati jacent in tribus partibus; videlicet in Harden-hole j particula; et in le karr, qui vocatur Seleeyge, alia particula; et ex parte bor., subtus gardinum, tertia particula.

Libertates tenentium in Barousford. Et tenens Prioris de prædictis terris ibidem molet bladum suum ad molendinum domini ibidem sine multura; et quietus erit a pannagio dando.

Habent etiam ibidem j grangiam decimalem, ex parte bor. villæ versus occid., juxta lez pottes, cum j gardino adjacente; et cont. in toto di. acræ terræ et plus; et dicta grangia est in manu Prioris pro garbis decimalibus observandis.

Et idem Johannes de Barassfurd t. prædicta ten. et terras, cum vestura gardini grangiæ decimalis, et r. p. a. xxs.; unde officio bursarii ijs.; et speciebus Conventus, xviijs.

GUNWARDTON.

Tenent etiam in Gunwardton j ten. ædificatum ex parte austr. villæ et capellæ, cum j gardino; in cujus parte austr. stat grangia decimalis; et cum j crofto adjacente cont. in toto per æst. iiij acras terræ. Et ij terræ husband cont. in acris sicut cæteræ terræ husband ibidem; quarum v acræ, vocatæ le Prior-flatte, jacent ex parte austr. juxta dictum croft. Et ex parte bor. viæ inter Barousford et Chipches, super lez Wyndilandes, iij acræ. Et super lez Sandilandes, ex parte austr. Schirrewel-strandes, buttando super aquam Tyna, v acræ. Et ex parte occid. le milnsyd ij acræ. Et super lez Schol-brades ij acræ. Et ex parte or. juxta Fulfurd-syde j acra. Et super le Gibbis-more, ex parte or. de Michels-bank, buttando super le Sclate-ford, viij acræ. Et super Harden-way, fere in medio, ex transverso viæ ibidem quæ ducit de Gonwarton ad Chipches, ij acræ. Et ex parte austr. de Mullan-wod, super le dyk, iij acræ.

Et ad le heuede del Schirrewell j acr. prati. Et in Fulfursyde, juxta prædictam acram terræ arab. ibidem, di acræ prati. Et est in tenura xxjs.

BYRTELYE.

Tenent etiam in Byrtelye j ten., ædificatum ex austr. parte villæ versus finem or., cum j gardino et j crofto ex parte austr. ejusdem ten. Et croftum cont. vj acras terræ arab., quæ jacent inter tenuram Willelmi Lyghtfote ex parte occid., et terr. Adæ de Lee ex parte or.; et buttat super Dunley ex parte austr. Et tenentes Prioris molent blada sua ad molendinum domini ibidem sine multura; et quieti erunt a pannagio dando. Et est modo in tenura vs.

CHIPCHES.

Tenent etiam in Chipches j grangiam decimalem ad finem or. villæ, ex parte bor. viæ quæ ducit ad Gonwarton, et cum j gardino adjacente; et cont. in toto minus j rod. terræ; et est in manu domini pro decimis garbarum intrandis.

COLDEN.

Tenent etiam totum Colden, et est seperalis omni tempore anni, et includitur infra has divisas; videlicet, incipiendo ad finem or. del Trow-hille. Et inde, sicut antiquum fossatum tendit, ad le Trowe-burne; et inde per le dictum Trowe-burne versus occid. usque le Ley-acre-dyk: et inde versus austr. per lez Standand-stanes, stantes inter moram de Britle et le Newfeld de Colden, usque le Lange-syk: et exinde per le Lange-syk versus or. usque Colden-burne: et inde per quoddam antiquum fossatum inter moram de Gonwarton et dictum Colden, usque quoddam parvum siketum ex parte bor. cujusdam parvæ rupis vocatæ Colden-kyrk, usque le Der-strete. Et inde per le Derestrete versus bor. usque le Trow-hill prius nominatum.

Habent etiam liberos introitus et exitus de dicto Colden usque moram de mora de Gonwarton ad v score averia, videlicet, boves et vaccas, ad prædictam moram, cum dictis averiis omni tempore depascendum. Et, si prædicta averia intraverint le Frithe aliquo tempore prohibito, pro eschape non ideo inparcabuntur, sed sine strepitu vel dampno libere et pacifice rechaciari debent (per cartam indentatam et concordiam factam inter Priorem et Conventum et Johannem filium Johannis de Gonwarton. *In marg.*)

Dimissio. Et est in tenura Alani del Strothre prædictum Colden cum omnibus suis pertinentibus, et r. p. a. lxvjs. viijd.

STELDEN.

Johannes de Midelton, dominus de Swynburn Est, t. totam Steldene per homagium et fidelitatem, simul cum tofto et crofto quod Samson de Swynburne aliquando tenuit, cum omnibus pertinentiis suis, extra barcariam Prioris et Conventus in Stelden, et pasturam dictorum Prioris et Conventus in mora de Gonwarton, cum liberis introitu et exitu ad oves dictorum Prioris et Conventus ad dictam barcariam commorantes; et r. p. a. pro terris prædictis xls.; unde Abbati de Newmostre per annum xxxiijs. iiijd.: et, in defectu solutionis, dictus Abbas reintravit et dimisit dictum Stelden, ut jus suum proprium et justitia requirebat.

SWYNBURN EST.

Habent etiam quamdam parcellam terræ ibidem, cont. iiij^{xx} pedes in longitudine, et iiij^{xx} pedes in latitudine, pro grangia decimali ibidem construenda; et est ad finem occid. cimiterii capellæ Omnium Sanctorum ibidem versus bor. Et Jordanus de Barousford t. prædictam placeam, et r. p. a. jd.

COLLEWELLE.

Habent etiam in Collewelle pasturam ad quadringinta oves ubique in communi pastura ibidem, et ad xxx boves et x vaccas cum j tauro in eadem villa, cum liberis introitu et exitu de villa de Byngfeld ad prædictam pasturam communicand' omni tempore anni [per cartam Gilberti de Umfravill *in marg.*]

Habent etiam ibidem j grangiam decimalem cum j gardino adjacente; et cont. in toto minus roda. Et est ex parte bor. juxta Chollirton-waye ad le south-west-end ejusdem villæ, et buttat super les meres ad le south-end eorumdem. Et Willelmus Smert tenet vesturam dicti gardini, et r. jd.

Dimissio. Hæres Rogeri de Wodryngton t. j messuagium in villa de Swynburne West, cum certis acris terræ eidem pertinentibus in campo ibidem, per homagium et fidelitatem; quod quidem mesuagium jacet ad finem occid., ex austr. parte viæ, et ex opposito le north-est-corner muri circumdantis castrum ibidem. Et nuper erat in tenura Adæ Scibald, et r. p. a. iijs. speciebus Conventus.

Grangia decimalis. Habent etiam in eadem villa j grangiam decimalem, et jacet ex parte del north-est capellæ ibidem, et est vastum.

Acra terræ in Swynburn West. Habent etiam in campo

ejusdem villæ j acram terræ, et jacet ex parte bor. juxta le crosse; et jungitur tenuræ Hugonis Colstan in Chollirton, ut ibidem patet.

KYRKHETON CUM CALDSTROTHRE.

Tenent etiam in Kyrk-heton et Cald-strothre integrum dominium, videlicet in homagiis, servitiis, releviis, custodiis, escaetis, villinagiis, cum omnibus libertatibus ad dictam villam pertinentibus, et cum omnibus servitiis forincecis quibuscumque.

Johannes de Strevelyne, miles, t. certas terras in Kyrkheton pro homagio et fidelitate. Thomas de Horsle t. ibidem certas terras pro humagio et fidelitate. Johannes Kemp t. ibidem certas terras et ten. pro homagio et fidelitate. Johannes de Marlaye t. ibidem certas terras et ten. pro homagio et fidelitate. Thomas de Beckeburne t. certas terras et ten. in Caldstrothre pro hom. et fid., et r. singulis annis ad festum Natal. Domini jd. Johannes de Dalton t. certas terras et ten. pro hom. et fid. Thomas de Hildreton, miles, t. certas terras et ten. ibidem pro hom. et fid. Et omnes prædicti debent sectam curiæ Prioris ibidem.

TERRÆ HUSBAND. Et sunt in eadem villa xxxiij terræ husband, et quælibet terra cont. xxxiiij acras terræ arab. et prati, excepta terra in tenura Ricardi Atkynson; quæ quidem terra continet vij acras quondam adjacentes cuidam cotagio, et xviij acras de for-land; et nunc adjunguntur terr. husband. Unde in tenura.

Johannes Hastynsone t. iij terras husb., et r. p. a. xxxs. Ric. Atkynsone t. j terr., quæ jungitur terr. husb., et r. p. a. viijs. Johannes de Akome et Christiana Scot t. j terr., et r. p. a. ixs. Rogerus Johnson t. ij terras, et r. p. a. xxs. Johannes de Esschelez t. j terr., et r. p. a. xs. Willelmus de Babynton t. j terr., et r. p. a. xs. Willelmus Gilessone t. iij terr., et r. p. a. xs. Henricus de Schaftow t. j terr., et r. p a. xs. Johannes Wilkynson, nativus domini, t. iij terr., et r. xxs. Robertus Seemane t. j. terr., et r. per a. xs. Willelmus Jonson, nativus domini, t. ij terr. et r. xxs.

Sunt ibidem viij cotagia et ij crofta. Unde in tenura.

Johannes Hastynson t. j cotagium ædificatum cum iiij acris terræ et di., et r. ijs. Idem t. j cot. vastum et v acras terræ, et r. p. a. ijs. Johannes Wylkynson, nativus domini, t. j cot. vastum et iij acras, xviijd. Johannes de Babinton t. j. cot. et xiij acras terræ vastæ, et r. p. a. iijs. Johannes Morell t. j cot. ædificatum, et iij acras terræ et di., et r. p. a. iijs. Willelmus Dudden t. j cot. ædificatum et vij acras, et r. p. a. vjs. Christiana Scott t. j. cot. vastum, et iij acras terræ et di., et r. p. a. xijd. Willelmus Beene t. j cot. ædificatum et vij acras terræ, et r. p. a vs. Robertus Atkinson t. j croftum vocatum le Cotgarth, et r. p. a viijd. Item t. j croftum vocatum Natrescrofte, et r. p. a. xijd.

Prata dominica. Omnes tenentes villæ tenent conjunctim vij acras prati et di. de dominicis, et r. p. a. vjs.

Vast' prat'. Habent etiam quandam portionem prati dominici, vocatam le Hegh-sid-lech, et est vastum.

Libertates de Kyrkheton et Caldstrothre. Et sciendum quod neque comes de Riddesdale, nec hæredes sui, aut eorum ballivi, in villa de Parva Heton et Cald-strothre, pro aliquo servitio forinceco domino regi debito, vel pro communi ammerciamento coram justiciariis itinerantibus ad dominum regem pertinente, seu aliquo alio modo, suis propriis auctoritatibus, secundum confirmationem cartarum antecessorum domini comitis qui nunc est, aliquatenus distringere debeant.

PARVA BABYNTON.

Tenent etiam in Parva Babyngton ij tofta ædificata ad finem occid. villæ, et ex parte bor. ejusdem, cont. in toto per æst. j acram terræ. Et j toftum vastum, prope finem or. villæ, et ex parte bor., cum j gardino adjacente; et ix acras terræ arabilis et di., quarum iij acræ jacent super le Toftes. Et super le Hony-landes di. acræ. Et juxta le Hare-well j acra. Et super lez Chestres prope Gibbis-kilne j acra et di. Et super Gose-croft j acra et j roda. Et super Godi-lawe ij acræ. Et super lez Morilandes j roda.

Pastura. Habent etiam communam pasturæ in territorio ejusdem ad xv averia et lx oves, et ad ij equos, omni tempore anni.

Et Willelmus de Schafthow de Babyngton tenet prædicta tenementa et terras ad voluntatem domini, et r. p. a. ijs. officio elemosinarii.

NEUTON IN COOKDALE JUXTA HARBOTELL.

Tenent etiam in Neuton in Cookdale j toftum vastum cum j crofto adjacente, vocato Dians-croft; et jacent ad finem occid. de Suthre Neuton, ex parte austr. le lonyng ibidem, inter toft' et croft' Johannis de Berehalgh, sicut dividitur per unum balk ex parte or.; et quoddam siketum inter terr. dominic. comitis de Angose in Hirbotle ex parte austr.; et communam moræ dictæ Neuton ex parte occid.; et le lonyng quæ ducit ad dictam moram ex parte bor.; et cont. in toto per æst. iiij acras.

Tenent etiam in campo ibidem j carucatam terræ arabilis et prati, et jacet inter has divisas, ad finem or. de North-Newton-felde; videlicet, incipiendo ad quendam parvum siketum inter campum Walteri Tailboise et campum de North Newton prædictum, versus bor., per metas lapideas positas inter campum de North-Newton et dictam carucatam terræ, usque viam quæ ducit de Nethreton ad ecclesiam de Alwenton. Et inde, sequendo dictam viam, versus or., usque quendam parvum siketum descendentem inter dictam carucatam terræ et campum de Buroudon. Et exinde per dictum siketum, versus austr., usque quendam siketum vocatum Dians-dene. Et sic, sequendo dictum siketum versus occid., sicut descendit inter quamdam portionem terræ Johannis de Berehalgh, et dictum campum Walteri Tailboise, usque metas lapideas prius nominatas. Et Johannes de Berehalgh t. prædicta toft' et crofta cum dicta carucata terræ, et r. p. a. xiijs. iiijd.

TEMPLE THORNTON.

Tenent etiam in Temple Thornton diversa tofta et terras, de quibus j toftum ædificatum, cum j gardino et j crofto adjacente, jacet in West-gat, prope finem bor., ex parte occid. ejusdem; et cont. in toto per æst. v rodas. Et aliud toftum ædificatum jacet directe ex parte austr. dicti tofti, cum j gardino et crofto adjacente, et cont. in toto iij rodas. Et tertium toftum jacet vastum directe ex parte austr. dicti tofti, cum gardino et crofto adjacente; et cont. in toto per æst. iij rodas. Et ij tofta vasta cum ij gardinis adjacentibus jacent in eodem vico adinvicem, ad finem austr. dictæ viæ, et ex parte or. ejusdem; et cont. in toto j acram terræ et di. Et ij acræ terræ, pertinentes dictis ij toftes vastis, vice croftorum, jacent adinvicem, ex transverso Wotton-deene, buttando super le West-deene.

Tenent etiam diversas terras arabiles et prata, quarum j acra jacet super le Ridyng, buttando super le West-deene. Et super Jakis-flatt, ex parte occid. del Crosse-lande, v acræ. Et super lez Wlle-pottes, ex parte bor. viæ vocatæ le Monkes-way, ij acræ et di. Et Ake-wel-syd, ex parte occid. ejusdem, buttando super lez Medou-bank, ij acr. et di. Et in le Hyngand-syde, quia in medio, j acra et j roda. Et super le Kyrk-way, ex transverso ejusdem, j acra et di. Et ad partem austr., juxta le Well ij acræ et di. Et super le South-deene, buttando super le deen, vij acræ vocatæ le South-croft et North-croft; et super le Toft-thorne ij acræ et di. Et super le Wel-myre, ex parte austr. ejusdem, ij acræ et di. Et apud le est-end del Well-myre iij rodæ. Et apud le est-syde ejusdem iij rodæ. Et ex parte occid. dictæ myre v rodæ. Et ex parte austr. ejusdem well ij acræ et di. Et super lez Furlanges j acra et di. Et apud Elges-well v rodæ. Et super lez South-deen-bank, buttando super Hartburn, v acræ. Et super lez Miln-hill v rodæ. Et super Hildes-well, del north-end ejusdem, ex transverso Morpeth-way, j acra. Et apud Ald-thorn-law, ex parte occid. ibidem, v rodæ. Et super lez Flores v rodæ. Et ex parte bor. lez Flores ij acræ et di. Et in lez Furthalgh v rodæ. Et super lez Twystes, buttando super Brere-law-medou, ij acræ et j roda. Et super lez Seven-acresse, ex parte austr. eorumdem, v rodæ. Et super Lynt-lawes, quia in medio, iij acræ. Et super le Hole-medoue, ex parte austr. ejusdem, ij acræ et di. Et ex parte occid. ejusdem medowe j acra et di. Et ex parte austr. de Halton-lawe iij acræ. Et super Hunguge, ex parte austr. ibidem, iij rodæ. Et super le Forlanges, juxta le Miln-waye, v rodæ. Et super lez Furlandes, ex parte or. ibidem, v rodæ. Et super lez Threp-more, ex parte occid. ibidem, iij acræ. Et ex parte bor. ejusdem ij acræ et di. Et super le Schelle-lawe ij acræ et di. Et super lez Smal-half-acre, quia in medio, ex parte austr. del Morpeth-way, ij acræ et di. Et ex parte occid. del Cot-walles v acræ. Et in Hesewell-croftes, ex parte austr. ibidem, ij acræ et di. Et in Sewell-syd, quia in medio, ij acræ et di. Et apud le Propp, ex parte austr. de Morpeth-way, iij rodæ. Et ex parte austr. de Clough-lech ij acræ et di. *Summa totalis acrarum* iiij^{xx} xj acræ, et iij rodæ terræ.

Prata. Et in Hessewell-strothre iij acr. prati : et prædicta tofta et terræ dividuntur in quinque terras husband. Unde in tenura.

Willelmus Smyth t. j toftum ædificatum, j toftum vastum, et ij terras eisdem pertinentes, et r. p. a. xxxs. ; unde, pro qualibet terra husband, xs.

Dimissio. Thomas de Hertburn t. j toftum ædificatum, et j toftum vastum, et ij terras eisdem pertinentes, et r. p. a. xxs.

WHALTON.

Tenent etiam in Whalton j toftum ædificatum, cum j crofto et gardino adjacente; et jacet prope finem occid. ex austr. parte villæ, et ex parte or. communis viæ; et cont. in toto iiij acras. Tenent etiam in campo ejusdem villæ di. carucatæ terra, videlicet lij acras terræ et di.; quarum super Lindes-lawe, ex parte occid. ejusdem villæ, jacent iiij acræ. Et super le Flores, ex parte occid., prope dictas acras, ix acr. Et in le West-feld, inter Walwyk et Leverchild, xiij acræ, vocatæ le Burn-flatt, ex parte austr. molendini ibidem, xiij acr. *(sic)*. Et super le Farne-law, ex parte or. villæ ejusdem, xiij acras.

Prata. Et ex parte bor. molendini, inter Midrige et le Miln-dame, jacent j acra et iij rodæ prati. Et super Ellisdun-syd iij rodæ.

Habent etiam communem pasturam ad trescentas oves omni tempore anni, et agnis earumdem, usque festum Nat. Sancti Johannis Baptistæ. Et tunc erat in libito retinere agnos in eadem pastura, et removere de ovibus juxta numerum agnorum. Et Robertus Milner t. prædicta tofta et terras cum pertinentiis, et r. p. a. xs. officio coquinæ.

Redditus viiis. in villa de Whalton. Habent etiam ibidem annuum redditum viij solidorum, annuatim exeuntem de manerio ejusdem villæ, solutum per Henricum Scrope, dominum villæ prædictæ, officio sacristæ.

NEWBIGGYNG SUPER MARE.

Tenent etiam in villa de Newbiggyng, prope finem or. villæ, et ex parte austr. ejusdem, j burgagium; et jacet inter burgagium Julianæ Puddyng et burgagium Marjoriæ Bane; et est vastum; et cont. v rodas terræ juxta moram burg. ibidem.

Tenent etiam j burgagium ibidem, in le south-west-end ejusdem villæ, inter ij molendina ventritica; et jacet inter burgagium Johannis de Wangesford et burgagium Willelmi Serjant; et cont. iij rodas, juxta morem burg. ibidem; et dimittitur pro ijs., unde pro libera firma dictorum burg. domino villæ r. p. a. xvjd., videlicet pro j roda ijd., officio cellararii.

STANYNGTON.

Tenent etiam in Stanyngton j toftum vastum, ad finem occid. del Cat-rawe, cum j gardino adjacente, et ex parte bor. ejusdem; et cont. per æst. j rodam et di. Tenent in campo hujus villæ j terram husband, et cont. in acris, sicut cæteræ terræ husband ejusdem villæ; quarum in le West-feld, super le Castell-flatt, ex parte or. lez Castell-way, buttando super eandem, jacet di. acr. Et ad finem or. di. acra, j rode. Et super le Dug-knoll, ex parte occid., prope Maym-medow, j rud. Et super Esshen-doneyard, buttando super le Wod-way, j roda. Et ex parte occid. del Burn-way quæ ducit ad Belacys, buttando super dictam viam, j roda. Et ex parte occid., prope le Foul-brig, juxta Raysland, j roda. Et super Dunscale, quia in medio, di. acræ. Et ad finem de Dunscale sunt ij buttæ, quarum j butta jacet juxta le balk de miln-fleme, et alia butta jacet ad finem bor. de Dunscale, cont. j rodam terræ. Et super lez Flores, ex parte bor. del Belasys-way, buttando super le Wedloch, di acræ. Et ex parte occid. del Flores di. acræ. Et super lez Wyndy-hepes, ex parte bor. ibidem, j acra et di. Et ex parte austr., juxta Belysys-way, di. acræ. Et super lez Over-flores, quia in medio, buttando super Whyt-rig-way, di. acra. Et ex parte austr., prope le El-crosse, di. rodæ. Et ex parte bor., juxta le Lame-pottis, j roda. Et ex parte occid. de Killes-crok, buttando super Blyth, di. rodæ. Et ex parte occid., juxta Gren-law-dykes, di. acræ. Et ex parte occid., juxta Blak-law-more, j roda. Et in le Crok, videlicet ad fidem or. villæ, j roda. Et ex parte bor. de Methrelech-brig j roda. Et, super Nethre-pes-landes j roda. Et super lez Over-pess-land, juxta rodam prædictam, di. acræ. Et ad finem austr. juxta le Hall-flatt, j roda. Et ex parte bor. de Brade-mere, buttando super le medow, j roda et di. Et ex parte or. dictarum rodæ et dimidiæ, ex transverso del Fennes-wray, j roda et di. Et ex parte or. de Vikeris-flatt, buttando super eandem, di. acræ. Et super le Heretherne, quia in medio, di. acræ. Et ex parte or. de Brad-miere, buttando super eandem, j roda. Et ex parte or., buttando super Whytt-horn-lech, di. acræ. Et ex parte bor., juxta le Akin-schawe j roda. Et ex parte occid., juxta le Lady-dene, j roda. Et ex parte austr. del Lady-den-more, j roda. Et ex parte or. del Blak-lawe, buttando super lez Iles, di. acræ.

Et, memorandum, quod residuum terræ husband prædictæ, hic non specificatæ, jacet inter vastum prædicti campi; ubicumque jacet aliqua portio terræ de Raysland ibidem, ex parte occid. immediate jacet æqualis portio terræ Prioris per totum campum ejusdem villæ.

Tenent etiam ad finem occid. de Clifton-medowe, et ex parte austr. ejusdem, ij acras prati, pertinentes ad terram supradictam.

Dimissio. Et Ricardus Addi t. prædicta tofta et terras cum omnibus suis pertinentiis, et r. p. a. vjs. cellerario.

CLIFTON.

Item habent in Clifton unum annuum redditum xviijd., exeuntem annuatim de cantaria B.M. in ecclesia de Stanyngton, pro quibusdam terris et ten. quas capellanus deserviens dictæ cantariæ t. in Clifton, ex concessione Bernardi, quondam Prioris de Hexham. Et dictus capellanus tenetur dictum annuum redditum, qui pro tempore fuerit, ad festum est Petri ad Vincula dumtaxat solvendum. Et Rogerus de Both, capellanus, occupat prædicta ten. et terras dictæ cantariæ pertinentia, et est vasta.

SETON, WODHORN JUXTA NEWBIGGYNG.

Habent etiam in villa de Seton unum annuum redditum xls. annuatim exeuntem de tota villa de Seton, ex dono Bernardi de Balliolo. Quæ quidem villa modo dividitur inter tres dominos, videlicet Elenam de Seton, relictam Willelmi de Burgoyne, quæ t. tertiam partem prædictæ villæ; et Adam de Seton, qui t. aliam tertiam partem ejusdem; et Robertum de Ogle, Johannem de Wodburne, et prædictam Elenam, qui tenent inter se divisim reliquam tertiam partem; unde quilibet prædictorum tenetur solvere pro rata portionis tenuræ suæ in villa supradicta officio celerarii.

Et notandum quod in cartis prædictorum dominorum habetur plenarie expressum de dicto redditu solvendo pro dictæ suæ tenuræ rata portione.

BRENKLAWE.

Habent etiam unum annuum redditum xiijs. iiijd. in molendino de Brenklawe, ex dono Henrici de Ferlyngton; quia vastum.

NORTH MILNBURN.

Tenent etiam totam grangiam de North-Milnburne cum omnibus pertinentiis, in pratis, pascuis, pasturis, merleriis, aquis, viis, semitis. Et includitur infra has divisas: videlicet, incipiendo ad partem or. dictæ grangiæ ad quemdam locum vocatum le Rede-hogh. Et inde, per quoddam fossatum versus or., inter campum de Hegham et dictum Milneburne, usque perveniatur ad quoddam fossatum vocatum le mayn-dyk de Craklawe. Et inde, sequendo dictum mayn-dyk, inter terram dominicam de Craklawe et dictum Milnburne, versus bor., usque perveniatur ad le estemer del Mydil-more. Et exinde, sequendo unum antiquum fossatum versus (—), inter campum de Craklawe et Newham, usque perveniatur ad le Lang-syk. Et inde, sequendo dictum syk, versus occid., usque quoddam antiquum fossatum jacens ad finem occid. campi dicti Milnburne, inter campum de Newham et campum dictæ Milnburne. Et inde, versus austr., sequendo dictum fossatum, usque perveniatur ad le burne vocatum Milneburne. Et exinde, sequendo dictum burne, versus or. usque perveniatur ad le Rede-hogh prius nominatum.

Habent etiam communam pasturæ infra moram de Craklaw et turbariam de Mordes-fene pertin. ad grangiam prædictam.

Habent etiam per cartam licentiam situandi unum molendinum super le burne de Milnburne infra dominium ibidem, quum et ubi sibi viderit melius expedire.

Et Robertus Horsle t. prædictam grangiam cum pertinentiis, et r. v*l*. vjs. viijd. Item sol. habere j barcariam ibidem ad opus domini.

BYRESFELD DE MILNBURNE.

Tenent etiam juxta prædictum Milnburne, extra divisas prænominatas, quemdam campum terræ arab. et prati vocatum le Byresfeld; et est particula dictæ grangiæ et pertinens eidem, et jacens infra has divisas; videlicet, incipiendo ad le fote de Whityngdon-syk, ubi descendit in le burne de Milnburne. Et inde, sequendo dictum syk de Whyttyndon, sicut descendit usque austr. inter del South-Mylnburne et lez Byresfeld, usque perveniatur ad le kyrk-way de Ponteland. Et inde, sequendo dictam waye, versus or. usque perveniatur ad le Ded-manis-dyk. Et inde, sequendo dictum dik, sicut jacet inter campum de Caldcotes et lez Byresfeld, usque viam quæ ducit de Dysyngton ad dictam Caldcotes. Et inde, sequendo dictam viam, usque perveniatur ad j siketum ad finem or. dicti Byresfeld, inter dictum feld et dictum Caldecotes. Et exinde, sequendo dictum siketum, versus bor., usque perveniatur ad le burne de Milnburne. Et inde, sequendo dictum burne, versus occid., usque le fote de Whyttiden-syk prius nominatum.

Et dominus Radulphus de Euere t. prædictum Byresfeld in allocatione xiijs. iiijd. pro certis terris ibidem in manu Prioris, et r. p. a. xviijs.

Habent etiam unum redditum duorum corporalium annuatim per uxorem domini de Dissington, et uxores hæredum suorum ad festum Sancti Andreæ summo altari in ecclesia conventuali offerendorum, pro multura hominum Prioris morantium in villa de Echwyk, excepta multura de dominic. ibidem Prioris, quorumcumque manibus fuerit. Qui quidem tenentes dictarum terrarum dominicarum ad molendinum de Dissyngtone, proximo post dominum et sine multura *(sic)*. Et, similiter, idem dominus de Dissington, qui pro tempore fuerit, pro dicta concessione multuræ tenetur assurgere Priori de Hexham supervenienti in curiam, vel ubicumque fuerit, et sedem suam eidem offerre, nisi fuerit præventus districtione superioris.

Et, si aliquis dictorum tenentium de Echwyk abstulerit multuram suam de molendino dicti domini de Dissington, debet propter hoc in curia Prioris justificari. Et, si convictus fuerit, debet ad restitutionem dictæ multuræ dicto domino faciendam compelli per senescallum dicti Prioris, et dicto Priori de forisfacto satisfaciet.

ECHWYK.

Habent etiam in Echwyk j capitale mesuagium, cum iiij gardinis et ij toftis eidem adjacentibus, et cum ij croftis dicto capitali mesuagio pertinentibus; quorum j croftum jacet ex parte bor. del Hellilaw-thornes, et cont. di. acræ terræ. Et alterum jacet ex parte bor., prope dictum mesuagium, cont. j rodam prati. Et j aliud croftum jacet ex parte occid. super le Hogh-lawe, et cont. di. acræ.

Habent etiam ibidem iiij^{xx} viij acras terræ dominicæ, quarum iiij acræ et j roda jacent super le Park-flatt. Et super le Strothre-flatt iiij acr. Et in le Hope ij acr. Et ad Chere-yard-syd et ad Dalton-hogh ij acr. et iij rod. Et super Swardon-syde ij acr. Et super Gose-acre j acr. Et super Medeburne-syde v acr. et di. Et ad le Honnle-therne j acr. Et super lez Brome-landes iiij acr. Et super le Schot-well j acr. et di. Et super le Ra-syd iij rod. Et in Calf-strothre di. acr. Et ad le Lonyngton-heued di. acr. Et le Hare-law j acr. Et super Hobbis-flatt, versus partem or., quatuor acræ et di. Et ex utraque parte del Gladin-croke iiij acr. et di. Et apud le Out-ganges vj acr. Et ex utraque parte del Gladin-crok iiij acr. et di. Et super le Hegh-lawes, ex parte austr. ibidem, j acr. Et ex parte bor. gardini Johannis de Naffirton, in duobus locis, iij acræ. Et super le Stane-flatt iij acr. j rod. et di. Et ex parte bor. del Brad-medowe j acr. Et super lez Lame-rodes, quia in medio, j acr. Et super lez South-kelawes, quia in medio, quatuor acr. et di. Et ex parte austr., super le Hegh-lawes, in lez Lang-landes iij acr. Et super le Treuen-brige di. acr. Et super Elly-balk j acr. Et ad finem occid., super le North-hope, j acr. Et ex parte occid., super le Hare-lawe, j acr. et di. Et ad finem occid., super le Ra-syd, iij rod.

Prata. Item habent in Calf-strothre di. acr. prati. Et in le Lym-kylne-medow iij rodas prati.

Dimissiones. Et notandum quod omnia prædicta, videlicet capitale mesuagium, cum gardinis, croftis, terris, et pratis prænominatis, dividuntur in quatuor terras husband.

Johannes de Aynwyk t. j toft. ædificatum, modo vocatum capitale mesuagium, cum j gardino et crofto adjacenti crofto uno cont. di. acr. prati et xxix et di. acr. terræ arab. et prati, et r. p. a. xvjs.

Johannes de Brenklaw, Robertus Watson, et Rogerus Smyth t. totum residuum terrarum prædictarum, videlicet lvij acras, cum iij toftis vastis, gardinis, et croftis eis pertinentibus, et r. p. a. pro omnibus, xvijs.

Prata dominica. Habent etiam ibidem vij acras prati

dominici in manu domini, et dimittuntur tenentibus villæ ad voluntatem domini, et r. p. a. ixs. Solebant reddere p. a. xs.

LIBERA FIRMA. Johannes de Brenklawe t. j cot. et viij acr. terræ liberæ per fidelitatem, et r. p. a. viijd.

FRE-MAYDENS-LAND, VEL BELLINGEHAMS-LAND. Johannes Annotson t. j toftum ædificatum, vocatum Fre-maydens-land, cum xviij acris terræ eidem pertinentibus, et r. p. a. vjs. Solebat r. p. a. xijs.

Habent etiam ibidem vij bondagia, quorum quodlibet cont. xxiiij acr. terræ arab. et prati; et debent molere blada sua ad molendinum de Dissyngton ad xiij vas, ut supra notatur in Dissyngton; unde in tenura.

BONDAGIA. Johannes Syre, nativus domini, t. j bondagium vastum cum tofto, et r. p. a. viijs. Rob. Watson t. j bond., cum tofto, ædificatum, et r. p. a. ixs. vjd. Solebat r. xiijs. oneris isti(us) tenentis. Adam Milner t. j bond., cum tofto, ædificatum, et r. p. a. vjs. Johannes Brenklaw t. j bond. cum tofto vasto, et r. p. a. vjs. Willelmus Hogissone t. j bond. cum tofto vasto, et r. p. a. vjs. Matheus Waller t. j bond. cum tofto, ædificatum, et r. p. a. viijs. Johannes Syre, nativus, t. j bond., cum tofto, ædificatum, et r. p. a. xs. vjd.

COTAGIA. Sunt ibidem viij cotagia cum terris certis eisdem pertinentibus; et molent blada sua ubi melius illis placuerit: unde in tenura.

Johannes Annotson t. j cot. cum tofto vasto, et ij acr. terræ vocatas le Brewing-land, et r. p. a. ijs. Amabill de Rosse t. ij cotagia, quorum j ædificatur, cum vj acr. terræ arab. et prati, et r. p. a. iijs. vjd. Johannes de Brenklaw t. j cot., cum crofto, ædificat., et iij acras terræ, et r. xijd. Idem Johannes t. ij cot., cum crofto vasto, et vj acras terræ, et r. p. a. iijs. Johannes Syre t. ij cot., quorum j ædificatur, cum vj acr. terræ, et r. p. a. ijs.

[HUSBAND-LANDS]. Sunt ibidem v terræ husband quæ fuerunt Johannis de Faudon, modo mortificatæ per cartam domini regis Edwardi Tertii post Conquestum; et quælibet terra cont. xxiiij acr. terræ et prati: unde in tenura.

Willelmus Hogisson t. j terr. cum crofto ædificat., et r. p. a. vs. Idem Willelmus t. j terram, et r. p. a. vs. Johannes Syre t. j terr., et r. p. a. vjs. Idem Johannes t. j terr., et r. p. a. vjs. Willelmus de Rosse t. j terr. ædificat., et r. p. a. vjs.

COTAGIA. Sunt etiam ibidem ij cotagia pertinentia prædictis v terris: unde in tenura.

Willelmus Hogisson t. j cot., cum crofto adjacente, et r. p. a. iijd. Robertus Watsone t. j cotagium et j acram terræ, et r. p. a. vjd.

Bracinagium. Johannes de Brenklaw t. bracinagium villæ ejusdem, et r. p. a. xijd.

Communa pasturæ in Whitchestre. Item Prior et Conventus, et tenentes sui in Echwyk, habent communam pasturæ super communi mora, jacente inter Echwyk et Whytchestre, ad communicandum cum bestiis et averiis suis ibidem omni tempore anni.

Turbaria. Idem etiam Prior et Conventus accipient brueram de prædicta mora et turbas, ad omnia sua necessaria. Tenentes vero de Echwyk non accipient brueram sive turbas in prædicta mora, nisi tenentes domini de Whytchestre inde capiant.

Memorandum, quod Johannes de Faudon, dominus de eadem, dederat cuidam Willelmo de Hoghton, et hæredibus suis de corpore suo legitime procreatis, omnia terras et tenementa sua in Whytchestre et Hirlaw; reddendo inde annuatim dicto Johanni, hæredibus et assignatis suis, xxvjs. viijd. Et si contingat dictum Willelmum, sine hærede de corpore suo legitime genito, decedere, dicta tenementa et terræ prædicto Johanni et rectis hæredibus suis integre reverterentur. Et, postmodo, dictus Johannes de Faudon dederat Priori et Conventui prædictis redditum xxvjs. viiijd.; ac etiam reversionem prædictorum tenementorum et terrarum, si accederit, dederat domino Gilberto de Minstre-acres, capellano, et Thomæ de Raneton, hæredibus et assignatis suis; qui quidem Gilbertus et Thomas concesserunt et dederunt dicto Priori et Conventui reversionem dictorum tenementorum et terrarum, una cum servitiis omnium liberorum tenentium ibidem. Et dictus Willelmus de Hoghton obiit absque liberis de corpore suo genitis; sic reversio dictarum terrarum et tenementorum remanet dicto Priori et Conventui; sed possessionem terrarum (et) tenementorum prædictorum nondum sunt consecuti, per defectum licentiæ intrandi comitis de Angos, domini immediati, nondum petitæ. Et prædicta tenementa et terræ sunt mortificatæ abbathiæ de Hexham per cartam domini regis, prout patet in carta ejusdem regis facta super mortificatione terrarum in Echewyk. Et sciendum quod omnia prædicta tenementa et terræ, quondam Johannis de Faudon, concessa Priori et Conventui, jacent discontinue per campum ibidem in quolibet loco suo semper propinquius soli.

DALTON.

Habent etiam totum manerium de Dalton, in quo est j capitale mesuagium, et diversæ domus ædificatæ, cum diversis gardinis adjacentibus, et vij^{xx} acris terræ arab. et prati dominic.;

quarum ix acræ jacent super le Bern-flatt. Et super Lint-lawes iiij acræ. Et super Schib-ever-lawe iiij acr. Et super Kiplaw-flatte xvj acr. Et super lez Miln-dykes x acr. Et super lez Toftes xij acr. Et super Skuttesklene vj acr. Et super Ded-mans-lau-crok iij acr. Et super North-de-man-lawe iiij acr. Et super Half-forlang ij acr. Et super le Cros-flatte xij acr. Et super Cok-lawe iij acr. Et super lez Cart-rige ij acr. et di. Et super Sterling-strothre-flatt iiij acr. Et super lez Breches iiij acr. et di. Et super le Cros-flatte invicem jacent vastæ xxx acr.

Prata. Et in le Miln-medowe iij acræ prati. Et in le Brad-medowe iij acræ prati. Et in Horse-pol-medowe ij acræ, iij rod. Et in le Flore-medowe j roda. Et in le Toft medowe iij acræ. Et in Sterling-strothre-medowe ij acræ.

Et Willelmus Scot, Johannes Bigle, Thomas de Heworth, et Johannes Elder t. omnia prædicta ten. et terras inter se, et r. p. a. ls.

Johannes de Dalton t. libere ibidem j mes., cum certis acris terræ, videlicet vij acris et iij rodis terræ, nuper in tenura Agnetis de Johnby, et r. p. a. vd.; et non plus, quia dicta Agnes et Willelmus Nippet dederunt Priori et Conventui xj acras et j rodam terræ, quæ olim insertæ erant tenuræ prædictæ; et tunc solebant r. p. a. xd.

Libera firma. Robertus Ogle t. libere j mess. voc. John-Colynson-land, et viij acras terræ eidem pertinentes, et r. p. a. viijd. Agnes Baxter t. libere ij mes. et xviij acras terræ, et r. p. a. xviijd., sed remittuntur eidem pro vita sua per dominum, eo quod dicta mes. et terræ remanebunt Priori et Conventui post mortem dictæ Agnetis. Johannes de Dalton t. libere iij acras terræ, et r. p. a. iijd. Idem Johannes libere (t.) j toftum et j acram terræ, in quo tofto Robertus Batirsuys residet, et r. p. a. jd.

Terræ husband. Sunt etiam ibidem xix terræ husband, de quibus quælibet terra de xj terris cont. xxiij acras; et quælibet terra de viij terris cont. xvj acras terræ arab. et prati; et tenentur cariare molares molendini ibidem, et facere parietes ejusdem, et cooperient ibidem propriis suis expensis.

Alanus de Galleway t. j terr. husb., cont. xvj acr., et r. p. a. vjs. viijd. Idem Alanus t. j terr. et cont. xxiiij acr., et r. p. a. iiijd. Solebat r. ixs. iijd. ob. Thomas de Heworth t. j terr., cont. xvj acr., et r. p. a. vs. viijd. Idem t. j terr., cont. xxxiiij acr. terr., et r. p. a. iiijs. Johannes Eldare t. ij terr., utraque cont. xvj acr., et r. p. a. xijs. Idem Johannes t. j terr., cont. xxiiij acr., et r. p. a iiijs. Johannes Bygglye t. j terr., cont. xvj acr., et r. p. a. vs. Idem Johannes t. ij terr. husb., utraque cont. xxiiij acr., et r. xs. Johannes Todde t. j terr., cont xvj acr., et r. p. a. vs. Idem t. iij terr. husb., qualibet terra cont.

xxiiij acr., et r. p. a. xviijs. Willelmus Scotte t. ij terr. husb., utraque cont. xvj acr., et r. p. a. xiijs. iiijd. Idem t. ij terras husb., utraque cont. xxviij acr., et r. p. a. xs. viijd. Alanus de Galleways t. j terr., cont. xxiiij acr., et r. p. a. vs.

[Cotagia.] Sunt ibidem vij cotagia, et quodlibet eorum faciet opera in reparatione molendini, sicut terræ husb. superius notatæ: unde in tenura.

Mauritius Scotte t. j cot. ædificatum, et iij terras, et r. p. a. xxjd. Idem Mauritius t. j. cot. cum tofto vasto et iij acras terræ, et r. p. a. ijs. ijd. Alanus de Gallewaye t. j cot. ædificatum et iij acras terræ. Idem t. j cot. cum tofto vasto et iij acr. terræ—et r. p. a. iijs vjd. Willelmus Scott t. j cot. ædificatum et iij acras terræ, et r. p. a. ijs. vjd. Alanus de Gallewaye t. j. cot. cum gardino, et r. p. a. xijd.

Molendinum aquaticum. Robertus Batirsyse t. molendinum aquaticum ibidem, et. r. p. a. lvjs. viijd.

VILLA DE HOGHE.

Habent in ville de Hoghe quamdam portionem terræ, vocatam Dedisyd, cont. xxx acras terræ arabilis et prati, et jacentem inter has divisas; videlicet, inter viam quæ ducit de Heddon ad dictam villam de Hoghe, ex parte occid.; et Heddirslaw-medow ex parte bor.; et Dedisyde-leche ex parte or.; et le Lang-strothre ex parte austr. Et Johannes Robinson del Hoghe t. prædictas terras, et j toftum cum crofto in villa de Stanfordham, ut ibidem patebit inferius, et r. p. a. iiijs.

Tenentes in Hoghe. Habent etiam in eadem villa diversa ten. jacentia ex parte bor. in villa ibidem; videlicet inter tenuram clericorum Baliol., Oxon., ex parte occid., et tenuram Thomæ de Falofeld ex parte or. Et etiam quædam ten. jacentia ex parte austr. villæ ejusdem, inter tenuram Johannis de Dalton ex parte or., et tenuram vocatam Thrillwalles-land ex parte occid.: et omnia ten. prædicta dividuntur in vij terras husband et ij cotagia, prout inferius patet.

Habent etiam in campo ejusdem villæ viij^{xx} acras, ix acras et di. terræ arabilis et prati; quarum super lez Lint-lawes in duobus locis jacent ij acræ. Et in le Midel-kenyll, in ij placeis, ij acræ. Et super lez Northre-yardes del Hoghe j acra. Et ex parte occid., super le Brery-syde, j acra. Et ex parte bor. de Dalton-medowe j acra. Et ex parte bor. dictarum acrarum ij acræ. Et ex parte austr. de Dalton roda.

Et ex parte or. super lez Elichestrez, juxta marchiam de Dalton, in diversis locis ij acræ. Et ex parte austr. dictorum Chestrez, buttando super ponte, in diversis locis vj acræ. Et super Lustre-law-syde, quia in medio, ex transverso viæ de Dalton, j acra. Et ex parte occid., juxta dictam acram, j acra. Et ex parte occid. le Lustre-law-syde in diversis locis ij acræ. Et in le Estre-leche, buttando super Hec-leche, j acra. Et ex parte or. dictæ leche j acra. Et ex parte bor. le lonyng de Standfordham j acra iij rodæ. Et ex parte occid., juxta lez Mayns de Standfordham, j acra. Et ex parte or., juxta le Standdandstane, j acra. Et ex parte occid., juxta le Kyrk-waye, prope villam, j acra. Et ex parte austr., prope dictam acram, ex transverso dictæ viæ, j acra. Et ad finem occid. villæ j acra. Et ex parte or., juxta Mabchestre-lawe, j acra. Et super le Thornelawe j acra. Et ex parte or., juxta le Gren-waye, j acra. Et sub le Bla-furlang in diversis locis iij acræ. Et ad le Bony-lech et super lez Mony-laus, in duobus locis, ij acræ. Et ex parte occid. le Netly-lawe j acra. Et ex parte or. dictæ lawe di. acræ. Et in le strothre de Netteli-lawe j acra. Et super lez Cranelandes in ij locis iij acræ. Et super lez Bak-stanes in diversis locis iiij acræ. Et super lez Ri-landes, ex transverso viæ de Stanfordham, j acra. Et sub lez Hallyardes, buttando super dictum yard, j acra. Et super Scherwent-dimpyls in diversis locis iij acræ. Et ex parte austr., super Scherwent-law, j acra. Et super Scherwent-law-syd ij acræ et di. Et super Redelandes in ij locis ij acræ. Et super le Half-furlang in diversis locis vj acræ et di. Et super le Hollawe, ex parte occid. ibidem, j acra. Et super lez Elichestres, ex parte occid. ibidem, ij acræ. Et ex parte or. dictarum acrarum ij acræ et di. Et super dictum Elichestre-law j acra. Et super le Stobbe in diversis locis viij acræ. Et super le Knott-lawe j acra. Et ex parte occid., super Bla-lang-furlang-dyk, j roda. Et ex parte occid., juxta Heddon-way, in ij locis ij acræ. Et super Langstrothre-syd in diversis locis iij acræ. Et super dictum strothre, ad le Flore-welle, j acra. Et sub gardino Johannis Nippet, buttando super eundem, j acra. Et ad finem or. de Ovyrgrip-chestres, juxta moram, iiij acræ. Et ex parte occid., super Dedi-syde, juxta Heddon-way, in diversis locis iij acræ, et di. Et ex parte or. de Thrilliswall-land, buttando super Wrechitman-medow, j acra. Et ex parte austr., juxta dictum medow, j acra. Et super le Cros-furlang in diversis locis v acræ. Et ex parte occid. de Crosse j acra. Et ex parte or. dictæ Crosse, buttando super Heddone-burne, j acra. Et in Hethreslawchestres, et in lez Hemp-twystes, super dictum burne, in diversis locis v acræ. Et super Hordlaw-syde, ex parte or. ibidem, in diversis locis iij acræ. Et ex parte occid. del Havyrbalk j acra. Et super lez Farlaws in diversis locis v acræ. Et super Goneld-chestres, inter quamdam portionem terræ Galfridi de Farlawe ex parte or., et quamdam portionem terræ de terris dominicis ejusdem villæ ex parte occid., jacet quædam portio terræ cont. per æst. xvj acras. Et super Wythopp, inter quamdam moram vocatam Raven-stan-more ex parte or., et quamdam portionem terræ vocatæ Thrillwall-land ex parte occid., jacet quædam portio terræ per æst. v acræ. Et super Ravenstan-more, ex parte occid., juxta Four-stanes, jacet quædam portio terræ cont. per æst. viij acras. Et ad finem or. dictæ moræ jacet quædam portio terræ cont. per æst. v acras. Et ad finem or. del Ybrakes jacet quædam portio terræ cont. per æst. v acras.

Prata. Habent etiam ibidem quamdam (portionem) prati, vocatam le Hol-medow, cont. per æst. iij acras, et r. p. a. iiijd.

Seperalis Pastura. Habent etiam quamdam portionem moræ seperalis, et jacet ex parte or. del North-more, juxta Yngow-lech; in qua nullus tenens ibidem debet fodere turbas, vel capere brueram, sine licentia Prioris vel Terrarii.[g]

Adhuc de Matfen Est. Sciendum quod si dominus de Fenwyk, qui est, et dominus de Matfen voluerint redigere in culturam vastum in prædicto campo, quod dicti Prior et Conventus accipient partem suam pro portione sua in illa cultura secundum sortem; sicut primo fecerunt in aliis culturis; videlicet juxta assertionem veterum, in omni loco tertiam partem.

Prata. Habent etiam apud Knoker-hill, ad finem occid. ibidem, x acras prati. Et in medio magni prati ibidem vij acras prati. Et apud lez Yles, prope finem or., vj acras. Et apud le Rou-brig, ex parte or. ejusdem, in quodam prato vocato le Litil-medow, quia in medio, j rodam.

Habent etiam ibidem iij tofta cum gard' adjac., quæ jacent adinvicem inter tenuram vocatam Yngow-lande ex parte or., in tenura Thomæ Matfen ex parte occid. Quorum quidem j toftum limitatur pro j terra husb. ab antiquo, et ij tofta limitantur pro ij cotagiis.

Habent etiam vij cotagia vasta ex parte austr. villæ ibidem, et ad finem occid. ejusdem. Et jacent inter tenuram quondam Knokers-land ex parte or., et tenuram quondam vocatam Yorkesland ex parte occid., adinvicem jac., cum vij gardinis adjacentibus; et cont. in toto per æst. x acras terræ: quæ quandoque erant in tenura; redd., prout inferius patet. Unde,

Willelmus Troute t. j toftum ædificatum, limit. pro j terra husband, et xiiij acras terræ arabilis et prati de terris superius specificatis dicto tofto assignat., et r. p. a. xiijs. iiijd. Idem t.

[g] After this there is a blank page; which, judging from the next entry, ought to have been filled.

ij cotagia juxta dictum toftum, et iiij acras terræ et di. de terris, ut supra, eisdem assignatis, et r. p. a. vjs. viijd.

Et vij cotagia vasta, ut præmittitur, quondam erant, videlicet—

Radulphus Schiphrd tenebat j cot. et j acram et j rodam terræ, ut supra, et r. p. a. ijs. Johannes de Galleway tenebat j cot. et j acr. j rodam terræ, ut supra, et r. ijs. Johannes Kitteson t. j cot. et j acr. terræ de terra, ut supra, et r. ijs. Issabell de Tynmouth t. j cot. et j acr. terræ, ut supra, et r. ijs. Agnes de Rome t. j cot. ij acras terræ, ut supra, et r. iijs. Willelmus de York tenebat j cot. et ij acr. et di. terræ, ut supra, et r. iijs. Johannes Rue t. j cot. et j rodam terræ, ut supra, et r. xijd.

Dimissio. Et Johannes de Fenwyk, dominus de eadem, t. omnia prædicta ten. et terras, et r. p. a. iiijli. xiijs. iiijd.

Pastura communis. Habent etiam communam pasturæ ibidem, ad communicandum eandem cum xxiiij bobus, et quatuor equis, et cum j equo, et ij vaccis custodis dictæ grangiæ. Et cum uno ovili ovium. Et cum uno flok porcorum omni tempore anni.

Habent etiam communam pasturæ ibidem ad communicandum eandem a festo Omnium Sanctorum usque festum Inventionis Sanctæ Crucis, quolibet anno, cum j armento sive de bovettis, stirketis, aut vaccis, ad placitum Prioris; excepto quod si dominus de Fenwyk voluerit claudere terram de Westirmost-Wlflatt ab occid. parte moræ usque ad novam crucem lapideam versus occid., ei bene licebit; ita quod dicti Prior et Conventus habeant communam in illa pastura, quousque clausa fuerit competenter. Et si, propter defectum clausuræ, averia dictorum Prioris et Conventus, vel hominum suorum, pasturam ipsam intraverint, sine calumpnia vel impedimento aliquo rechacientur.

Item habent communam de Pet-myre ibidem pro se et hominibus suis ad fodiendum et capiendum inde petas in austr. parte dicti Pet-myre ad omnia sua necessaria.

HAUKEWELL.

Habent etiam in campo de Haukwell j acram terræ arabilis; et jacet versus finem or. campi ibidem, juxta viam quæ ducit de Haukwell usque Dalton, ex parte austr. dictæ viæ; et buttat super Cherlaw-leche ex parte occid. de Charlawe.

ULKESTON.

Habent etiam in campo de Ulkeston j acram terræ arabilis, et jacet super Beryng-flatte ad finem or. campi ejusdem; et ex parte del north-est, prope le Deryng-thorne; et buttat super le Warynere, quia in medio.

PETARIA IBIDEM. Habent etiam ibidem iiij acras petariæ: quæ quidem acræ jacent in petaria ibidem, et extendunt se versus occid. ad petariam de Matfen versus or., et communam pasturæ de Ulkeston.

CHESEBURGHE.[h]

Habent etiam maneriam de Chereburghe, cum omnibus suis pertinentiis, in quo diversæ domus ædificantur, cum j capella et j columbari, et quicquid includitur infra has divisas; et est seperale omni tempore anni; videlicet, incipiendo ad le south-est corner muri dicti manerii; et inde, sequendo viam quæ ducit a dicto manerio usque viam quæ ducit ad villam de Nesbit, quousque perveniatur ad quoddam siketum quod descendit ad finem or. del Stob-flatte, inter campum de Echwyk et lez Maynes dicti manerii; et exinde versus occid., sequendo viam quæ dicitur Corbrig-way, per metas et limites inter campum de Nesbitt et campum dicti manerii, usque perveniatur ad quemdam balk qui jacet inter campum de Ulkeston et lez Mayns dicti manerii; et inde, sequendo dictum balk versus bor., per metas lapideas et antiquos limites usque perveniatur ad finem bor. del Wet-flatt: et exinde versus or., sequendo j balk inter campum de Haukwell et lez Mayns dicti manerii, usque perveniatur ad quoddam law vocatum Schapp-law; et inde, sequendo j balk, usque perveniatur ad quemdam fontem fluentem usque ad finem or. del Threp-heued-land: et inde, sequendo quemdam parvum rivulum descendentem de dicto fonte, et per metas lapideas ibidem, usque perveniatur ad quemdam rivulum vocatum Cherlaw-lech: et inde, sequendo dictum leche, usque perveniatur ad rivulum vocatum Pont: et inde, sequendo dictum rivulum, versus or. usque perveniatur ad pedem cujusdam leche, descendentis de quodam fonte in dicto manerio in prædictum rivulum de Pont: et inde, sequendo dictum lech versus austr., usque perveniatur ad le est corner muri manerii antedicti: et inde, sequendo dictum murum, usque le south-corner prius nominatum.

TERRÆ EX PARTE ORIENTALI GRANGIÆ. Habent etiam alias terras ex parte or. dicti manerii, non seperales; videlicet, ad

[h] Erroneously Chereburghe in the MS. Hodie Cheeseburn.

capud austr. del Helawes ij acras. Et ad finem occid., super lez brokes juxta moram, iiij acras. Et super eandem flatte, ex parte or., prope dictas acras, iiij acras. Et super Niks-flatt xx acras. Et est ibidem quoddam strothre, vocatum Whitlaw-strothre, et est pastura boum manerii prædicti. Et inter le lech quæ descendit de manerio prædicto et Dalton-way juxta rivulum de Pont iiij acras. Et ex parte or. super Whitlaw-flatte iiij acras. Et inter Whitlaw-thornes ij acras. Et ex parte bor. de Whitlaw-thorns ij acras. Et ad le est-heued de Whitlaw-flatte, super lez Lame-rodes, ij acras. Et ex parte occid. de Wart-heghe, super lez Knokes, iij acras. Et super dictum Wart-hege iiij acras. Et ex parte or. dicti Wart-heghe, buttando super Pont, ij acras. Et ad finem or. dictarum acrarum, super le Homel-thierne, j acram. Et ex parte or. dictæ acræ, juxta rivulum de Pont, v acras. Et super Lynt-lawes xv acras. Et ex parte occid. de Lynt-laws ij acras. Et ex parte bor. dictæ Lynt-laws, buttando super Pont, ij acras et di. Et in Lynt-law-hope iiij acras. Et sub le Tod-hoghe, in le Half-acre-medow juxta Pont, j rodam prati.

Peslaw flatt. Et in campo de Nesbit est quædam flatt vocata Peslaw-flatt, et cont. per æst. vj acras, et dimittitur ad firmam ten. de Nesbitt, ut inferius patebit—et in Grimescrok *(sic)*.

Pasturæ et vastæ. Et sciendum quod omnes vastæ jacentes juxta rivulum de Pont, vocatæ le Hughs, ab or. parte de Lynt-law-hopp, usque murum manerii prædicti, sunt pertinentes et appendentes terris manerii antedicti.

Johannes Rothrefurth, Ricardus Clark, Thomas Cristall et Johannes Cristall t. inter se totum prædictum manerium cum pertinentiis, et r. p. a. vjli. Tenentes prædicti molent blada sua crescentia super terras dicti manerii ad molendinum de Dalton ad vicesimum vas.

NESBITTE.

Habent etiam totam villam de Nesbit cum omnibus suis pertinentiis et servitiis liberorum hominum in eadem: unde,

Libera firma. Ricardus Freman t. libere j mes. et xij acras terræ per homagium et fidelitatem, et faciet sectam ad tres capitales curias in Aynwyk, et r. p. a. iiijd.

Terræ husband. Et sunt ibidem xix terræ husband, quarum quælibet cont. xxv acras terræ arabilis et prati: unde in tenura,

Willelmus Hamlyn t. ij terras cum tofto ædificat., et r. p. a. xviijs. Johannes Netehird t. ij terras cum tofto ædificat., et

r. p. a. xvs. Johannes de Pikryng t. ij terras cum tofto ædificat., et r. p. a. xvjs. Johannes Jacson t. j terram cum tofto ædificat., et r. p. a. viijs. Ricardus Freman t. j terram cum tofto ædificat., et r. p. a. ixs. Johannes Michelson t. j terram cum tofto vast., et r. p. a. vjs. Willelmus Thomson t. j terr. cum tofto vast., et r. p. a. vjs. Idem Willelmus t. j terram cum tofto ædificat., et r. p. a. ixs. Michael de Whitchestre t. ij terras cum tofto ædificat., et r. xvjs. Johannes Michelson t. j terram cum tofto ædificat., et r. p. a. vjs. viijd. Willelmus Brade t. j terram cum tofto ædificat., et r. p. a. ixs. Ricardus Freman t. j terram cum tofto ædificat., et r. p. a. vjs. viijd. Johannes Jacson t. j terr. cum tofto ædificat., et r. p. a. xiijs. vjd. Robertus de Redesdale t. j terram cum tofto æd., et r. p. a. ixs. Ricardus Freman et Willelmus Hamelyn t. j terram cum tofto vast., et r. iiijs. Robertus de Redisdale t. ij acras et di. prati, vocatas Maldes-medow, et r. p. a. ijs.

Peslaw-flat. Omnes tenentes villæ tenent inter se vj acras terræ dominicæ, vocatas Priors-pes-flatte.

[Cotagia]. Sunt ibidem quatuor cotagia et j gardinum; in tenura.

Willelmus Hamelyne t. j gardinum, et r. p. a. ijd. Johannes Nouthird t. j cotagium vastum et iij acras terræ, et r. p. a. xvd. Willelmus Thomson t. j cotagium vastum, vocatum Smyths-cotage, et iij acras terræ, xviijd. Ricardus Freman t. j cotagium vastum, vocatum Carrous-cotage, et iij acras terræ, et r. xviijd. Ricardus Freman, jun., t. j cotagium ædificatum, et iij acras terræ, et r. p. a. xvd. Johannes Jacson t. j cotagium et iij acras terræ, et r. p. a. xvd.

Multura. Et quilibet tenens ejusdem villæ molet blada sua crescentia super prædictas terras ad molendinum de Dalton ad xiij vas.

STELLYNG.

Habent etiam totum manerium de Stellyng cum omnibus suis pertinentibus; in quo diversæ domus ædificantur; et est seperale omni tempore anni. Et continetur infra has divisas; videlicet, incipiendo ad finem or. campi dicti manerii, ad quemdam fontem vocatum Holburne-well: et inde, ascendendo versus occid., per j parvum siketum et per metas lapideas positas inter campum dicti manerii et quemdam campum de Neuton-hall, vocatum le More-hous-felde, usque perveniatur ad quamdam balk jacentem ad finem or. del Lampot-lech: et inde, sequendo dictam balk versus austr., per metas lapideas positas inter campum dicti manerii et campum de Neuton-hall, usque perveniatur ad le Whye-well: et exinde, sequendo unam aliam balk, sicut jacet ex parte occid. del Notthyng-lawe, usque perveniatur ad le Thornlaw-flatt: et inde, sequendo aliam balk, sicut jacet ex parte occid. del Farnelawe, inter prædictum law et quamdam flatt vocatam Cokis-how, usque perveniatur ad Akom-leche: et inde, sequendo dictum leche versus or., usque le Stokwell: et inde, sequendo j antiquum fossatum, usque ad capud clausuræ campi dicti manerii: et inde, sequendo j antiquum fossatum versus bor., usque perveniatur ad dictum fontem, vocatum Holburn-well, prius nominatum.

Pastura. Habent etiam communam pasturæ dicto manerio pertinentem per totam baroniam de Bywell, ad communicand. dictam pasturam cum averiis suis omnimodis, dicto manerio pertinentibus, omni tempore anni.

Dimissio. Adamarus de Athedell, miles, t. prædictum manerium cum omnibus suis pertinentiis, et r. p. a. iiij marcas.

Item solebant habere molendinum aquaticum in Naffirton; ad quod pertinebat tam multura de Naffirton quam de Whithill, et j cotagium ibidem vocatum Milner-crofte; et sunt vasta.

THROKELAW.

Habent etiam in villa de Throkelaw j toftum et croftum cont. in toto j acram, et medietatem unius tofti et crofti ibidem.

Habent etiam in campo ejusdem villæ lj acras terræ et prati et di. acræ et di. rodæ. Quarum iij rodæ et quarta pars rodæ jacent ex occid. parte de lonyng, et se extendunt usque ad murum. Et in or. parte ejusdem lonyng jacent v acræ et di., et j roda et quarta pars rodæ. Et se extendit usque ad Schukeslade. Et inter muros j acr. Et super Throkerige j acr. Et super Morige v acr. Et super lez Fletes iiij acr. et j rod. Et in or. parte de Midel-flatt v acr. et di. Et in or. parte de Deulaw-rige ij acr. et j. rod. et di., quæ se extendunt usque le Bradischawe, juxta pratum ibidem. Et viij acræ jacent in campo ejusdem villæ. Et sunt illæ acræ quas quondam Woldewes[1] tenuit, quæ vadiatæ fuerant leprosis de Novo Castro cum tofto. Et vj acræ jacent in Bakstan-schaw. Et iiij acræ jacent in Grunis-flatt, juxta le Law, prox. orient. Et iiij acræ in medio de Schele-flatt. Et ij acræ in medio de Sigges-flatt. Et ij acræ in le Lang-schawe, prox. campo de Newburne.

Prata. Habent etiam j rodam prati in Wallynges, et totum pratum jacens inter le Brade-schawe et le Brade-gate; et pratum jacens inter muros ibidem.

[1] *i. e.*, Waldevus or Waldeve.

NEWBURNE.

Habent etiam in Newburne duas piscarias vocatas Fuyle et Drypintille, cum quadam portione prati ex parte bor. Tyne ibidem pro siccatione retium piscatorum: et jacent inter quamdam portionem prati, vocatam Grunes-grene ex parte occid.; et terras dominicales de Est-halgh ex parte bor.; et quamdam portionem prati vocati les Crokyt-spechynes ex parte or.; et Bladen-bankes ex parte austr. Et portio prati prædicti cont. per æst. di. acræ.

Et dominus Ricardus, vicarius ibidem, tenet prædictas piscarias cum prædicto prato, et r. p. a. xxvjs. viijd.

BENWELL.

Habent etiam infra territorium de Benwell quamdam placeam vocatam Wodhall, in qua una domus ædificatur; et cont. in toto, cum bosco, quatuor acras et plus; et non est seperalis omni tempore anni. Et continetur infra has divisas: videlicet, incipiendo ad pedem cujusdam parvi rivuli descendentis in Tynam inter dictam placeam et boscum Willelmi del Vale, militis, ex parte occid.: et inde, sequendo dictum rivulum versus bor., usque perveniatur ad quoddam antiquum fossatum stans inter dictam placeam et quemdam boscum vocatum Harpareswode: et inde, sequendo dictum fossatum versus or., sicut jacet inter dictam placeam; et per dictum boscum vocatum Harparswod usque perveniatur ad le lonyng vocatum le Mere-lonyng: et exinde, sequendo dictum lonyng versus austr., usque in Tynam: et inde, sequendo ripam de Tyne versus occid., usque ad pedem dicti rivuli prius nominati.

Et r. p. a. absque vasto inibi faciendo vs.

NOVUM CASTRUM.

Thomas Wodman t. j burgagium in Novo Castro, ex parte occid. del Cale-crosse, inter le Coke-rawe et le Souter-raw. Et jacet inter burg. quondam Hugonis de Sadlyngstanes, modo Rogeri de Fulthropp, ex parte austr., et burg. Laurentii Akton ex parte bor.; et r. p. a. iiijs. officio Sacristæ.

Idem tenet ij burgagia ex parte or. de Sandhill, prope le Keye, nuper Henrici Wodman; et jacent inter burg. Roberti de Kellessowe ex parte austr., et burg. Johannis de Bulkham ex parte bor., et r. p. a. iiijs. officio Sacristæ.

Et, nota, quod dictus annuus redditus creditur veraciter exire debere annuatim, quamquam dictus Thomas astruat dictum annuum redditum de aliis burgagiis provenire.

Robertus Fleshewer t. j burg. ad voluntatem Prioris in Fleshewer-gate, ad finem austr. ejusdem, inter burg. Ricardi Scott ex parte bor., et quamdam parvam venellam jacentem inter dictam Fleschewer-gate et Skynnar-gate; quæ venella est introitus de dictis viis ad le Bere-markate-gate, et r. p. a. xxs.

Johannes de Howdene t. libere j burg., et r. p. a. xijs. Idem t. j burg. juxta prædictum burg., ex parte austr. ejusdem, et r. p. a. vjs.

Henricus Barbor, alias Wyngatis, t. libere j burg. ibidem, nuper in tenura Roberti de Penreth, et r. p. a. iijs. vjd.

Item solebant habere j annuum redditum, exeuntem de burgagio quondam Johannis Cornfurth, et modo nil, eo quo situs loci dicti burg. ignoratur. Solebat r. p. a. iiijs.

Item solebant habere unum annuum redditum de le stanhous in Westgate; modo nil, quia situs loci ignoratur.

EPISCOPATUS DUNELMENSIS.

GREN HELEY JUXTA MUGILSWORTH.

Habent etiam j toftum cum j crofto adjacente in Heley. Croftum vero cont. per æst. j acram terræ, et jacet ex parte bor. villæ ex parte or., proximum tofto vocato le Almor' place Dunelm. Et habent j acram terræ boscosæ in Alden-crok, vocatam Deven-crofte; et jacet ex parte occid., prox. le Almoners-land Dunelm. ibidem.

Habent etiam xx acras terræ arab. et prati cum omnibus aisiamentis in pasturis, aquis, boscis, et similibus; quarum xij acræ et iij rodæ jacent in le Scele juxta le Segge-strothre, buttando super Yman—le north-west. Et vij acræ et j roda jacent juxta stangnum veteris molendini, descendendo versus bor., ex parte or. parvi siketi vocati Chapell-well.

Dimissio. Johannes de Strevelyn, miles, et domina Jacoba, uxor ejus, t. omnia prædicta ten. et terras, ad totam vitam ipsorum, et utriusque diutius viventis, et r. p. a. vs. Sacristæ.

FENHALL IN GRENCROFT.

Habent etiam in Grencrofte unum mes., vocatum le Fenhall, cum certis pratis et boscis; et includuntur infra has divisas: incipiendo, videlicet, ad finem bor. de Gregori-croft, ubi le hege-garth descendit in Smalhop-burne. Et inde, sequendo dictum burne de Smalhopp, versus bor. usque le fote del Stolerydyng-leche. Et inde, sequendo dictum lech, versus or. per metas lapideas positas in dicto lech inter campum Roberti de Kellow et campum de Fenhall prædicto, usque perveniatur ad quemdam campum vocatum Dawbler-feld. Et inde, sequendo j fossatum antiquum, versus austr., usque perveniatur ad Holdenburne; et inde, sequendo j fossatum antiquum, versus le southwest, inter campum de Fenhall prædictum, et Maldes-close, et communem pasturam ibidem, et le lonyng de Langchestre, usque perveniatur ad le fote dictæ hegge-garth prius nominatæ. Et quicquid includitur infra has divisas est seperale Prioris et Conventus omni tempore anni; excepto quod ecclesia de Lanchestre habet di. acram terræ arabilis eidem pertinentem infra has divisas prædictas.

Dimissio [et] servitium ejusdem. Et Nicholaus de Moresyd t. omnia prædicta mesuagia et terras, et r. p. a. xxviijs.; unde libera firma iijs. Inde domino de Grencrofte pro feodi—

firma exeunte annuatim de dicta Fenhall iijs. Et inveniet domino Priori et Terrario sufficiens hospitium in dicta placea, fœnum pro equis, stramentum pro lectis, focalia et albam candelam, quotienscumque illuc declinare contigerint.

MAYDENSTANHALL IN LANGCHESTRE.

Habent etiam in Langchestre j mes. vocatum Maydenstan-hall cum terris, pratis, boscis, seperalibus omni tempore anni, eidem pertinentibus. Et includuntur infra has divisas: videlicet, incipiendo ad le West-lyd-yete dicti campi stantem super Smalhop-burne: et inde, ascendendo versus le north-est, per quoddam antiquum fossatum inter terram dominicalem pertinentem decano de Lanchestre, et campum de Maydenstan-hall prædicto, usque ad commune stratum quod ducit de dicta villa de Langchestre versus Dunelm. Et inde, sequendo quoddam fossatum antiquum, versus austr. inter communem pasturam dictæ villæ de Lanchestre, et quamdam flatt in campo de Maydenstan, vocatam le Kemster-leyghes, et lez Rydynges, usque perveniatur ad campum Johannis de Lewyne. Et inde, sequendo quoddam antiquum fossatum, inter dictam flatt del Rydyng, et tenuram dicti Johannis Lewyne, usque perveniatur ad quemdam rivulum vocatum Broune. Et inde, sequendo dictum rivulum, versus occid., sicut dictus rivulus descendebat ab antiquo inter campum dictæ Maydenstan-hall et campum de Hamstell, et le Forthe-feld, usque perveniatur ad locum ubi dictus rivulus de Brone descendit in Smalhop-burne. Et inde, sequendo dictum burne, versus bor. usque le West-led-yate prius nominatum.

Ricardus de Aldwod t. dictum mes., cum terris, pratis, et boscis eidem pertinentibus, et r. p. a. xxxjs. iiijd.: unde scaccario Dunelm. iiijd. *(in marg.)*. Unde scaccario Dunelm. episcopi, pro libera firma annuatim exeunte xxiijs. Et speciebus Conventus de Hexham, annuatim, viijs.

KYMESWORTHE.

Habent etiam in villa de Kymelsworthe j toftum ædificatum ex tribus domibus, cum j pomerio et j crofto adjacente; crofto vero cont. per æst. j acr., et jac. ad finem austr. de West-rawe; et habent ibidem iij acras terræ ex parte occid. dicti tofti. Et omnia prædicta includuntur infra has divisas: incipiendo, videlicet, ex parte bor. dicti tofti, ad quoddam antiquum fossatum inter dictum toftum et terr. Roberti Coksyde. Et inde, sequendo dictum fossatum, versus occid. usque le Lang-felde del Erle-house. Et inde, sequendo j antiquum fossatum, versus austr. usque le Deen-burne. Et inde, sequendo dictum burne, versus or., usque ad quamdam balk heggeatam inter dictum toftum et terram Roberti de Coksyde. Et inde, sequendo dictam balk, versus bor., usque introitum villæ de Kymelesworth antedictæ.

Terræ arabiles et prata. Habent etiam j acram terræ arabilis et ij acras prati per æst., jacentes ex parte or. le lonyng quæ ducit de Kymelesworth ad villam Dunelm., juxta communem pasturam.

Habent etiam communam pasturæ ad ccc oves et octo boves pro carucis Prioris aut ejus tenentium, ad communicandum omni tempore anni, ubicunque animalia domini dictæ villæ pasci contigerint. Et habent estoveria in boscis ejusdem villæ pro se et tenentibus suis, ad ædificandum et comburendum, per visum et liberationem forestarii ibidem, ubicumque dominus dictæ villæ estoveria sua accipere contigerit.

Dimissio. Et dominus Radulphus de Euere et Johannes Lewyne, mason, executor Thomæ de Coksyd, tenent prædicta ten. et terr., ad term. contentum in indenturis dicti Thomæ, et r. p. a. xs.

Et invenient domino Priori et Terrario sufficiens hospitium in dicta placea, fœnum pro equis, stramentum, focalia, albam candelam, quotienscumque illic declinare contigerint.

STAYNTON IN STRATA.

Habent etiam ibidem ij tofta ædificata in iij domibus, cum j gardino adjacente; et jacet super le West-rawe, prope finem austr., inter ij placeas vocatas Mason-places ex utraque parte. Et aliud toftum jacet super eandem rawe, inter toftum Willelmi Smyth ex parte austr., et toftum Thomæ de Elstobbe ex parte bor.

Bovata terræ. Item habent ibidem iiij bovatas terræ; et quælibet cont. xviij acras terræ et prati; quarum super Northman-crofte, inter Aukeland-gate et Grenden-more, jacet di. acræ. Et super le Mor-acre-fore j acra et di. juxta Aukeland-gate, prope di. acram prædictam. Et in lez Crokes, juxta dictam gate, di. acr. Et super Nethir-ozrowe, ex parte bor. ibidem, j acra. Et ex parte occid. de Durham-gate, buttando super dictum Ozrowe, di. acra. Et ex parte or. dictæ gate j acra et j roda. Et ex transverso, super Elstob-rode, j acra. Et ex parte bor. del Gren-dyke, buttando super eandem, iiij acræ. Et super Brakenbery, ex parte bor. ibidem, ij acræ: et inter le Ledy-flatt, cum terr. cotag., buttando super Stillyngton-gate, ij acræ. Et super le Wathorn-flatt iij rodæ. Et super North-den-bank j roda. Et super le Lang-flatt et le Clay-bothum j acra et di. Et circa ecclesiam j acr. et di. Et super lez Fiche-buttes et le Miln-way, buttando super prædictas Fiche-buttes, j acra et di. Et ex parte austr. de Aukland-gate, inter dictam gate et le Miln-way, j acra. Et super le Lousy-lawe ij acræ et j roda. Et super le Ley-brakes iij rodæ.

Et ex parte bor. del Lytil-medowe iij rodæ. Et ex parte austr. ejusdem medowe iij rodæ. Et ex parte or. ibidem di. acra. Et in Okir-den-bank, ex parte bor. ejusdem, x acræ. Et ex utraque parte de Okir-den-bank ij acræ. Et super le Pot-syde j acra. Et super le Bradeley j acra. Et super Thomas-hous iij rodæ. Et ad finem or. de Thomas-hous j roda. Et ad finem or. de Sandi-flatt di. acra. Et super le Schort-alf-acre di. acra. Et ad finem occid. de Sandi-flatt di. acra. Et super le Medous-syd iij acræ. Et super le Severell, buttando super eundem, ij acræ. Et super le Dunwell et le Forgar j acra. Et super le Croftes, ex parte occid. dictorum toftorum, ij acræ. Et super Gilbertes-flatt vj acræ. Et in Lousy-law-carre, ex parte austr. ejusdem, di. acra. Et super Harth-stan-flatt j acra. Et super Owthorne j roda.

Et ad finem or. de Grantirs-dane-heued, et super le Brig-flatt, in diversis locis, iij acræ. Et ex parte austr. de Derlyng-ton-way, super le Mildil-furlange, j acra. Et super Red-knoll di. acra. Et ex parte austr. de Smaldene-grave j roda. Et ex parte or. de Crokyt-half-acre di. acra. Et super le Red-knoll j acra. Et super le Schort-bothum, ex parte bor. de Man-flatt, j acra et di. Et super Hauks-lawe, buttando super eandem, j acra. Et ex parte occid. del Hans-medowe j acra. Et ex parte austr. de Waldy-way j roda. Et super le Lang-flatt j acra et di. Et ex parte occid. de Derlyngton-way di. acra.

Prata dominica. Et in le Lytil-medow juxta Bisschopton j acra. Et in le Forgare di. acra. Et in le Brad-medow di. acra. Et ad finem austr. de Grantirs-den-heued di. acr. Et in Ballok-karre di. acra.

Et notandum quod cæteræ portiones prati pertinentes ij bovatis terræ jacent proportionaliter inter lez husband-dales, juxta quod aliæ terræ husbandorum ibidem inter se capiunt. Et notandum quod tenentes Prioris et Conventus ibidem habe-bunt j equum pascentem in le Oxon-pasture, præter boves per-tinentes ad quatuor bovatas terræ ibidem; quamvis cæteri tenentes ibidem nullum equum habebunt in prædicta pastura.

Et Thomas de Legiard t. omnia prædicta terras et ten., et r. p. a. xls. officio Celerarii.

HERTYLLPULL.

Johannes de Hesilden t. j ten. in Hertilpole in le Southgate; et jacet inter ten. quondam Roberti de Seton ex parte occid., et ten. Petri Legeate ex or., et r. p. a. xijs. Johannes Dible t. j ten. et jacet inter ten. Petri Legeate ex parte occid., et ten. Willelmi de Heddone ex parte or., et r. p. a. ijs. Celerario.

Libera firma. Habent etiam j annuum redditum in dicta tenura dicti Petri, modo vastum, et modo nil; et solebat reddere p. a. vs.

SILKYSWORTH.

Habent etiam infra territorium de Silkysworth unam grangiam, vocatam Farendon-grange, jac. inter villam de Heryngton et dictam villam de Silkysworth; et dicta grangia cum terris arabilibus suis includuntur *(sic)* infra has divisas: incipiendo, videlicet, ad portam austr. dictæ grangiæ, et inde, sequendo j antiquam fossatam ex parte occid. del Barn-crofte, juxta situm veteris orrei versus austr., usque perveniatur ad quamdam fossatam antiquam descendentem de Halmer-stank. Et inde, sequendo dictam fossatam, versus or., sicut jacet inter dictum Barn-crofte et terras de Silkysworthe, usque de Rodesmore. Et inde, sequendo j sulcum inter terras husband ibidem, et Rod-landes et le Gren-syd villæ prædictæ, et quam(dam) flatt grangiæ prædictæ, vocatam Stephanes-flatt, usque le Kylnsele. Et inde, sequendo unum sulcum inter dictas Rede-landes et quamdam flatt dictæ grangiæ vocatam le Wharell-flatt, usque Grendon-rode. Et inde, sequendo dictum rode, inter dictum Wharell-flatte et dictas Red-rodes, usque le north-ende dictorum Red-landes. Et sequendo j sulcum versus le—, inter dictum Wharell-flatte et campum de Silkisworth, usque viam vocatam Castel-way. Et inde, sequendo dictam viam, versus bor. usque le Ca—. Et inde, sequendo oram dictæ moræ, inter dictam moram et le Wharel-flatt, usque quemdam antiquum fossatum inter dictam moram et le Park-flatte. Et inde, sequendo dictum fossatum, versus bor., usque le Loury-bush. Et inde, sequendo j antiquum fossatum, inter dictam Park-flatte et dictam moram, versus occid., usque le Pillemore-flatte. Et inde, sequendo oram de Canon-more per dictum Pilmor-flatte et le Miln-flatte, usque perveniatur ad quemdam parvum siketum inter le Miln-flatte et Basset-flatte. Et inde, sequendo dictum siketum, versus occid., inter dictum Basset-flatte et le Miln-flatte, usque quoddam fossatum vocatum le Canon-dyk. Et inde, sequendo dictum Canon-dyk, versus austr., usque quemdam more vocatum Harlaw-more. Et inde, sequendo j fossatum inter dictum more et campum dictæ Farondon-grange, usque perveniatur ad portam austr. dictæ grangiæ prius nominatæ.

Habent etiam unum more vocatum Canon-more; et jacet ex parte or. de Farondon-grange, versus Wermouth, inter villam de Silkisworth et le Ford. Et est seperale Prioris et Conventus omni tempore anni, excepto quod dominus de Silkisworth, vel qui tenuerit terras dominicas ibidem, habebit xxiiij boves pro carucis pascentes in dicto moro, sine additamento quorumcumque aliorum animalium.

Seperale de Morhous-pott. Habent etiam ibidem quamdam portionem terræ, vocatæ Morhous-pote; cont. per æst. ij acras et di.; et est seperale Prioris et Conventus.

Dimissio. Willelmus Mortimer et Willelmus del Hall tenent inter se omnia prædicta ten. et terras cum pastur', et r. p. a. lxxiijs. iiijd.

Multura ejusdem. Et prædicti tenentes molent blada sua crescentia super prædictas terras ad molendinum Prioris ibidem ad xx vas.

Habent etiam ibidem molendinum ventriticum et emolumentum ejusdem, et r. p. a. xxvjs. viijd.

Habent etiam in villa de Silkysworth iiij terras husband, jacentes discontinue inter cotagia ibidem et tofta dictarum terrarum husband; cum cotagiis jacentibus adinvicem ad finem bor. dictæ villæ: et quælibet terra evacuabit terram circa le miln-post; et cariabit molares molendini prædicti, et le post ejusdem, et omne meremium versatile sive currens pertinens dicto molendino.

Et molent blada sua crescentia super terram prædictam ad molendinum prædictum; videlicet, frumentum quod expendunt domibus suis ad xiij vas. Item super terras Prioris ad xvj vas; et dabunt pro quolibet quarterio ordei vendito di. — ordei pro multura: unde in tenura,

Willelmus Wedowson t. j toftum ædificatum et lxj acras terræ arabilis et prati, et r. p. a. liiijs. iijd. Robertus Wilkynson de Tunstale et Johannes de Hoghton tenent inter se j rodam ædificatam et xx acras terræ arabilis et prati, et r. p. a. xxs. Ricardus de Durham t. ij tofta, quorum j ædificatur, et lxiiij (acras) terræ arabilis et prati, et r. p. a. xli. vjs. viijd.

Habent etiam in eadem villa xij cotagia; et quilibet cotarius molet blada sua ad molendinum Prioris; ut supra.

Matildis Marmeduk t. iij cot. ædificata et viij acras terræ et iij rodas, et r. p. a. ijs. Robertus de Berdene t. j cot. ædificatum et ij acras et iij rodas terræ et di., et r. p. a. iiijs.

Willelmus Deye t. j cot. ædificatum et v acras terræ et di., et r. p. a. vijs. vjd. Willelmus Wedowson t. ij cot. ædificata et v acras terræ et di., et r. p. a. vijs. vjd. Johannes Souter t. j cot. ædificatum et iiij acras terræ et di., et r. p. a. vs. Willelmus Wedouson t. j cot. et ij acr. et j rodam terræ, et iij rodas terræ jac. super le Lang-dene, et r. p. a. iijs. Ricardus Hunter t. j cot. sine gardino et j rodam terræ, et r. p. a. xiiijd. Agnes Richards-wyfe t. ij cot. ædificata et iiij acras terræ, et r. vjs.

Est ibi etiam j parvum cot. vastum juxta commune furnum; solebat reddere viijd.

Habent etiam ibidem unum commune furnum pro tenentibus Prioris ibidem.

Habent etiam ibidem commune bracinagium pro dictis tenentibus.

Habent etiam in villa de West-Heryngton xiij acras prati secundum cartas, jacentes discontinue inter prata dictæ villæ, circa le Karre; cum liberis introitu et exitu ad fœnum dictarum acrarum falcandum, levandum, et cariandum, ubicumque videbitur expedire; cum omnibus aliis libertatibus ad dictum pratum pertinentibus.

Dimissio pratorum. Willelmus Mortimer et Willelmus del Hall t. inter se prædicta prata, et r. xxvs. Item habent curiam suam de tenentibus suis in Silkisworth, cum amerciamentis eidem pertinentibus: et etiam omnia amerciamenta dictorum tenentium, si amerciati fuerint in curia domini de Silkisworth, nisi tangat propriam personam prædicti domini.

CLEVELAND. COMITATUS EBORACENSIS.

PARVA BROGHTON.

HABENT etiam manerium totum de Parva Broghton, cum homagio et servitiis Nicholai de Semer et hæredum suorum, Willelmi de Flaxton hæredumque suorum, cum molendino, cum cursu aquæ ad dictum molendinum. Et cum tota secta et soca, et cum toto prato et pastura in eadem villa et extra. Et cum wardis et releviis, eschaetis, servitiis forincecis, sectis curiarum et molendinorum, cum omnimodis libertatibus et aysiamentis in boscis, planis, pratis, viis, semitis, pascuis, aquis, moris, in omnibus locis eidem manerio pertinentibus. In cujus tofto dominico diversæ domus ædificantur, cum j pomerio in quo tremuli crescunt in numero copioso. Et cum j columbari et j gardino adjacente, vocato le Barly-garth, cum j crofto dicto tofto adjacente, cont. per æst. vij acras terræ arabilis. Et etiam diversas flattes terræ arabilis et prati, cum vastis eorumdem, quæ sunt seperales omni tempore anni; videlicet, super le Cotes-flatte xx acras terræ arabilis. Et super le Lang-flatte xxx acras. Et super le Threpland-flatte xx acras. Et super le Whete-hill et le Brant-thorne, et le Schole-brade xxx acras. Et ex parte austr., juxta le Whete-hill, ij acras prati. Et ad finem bor. de Brant-thorn-flatte j acram prati.

Sunt etiam diversæ flattes, non seperales, jacentes inter terras husbandorum; unde super Moubray-flatte, juxta toft. dominic., vj acræ. Et super aliam Moubraye-flatte iiij acræ. Et ad finem occid. del Spanlang-crofte j acra. Et super le Dale-bank iij acræ. Et super le West-lang-crofte, ex parte or. de Lind-bek, ij acræ. Et super le Croft-syk-flatte iiij acræ. Et super le More-syk j acra et di. Et super Ravens-acre j acra et di. Et super le Langland-heued-land j acra. Et super lez Lang-landes ij acræ. Et ad le Miln-dore j acra et di. Et super la Mecote-heued-land di. acra. Et ex parte bor. del Milne, buttando super le Miln-syk, iij acræ. Et super le Miln-gote iij acræ. Et super Hastyng-garthe x acræ. Et super Whyt-lawe, ex parte bor. del Skald-thorne-more, j acra et di. Et super Bes-karre iij acræ. Et super Whit-law viij acræ. Et super Whitlaw-syke iij acræ. Et super le More-syk ij acræ. Et super lez Pes-landes iij acræ. Et super Hercotte iiij acræ. Et super Cok-thorne ij acræ. Et super Bentes-crofte et Bentes-flatte vj acræ. Et super Halle-burne-gavell iij acræ. Et super Feldyng-wath, buttando super Ellerbek, j acra et di.

CASSEHOLME. Et est ibidem unus locus vocatus Casseholme, et cont. ij acras et di. Solebat r. p. a. xd.

PRATA. Et in le Trenches et lez Dammes v acræ prati. Et in Alanes-acre-yng j acra et di. Et super Whathill ij acræ. Et super Bentes-yng j acra et di. Et prædictæ acræ prati sunt quietæ a solutione decimæ, pro qua quædam portio prati assignatur parochiali ecclesiæ ibidem.

DIMISSIO. Thomas Hunter t. prædictum toftum dominicum cum terris prænominatis, et r. p. a. lxxiijs. iiijd.

SERVITIA MANERII. Et etiam inveniet domino Priori et Terrario hospitium sufficiens in dicto manerio, et fœnum pro equis suis, et stramentum, focalia, et albam candelam, quando et quotienscumque illuc declinare contigerit.

LIBERA FIRMA CUM SECTA CURIÆ. Thomas Hunter t. j toftum — bovatas terræ liberæ, quondam Henrici Foxdon, per homagium et fidelitatem, et r. p. a. jd. Idem t. j ten. et vj bovatas terræ liberæ, quondam Nicholai Semer, per homagium et fidelitatem, et r. p. a. iijs. viijd.

Et sunt ibidem ix mesuagia husband et xxvj bovatæ terræ; de quibus quælibet bovata terræ de xxiiij bovatis cont. viij acras terræ arabilis et prati; et de duabus bovatis remanentibus utraque cont. ix acras. Et quælibet bovata pro portione sua cariabit molares molendini, et faciet parietes ejusdem; et dictum molendinum cooperiet, præter super le louthre, suis propriis sumptibus et expensis, quotiens et quando necesse fuerit; et mundabit stagnum molendini prædicti; et molet blada sua ad xiij vas. Unde in tenura,

Johannes Whyte t. j mes. et ij bovatas terræ, quondam in tenura Roberti Whytheued, et r. p. a. viijs. Adam Maner t. j mes. ædificatum et v bovatas terræ, et r. p. a. xviijs. Johannes (*sic*) t. j toftum ædificatum et quatuor bovatas terræ, quondam in tenura Nicholai Snawball, xvijs. Idem t. j flatte, vocatum Moubraye-flatte, et r. p. a. xvijs. Idem t. ij bovatas terræ cont. xviij acras, et r. p. a. xvijs. Idem t. j mes., quondam Johannis Snawball, et iiij bovatas terræ, et r. xiiijs. Idem t. j mes. et j bovatam terræ, quondam Thomæ de Colte, et r. p. a. vs. Rogerus de Berwyk t. j mes. ædificatum et j bovatam terræ, et r. p. a. vs. Johannes Whyte t. j ten. et ij bovatas terræ, voc. Carlton-place, r. p. a. ixs. Thomas Gollane t. j mes. ædificatum et iij bovatas terræ, et r. p. a. xijs. Johannes Whyte t. j mesuagium et ij bovatas terræ, quæ quondam tenuit Petrus Mody, et r. p. a. vjs.

OPERA. Sunt ibidem xj cotagia; et quodlibet cotagium molet blada sua ad molendinum ibidem; et faciet opera et consuetudines ad dictum molendinum, sicut tenentes faciunt pro bovatis terræ superius prænominatis; et faciunt servitia, ut inferius patet; unde in tenura,

Johannes Whyte t. j cot., quondam Johannis Mek, et v acras terræ, et r. p. a. vs. Idem t. j cotagium, vocatum Pondar-place, et ij acras terræ et di., et r. p. a. iijs. (opera in autumpno—*in marg.*) Idem t. j cotagium, quondam Johannis Gelle, et iiij acras terræ, iijs. Idem t. j cotagium, quondam Matildæ Parlien, et v acras terræ cum crofto, r. p. a. iijs. Idem t. j cotagium, quondam Roberti Netehyrd, et v acras terræ cum crofto, et r. p. a. vs.; et quatuor opera. Idem t. j cot., quondam Willelmi Milner, cum j crofto et iij acras terræ, r. p. a. vs. et iiij opera. Idem t. j cot. cum j crofto, quondam Christianæ Skanser, r. p. a. xviijd. Idem t. j cot. cum crofto et iiij acras terræ, quondam Johannis Walkar, r. p. a. iijs. iiijd. et opera. Idem t. j cot. cum j crofto et viij acras terræ, quondam Aliciæ Abbote, r. p. a. vs. et opera. Idem t. j cot. et iiij acras terræ, quondam Thomæ de Bekke, r. p. a. iiijs. Idem t. j cot. de novo appropriatum per Thomam Jonson ibidem, r—.

Dimissio. Et dictus Johannes Whytte t. omnia prædicta tenementa et terras, cum bovatis terræ prænominatis, prout superius specificatur per tenuras suas; et r. p. a. in grosso pro omnibus lxxs. viijd.

Est etiam ibidem unum molendinum aquaticum pertinens manerio prædicto, et iij acras terræ prædicto molendino pertinentes, vocatas le Miln-holme, et jacentes versus occid. a dicto molendino, et ex parte bor. de Ellerbek in campo Magni Broghton, et r. p. a. xiijs. iiijd.

Et sciendum quod vicarius de Kyrkbe in Cleveland habet ibidem diversa tenementa et xxviij acras terræ, pro quibus idem vicarius tenetur facere qualibet sexta feria celebrari unam missam in capella Sanctæ Margaretæ ibidem; et etiam faciet pronuntiari in dicta capella Evangelium dictis parochi(an)is qualibet die Dominica; et aquam benedictam cum pane consimili eis fieri et ministrari; et in festo Pur. B. M. inveniet unum capellanum ad recipiendum oblationes candelarum ibidem annuatim; et etiam oblationes palmarum in Dominica in Ramispalmarum; et etiam ad audiendum confessiones parochianorum ibidem singulis annis tempore Quadragesimali.

BROGHTON.

Habent etiam (in) Magna Broghton j capitale mes. ædificatum, et jacens ex parte or. ejusdem villæ et ex parte austr., juxta le owt-gang versus Parvam Broghton, cum j gardino et j crofto adjacent., crofto vero cont. ij acr. prati.

Habent etiam iij bovatas et di. terræ arabilis et prati dicto mes. pertinentes; unde ij acræ et j roda prati jacent discontinue inter prata communia husband ibidem: et quælibet bovata cont. xviij acras terræ arabilis et prati: unde super le Lyng-hill in ij locis jacent iij acræ. Et ex parte or. del Mykil-mere, super Whit-lawe, j acra et di. Et super Mykill-mer-hill, versus or., cum j butta super le Post, j acra et j roda. Et super Gude-monondayes, ex parte or. ibidem, j acra et j roda. Et super le Crosse-gart-hill, quia in medio, j acra. Et ex parte or. del Hell-karre, juxta Lytil-broghton feld, j acra. Et super lez Postes di. acra. Et super lez Toft j acra. Et super le Standand-stane, quia in medio, j acra. Et super Schof-furdale et le Dale-acre j acra. Et super Braubi-forris iij rodæ. Et super Mikil-rigge, quia in medio, ij acræ in diversis locis. Et ex parte occid., juxta Trans-syke, j acra. Et ad Jacgart-heud, super Mal-knoll, di. acra. Et super lez Flores di. acra. Et super lez Schort-hordes di. roda. Et super Schort-mosse-fen di. roda. Et super Lang-mos-fenne j roda. Et super lez Schort-rodes di. roda. Et super le Ovyr-wendikes di. acra. Et super le Wych-busk, in diversis locis, j acra. Et super le Miln-hill, versus finem or., j acra. Et super lez Lathe-buttes, quia in medio, j acra et di. Et super lez Lang-landes ij acræ et di. Et super lez Lenendales di. acra. Et super Wyndes-herse di. acra. Et super Smyth-stedes di. acra. Et super le Miln-gavell j acra et j roda. Et super le More-brek di. acra. Et super lez Smyth-stedes, ex parte austr. ibidem, iij rodæ. Et juxta Hillerbek-brigges, ex parte bor., j roda. Et super lez Schort-rodes ij buttes j roda. Et super Sande-landes j acra et di. in diversis locis. Et super Row-carre di. roda. Et super Alward-acre in tribus buttis iij rodæ. Et ad le Falu-crosse di. acra. Et super le Thorne-dyk di. acra. Et super le Lang-half-acre j acra et j roda. Et super le Thorn-bank iij rodæ. Et super Kim-acre iij acræ. Et super lez Big-landes in diversis locis j acra et di. Et super Lang-abbow j acra j roda. Et super Schort-abbow j roda. Et super le Canon-flatte iiij acræ. Et super Nauware-law iij rodæ. Et super Gosmodre di. acra. Et super lez Layre-pittes in diversis locis j acra. Et super le Lang-pole j acra. Et Nocthorne j roda. Et super le Wattir-fall in diversis locis j acra. Et super Gren-rige j acra et di. Et super Swyn-holmes in ij locis j acra j roda. Et super Lambe-lez j roda. Et super Estwyn-holme j acra. Et super Skal-rige di. acra. Et ex parte bor. dictæ di. acræ j acra. Et super Litil-holdale j acra. Et ex parte occid. le Cot-garth, ante portam grangiæ Abbatis de Ryvaux, buttando in le miln-dam, di. acra. Et super le Mir-syk j acra. Et in medio terrarum dominicarum grangiæ prædictæ, buttando super le cote, versus occid. Et super Eller-syk, versus or., j acra. Et super Hurig-leyse, in ij locis, j acra. Et ex parte occid., juxta le Grange-flatte, di. acra. Et super Whayt-hill j roda.

Cotagia cum terra adjacente. Habent etiam ibidem ij cotagia in eadem villa; quorum j jacet ædificatum prope finem bor. dictæ villæ, inter placeam Abbatis de Ryvaux ex parte bor., et placeam Templariorum ex parte austr. Et sunt acræ terræ arabilis pertinentes dicto cotagio; quarum super lez Hert-breks jacet j acra. Et super le Standand-stan di. acra. Et ex parte or. de Mikle-rige j acra. Et super lez Schort-hordes, buttando super Tran-syk, di. acra. Et in le Helle-karre j roda.

Et aliud cot. vocatum Tabard-place jacet juxta grangiam Abbatis ibidem versus occid., cum j crofto adjacente, et r. p. a. xviijd.

Et Johannes de Appilton t. omnia prædicta tenementa et terras, et r. p. a. in grosso xxiiijs.

Habent etiam in campo Magni Broghton xiiij acras terræ arabilis sine tofto, quæ solebant esse in manu domini, eo quod sunt terræ dominicæ, ad dimittendum ad firmam cuicumque placuerit; quarum super Godemononday, ex parte or. ibidem, jacent vj acræ. Et ex parte occid. del Crosse, ex una parte viæ de Kyrk-gate, j acra et di. Et ex parte austr. del Lowyk-karre, buttando super eundem, ij acræ. Et ex parte bor. dictæ Karre j acra et di. Et super le Lang-mos-fene, buttando super Tran-syk, versus occid., j acra et di. terræ arabilis et prati. Et super Schort-mos-fene, ex parte or. ibidem, ij acræ terræ arabilis et prati.

Prata dominica. Habent etiam ij acras et iij rodas prati dominici ibidem, pertinentes prædictis acris terræ dominicæ; quarum in le Lang-strothre, ex parte austr. ejusdem, jacent j acra et iij rodæ. Et ex parte occid. de Lyn-bek, buttando super Lyn-bek-wathe, iij rodæ. Et ex parte bor., juxta easdem rodas, j roda.

Dimissio. Et Johannes Whyt t. prædicta terras et prata cum terris specificatis in tenura sua in Parva Broghton, et r. pro omnibus in grosso, ut patet.

INGLEBY.

Habent etiam in villa de Ingleby j toftum ædificatum, et jacens ad finem austr. villæ, ex parte occid. ejusdem, cum j gardino et j crofto adjacente, cont. in toto per æst. j acram et di.

Habent etiam in campo ibidem j bovatam terræ arabilis et prati, cont. xv acras terræ; quarum, ex parte occid. de May-bek, jacent v acræ. Et super Lilil-red-howe, quia in medio, buttando super Rede-how-syk, iij rodæ. Et ex parte or. de Belrige, buttando super Me-bek, iij rodæ. Et ex parte bor. de Redhow-gate ij acræ et di. Et super le Bryg-syk, quia in medio, buttando super le Blind-keld versus austr., j acra. Et super lez Wate-landes, buttando super Esby-marche, j acra. Et super Haystangarth, ex parte bor. de Ingleby-feld, j acra. Et super Haystangarth-hill, buttando super Esby-waye, j acra. Et super dictum Hastyngarth, ex parte austr. del Thornes, di. acra. Et super dictum Hastyngarth, ex parte austr. prope di. acram prædictam, buttando super le Round-holme, j acra.

Cotagia. Habent etiam j cot. ædificatum ibidem et jacens ex parte or. villæ, et ad finem bor. ejusdem, cont. in toto per æst. di. acram.

Habent etiam ij acras terræ et di. pertinentes eidem cotagio; quarum super lez Lam-cotes jacent j acra et j roda. Et super Gildre-cost j acra et j roda.

Dimissio. Et Petrus de Bathebon t. prædicta ten. et terras, et r. p. a. viijs. Unde pro bovata terræ vs. Et pro cotagio cum terra eidem pertinente iijs.

KYRKBE IN CLEVELAND.

Habent etiam j ten. ædificatum cum j gardino et j crofto adjacentibus, cont. in toto per æst. j acram; et jacet ex parte or. villæ, inter placeam vicariæ dictæ villæ, ex parte austr., et placeam Johannis Turim ex parte bor.

Habent etiam j bovatam terræ arabilis ibidem cont. xij acras terræ; quarum super Fulburne et lez Dykes j roda. Et super Hay-bek di. acra. Et super Dymples j roda. Et in le sclak del gate j roda. Et ad le Wynd-myln-hill, ex utraque parte viæ quæ ad Stokeslaye (ducit), di. acra. Et ad Hellerberkheued, ex transverso dictæ viæ, di. acra. Et super Hillerbeklandes iij rodæ. Et ex parte occid. dictæ Hillerbek-landes j acra j roda. Et super Helle in duobus locis di. acra. Et super Lang-span-how di. acra. Et super Schort-span-how j roda. Et in lez Bothomes j roda. Et super Magodes-leyse, buttando super lez Dykes, di. roda. Et super Wyndynges, juxta le Aldbek, in diversis locis, vj acræ. Et in lez Pet-pottes di. acra. Et ex austr. dictarum Pet-pottes j roda. Et super le furlang de Wese-bek, in diversis locis, di. acra. Et ex parte austr. del Acre-thorne di. roda. Et super lez Over-toftes j roda. Et super Somerell-buttes iij rodæ. Et in lez Over-brotes, quia in medio, j roda. Et ex parte occid. del Bere-rige di. acra. Et in medio ejusdem di. acra. Et in lez Brotes j roda et di. Et super Schort-berige j roda. Et super Lang-lillynges j roda. Et super Schort-lillinges di. roda. Et ex parte or. le lonynge de lez Enge-gates j roda. Et ad finem austr. villæ, ex parte or. del Dykes, di. acra.

Prata ibidem. Habent etiam iij rodas prati jacentes discontinue inter husband ibidem; videlicet in lez Flodres j roda. Et in lez Lang-rodes j roda. Et in lez Schort-rodes j roda.

Cotagium. Habent etiam j cotagium ibidem cum j crofto adjacente, et jacet ex parte occid. villæ prædictæ, versus finem austr. ejusdem villæ, inter placeam Johannis de —— ex parte bor., et placeam Johannis —— ex parte austr.

Dimissio. Et Robertus de Yngrame t. omnia prædicta ten. et terras, et r. p. a. in grosso pro omnibus ixs.[j]

Opera et consuetudines, ut prius. Johannes Talyor t. j. mess., et facit opera in autumpno, et r. p. a. ad festum Nat. Domini xx ova, et ad festum Paschæ; et etiam r. p. a. ad terminos consuetos xijd. Johannes Drewery t. j cot. iij acras terræ et prati cum j herbar', r. vd. et opera. Johannes Kyell t. j cot., et r. p. a. xijd. et opera, ut supra. Johannes Colynson t. j cot. iij et di. (acras) terræ, et r. p. a. iiijs. vjd. et opera. Johannes Hare t. j cotagium, ij acras terræ, et r. p. a. ijs. vjd. et opera, ut supra. Johannes Kyrkbe t. j cot. iij acras terræ et di., et r. p. a. iijs. xd. et opera, ut supra. Idem t. virgas juxta ripas de Doufe, vocatas spechyns, vjs., sine operibus. Raynaldus Robertsun t. j cot. et j acram terræ, et r. p. a. iijs. et opera, ut supra. Issabella de Stanegreve t. cotagium, et r. p. a. xijd. et opera. Nichol Nettehird t. j cotagium, et r. p. a. xijd. et opera. Johannes Lepare t. j cotagium, et r. p. a. ijs. et opera, ut supra. Idem Johannes t. herbar' ortorum ad finem villæ, et r. p. a. in festo S. Martini iijs., sine operibus. Willelmus Talyor t. ij ortos, et r. p. a. ijs., sine operibus. Cel Ferung' t. j cot., et r. p. a. ijs., sine operibus. Johannes Wayde t. j cot. iiij acras terræ et di. acram prati, et r. p. a. iijs. vjd. et opera. Johannes Moris t. j cot. cum diversis gardinis herbarum ad finem villæ, et r. p. a. iiijs., sine operibus. Willelmus Milner t. j cot., et r. p. a. xijd. et opera, ut supra. Johannes Mere t. j cot. j acram terræ, et r. p. a. ijs. et opera. Dominus Petrus, vicarius, t. lez Peel-garth, et r. p. a. iiijd., sine operibus. Willelmus Acastre t. j cot. juxta cimiterium, et r. p. a. ijs., sine operibus. Johannes de Kyrkbe t. j cot. et j gardinum ad occid. finem villæ, et r. xxd., sine operibus. Ricardus Durefu t. ij gardinos ad occid. finem villæ, et r. p. a. xviijd., sine operibus. Willelmus Durefu t. Ketilgarth, et r. p. a. xiijd., sine operibus.

[j] After this there is a blank page, and a leaf has been cut out of the MS.

Redditus solitus ex antiquo. Et sciendum est quod quodlibet cotagium de prædictis cotagiis, jacens absque terris adjacentibus, solebat antiquis temporibus dimitti ad firmam pro xijd. per ann. et operibus, vel pro ijs. sine operibus, ut patet in antiquo rotulo. Et omnes gardini prædicti solebant dimitti ad firmam altiorem.

Dominus vicarius tenet Ades-crofte, et cont. ij acras terræ et di. per æst., et r. p. a. iiijs. iiijd., sine operibus. Solebat reddere vjs.

Commune furnum. Johannes Moris t. commune furnum villæ, et r. p. a. iijs. vjd.

Et quilibet brasiatrix, sive super terram bond' vel cotagiorum, de quolibet bracionagio dabit domino ex consuetudine ij lagenas cervisiæ.

Johannes del Stable t. molendinum aquaticum.

MANARIUM DE SALTON.

Habent etiam manerium in villa de Salton, ubi diversæ domus ædificantur, videlicet una aula cum tribus cameris et una capella, coquina, pistrina, bracina, magnum stabulum, unum pomerium, et unum gardinum vocatum le pen-garth. Et, ex parte bor. dicti manerii, una aula vocata le gest-hall, cum una camera in fine, et le gate-hous, et una magna grangia, boscar', porcar'; et unum torale noviter ædificatum; unum pomerium vocatum le kyln-garth; et unum gardinum vocatum le ben-garth.

Sunt etiam ibidem xvj bovatæ terræ dominicæ arabilis; quarum quælibet cont. ix acras terræ: unde octo bovatæ jacent in quatuor flattes, vocatis lez Dikes et lez Miln-croft. Istæ prædictæ flattæ, vocatæ Bla-pule, jacent juxta Crossow-brigge, inter terras tenentium, et sunt seperales. Et cæteræ viij bovatæ terræ jacent discontinue per diversas partes inter terras tenentium ibidem.

Sunt etiam ibidem xij acræ prati et di. in le W——, præter duas seliones redactas in pratum, et sunt seperales omni tempore anni. Sunt etiam ibidem viij acræ prati in lez South-enge, jacentes in una flatta inter prata tenentium, non seperalia.

Est etiam ibidem una clausura, vocata lez Miln-clos, et est seperalis omni tempore anni.

Frensholme. Est etiam ibidem j boscus vocatus Frens-holme, cont. per æst. ij acras et di.; et est seperalis omni tempore anni.

Barcaria juxta campum de Edeston. Est etiam in campo ibidem j placea terræ, vocata Cote-garth, ubi dominus solebat habere unam barcariam.

Dimissio. Willelmus de Daventre t. lez gest-hall cum omnibus aliis domibus ibidem, ex parte bor. antedicti manerii, cum lez kyln-garth et lez been-garth; excepto quod dominus habebit finem australem magnæ grangiæ pro decimis suis intrandis, quotiens opus fuerit. Et etiam dictus Willelmus t. omnia terras et prata prædicta, excepto quod dominus habebit vj acras prati in Weste-rige pro equis suis; et exceptis Frens-holme et placea pro barcaria juxta campum de Edeston; et r. p. a. ad terminos S. Martini et Pentecostes xxxiijs. Et etiam r. p. a., videlicet ad Pur. B.M.V. et Pasca, per æquales portiones, vj quarteria frumenti et mixtilionis, iiij quarteria ordei, et x quarteria avenarum; et molet blada sua ad molendinum domini ad — vas; et faciet sectam ad curiam ibidem. Sunt etiam in villa ibidem lxxiij bovatæ terræ, unde liiij bovatæ sunt de bondagio, et iiij bovatæ per æst. sunt in lez For-landes; et tenentur ut bondagiæ: et xv bovatæ terræ sunt de dominicis; unde quælibet bovata terra de dominicis cont. vij acras et di. terræ arabilis et prati. Et quælibet bovata de bondag. et de lez For-landes cont. ix acras. Et, præter hæc, ij bondagiæ et di. per æst. divisæ sunt inter cotagia ibidem.

Et quælibet bovata terræ, secundum consuetudinem manerii ibidem, pro portione sua, cariabit victualia domini ubique infra comitatum Ebor. pro domino et equitaturis suis. Et etiam carriabit meremium serratum et quadratum pro ædificatione manerii de Salton; et etiam molendini ibidem. Et carriabit molares ejusdem molendini; et reparabit stagnum ejusdem molendini; et faciet omnia opera terrea pertinentia dicto molendino. Et mundabit conductum aquæ ejusdem stagni ex utraque parte. Et cooperiet dictum molendinum coopertura domini. Et etiam inveniet lectos honestos pro hospitibus domini quotiens illuc accesserit. Et carriabit petras et calcem latomorum, et omne meremium pro domibus in prædicto manerio construendis et reparandis. Et etiam eliget unum ydoneum servientem pro manerio prædicto custodiendo, et alios præpositos pro denariis colligendis. Et ale-graves, watere-graves, et iiij juratos, omnia præsentatilia *(sic)* in curia et in capitulo de Salton; et unum staurarium pro stauro domini custodiendo ibidem. Pro quibus supradictis sic electis tenentes ibidem respondere tenentur. Et etiam nullus tenens ibidem carriabit bladum suum in autumpno, priusquam bladum domini fuerit carriatum, nisi licentia a domino petita et optenta. Et etiam quælibet bovata pro parte sua mundabit fossatum circa Frens-holme, et molet blada sua ad molendinum domini ad xiij vas.

Bondagia. Johannes de Cravin t. j mess. et ij bovatas terræ et di. de bondagiis, et r. p. a. xs. Idem Johannes t. ij acras terræ de for-land, et r. p. a. ixd. Idem Johannes (t.) j rodam et di. prati, et r. p. a. ijs. Idem Johannes t. j cotagium cum fore-land, et r. p. a. ijs. vj½d. Rogerus Bell t. j mess. et iij bovatas terræ de bond., et r. p. a. xijs. Idem Rogerus t. j bovatam terræ de dominicis, et r. p. a. vjs. Idem Rogerus t. j herbariam cum mess. et ij bovatis terræ de bond., et r. p. a. jd. Johannes Elynson t. j mess. et ij bovatas terræ de bond., et r. p. a. viijs. Idem t. j. bov. terræ de dominicis, et r. p. a., cum j herbar., vs. ob. Idem t. j placeam terræ, vocatam Hawykes-crofte, ad voluntatem domini, ad incrementum tenuræ suæ, quia debilis; et nil; sed solebat reddere ijs. iiijd. Relicta Roberti Watson t. j mess. et iiij bovatas terræ de bond., cum harbaria et for-land, et r. p. a. xvjs. jd. ob. Johannes filius Roberti Watsun t. j mess., xijs. jd. Idem Johannes t. j bovatam terræ de dominicis, et r. p. a. vjs. jd. Robertus de Malteby t. j mess. et ij bovatas terræ de bondagiis, et r. p. a. viijs. Idem Robertus t. j bovatam terræ de dominicis, et r. p. a. vjs. Idem Robertus t. j chere-garth, di. Wodli-busk, et j Wildir-land, et r. xiiijd. Johannes Smyth t. j mess. et iij bovatas terræ de bond. cum j herbaria, et r. p. a. xjs. ob. Alicia de Ottrington t. j mess. et ij bovatas terræ de bond., et r. p. a. viijs. Eadem Alicia t. iij bovatas terræ de dominicis, cum le for-land, ut in rotul' curiæ, et r. xvijs. qua. Willelmus de Thirneham t. j mess. cum j girs-garth, inclusum, et iij bovatas terræ bond., r. xiijs. Idem Willelmus t. j parcellam de for-land, vocatam le Brade-tofte, et r. p. a. xviijd. Idem t. ij acras terræ de dominicis, et r. p. a. ijs. Thomas Enysun t. j bovatam terræ de dominicis, et facit ij opera in autumpno, et r. vs. Johannes de Stable t. j mess. ij bovatas terræ de bond., et r. p. a. viijs. Idem Johannes t. j bovatam terræ de dominicis, et r. p. a. vjs. Willelmus Talyor t. j bovatam et ij bovatas terræ de bond., et r. p. a. viijs. Walter Cattesun t. j mess. et ij bovatas terræ de dominicis, et di. bovatæ terræ bond., xjs. Johannes de Craven t. j mess. iij bovatas terræ de bond., cum le for-land, j herbar., xs. vjd. Henricus Wyotte t. j mess., iiij bovatas terræ bond., et r. p. a. xvjs. Johannes Ganton t. j mess. iij bovatas terræ de bond., et r. p. a. xijs. Idem Johannes t. iiij acras terræ de dominicis, et j Brade-tofte, et r. p. a. vs. Willelmus Durifen t. j mess., iij bovatas de bond., et r. p. a. xijs. Idem Willelmus t. j bovatam terræ et dominicis, et j acram de for-land, r. vjs. Idem Willelmus t. j parcellam prati juxta le West-yng, vocatam Crok, ijs. Willelmus Riotte t. j mess. ij bovatas terræ de bond., quarum j bovata nuper in tenura Reginaldi Lowe, cum for-land, et r. p. a. xijs. viijd. Idem Willelmus t. j acram terræ de dominicis in le North-feld, et r. p. a. ixd. Idem Willelmus t.

j acram terræ, vocatam Stoure-land, et r. p. a. xd. Idem Willelmus t. j buttam terræ ad le West-croft-yet, et r. p. a. ijd. Ricardus Durifen t. j mess., iiij bovatas terræ de bond., et r. p. a. xvjs. Idem Ricardus t. Brade-tofte, cum quadam parcella prati, vj buttas terræ super Doufe, et v buttas in le South-feld, et r. p. a. iijs. iiijd. Dominus Petrus, vicarius, t. ij bovatas terræ de bond., et r. p. a. viijs. Et sunt in manu domini, defectu, ij bovatæ terræ bond.: solebant r. p. a. viijs. Item in manu domini j bovata terræ dominicæ, cum for-land: solebat r. vs. ijd.

Cotagia. Et sunt in eadem villa xxxix cotagia, unde xvij ædificantur, xix non ædificantur, dimissa pro herbagio; et iij cotagia omnino vasta et sine tenura; et quodlibet cotagium facit opera ad molendinum et stagnum ejusdem, pro parte sua, sicut et bondi; et alia opera et consuetudines, sicut inferius patet.

Johannes Talyor t. j cot., et facit iiij opera in autumpno, et r. ad festum Nativ. iiij gallinas, et ad festum Paschæ xx ova, et etiam r. p. a. ad consuet. xijd. Johannes Drury t. j cot., iij acras terræ et prati, cum j herbaria, et r. p. a. iiijs. vd. et opera. Johannes Kyell t. j cot., et r. p. a. xijd. et opera, ut supra. Johannes Colynson t. j cot. iij acras terræ et di. terræ, r. p. a. iiijs. vjd. Johannes Hare t. j cot. ij acras terræ, et r. p. a. ijs. vjd., et opera, ut supra. Johannes Kereby t. j cot. iij acras di. terræ, et r. p. a. iijs. xd. et opera. Idem t. virgas juxta ripas de Doufe, vocatas lez spechyns, r. p. a. iiijs., sine operibus. Raynaldus Robertsun t. j cot. et j acram terræ, et r. p. a. iijs. et opera. Isabella de Stayngrafn t. j cot., et r. p. a. xijd. et opera. Nicholaus Netehird t. j cot., et r. p. a. xijd. et opera. Johannes Lepar t. j cot., et r. p. a. ijs. et opera. Idem Johannes t. herb. ortorum ad finem villæ; r. p. a., ad festum S. Martini, tantum iijs., sine operibus. Willelmus Talyor t. ij ortos, r. p. a. ijs., sine operibus. Ceell Ferung' t. j cot., et r. p. a. ijs., sine operibus. Johannes Waude t. j cot., iiij acras terræ et di. acram prati, r. p. a. iiijs., sine operibus. Johannes Moris t. j cot., cum diversis gardinis herb. ad finem villæ, r. p. a. iiijs., sine operibus. Willelmus Milner t. j cot., et r. p. a. xijd. et opera. Johannes Frere t. j cot. et j acram terræ, et r. p. a. ijs. et opera. Dominus vicarius t. le Peele-garth, et r. p. a. iiijd. Willelmus Acastre t. j cot. juxta cimiterium, et r. p. a. ijs., sine operibus. Johannes de Kirkbe t. j cot. et j gardinum, ad austr. finem villæ, r. p. a. xxd. Ricardus Durefene t. ij gardina, ad occid. finem villæ, r. p. a. xviijd. sine [operibus]. Willelmus Durefa t. Ketil-garth ad voluntatem domini, r. p. a. xiijd., sine operibus.

Et sciendum quod quodlibet cotagium de prædictis cotagiis, jacens absque terris adjacentibus, solebat antiquis temporibus dimitti ad firmam pro xij denariis p. a. et operibus, ut patet.

Et omnes gardini prædicti solebant dimitti ad firmam altiorem.

Dominus vicarius t. Ades-crofte, et cont. ij acras terræ et di., et r. p. a. iiijs. iiijd., sine (operibus).

Commune furnum. Johannes Morise t. commune furnum villæ, et r. p. a. iiijs. iiijd., sine operibus.

Bracinagium. Et quilibet bracionatrix super terras bond. vel cotag. de quolibet bracionagio dabit duos, ex consuetudine, lagenos servisiæ.

Molendinum aquaticum. Johannes del Stable t. molendinum aquaticum ibidem cum secta multuræ ejusdem, et r. p. a. iiijli. vjs. viijd.

Dominus vicarius de Salton t. piscariam ibidem, et r. p. a. ijs.

Agistamenta in lez Est More. Et notandum quod lez Est-more est seperale domini, a festo Inventionis Sanctæ Crucis usque festum Sancti Petri ad Vincula, excepto quod quilibet tenens de j bovata in Salton habebit in eadem per dictum tempus, pro qualibet bovata quam tenet, ij boves et vaccas, ex consuetudine. Et si aliquis tenens ibidem habeat aliquas bestias, ultra quod habet ibidem pro tenura sua, ut præmittitur, solvet pro qualibet bestia vjd. Et pro quolibet stirk ij annorum iijd. Et quilibet tenens ibidem habebit unum jumentum ibidem post pullulationem per iij dies, ex consuetudine, infra dictum tempus.

Opera et consuetudines. Et notandum quod singulæ binæ bovatæ terræ ibidem de bond. facient j carectam pro carriagio domini de meremio quadrato. Et pro victualibus domini carriandis quælibet bovata terræ bond. inveniet j equum. Et iiij bovatæ terræ invenient j bigam pro dicto carr', cum opus fuerit, super le Burd-land, nil faciendo de dictis operibus.

Commune auxilium. Et prædicti tenentes, secundum antiquam consuetudinem dictæ prebendæ, debent dare portionem de summa decem marcarum argenti pro palefrido emendo domino Priori, cum noviter fuerit electus : vel alias ad commune auxilium, cum necessitas cogerit ipsum petere ab eisdem; videlicet, quilibet juxta portionem tenuræ suæ.

Virgultum cum vasto. Communitas villæ t. virgas circa ripas aquæ de Doufe, et herbagium de vasto in campo de Salton, et r. p. a. —.

BRAWBY.

Sunt etiam in villa de Brawby lj bovatæ terræ et iij acræ terræ, unde octo bovatæ et iij acræ terræ sunt de terris dominicis, et xliij bovatæ de bondagiis. Unde tres bovatæ terræ per æst. dividuntur in for-land, quæ dimittuntur inter tenentes villæ, ut inferius. Est etiam ibidem una clausura in tenura Roberti Acastre, quæ cont. in (se) j bovat. terræ. Et quælibet de prædictis bovatis cont. in se in terra arabili et pratis ix acras. Item est ibidem una clausura in mora vocata lez Cot-garth, ubi solebat haberi una barcaria ædificata. Item dominus habet ibidem pistrinum commune, et r. p. a., prout continetur inferius. Item quilibet tenens prædictarum bovatarum terræ faciet singula opera et consuetudines pro portione sua ad molendinum de Salton, sicut tenentes de Salton faciunt pro bondagiis suis ibidem, prout superius specificatur. Et quilibet tenens in villa de Brawby tenetur molare blada sua ad molendinum de Salton, quamdiu non habetur molendinum apud Brawby, sub pœna perditionis totius grani versus lez multir-grafe, et sacelli versus molendinarium, et amerciamenti versus dominum. Et cum fuerit molendinum apud Brawby, tunc tenentes ibidem debent molare blada sua ad id molendinum, et facere opera et consuetudines ad dictum molendinum, sicut tenentes de Salton faciunt ad molendinum domini de Salton. Et, durante molendino apud Brawby, tenentes ibidem non tenentur ad aliqua opera vel consuetudines, neque sectam cum blado molend. de Salton, prout ordinatur in curia domini ibidem. Et quælibet bovata terræ ibidem faciet omnia opera et consuetudines, tam carriagio quam in aliis servitiis, pro portione sua, secundum quod tenentes de Salton faciunt pro bovatis terræ ibidem, ut superius est expressum. Et tenentur dare ad commune auxilium et pro palefrido emendo domino Priori, quilibet juxta portionem tenuræ suæ, prout tenentes de Salton, sicut superius est notatum.

Willelmus Courtman t. j mess., iiij bovatas terræ, j herbariam, et for-land, et Hors-poile, r. p. a. xvijs. vjd. Thomas Talyor t. j mess., ij bovatas terræ, cum for-land, r. p. a. viijs. vjd. ob. Johannes Wath t. j mess., ij bovatas terræ, cum lez for-land, cont. di. acram, et r. p. a. ixs. Johannes Knapton t. ij mess., iij bovatas terræ de bond., cum lez for-land, et r. p. a. xijs. ixd. ob. Idem Johannes t. j bovatam terræ de dominicis, r. p. a. vs. Johannes Water et Johannes Knapton t. iij bond. terræ cum for-land, et r. p. a. xijs. xjd. ob. Thomas Brown t. j mes., ij bovatas terræ, cum for-land, r. p. a. ixs. ijd. Thomas Ronfere t. j mess., iij bov. terræ de dominicis, cum for-land, r.

p. a. xvs. jd. Robertus Castre t. j mess., ij bovatas terræ de bond., cum for-land, iij acras terræ dominicæ cum j crofto, r. p. a. xiiijs. iijd. ob. Idem Robertus t. ij bovatas terræ de dominicis, r. p. a. xs. Johannes Symson t. j mess., ij bovatas terræ, et for-land, r. p. a. viijs. vijd. Robertus Walsch t. j mess., ij bovatas terræ de dominicis, cum for-land, r. xs. jd. Johannes de Halton t. j mess., iij bovatas terræ, cum for-land, r. xiijs. jd. Johannes Huge t. j mess., ij bovatas terræ de bond., cum for-land, viijs. vjd. ob. qu. Johannes Raynerson t. j mess., ij bov. terræ bond., cum for-land, viijs. vjd. ob. qu. Thomas Talyor t. j mess., ij bovatas terræ bond., cum for-land, r. viijs. vjd. ob. qu. Willelmus Symson t. j mess., ij bov. terræ, cum for-land, viijs. xd. Robertus Loge t. j mess., ij bovatas terræ cum pistrino, iij bov. terræ, et cum for-land, xvjs. iijd. Johannes Water t. j mess., ij bov. terræ, cum for-land, viijs. vjd. ob. Robertus Talyor t. j mess., ij bov. terræ, cum for-land, r. p. a. viijs. vjd. ob. Willelmus Symson t. j mess., ij bov. terræ, cum for-land, r. p. a. viijs. vjd.

Cotagia de Brauby. Opera et consuetudines. Adam Schephyrd t. j cot., iij acras terræ, et r. p. a. xxjd., j gallinam, et ova. Idem t. j gyrs-garth et j acram terræ, et r. p. a. xvd., sine operibus. Idem t. cot., ij acras terræ, et r. p. a. xiijd. et opera. Alicia Northyrn t. j cot., iij acras terræ, r. p. a. ijs. jd. et opera. Johannes Kent t. j cot., vj acras terræ cum prato, et r. p. a. vjs. iijd. et opera. Johannes Broune t. j cot., vj acras terræ, r. p. a. iijs. xd. et opera. Isolda Berear t. j cot., vj acras terræ, j acram prati, r. vjs. iiijd. et opera. Cecilia Liepare t. j cot., j buttam terræ, r. p. a. ijs. iijd. et opera. Thomas Broune t. j cot., r. p. a. vjd., sine operibus. Idem t. iij acras terræ, r. p. a. xijd., sine operibus. Communitas villæ t. virgas juxta aquam, et vastum ibidem, r. xjs. xd. Thomas Talyor t. le Cot-garth in heremo, et r. ijs. pro voluntate domini. Johannes Water t. j cot. vastum cum j crofto, r. ijs. Johannes Knapton, t. j cot. vastum, et r. p. a. xijd. Robertus Talyor t. j cot. vastum, et r. p. a. ixd., et opera. Willelmus Courtman t. j cot. vastum, r. xd. et opera. Johannes Raynerson t. j cot. vastum, et r. p. a. xijd. et opera. Sunt ibidem v acræ terræ, vocatæ Gild-land, in manu domini. Solebat r. p. a. iijs. iiijd.

Bracinagium ibidem. Piscaria ibidem. Milnclose —.

EDESTON.

Sunt in villa de Edeston xl bovatæ terræ, unde quælibet bovata cont. ix acras terræ et prati; quæ nulla opera faciunt neque consuetudines, sicut aliæ bovatæ pertinentes manerio de Salton, eo quod non sunt de præbenda.

Dimissio. Henricus Gamill t. j mess. et vj bovatas terræ, r. xxvijs. Johannes filius Walteri t. iiij bovatas terræ, et r. p. a. xxs. Johannes Wilcocsun t. unum. mess., iiij bovatas terræ et di., xxs. vjd. Johannes Gamill t. j mess., iiij bov. terræ et di., r. p. a. xxs. Robertus Oven t. j mess., iiij bov. terræ, et r. p. a. xxs. Willelmus Arnald t. j bov. terræ, et r. p. a. iiijs. Robertus Michell t. j mess., iiij bov. terræ, r. xviijs. Robertus de Oven t. iij bovatas terræ, et r. p. a. xijs. Johannes filius Aliciæ t. iiij bov. terræ, r. p. a. xvjs. Item sunt ij bovatæ terræ, assignatæ vicario de Salton in relevamen portionis suæ, pro beneplacito domini.

Susanna Wilkynson t. j bovatam terræ, r. p. a. iiijs. Willelmus filius Walteri t. ij bov. terræ, et r. p. a. viijs. Alicia Dauson t. j buttam terræ, et r. p. a. ijd.[k]

Sunt ibidem ix cotagia.

Willelmus Arnald t. j cot., et r. p. a. ijs. Dominus Willelmus, vicarius ibidem, t. j cot., et r. p. a. ijs. Eufamia Wilkynson t. j cot., et r. p. a. ijs. Willelmus Arnald t. iij cot. vasta. Solebat r. p. a. vjs.

Prata dominica. Johannes Watsun t. viij acras prati dominici, vocatas le Savage-yng, et r. p. a. xxiiijs.

Terra libera. Dominus Peert t. j parcellam terræ inclusam infra manerium Johannis Holme, et r. p. a. vjs.

MAGNA BERGH.

Bondagia. Sunt in Magna Bergh xxiiij[or] bovatæ terræ, et quælibet bovatarum prædictarum faciet universa et singula servitia, tam ad carruc' quam ad molendinum de Salton, sicut bovatæ faciunt manerii de Salton prædicto, ut superius est notatum; unde in tenura,

Dimissio. Walterus Colman t. j mes. et ij bovatas terræ, r. p. a. vjs. jd. Johannes Smyth t. iij mes. vj bov. terræ, et r. p. a. xviijs. iijd. Willelmus Nyghtgale t. j mess., iiij bov. terræ, r. xijs. ijd. Thomas Carre t. j mess., ij bov. terræ, r. p. a. vjs. jd. Willelmus Wand t. j mess., iiij bov. terræ, r. p. a. xijs. ijd. Johannes Tynk t. j mess., iiij bov. terræ, r. p. a. xijs. ijd. Adam Hogh t. j mes., ij bov. terræ, r. p. a. vjs. jd.

Cotagium. Est ibidem cotagium quod faciet omnia servitia et opera, sicut cotagia manerii de Salton, ut superius expressatur.

[k] After this there is a blank page.

Dimissio. Adam filius Hugonis t. j cot., et r. p. a. iijs. Libera terra. Walterus de Bergh t. ij tofta, super quæ ædificatum est manerium ipsius Walteri, r. p. a. ijs. Idem Walterus t. j placeam terræ, vocatam Schor-place, quæ jacet inter gardinum suum et gardinum nuper Adæ de Whytton, r. p. a. iijs.

LYTILL BERGH.

Bondagiæ. Sunt in Parva Bergh iiij bovatæ terræ, quarum iij bovatæ sunt de bondag: et faciunt opera et servitia, sicut inferius patet. Et una bovata terræ extra bond., quæ nuper erat in tenura Walteri de Bergh, ut inferius patet.

Est ibidem j bovata terræ, nuper in tenura Walteri de Bergh per cartam, quæ solebat r. p. a. xjs. viijd.: et quia videbatur ei nimis cara, jacuit vasta nil reddendo; sed modo dimittitur per custodem manerii Johanni Proude, r. inde p. a. iiijs. vjd.

Bond. Sunt ibidem iij bovatæ terræ de bond., quarum quælibet facit opera et servitia, tam in carrecta quam ad molendinum de Salton, ut bovatæ manerii de Salton prædicta, prout superius est expressum.

FLAXTON.

Libera firma. Ricardus Plaice t. per cartam j toftum et j bovatam terræ, r. p. a. viijs.; et inveniet domino, quotiens illuc accesserit, cameram competentem et honestam pro se et familia sua, stramen pro lectis, albam candelam, fœnum pro equis.

Terræ arabiles. Sunt etiam v bovatæ terræ de bond., et quælibet bovata cont. per æst. xv acras terræ et prati; quarum iiij et iij rodæ jacent super le Lang-crofte in medio. Et super le Stob-keldes iij acræ et di.; super lez Lang-landes, in medio, iij acræ; super lez Hagge-brekes, in medio, iij acræ; super lez Thwaytes, in parte austr., j acra et di.; super lez Rongefordgates, in medio, iij acræ. Et ex parte austr. Thornton-more, buttando super Lilling-dik, j acra; super Grelemar-buttes, in medio, buttando super dictum dyk, j acra; super lez Angromes, inter Thornton-more et Flaxton-ryse, ij acræ, j roda. Item in le Brod-feld, super lez Crascildes, j acra. Super lez Diglandes iij acræ. Super le Ayk-buskes iij acræ. Super le Brakan-hill acra et di. Ex parte austr. de Thornton-more, buttando super Flaxton-dyk, ij acræ. Super Flaxton-buttes, ex parte bor., buttando super Thornton-feld, ij acræ. Super lez Ersbrayth, buttando super Thornton-balkes, iij rodæ. Ex parte occid. de lez Westil-carris j acra. Ex parte or. dicti Yle-carres, buttando super eundem, j acra. Super le North-brek, in medio, ij acræ, j roda. Super le Medel-dales iij acræ. Super le Westbrek j acra di. Super lez Wandales iij rodæ. Super lez Brotes, in duobus locis, vj acræ. Item in le Croft-feld, in lez croftes, vj acræ. Super lez Schol-brades j acra di. Super lez Hen-baynes di. acra. Super lez Coft-heuede-land j acra et di. Super lez Gray-stanes j acra et di. Super lez Fun-rodes j acra et di. Super lez Wrang-landes ij acræ, j roda. Ex utraque parte le Green-hill, buttando super eundem, di. acra. Super Petir-flatte, juxta le Coter-keld, iij acræ. Super lez Kirk-hilles iij acræ. Super lez More-buttes, inter le Kirk-hill et Barton-flatte, di. acra. Super le Swyn-sty-buttes di. acra. Super lez Clibberres j acra et di. Super Barton-flatte iij acræ. Super lez Ly-gates iij acræ. Super lez Wandales j acra et di. Et ultra, super lez Sindirli-buttes di. acra. Et super lez Sand-landes j acra et di.

Prata. Quædam portio prati jacet in le South-yng, et alia portio prati in le Schole-brad-yng; et tertia portio prati jacet in le North-yng; et in le Wandale di. acra. Et terræ et prata prædicta jacent discontinue per campos prædictos, inter terram Ricardi Bernard, et terras monialium de Burneholme, ut superius specificatur.

Dimissio. Ricardus Plaice t. ij tofta cum ij gardinis, prope finem austr. dictæ villæ, juxta placeam Ricardi Barnard ex parte bor., et ij bovatas terræ de prædictis v bovatis, superius nominatis, et r. p. a. xijs. Willelmus Raynersune t. ij tofta et reliquas iij bovatas terræ de superius nominatis, et r. p. a. xviijs. Et solebat reddere —.

Consuetudines et servitia. Et prædicti tenentes debent facere sectam ad curiam de Salton de tertia septimana in tertiam septimanam. Et etiam, si quis eorum notatus fuerit super aliquo delicto, cujus correctio tanget forum ecclesiasticum, debet citari ad capitulum de Salton, et ibidem puniri. Et etiam debent dare commune auxilium pro palefrido emendo domino Priori, cum noviter sit electus, vel alias rogati fuerint per dictum dominum Priorem pro aliquo auxilio conferendo.

MIL(L)INGTON.

Sunt ibidem ij bovatæ terræ, quarum utraque continet —, et j mes. vastum. Quod quidem mes. cum crofto jacet ex parte bor. cimiterii ecclesiæ ibidem. De quibus quidem bovatis j acra et di. jacent in Dun-holme. Et super lez Wrang-landes j acra et di. Et super lez Bla-landes j acra et di. Et super Swyn-gil-more j acra. Et super lez Lange-rodes et le Wod-heuede j acra. Et super lez Sugge-dales, in duobus locis, iij acræ di.

Et super lez Knolles, in duobus locis, j acra. Et ex parte bor. ecclesiæ iij rodæ. Et ad finem occid. villæ j rode. Et ad Fukel-heued iij rode. Et super le Swynes j rode. Et super lez Eggis iij rod. Et super Kiln-will-miln-buttis j rod. Et ex utraque parte Fulkel-syk j rod. Et super le Peter-hill di. rod. Et Lillyng-brest di. acra. Et super Skilburn-keld-heued di. acra. Et ad Scla-thorn-heued di. acra. Et super Cliffton in duobus locis j acra. Et super lez Bland-corn-land di. acra. Et ad Threle-dale-heuedes j acra. Et super lez Houle-landes di. acra. Et super lez Foul-dayles ij acræ. Et in lez Brotes j acra et di. Et super Haver-flek-more di. acra. Et in lez Dales j acra. Et sciendum quod dictæ portiones terræ prænominatæ et diversæ portiones terræ vastæ super ——.

GEVELDALE IN LE HOLE.

Est ibidem j toftum, diversis domibus ædificatum, cum j gardino; quod quidem toftum jacet inter placeam baronis de Graystok ex parte or., et placeam Sancti Petri ex parte occid. Et sunt iiij bovatæ terræ, quæ jacent in campo ejusdem, quarum quælibet bovate cont. —: unde in Grindell-dikes jac. . . . acr. Et super lez Hou-landes j acra. Et super lez Hul-landes ij acræ. Et super lez Wandels j acra et di. Et super lez Graynes j acra. Et super le For-land, ex parte austr., iij rodæ. Et super lez Brekes j acra. Et ex utraque parte del Hungir-hill iij acræ. Et super le North-wlfe-acre ij acræ. Et super lez South-pese-landes j acra. Et super lez Crosse-landes ij acræ. Et ex parte austr. lez Gren-gat-landes ij acræ. Et super Thorn-hous-buttes j acra. Et super lez Staan-landes, ex parte austr. le Staane, j acra. Et ex parte austr. le Green-gate ij acræ. Et ex parte bor. le Mykill-syk j acra. Et super le Gare, buttando super le miln-dam, ij acræ. Et super lez Lynakes di. acra. Et inter le Brig-keld et lez Keldes di. acra. Et super lez Cattetayle-landes di. acra. Et sub le Prest-garth j roda. Et super le Clerk-myn-landes j acra. Et super lez Kape-keld-hilles j acra. Et super lez Gyast-landes j acra et di. Et super lez Bul-dayles j acra. Et super lez Over-bul-dayles j acra. Et super lez Skal-beres j acra. Et super lez Lang-landes, versus le Swyn-keld, iiij acræ. Et super le Schere-brath et lez Stand-land-buttes j acra. Et super le Northir-skald-beres et le Garth-heued-land di. acra. Et in le Clerk-myln-dame j acra prati. Et sciendum quod residuæ terræ pertinentes iiij bovatis prædictis jacent inter terras husband loci ejusdem discontinue, sed nescitur quot acras continent.

CHARTERS AND OTHER DOCUMENTS.

I.—A SURVEY OF THE LANDS BELONGING TO THE PREBEND OF SALTON IN YORKSHIRE, WHICH WAS ATTACHED TO THE PRIORATE OF HEXHAM.[l] [MSS. Cotton, Claudius, B, iii., 117 *a*, *b*.]

PRÆBENDARIUS de Saltona habet ecclesiam de eadem, et percipit omnes decimas, tam majores quam minores; et habet jurisdictionem ibidem in omnibus causis spiritualibus. Habet etiam in villa de Saltona manerium suum dominicum. Habet etiam de terra dominica, quæ culta est, duas carucatas, et de prato xiij acras. Habet etiam quandam placeam inclusam, quæ vocatur Frensholm, quæ continet ij acras et dimidiam. Et habet molendinum suum. Habet etiam garennam in omnibus terris suis. Habet etiam in Saltona xx husband, quorum quilibet tenet unum toftum et ij bovatas terræ, et reddit per annum viij solidos. Et cariabunt meeremium domini ad domum construendam, et ædificia reparanda, ubicunque fuerit emptum. Et cariabunt cybum domini ad Ebor., et alibi, quotienscunque fuerint requisiti. Habet etiam unum tenentem, qui tenet iij bovatas terræ, et reddit per anum xijs., et facit servitium, ut supra. Habet etiam unum tenentem qui tenet unam bovatam terræ, et reddit per annum iiij solidos, et facit, ut supra. Et reparabunt stagnum molendini quotiens opus fuerit.

Habet etiam in eadem x gresmanni *(sic)*, quorum quilibet tenet unum toftum, et unam acram terræ, et reddit per annum xvj denarios, et facit iiij opera autumpnalia, et dat unam gallinam et xx ova per annum.

Habet etiam dictus præbendarius in Brauby xj tenentes, quorum quilibet tenet unum toftum et ij bovatas terræ, et reddit per annum viij solidos, et facit in omnibus sicut et cæteri de Saltona. Item habet in villa de Brauby duos tenentes, quorum quilibet tenet iiij bovatas terræ, et reddit per annum

[l] This survey is written in a bold and beautiful hand, probably in the twelfth century. There are similar documents in existence relating to the other stalls at York.

xvij solidos, et facit, ut supra. Item habet in eadem iij tenentes, quorum quilibet tenet iij bovatas terræ, et reddit per annum xijs., et facit servitium, ut supra.

Item idem præbendarius habet in villa de Brauby viij gresmenni, quorum quilibet tenet unum toftum et unam acram terræ et dimidiam, et reddit per annum xviij denarios, et facit duo opera autumpnalia, et dat unum gallum ad Natale Domini, et xx ova ad Pascha.

Habet etiam dictus præbendarius in Bergh Magna iiij tenentes, quorum quilibet tenet iiij bovatas terræ, et reddit per annum xij solidos, et facit in omnibus ut homines de Saltona. Habet etiam in eadem iij tenentes, quorum quilibet tenet ij bovatas terræ, et reddit per annum vj solidos, et facit in omnibus, ut supra. Habet etiam in eadem unum tenentem qui tenet unam bovatam terræ et reddit per annum iij solidos.

Habet etiam in Litel-bergh unum tenentem, qui tenet ij bovatas terræ, et reddit per annum viij solidos, et facit servitium, ut supra. Habet etiam in eadem ij gresmanni, et quilibet istorum reddit per annum xij denarios.

Willelmus de Neutona tenet de eodem præbendario in villa de Neutona xxiiij bovatas terræ, et reddit per annum l solidos, et facit sectam ad curiam de Saltona.

Item dominus J. de Steyngrave tenet de eodem in villa de Neutona unam culturam quæ vocatur Scarlet, et continet in se vj bovatas, et reddit per annum xiij solidos, iiij denarios.

Idem præbendarius habet in villa de Flaxtona iij tenentes, quorum quilibet tenet ij bovatas terræ, et reddit per annum de toto lxvj solidos, viij denarios.

Item hæredes Gilberti de Gevildal tenent de eodem præbendario in villa de Milington vj bovatas terræ, et reddunt per annum x solidos pro omnibus, sed quod facit sectam ad curiam de Saltona.

II.—A GRANT OF CARRAW FROM RICHARD CUMIN TO THE PRIOR AND CONVENT OF HEXHAM.[m] [MSS. Dodsworth, xlv., 33 *a*.]

Ricardus Cumin omnibus hominibus suis salutem. Notum sit omnibus vobis me, concilio et assensu uxoris meæ Hextild, et amicorum, et hominum meorum, concessisse et dedisse, et

[m] A deed of the twelfth century taken from one of Dodsworth's MSS. in the Bodleian Library. It also appears in a volume of the collections of the same learned antiquary among the Lansdowne MSS., No. cccxxvi., 108 *b*. He there states where he found it *In cartis Johannis Fenwyke, militis et baronett, apud Hexham reservatis*, 5° *Febr.* 1638, *in a white box marked* φ. In dorso; *Prima Carta.* This charter has been printed in Dugdale's Monasticon, vi., 184, and in

præsenti carta confirmasse ecclesiæ Sancti Andreæ de Hextadelsham, et canonicis ibidem Deo servientibus, de campis villæ meæ de Stancroft terram illam quæ jacet juxta locum qui dicitur Charrau, et tendit juxta murum Romanorum versus occidentem per divisas eis ostensas, in elemosinam perpetuam, etc. Confirmo etiam eis dimidiam carucatam terræ de feudo meo in Hedeneshalch, quam Aguilfus, miles meus, dedit eis in elemosinam. Hoc autem beneficium eis confero, quia me, et uxorem meam Hext', et fratrem meum Walterum, et hæredes meos, in plenariam fraternitatem receperunt, et in vita, et post mortem. Testes sunt Hugo de Morevilla, Gillebertus de Umframvill, Odonell de Umframvill, Willelmus de Sumervill, Walterus de Ridall, Willelmus de Lindeseia, Walterus Cumin, Aguilfus et Nicholaus frater ejus, Walterus filius Ranulfi, et multi alii.

III.—A GRANT OF LAND AT WHITLAW TO THE CHURCH OF HEXHAM BY ADAM DE TINDALE.[n] [MSS. Dodsworth, xlv., 33 *a*.]

Sciant præsentes et futuri quod ego Adam de Tindale dedi, etc., ecclesiæ Sancti Andreæ Haugustaldensi, et canonicis ibidem Deo servientibus, totam de Witelawe, quam emi, cum pertinentiis; per eas divisas, etc.; et cum libero communione in toto feodo de Fetherstanhalc, cum nemore ad ædificandum et comburendum. Testibus W° de Ravenest, Hugone de Grendon, Ada de Thorngrafton, Ranulfo filio ejus, Matheo de Witefeld, Hudardo de Willimothwic, etc.

Hodgson's Northumberland, iii., part ii., 396. At p. 416 there are some notices of Cumin and his family.

Dodsworth saw also the following charter among Sir John Fenwick's deeds (MSS., xlv., 33 *b*, and MSS. Lansdowne, cccxxvi., 109). It was marked on the back vj[ta] carta:—"Omnibus Christi fidelibus, etc., Ricardus Cumin salutem. Noveritis me concessisse, etc., ecclesiæ Sancti Andreæ, etc., terram de Karrawer a prædecessoribus meis inde collatam, per divisas perambulatas a quatuor legalibus hominibus sacramento super Rubrum Librum de Hexteldesham, etc. Testibus domino Willelmo Cumin comite de Buchan, Ada de Tindal, Roberto de Aubeny, Johanne Prat, Nicolao de Willemotewic, Simone de Rumecestre, Matheo de Witefeld, Adamo de Elrington."

[n] See, also, MSS. Lansdowne, cccxxvi., 109 *a*. Taken from Sir John Fenwick's charters, and endorsed *Prima Carta*.

There is an account of the Tindales in Hodgson's Northumberland, iii., part ii., 364-5. Among Dodsworth's extracts from the chartulary of Lanercost it is said that Adam de Tindale confirmed to that abbey "calumpniam suam in mora de Brenkibeth versus Robertum de Vallibus" (MSS. Dodsw., xlv., 8 *b*): and Ivo de Veteriponte, knight, at the request of Robert de Veteriponte, his brother, granted to him the vill of Renegill, which his mother, Matilda de Veteriponte, gave him (ibid., 18 *b*). To the first of these two deeds a seal is appended, a bar between two chess rooks. See Hodgson's Northumberland, iii., part ii., 356-7.

IV.—A QUIT-CLAIM FROM JOHN THE PRIOR, AND THE CONVENT OF HEXHAM, OF THE PENSION PAYABLE TO THEM OUT OF THE ARCHDEACONRY OF THE WEST RIDING. [Reg. Magnum Album penes Dec. et Cap. Ebor., pars i., fol. 40 *a*, *b*.]

Johannes, Prior, et Conventus ecclesiæ Sancti Andreæ Algustadii,[o] omnibus has literas visuris vel audituris salutem. Ad notitiam vestram pervenire volumus nos quietum clamasse dominum Rogerum Ebor. archiepiscopum, et omnes successores suos, a præstatione centum solidorum, quos ipse de archidiaconatu Westrithing nobis solebat reddere ad vestitum fratrum, ex constitutione prædecessorum suorum, Thomæ junioris, et Turstini, archiepiscoporum: ipse namque, prætaxatus archiepiscopus, sicut vir bonus et prudens, volens providere tam utilitati et quieti ecclesiæ nostræ, quam ecclesiæ Eboracensis (et) successorum suorum, ad petitionem nostram, hoc intuitu concessit nobis et ecclesiæ nostræ imperpetuum ecclesiam de Edestona, cum omnibus pertinentiis, quietam ab omni servitio et consuetudine, præter iiij solidos sinodales, et præter ij solidos quos annuatim debemus reddere ad Conred archidiaconum. Ita videlicet quod nos præsentabimus archiepiscopo capellanum, qui ei respondebit de cura animarum. Cætera autem omnia in usus nostros cedent. Hiis testibus Roberto decano, Willelmo cantore, Johanne archidiacono, Alano, Mainardo, Geroldo, Hamone, Nicholao, Stephano, canonicis Ebor., David, Ricardo, canonicis Augustald'.

V.—A CHARTER OF WILLIAM THE LION, KING OF SCOTLAND, GRANTING THE MANOR OF WHITFIELD, ETC., TO THE PRIOR AND CONVENT OF HEXHAM. [From the original in the possession of Mr. Orde, of Whitfield hall.]

W. rex Scottorum,[p] omnibus probis hominibus totius terræ suæ, salutem. Sciant præsentes et futuri me concessisse, et hac carta mea confirmasse Deo et ecclesiæ Sancti Andreæ Hagustald', et canonicis ibidem Deo servientibus, in perpetuum, totam Witefeld, cum bosco et plano, cum prato et pastura, cum molendino, et cum omnibus eidem villæ de Witefeld adja-

[o] There is another copy of this deed in the same volume, part ii., 23 *a*, and in MSS. Cotton, Claudius, B, iii., 18 *a*. They vary but little. The two last read *Augustandii* instead of *Algustadii*, and the name of archbishop Thurstan is not inserted. This payment is mentioned in Vol. I., 58.

[p] Mr. Hodgson (Northumberland, iii., part ii., 17-18) gives extracts from some other charters relating to Whitfield. They are merely taken from transcripts.

centibus, præter illas terras quas Robertus filius Willelmi, et Johannes de Corebrig de matre mea tenent in villa illa. Tenendum de matre mea et hæredibus ejus in feodo firmo, et in perpetuum, libere et quiete ab omni servitio et consuetudine, et ab omnibus auxiliis, et ab omni geld, per easdem divisas per quas mater mea tenuit illam de Henrico comite, patre meo, et postea de me; et per illas divisas per quas Robertus, capellanus matris meæ, tenuit; et sicut illam quam mater mea et Robertus capellanus per eam de dominio gvast H. comitis, patris mei, coluerunt et inhabitaverunt. Reddendo inde annuatim matri meæ, et hæredibus suis, vj libras piperis, ad festum Sancti Michaelis, sicut carta comitissæ matris meæ testatur, et confirmat. Testibus David fratre meo comite, Wald(evo), Hugone Ridel, Ricardo Cumin, Rogero de Coigneres, Waltero de Windlesoure, Hugone Giffard, Liolfo filio Macc[s], Gileberto filio Rich', Gileberto de Umframvill, Willelmo de Haia, Willelmo de Mortemer. Apud logias de Duneliveshalch.

[Remains of the royal seal, much defaced and broken, appended by strings of white silk.]

VI.—A GRANT OF THE MANOR OF WHITFIELD FROM THE PRIOR AND CONVENT OF HEXHAM TO MATTHEW, SON OF ROBERT, THE CHAPLAIN OF THE COUNTESS ADA. [From the original in the possession of Mr. Orde, of Whitfield hall.]

J. Prior Hagustald' ecclesiæ, totusque Conventus canonicorum et fratrum, omnibus sanctæ matris ecclesiæ filiis, salutem. Notum vobis fieri volumus nos dedisse et concessisse, et hac carta nostra confirmasse Matheo filio Rodberti, capellani Adæ comitissæ, et hæredibus suis, totum Whitefeld, præter terram Hugonis et Rodberti, in feudo et hæreditate, tam plenarie quam illud tenemus de Ada comitissa; scilicet, cum bosco et plano, et prato et pastura, et cum molendino, et cum omnibus eidem willæ de Witefeld adjacentibus; libere et quiete ab omni servitio et consuetudine, et ab omnibus auxiliis, et ab omni geld, per easdem divisas per quas prænominata comitissa de Henrico comite, viro suo, tenuit; et postea de Willelmo rege, filio suo; et sicut modo nos tenemus; reddendo inde annuatim Deo, et Sancto Andreæ, et canonicis, unam marcam argenti ad duos terminos; scilicet, ad festum Sancti Martini unam dimidiam marcam, et ad Pentecosten aliam. Præterea vero in manu nostra toftum et sex acras terræ, unam acram de prato, et pasturam triginta vaccarum retinemus; quas prædictus Rodbertus capellanus coram comitissa nobis donavit. Volumus autem et concedimus ut hæredes ipsius Mathei, scilicet filius ejus vel filia, frater vel soror, nepos vel nepta, hoc prædictum Whitefeld post mortem ejus per unam marcam argenti relevent, et sic cum prædicto servitio sine occasione de hærede in hæredem, scilicet in omne posterum in perpetuum teneant et habeant. Testibus Abraham presbytero, Godefrido de Bingafeld et Paganero, Rodberto Bertram, Cospatricio Homal et Waltero et Gregorio filiis ejus, Thurkil filio Archilli, et Adam filio ejus, Ernebrand de Einewic, Benedicto clerico, Briano, Aschetillo, Johanne de Castelo, Johanne famulo Prioris, Reinaldo senescaldo, Horm de Whitefeld, et aliis multis.

[Sigillum deest.]

VII.—A DEED FROM JOHN PRIOR OF HEXHAM AND HIS CONVENT, GRANTING A HOUSE IN YORK TO WILLIAM, CHAPLAIN OF ARCHBISHOP GEOFFREY PLANTAGENET. [From the original in the possession of the Dean and Chapter of York.]

Johannes Prior, et Conventus Haugustaldensis ecclesiæ,[q] omnibus sanctæ matris ecclesiæ filiis, tam præsentibus quam futuris, salutem. Universitati vestræ notum fieri volumus nos dedisse, et concessisse, et præsenti carta nostra confirmasse Willelmo, capellano domini G. Eboracensis archiepiscopi, fratri nostro, et hæredibus suis, videlicet quos hæredes constituerit, unam mansuram terræ quam habemus in Eboraco, in vico qui vocatur Gudherimegata, in feodo et jure hæreditario; de nobis tenendam, pro tribus solidis annuatim reddendis, liberam et quietam ab omni alio servitio et consuetudine nos contingente. Reddet vero dimidium trium solidorum ad festum Sancti Martini et dimidium ad Pentecosten. Quisquis autem hæredum suorum hanc terram tenuerit, fidelitatem ecclesiæ nostræ et nobis faciet. Hiis testibus magistro Simone de Appulia cancellario Eboracensi, Willelmo archidiacono Notingahamiæ, Petro de Ros archidiacono Carliolensi, magistro Erardo, magistro Lisiardo, canonicis Eboracensibus, magistro Rogero Arundel canonico Suell, Alano capellano, Radulpho de Wigethot, canonicis de Ripum, magistro Johanne filio Otin, Nigello clerico, Benedicto capellano, Rogero de Bavent senescallo archiepiscopi, Radulfo de Wellewic, Hugone Gernagot, Ricardo de Wivill, Ricardo de Luterinton, Ricardo de Hudeleston, Henrico de Muhaut, militibus, et multis aliis clericis et laicis.

[A fragment of the seal.]

[q] See the Preface to Vol. I., clii-iii. This deed must have been executed between 1189 and 1194. I have engraved the fragment of the seal.

VIII.—A GRANT OF LAND AT FETHERSTANHAUGH TO THE PRIOR AND CONVENT OF HEXHAM BY ELIAS DE FETHERSTANHAUGH. [MSS. Dodsworth, xlix., 25 *b.*]

Ego, Helyas de Fethirstanhalcht,[r] do et concedo Deo et ecclesiæ Sancti Andreæ Hagustaldensis, et fratribus ibidem Deo servientibus, illam terram meam de libero feodo meo de Fetherstaneshalcht; quæ terra includitur per has divisas. Ab oriente, etc. Et iidem fratres receperunt me, et filium et hæredem meum post me, in fraternitatem ejusdem ecclesiæ. Testibus Eustacio, Papedi, Benedicto, et Willelmo, capellanis, Richardo archidiacono, Roberto, Rogero, Waltero Hamel', Huctredo de Herynton, Rannulfo de Elrinton, Reginaldo de Wardon, etc., Willelmo Luvell, et aliis.

IX.—A GRANT OF FREEDOM FROM TOLLS, ETC., TO THE HOSPITAL OF ST. GILES AT HEXHAM. [Rot. Chart., 2 John, m. ii.]

Johannes Dei gratia, etc. Sciatis nos concessisse leprosis de Estoldesham quietanciam de theloniis passagii, et pontagii per terram nostram de Ebor. et Northumbreland, de omnibus hiis quæ ad usus suos proprios emerint vel vendiderint. Et ideo firmiter præcipimus quod in quieti sint. T. Hugone Bard', et Eustacio de Vescy. Apud Estoldesham, xvj die Februarii.

X.—A GRANT OF LANDS TO THE CHURCH OF HEXHAM MADE BY THOMAS DE DEVILSTONE. [MSS. Cotton, Claudius, B, iii., 28 *b.*]

Sciant præsentes et futuri quod ego Thomas de Diveleston[s] dedi et concessi, et hac carta mea confirmavi, Deo et ecclesiæ Sancti Andreæ Haugustaldensis, et canonicis ibidem Deo servi-

[r] See Hodgson's Northumberland, vol. iii., part ii., 354, etc. This deed seems to have been made about 1215. There is another copy of it in MSS. Lansdowne, cccxxvi., 80 *b.* When Dodsworth saw the original at Fetherstanhaugh it had *a faire seale with a man on horsebacke.* Dodsworth gives two other deeds relating to Hexham (Ex cartis Albani Fetherstanhough de Fetherstanhough, esq., 1 Augusti, 1639). Mr. Hodgson has printed both of them pretty correctly. In the last, instead of antecessorum *suorum* read *meorum.*

[s] A deed made in the early part of the thirteenth century. There is another copy of it in the Reg. Magn. Album, part ii., 35.

Devilston is the same name as Dilston. In 1239 Simon de Devilstone pays £60 to Adam Bertram for his interest in Dilston. In the time of Edward I. Simon de Devilstone grants to Thomas his son and heir, and to Lucy daughter of Sir William Heron, his manor of Dilston. William de Tindale was the cousin and heir of this Thomas (MSS. Dodsworth, xlv., 116-17). There was formerly a monument to Thomas de Devilstone in the church of Hexham.

entibus, totam Eskilescales, cum omnibus pertinentiis suis; tenendam sibi in puram et perpetuam elemosinam, libere, quiete, et solute ab omnibus servitiis et consuetudinibus et exactionibus in perpetuum; pro salute animæ meæ, et antecessorum meorum, et hæredum meorum: salvo servitio domini Eboracensis archiepiscopi, et successorum suorum. Testibus hiis, Ricardo de Umframvilla, Hugone de Bolbec, Othuero de Insula, Roberto De la val, Roberto fratre suo, David de Graham, Matheo de Witefeld, Petro de Sancto Claro, Willelmo de Hawelton, Rannulpho de Diveliston, Roberto Bertram, Adam Bertram, Helia de Frinton de Cattedene, et multis aliis.

XI.—A QUIT-CLAIM FROM THE PRIOR AND CONVENT OF HEXHAM OF THEIR INTEREST IN ESKINGSELES. [MSS. Cotton, Claudius, B, iii., 29 *a*.]

Universis Christi fidelibus ad quos præsens scriptum[t] pervenerit Willelmus Prior de Hextildesham, et humilis ejusdem loci Conventus, salutem in Domino. Noverit universitas vestra nos remisisse, et quietum clamasse in perpetuum venerabili nostro domino, Waltero, Eboracensi archiepiscopo et Angliæ primati, et successoribus suis, totum jus et clameum quod habuimus, vel habere potuimus, in villa de Eskingseles, quam emeramus a Thoma de Diveleston; cujus instrumenta quæ inde habuimus eidem domino nostro archiepiscopo reddidimus. Et, in excambium dictæ villæ de Eskingesel, dedit nobis idem dominus archiepiscopus quater viginti et quinque acras terræ, secundum divisas in carta memorati domini archiepiscopi nobis inde confecta contentas. Præterea remisimus et quietum clamavimus sæpedicto domino archiepiscopo, et successoribus suis, in perpetuum, totum jus et clameum quod habuimus, vel habere potuimus, in uno millenar' ang(u)illarum,[u] et quatuor solidaturis redditus, quas singulis annis in Beverlaco percipere consuevimus; et, in excambium tam dictarum anguillarum quam quatuor solidaturarum redditus, dedit nobis idem dominus archiepiscopus triginta acras terræ, juxta rivulum subtus Yaru-rig, ad aquilonem. Quietas etiam clamavimus dicto domino archiepiscopo, et successoribus suis, tres acras et dimidiam et sexdecim perticas terræ, juxta fontem Sancti Andreæ, quas eis dedimus in excambium trium acrarum et dimidiæ, et sexdecim perticarum terræ in cultura, quæ vocant Sele.[v] Et, ut hæc nostra remissio

[t] There is a copy of this deed in the Reg. Magnum Album, part ii., 35 *b*. It must be taken in connection with the preceding document.

[u] See Vol. I., p. 56.

[v] "Quæ *vocatur* Sele" (Reg. Magn. Album). This is the field contiguous to the Priory.

et quieta clamatio rata et stabilis perseveret, eam sigilli nostri munimine duximus confirmandam. Hiis testibus Roberto de Gray, Ada de Tindal, Willelmo Marcel, P. de Vallibus, G. de Stanlak, canonicis Ebor., R. de Bereford, A. de Stanle, Ada Bertram, Ricardo le Fossur.

XII.—A GRANT BY KING JOHN OF A PENSION OUT OF THE CHURCH OF WARDON. [Rot. Chart., 16 John, m. 6.]

J. Dei gratia rex Angliæ, etc. Sciatis nos intuitu Dei concessisse, et, quantum ad nos pertinet, dedisse, et hac carta nostra confirmasse, dilecto clerico nostro, magistro Roberto Morell, viginti duas marcas de ecclesia de Wardon, percipiendas per annum per Priorem de Hextildesham; quas episcopi Dunolm. conferre consueverunt per compositionem quandam factam inter eos et Priorem et Conventum de Hextildesham, de prædicta ecclesia de Wardon; quam eis in proprios usus confirmaverunt: retentis sibi et successoribus suis prædictis viginti duabus marcis conferendis; et quæ de nostra sunt donatione, ratione episcopatus Dunolm. vacantis et in manu nostra existentis; habendas et tenendas omnibus diebus vitæ suæ in puram et perpetuam elemosinam, adeo bene, libere, quiete, et integre, sicut aliquis prædecessorum suorum eas unquam melius, liberius, quietius, et integrius tenuit. Testibus dominis W. London., P. Winton., J. Bath. et Glaston. episcopis, Willelmo de Kantil', Johanne Marelc', Simone de Kima, Henrico filio Comitis, Thoma de Muleton. Data per manum magistri Ricardi de Marisco, cancellarii nostri, apud Goldeford, xvij° die Jan., anno regni nostri sexto decimo.

XIII.—FOUR GRANTS TO THE PRIOR AND CONVENT OF HEXHAM FROM WALTER GRAY, ARCHBISHOP OF YORK. [Ex Rot. Majore archiep. Gray. In dorso, No. 2.]

I.

Omnibus, etc. Noveritis nos dedisse, concessisse, et præsenti carta nostra confirmasse Deo et ecclesiæ Beati Andreæ de Hextold', et canonicis ibidem Deo servientibus, septies viginti et quinque acras et dimidiam terræ; de quibus quadraginta acræ jacent inter villam de Aynewik et hayam nostram de Akwod usque aquilonem; et quater viginti et decem acræ desuper Dotelant versus austrum; et quindecim acræ et dimidia subtus Dotelant versus aquilonem; tenendas et habendas de nobis et successoribus nostris in perpetuum, libere et quiete;

reddendo nobis et successoribus nostris quatuor marcas argenti per annum, pro omni servitio et exactione, medietatem ad festum Sancti Martini, et medietatem ad Pentecosten. Præterea concessimus eisdem canonicis unam viam ab exitu villæ suæ de Aynewik per medium hayæ nostræ de Akwod, a bercaria sua directe versus aquilonem, usque ad communiam *(sic)* pasturam suam ultra Kirkeburn, quæ continet in latitudine decem perticatas. Pro hac autem donatione et concessione remiserunt nobis et successoribus nostris prædicti canonici, pro se, et successoribus suis, et hominibus suis in perpetuum, totum jus et clamium quod habuerint, vel habere potuerint, in haya nostra de Akwod; scilicet ab exitu villæ de Sandhou per divisas Petri de Vallibus usque Kirkeburn; et de Kirkeburn descendendo usque ad molendinum de Akum. Concesserunt etiam nobis iidem canonici quod non reclamabunt, neque contradicent de cætero, pro aliquo assarto quod hucusque fecimus inter Hextildesham et Doteland, vel alibi; vel quod fecimus, vel facturi sumus nos, vel successores nostri, ultra Doteland. Præterea dedimus et concessimus eisdem canonicis quoddam molendinum, quod de novo construximus super magnum rivulum inter Doteland et villam de Rulei, cum tota multura hominum nostrorum de Eskinseles, et omnium hominum manentium in omnibus assartis nostris, jam factis, vel in futuro faciendis, in australi parte de Tine, excepta tota Alwentedal cum omnibus ad eam pertinentibus: tenendum de nobis et successoribus nostris ad feodi-firmam pro decem marcis nobis et successoribus nostris annuatim ad prædictos terminos reddendis. Et si forte processu temporis idem locus fuerit minus congruus ad molendinum, liceat eis alibi super eundem rivulum molendinum construere, ubi magis sibi viderint expedire, per consilium nostrum et successorum nostrorum, vel capitalis senescalli nostri. Et ut hæc, etc. Data apud Knarreburg, pridie nonas Augusti, anno xj.

II.

Omnibus, etc. Noveritis nos dedisse —— Deo et Sancto Andreæ Hextold', et canonicis ibidem Deo servientibus, omnia amerciamenta, et omnes escaetas quas habuimus vel habere solebamus de hominibus eorumdem canonicorum, quando justitiarii nostri itinerantes placita in partibus illis tenere solebant; scilicet quandocumque dominus rex justitiarios suos itinerantes in Norhumbriam destinaverit ad placitandum. Ita quod omnia placita quæ coram justitiariis solebant teneri, in curia eorumdem canonicorum ad hostium ecclesiæ, de cætero teneantur in curia nostra coram justitiariis nostris; et quod una sit curia de hominibus nostris et suis, et amerciamenta hominum suorum ponantur per justitiarios nostrorum de consilio Prioris, secundum quantitatem delicti, et salvo wanagio et contenemento suo. Et ipsi canonici ea de eisdem hominibus suis recipiant per manum ballivorum suorum. Pro hac autem donatione et concessione dabunt nobis et successoribus nostris, ipsi, et successores sui in perpetuum, duodecim marcas argenti, quotienscumque justitiarii nostri, vel successores nostrorum, in partibus illis prædicto modo placita tenebunt. Et ut hæc, etc. Data quæ prius.

III.

Omnibus, etc., Noveritis nos, caritatis intuitu, dedisse —— Deo, et ecclesiæ Beati Andreæ de Hext', et canonicis ibidem Deo servientibus, lxiiij acras, quæ jacent inter villam de Doteland et e(s)sartum eorum de Tirsterl; tenendas et habendas de nobis et successoribus nostris in perpetuum in puram et perpetuam elemosinam, cum omnibus communibus, libertatibus et aysiamentis, scilicet, in communibus, boscis, et pasturis, sicut aliqua elemosina liberius et quietius dari vel possideri potest. Et ut hæc, etc. Data quæ prius.

IV.

Omnibus, etc., Noveritis nos, Divinæ pietatis intuitu, concessisse Deo et Beato Andreæ de Hextold, et dilectis filiis Priori et canonicis ibidem Deo servientibus, omnes decimas et decimationes tam bladi quam leguminis in omnibus essartis, quæ vel nos, vel homines nostri fecimus, vel in futuro faciemus ubicumque, in Hextoldsira. Et ut hæc, etc. Data quæ prius.

XIV.—A DEED FROM THE PRIOR AND CONVENT OF HEXHAM RELATING TO SOME EXCHANGES BETWEEN THEM AND ARCHBISHOP GRAY. [MSS. Cotton, Claudius, B, iii., 43 *b*.]

Omnibus ad quos præsens scriptum[w] pervenerit, Bernardus, Prior de Hextildesham, et ejusdem loci Conventus salutem in Domino. Noverit universitas vestra nos recepisse a venerabili patre nostro, domino Waltero Ebor. archiepiscopo, Angliæ primate, de dono et concessione ejusdem, septies viginti et quinque acras terræ et dimidiam; de quibus quadraginta acræ jacent inter villam de Ainewik et haiam suam de Acwde versus aquilonem; et quater viginti et decem acræ desuper Doteland versus austrum; et quindecim acræ et dimidia subtus Doteland

[w] This deed must be taken in connection with the preceding number. There is a copy of it in the Reg. Magn. Album, part ii., 51 *b*.

versus aquilonem; tenendas et habendas de ipso domino archiepiscopo et successoribus suis in perpetuum, libere et quiete; reddendo sibi et successoribus suis quatuor marcas argenti per annum, pro omni servitio et exactione, medietatem ad festum Sancti Martini, et medietatem ad Pentecosten. Præterea concessit nobis unam viam ab exitu villæ nostræ de Aynewik, per medium haiæ suæ de Acwde, a bercaria nostra directe versus aquilonem, usque ad communem pasturam nostram ultra Birkburn, quæ quidem continet in latitudine decem perticas. Pro hac autem donatione et concessione remisimus ei et successoribus, pro nobis, et successoribus, et hominibus nostris in perpetuum, totum jus et clameum quod habuimus vel habere potuimus in haia sua de Acwode; scilicet, ab exitu villæ de Sandhow per divisas Petri de Val(l)ibus usque ad Kirkeburn; et de Kirkeburn descendendo usque ad molendinum de Akum. Concessimus etiam eidem domino archiepiscopo quod non reclamabimus neque contradicemus de cætero pro aliquo essarto quod hucusque fecit inter Hextildesham et Doteland, vel alibi, vel quod fecit, vel etiam facturus est ipse vel successores sui, ultra Doteland. Præterea dedit nobis et concessit quoddam molendinum quod de novo construxit super magnum rivulum inter Doteland et villam de Ruley, cum tota multura hominum suorum de Eskinschell, et omnium hominum suorum manentium in omnibus essartis suis jam factis, vel in futuro faciendis, in australi parte de Tine, excepta tota Alwentedale, cum omnibus ad eam pertinentibus: tenendum de ipso et successoribus in perpetuum ad feodi-firmam pro decem marcis, sibi et successoribus suis annuatim ad prædictos terminos reddendis. Et si forte processu temporis idem locus fuerit minus congruus ad molendinum, liceat nobis alibi super eundem rivulum molendinum construere, ubi nobis viderimus magis expedire, per consilium suum, vel successorum suorum, vel capitalis senescalli sui. Protestamur etiam quod in haia ejusdem domini archiepiscopi de Westwod nichil juris vendicamus, nec de cætero quicquam in ea vendicare poterimus. Ne igitur hæc in posterum in dubium possint converti, præsenti scripto sigilla nostra apposuimus. Testibus domino Nicholao quondam Manniæ et Insularum episcopo, magistris Ricardo cancellario, Godardo pœnitentiario, et Waltero de Taney, canonicis Ebor., Willelmo capellano, et Ada de Stavel, canonicis Suwell, Petro de Vallibus, Willelmo de Widindon, Petro Hareng', Ada Bertram, Rogero de Bingfeld, Thoma de Wytington, et multis aliis. Dat' apud Knaresburg, nonis Augusti, anno Domini m° cc° vicesimo sexto.

XV.—TWO GRANTS TO THE PRIOR AND CONVENT OF HEXHAM FROM ARCHBISHOP GRAY. [Ex Rot. Majore archiep. Gray. In dorso, Nos. 48, 49.]

Omnibus, etc. Noverit universitas vestra nos caritatis intuitu dedisse, concessisse, et præsenti carta nostra confirmasse Deo et ecclesiæ Beati Andreæ de Hextold', et canonicis ibidem Deo servientibus, in liberam et perpetuam elemosinam, ad emendationem firmæ quam nobis solverunt pro molendino quod de nobis tenent prope Doteland, sexaginta acras terræ, quæ jacent inter villam de Doteland et assartum eorum de Torneby, infra istas divisas; scilicet, inter Ormes-lecche et Smaleburne et Thysterley-burne, et prædictum assartum eorum de Torneby. Et, præterea, dedimus eis, et concessimus, et præsenti carta nostra confirmavimus, in liberam et perpetuam elemosinam, xxxiiij acras terræ residuas, quæ jacent infra easdem divisas, cum omnibus pertinentiis suis, libertatibus, et aysiamentis in boscis, et pasturis, et omnibus aliis communibus, solvendo nobis et successoribus de eisdem xxxiiij acris undecim solidos et quatuor denarios per annum, scilicet pro qualibet acra iiij denarios. Habendum et tenendum de nobis et successoribus nostris, libere et quiete ab omni servitio et exactione et demanda, prædictam tantummodo firmam reddendo. Et ut hæc, etc. T., etc. Data apud Hextold', ij kalendas Septembris, anno pontificatus nostri quartodecimo.

II.

Omnibus, etc., ——. Deo et ecclesiæ Sancti Andreæ de Hext', et canonicis ibidem Deo servientibus, in liberam et perpetuam elemosinam, duodecies viginti et quinque acras terræ inter Langhop et Elrinton; reddendo inde annuatim nobis et successoribus nostris pro qualibet acra quatuor denarios. Dedimus etiam eisdem, et concessimus, et præsenti carta nostra confirmavimus sibi, in liberam et perpetuam elemosinam, quadraginta acras terræ in eodem loco, reddendo inde annuatim nobis et successoribus nostris pro qualibet acra duos denarios. Et, præterea, dedimus eis —— viginti acras terræ in eodem loco pro decimis omnium dominicorum fœnorum nostrorum in Hexthansire ——. Nos autem, et successores nostri, prædictam terram cum pertinentiis suis contra omnes homines eis perpetuo warantamus et defendimus, nec de cætero terram aliquam dabimus nos vel successores nostri, nec ad firmam . . . . inter prædictam terram et villam de Catteden, sine eorum assensu et voluntate. Data apud Hext', per manum magistri Simonis, kalendis Septembris, anno quartodecimo.

XVI.—A LEASE OF THE DEMESNE LANDS AT HEXHAM, GRANTED BY ARCHBISHOP GRAY TO THE PRIOR AND CONVENT. [Ex Rot. Majore archiep. Gray. In dorso, No. 64.]

Anno gratiæ millesimo ducentesimo tricesimo secundo, ad Pentecosten, facta est hæc conventio inter dominum W. archiepiscopum Ebor., ex una parte, et Priorem et Conventum de Hextold', ex altera: scilicet, quod prædictus dominus archiepiscopus concessit et dimisit dictis Priori et Conventui totum dominicum suum de Hextold', infra culturas subscriptas contentum, ad firmam, usque ad terminum xv annorum. Videlicet, in magna cultura, inter dominicum mansum domini archiepiscopi et Tynam, lxij acras de avena seminatas: in cultura juxta Tynam, inter villam et hospitale, sex acras de frumento seminatas; in Heyning-croft quindecim acras de frumento seminatas: in cultura de Widhalc viginti acras de frumento seminatas: in cultura juxta fontem Sancti Andreæ, ex aquilonali parte exitus villæ, sex acras et dimidiam de siligine seminatas: in aquilonali parte Tyne, juxta pontem, quatuor acras de siligine seminatas: in occidentali et orientali parte pontis super Tynam novem acras de avena seminatas: in cultura juxta Harestan, in australi parte exitus de Preste-poffel, septem acras de avena seminatas: in australi parte de Preste-poffel, in una cultura, quinquaginta acras de terra wareccanda, cum precariis carucarum et herciarum, et cum messionibus et operibus autumpnalibus; et cum pastura ad sexdecim boves in Acwod; et cum estoveriis (?) ad tractus boum duarum carucarum in Westwod, per visum forestariorum capiendis; et cum omnibus aliis pertinentiis et aisiamentis ad dictum dominicum spectantibus, exceptis pratis dominicis, a festo Purificationis Beatæ Mariæ, quousque fœna carientur; reddendo inde annuatim pro qualibet acra frumentali et siliginosa apud Hext' unam tawam de frumento ejusdem terræ, vento et cribro pacabiliter purgato: et pro qualibet avenosa unam tawam farinæ pacabilem; medietatem ad Annuntiationem Beatæ Mariæ, et medietatem ad festum Sancti Johannis Baptistæ, pro omnibus aliis servitiis, consuetudinibus, et demandis. Completo igitur termino quindecim annorum, prædicti Prior et Conventus prædictum dominicum cum vestura tantummodo, sicut illud receperunt; et cum tanta terra wareccata, quantam receperunt wareccatam, domino archiepiscopo restituent. Si vero prædicti Prior et Conventus per werram, vel aliquo alio modo, per defectum archiepiscopi aliquid in dicto dominico amiserint, omnia perdita et dampna infra firmam proximo a Priore et Conventu pacandam, et in vestura restituenda, plene et integre computabunt per considerationem proborum virorum et legalium. Ut igitur hæc conventio, etc.

XVII.—TWO DEEDS RELATING TO BYRES, BETWEEN THE PRIOR AND CONVENT OF HEXHAM AND THE PRIORESS AND NUNS OF LAMBLEY. [MSS. Dodsworth, xlix., 25 *a*.]

I.

Anno gratiæ m° cc° xxxix°,[a] ad festum Sancti Martini. Noverit universitas fidelium quod hæc est conventio facta inter Priorem et Conventum de Hextild' ex una parte, Conventum et Priorissam Sanctimonialium de Lambeley, ex altera: scilicet, quod prædicti Prior et Conventus concesserunt, et præsenti scripto confirmaverunt, præfatis Priorissæ et Sanctimonialibus communiam pasturæ harbagii, cum ipsis et eorum tenentibus, ad averia sua propria infra divisas tenementi illorum de Byres nominatas et subscriptas; scilicet, de Maydene-gate per Blake-burne ascendendo usque ad Moriley-burne; et sic, ascendendo per Moriley-burne, usque ad Moriley-burn-heued. Et inde extra boscum, directe ex transverso moræ, versus austrum, usque in Glendewe, per divisas petrosas juxta Glendew positas. Et per Glendew descendendo usque in Maydene-gate; et sic per Maydene-gate versus aquilonem usque ad Blake-burne prius nominatum. Ita quod prædictæ Moniales, vel earum servientes, nichil capiant, vel aliquod dampnum in bosco prædictorum Prioris et Conventus alicubi faciant. Habendum et tenendum prædictis Priorissæ et Monialibus de præfatis Priore et Conventu ad feodi-firmam, reddendo inde annuatim præfatis Priori et Conventui, in recognitione hujus concessionis et gratiæ, unam tualiam decentem ad cameram Prioris die Sancti Andreæ apud Hextild'. Prædicta vero Priorissa fecit eisdem Priori et Conventui fidelitatem super præmissis, quod et ejus successores

[a] These two deeds, which are of the same date, were copied by Dodsworth on August 27th, 1639, from the muniments of Albany Fetherstonhaugh of Fetherstonhaugh, esq. There are transcripts of them in MSS. Lansd., cccxxvi., 79-80. See Hodgson's Northumberland, iii., part ii., 94.

The following document relates to the same place. "Anno gratiæ m° cc° lxxxv^{to}, die Sancti Petri ad Vincula, Sanctimoniales, fœmina Priorissa et Conventus de Lambeley, dimiserunt pro se et successoribus suis, quod Prior et Conventus de Hextildesham murum suum construant quotiens—necesse fuerit; quocumque casu dirutum, reædificent, etc., incipiendo, etc. Et pro hac concesserunt prædicti Prior et Conventus de Hextildesham, quod si averia prædictarum Sanctimonialium per escampium ultra rivulum de Morileyburne usque ad murum quem super eundem rivulum, etc. Testibus Thoma de Fetherstanhalch, Willelmo de Kellawe, Roberto de Boceland, Gilberto capellano, Uctred tunc serviente de Lambelly, Henrico del Syde tunc serviente del Byres, et aliis" (MSS. Lansdowne, cccxxvi., 80 *a*).

similiter facient. His testibus magistro A. archidiacono Northumbriæ, Henrico decano de Novo Castro, Hugone vicario de Ovingeham, Ricardo filio Alexandri ballivo de Hextildesham, Adam de Thirlewall, Thoma de Fetherstonhalt, Adam de Elrington, Hugone de Calflawe, Rannulfo de Blenkenehop, Johanne de Yngehowe, Richardo filio Thurstini, Roberto Mariscallo, Roberto de Elrington, et aliis.

II.

A., Priorissa et Conventus Sanctimonialium de Lambeleya salutem. Ad universitatis vestræ volumus devenire notitiam quod cum nos, ex mera liberalitate et permissione Prioris et Canonicorum de Hextildesham, aliquando habuimus aysiamenta pasturæ ad averia nostra intra divisas terrarum suarum de Byres, nos, liberalitate eorum et permissione ingratæ nullatenus existere volentes, recognoscimus, quod nullum jus vel clameum infra divisas terrarum prædictorum Prioris et Canonicorum habemus, nec debemus habere, nisi de mera eorum gratia et benignitate. Testibus magistro A. archidiacono Northumber', Henrico decano de Novo Castro, Hugone vicario de Ovingeham, Ricardo filio Alexandri ballivo de Hextildesham, Ada de Thirlewall, Thoma de Fetherstanhalt, Ada de Elrington, Hugone de Calflawe, Ranulfo de Blenkenehope, Johanne de Ynghowe, Ricardo filio Thurstini, Roberto Mariscallo, Roberto de Elrington, et aliis.

XVIII.—LICENCE FROM BERNARD, PRIOR OF HEXHAM, AND HIS CONVENT TO PETER AND ROBERT DE INSULA, AUTHORIZING THEM TO HAVE A CHANTRY AT CHIPCHASE. [MSS. Lansd., cccxxvi., 42 *b*.]

Nos B.,[y] Prior, et Conventus Haug', concessimus domino Petro de Insula et Roberto, filio ejus, et hæredibus suis, habere perpetuam cantariam in capella de Chipches, quolibet altero die in septimana, per unum capellanum, sumptibus matris ecclesiæ de Chelvertona; salvis in omnibus jure et indempnitate ejusdem matris ecclesiæ, secundum usum et consuetudinem archidiaconatus. Prædicti vero Petrus et Robertus, et eorum hæredes, omnia necessaria ad administrationem dictæ capellæ competentia, sufficienter in omnibus et per omnia, providebunt et invenient, exceptis capellano tantummodo et clerico. Testibus

[y] Dodsworth found this deed in the Chipchase box, among the deeds of Mr Heron, the owner of that place. On Sunday after the feast of St. Denis, 1348, Robert de Insula of Chipchase, clerk, quit-claimed to Sir William Heron of Ford, knight, all his interest in the manor of Chipchase.

domino S. abbate de Novo Monasterio, magistro H de Stanbrig rectore ecclesiæ de Stanfordham, magistro Abel rectore ecclesiæ de Symondburne, domino Othvero de Insula, Willelmo vicario de Biwell, Willelmo de Sancto Johanne, Symone de Hext', Willelmo capellano de Haydon, capellanis, Willelmo de Gunwarton, clerico, ... , et aliis.

XIX.—TWO DEEDS RELATING TO PROPERTY AT EDSTON BETWEEN THE PRIOR AND CONVENT OF HEXHAM AND THE PRIOR AND CONVENT OF MALTON. [Ex cartulario de Malton, MSS. Cotton, Vesp., D, xi., 114 *a*, *b*.]

I.

Omnibus[z]—Bernardus Prior, et Conventus Haugustald', salutem in Domino. Noveritis nos remisisse, et quietam clamasse Priori et Conventui Malton omnimodam exactionem de quibuscunque servitiis, ad quæ Willelmus filius Willelmi de Redeburn sex bovatas terræ in Minori Edeston per cartam suam nobis confectam obligaverat. Quas quidem bovatas idem Prior et Conventus Malton tenuit ex ipsius Willelmi dono jure perpetuo, cassata penitus omni objectione quam super prædictis servitiis movere possimus in perpetuum. In cujus, etc.

II.

Sciant universi—quod cum discordia esset mota inter Priorem et Conventum Malton, ex una parte petentes, et Priorem et Conventum de Haugustaldensem, et suos comparticipes, ex altera, tenentes, super pastura quadam, quæ dicitur Mariscus, jacente inter terram arabilem Majoris Edeston et pratum Minoris Edeston; et super quadam alia pastura jacente inter Colebecsike et terram arabilem Parvæ Edeston, sub hac forma sopita est. Videlicet, quod Prior et Conventus Haugustaldensis, et sui comparticipes, remiserunt a se et successoribus suis in perpetuum Priori et Conventui Malton, et suis successoribus, modicam illam pasturam quæ jacet inter Colebec-sike et terram arabilem Minoris Edeston, sine omni calumpnia in futurum. Ad pacis autem perpetuæ hinc inde conservationem, dimidiabitur alia pastura, jacens inter terram arabilem Majoris Edeston et pratum prædictum, simul cum tota terra arabili usque ad aquam de Dune versus occidentem linealiter inter partes prædictas adjecta medietati Prioris et Conventus Haugustaldensis

[z] The first of these deeds is endorsed *Quieta clamatio Prioris et Conventus Hagustaldensis de quibusdam exactionibus:* the second, *Compositio inter nos et Priorem et Conventum Haugustaldensem.*

et comparticipum suorum, de medietate Prioris et Conventus dimidia acra pasturæ. Hanc vero pasturam, simul cum terra arabili, poterunt partes prædictæ, vel altera, quæ voluerit, fossato includere, et ea uti pro sua voluntate. Concessit autem prædictus Prior Haugustaldensis, et sui comparticipes, prædicto Priori Malton, et suis successoribus, viam sufficientem ad occursum duarum bigarum onustarum, ex parte meridionali fossati Parvæ Edeston, ab egressu Parvæ Edeston versus meridiem usque ad Colbe-syck, eundo et redeundo versus pratum et pasturam Parvæ Edeston. Ita quod prædictus Prior et Canonici Malton facient fossatum novum sumptibus propriis, ab exitu villæ Edeston usque ad Colebec-sycke, ex australi parte prædictæ viæ. Pro concessione autem superius contentorum concessit Prior Malton, pro se et successoribus suis, adquietare Priorem et Conventum Haugustaldensem, et suos successores, de servitiis omnimodis, consuetudinibus, et exactionibus septem bovatarum terræ, quas habent de dono Willelmi filii Willelmi de Redburn: ad quarum defensionem assignavit dictus Prior Malton Willelmum de Kirkeby le Romayn, qui onus istud super se et hæredes suos suscepit, omnes terras suas, res, et possessiones, quas tempore hujus confectionis instrumenti habuit in Magna Edeston, et in Kirkeby Misperton, et alibi ubicunque terras habuit, obligando. Dicti autem Priores, pro se et Conventibus suis, bona fide concesserunt pacem mutuam inter se imperpetuum observandam de omnibus possessionibus, terris,— unde fuerunt in possessione tempore hujus scripti confectionis; cassatis omnibus quicquam pars altera possit objicere super prædictis in perpetuum. —— Acta apud Ebor. comitatum, anno gratiæ m° cc° xlij°, in octabis Sancti Michaelis, in præsentia domini H de Batho', tunc vicecomitis Eboracensis. Hiis testibus, etc.

XX.—A GRANT OF LAND FROM JOHN, THE PRIOR, AND THE CONVENT OF HEXHAM TO JOHN, SON OF RICHARD OF EAST SWINBURNE. [Ex MSS. Hodgson.]

Sciant præsentes et futuri quod ego Johannes, Prior, et Conventus Augustaldensis,[a] communi consilio Conventus nostri dedimus —— Johanni filio Ricardi de Swyneburne Orientali, pro homagio et servitio suo, totam terram nostram, cum capitali mesuagio quam Ricardus Fossator de nobis quondam tenuit: et totam terram nostram, cum tofto et crofto quam Sampson de

[a] Taken from the MSS. of Mr. Hodgson, the historian of Northumberland, who found the charter at Capheaton among the evidences of Sir John Swinburne.

Suyneburne de nobis aliquando tenuit in eadem villa: et totam terram nostram de Steldene cum pert. ——; excepta bercaria nostra de Steldene, et pastura nostra in mora de Gunewarton, sicut carta Abbatis de Novo Monasterio, quam inde habemus, testatur:—cum libero introitu et exitu ad oves nostras ad prædictam bercariam commorantes. Reddendo annuatim xls. et xijd.—Faciendo forinsecum servitium, quantum ad prædictas terras pertinet. Hiis testibus dominis Hugone de Bolebeck, Roberto de Insula, Thoma de Oggil, Thoma de Fennewyke militibus, Johanne de Swyneburne Occidentali, Waltero de Suetehope, Willelmo de Colewelle, et aliis.

XXI.—AN AGREEMENT BETWEEN ARCHBISHOP GRAY AND THE PRIOR AND CONVENT OF HEXHAM. [MSS. Cotton, Claudius, B, iii., 92 *b*, et Reg. Magnum Album, pars iii., 11 *a*.]

Notum sit omnibus præsentes literas visuris vel audituris,[b] quod cum contentio mota esset inter venerabilem patrem, dominum Walterum Ebor. archiepiscopum, Angliæ primatem, et Priorem et Conventum de Extoldesham, super quibusdam libertatibus quas idem Prior et Conventus dicebant ad se pertinere, tandem eadem controversia sub hoc fine quievit. Quod cum dictus dominus archiepiscopus miserit ballivos suos ad tenendum assisas suas apud Extoldesham, eligentur ab eisdem ballivis xij liberi et legales homines de manerio et de soca de Extoldesham; qui, jurati, veredictum suum facient de omnibus placitis quæ emerserint in manerio illo, et in soka, tam de terris archiepiscopi quam de terris Prioris et Conventus, ad Coronam spectantibus. Et (si) per illorum veredictum aliqua placita emerserint, quæ pertineant ad aliquos de hominibus Prioris et Conventus, ballivus Prioris et Conventus, vel canonicus ad hoc deputatus, exiget curiam ad ostium ecclesiæ: et hoc concedetur ei de omnibus hominibus Prioris et Conventus super omnibus placitis spectantibus ad Coronam quæ contra eos emerserint. Dabitur ei ad hoc dies certus ad prædictum locum. Finitis vero as(s)isis de hominibus archiepiscopi, ballivi archiepiscopi venient ad ostium ecclesiæ, et ibi placitabunt placita pertinentia ad homines Prioris et Conventus. Cum autem contigerit aliquos homines eorum esse amerciandos, amerciabuntur per sacramentum sex legalium hominum ex parte archiepiscopi, et sex legalium hominum ex parte Prioris et Conventus, salvo continemento et waynagio rusticorum; quæ videlicet amerciamenta pertinebunt ad archiepiscopum qui pro tempore fuerit.

[b] A very curious compact between the two great authorities at Hexham about the holding of assizes and trials there.

XXII.—A LICENCE FROM HENRY III. FOR THE PRIOR AND CONVENT OF HEXHAM TO ACQUIRE THE MANOR OF NESBIT. [Rot. Chart., 39th Hen. III., m. 2.]

Rex archiepiscopis, etc., salutem. Sciatis nos concessisse et confirmasse Deo et ecclesiæ Sancti Andreæ de Hextildesham, et canonicis ibidem Deo servientibus, donationes subscriptas eis factas: videlicet, de dono et concessione Johannis de Normanvile et Roberti de Insula, totum manerium de Nesebyte, cum omnibus pertinentiis suis et libertatibus, in dominicis, homagiis, servitiis, custodiis, releviis, et cum omnibus escaetis suis, sine aliquo retinemento; et, de redditione et assignatione Walteri filii Walteri de Nesebyte, totum jus et clamium quod idem Walterus, vel hæredes sui unquam habuerint, vel habere potuerint, in manerio prædicto, cum pertinentiis, sine aliquo retinemento; sicut cartæ prædictorum Johannis, Roberti, et Walteri, et confirmatio Johannis de Bayllol, quas prædicti canonici inde habent, rationabiliter testantur. Quare volumus et concedimus, pro nobis et hæredibus nostris, quod prædicti canonici, et eorum successores, in perpetuum habeant et teneant manerium prædictum, cum omnibus pertinentiis suis, sicut prædictæ cartæ et confirmatio prædicta rationabiliter testantur. Hiis testibus Willelmo de Fortibus comite Albemarl, Hugone le Bygod, Stephano de Mennyl, Johanne de Lexinton, Rogero Bertram de Mitford, Willelmo de Grey, Fulcone filio Warini, Bartholomeo le Bygod, Willelmo Gernum, et aliis. Data per manum nostram, apud Novum-Castrum-super-Tynam, xxv die Septembris (1255).

XXIII.—AN ORDINATION OF THE PARISH CHURCH OF HEXHAM. [Reg. archiep. Romani, 92 *b*.]

Universis pateat per præsentes quod nos, Johannes de Craucumbe, officialis curiæ Ebor., Robertus de Pikering, et Robertus de la Ford, clerici venerabilis patris, domini J., Dei gratia Eboracensis archiepiscopi, etc., in capella Beatæ Mariæ apud Hextildesham de tota libertate ejusdem visitationis et inquisitionis officium, vice et auctoritate prædicti patris, die Lunæ proximo ante festum Beati Cuthberti in Septembri, anno gratiæ m° cc° octogesimo sexto debite exercentes, ea quæ in capitulis corrigenda erant justitia correximus exigente. Et, inter cætera, per decretum pronuntiavimus statuendo, quod parochiani ecclesiæ Augustaldensis teneantur de cætero omnes capellas libertatis et parochiæ ejusdem, præter presbiterium seu cancellum earumdem capellarum, (quarum cancelli reparatio seu constructio ad Priorem et Canonicos de Hextildesham debet pertinere,) quotiens opus fuerit, construere et reparare, seu etiam reformare. Inveniendo in eisdem capellis Missale et calicem sub pœna c solidorum, pro parte parochianorum, et quadraginta solidorum, pro parte Prioris et Conventus, domino archiepiscopo solvendorum, si præmissa non fecerint, ut tenentur. In cujus rei testimonium sigillum prædicti patris præsentibus est appensum. Data apud Hextildesham, iij idus Septembris, anno gratiæ supradicto, et pontificatus ejusdem patris primo.

XXIV.—LICENCE FROM EDWARD I. FOR THE PRIOR AND CONVENT OF HEXHAM TO ACQUIRE LANDS IN NORTH MILBURN. [Rot. Pat., 13th Edward I., membr. 19.]

Rex omnibus ad quos, etc., salutem. Licet de communi consilio regni nostri providerimus, quod non liceat viris religiosis, seu aliis, ingredi feodum alicujus, ita quod ad mortuam manum deveniat, sine licentia nostra, et capitalis domini, de quo res illa immediate tenetur; volentes, tamen, dilecto et fideli nostro Thomæ de Develeston gratiam facere specialem, dedimus ei licentiam, quantum in nobis est, quod viginti libratas terræ cum pertinentiis in North-milneburn dare possit et assignare dilectis nobis in Christo Priori et Conventui de Hextildesham, tenendas et habendas sibi et successoribus suis imperpetuum; et eisdem Priori et Conventui, quod prædictas viginti libratas terræ ab eodem Thoma recipere possint, tenore præsentium similiter licentiam concedimus specialem. Nolentes quod idem Thomas, seu prædicti Prior et Conventus, ratione statuti prædicti, per nos vel hæredes nostros inde occasionentur in aliquo vel graventur; salvis tamen capitalibus dominis feodi illius servitiis inde debitis et consuetis. In cujus, etc. Teste rege apud Westmonasterium, vicesimo quinto die Maii (1285).

XXV.—A GRANT OF FREE WARREN FROM EDWARD I. TO THE PRIOR AND CONVENT OF HEXHAM IN THEIR ESTATES AT BYRES, WARDEN, MATFEN, ETC. [Rot. Chart., 14th Edward I., n. 13.]

Rex archiepiscopis, etc., salutem. Sciatis nos concessisse, et hac carta nostra confirmasse dilectis nobis in Christo Priori et Conventui de Hextildesham, quod ipsi, et eorum successores imperpetuum, habeant liberam warennam in omnibus dominicis terris suis de Byres, Wardon, Matfenn, Colden, Cheseburgh, et Milneburn in comitatu Norhumbriæ, et in omnibus dominicis terris suis de Saulton, et Broghton in comitatu Ebor.; dum tamen terræ illæ non sint infra metas forestæ nostræ. Ita quod nullus intret terras illas ad fugandum in eis, vel ad aliquid capiendum quod ad warrennam pertineat, sine licentia et voluntate ipsorum Prioris et Conventus, vel successorum suorum, super forisfacturam nostram decem librarum. Quare volumus, etc., dum tamen, etc., ita, etc., super forisfacturam nostram decem librarum, sicut prædictum est. Hiis testibus venerabilibus patribus R Bathon. et Wellenn., G. Wygorn., et W. Norwycensi episcopis, Edmundo fratre nostro, Willelmo de Valencia avunculo nostro, Edmundo comite Cornubiæ, Gilberto de Clare comite Glouc' et Hereford, Henrico de Lacy comite Linc', Rogero de Bigod comite Norff. et mariscallo Angliæ, Roberto filio Johannis, Petro de Chaumpvent, et aliis. Data per manum, apud Westmonasterium, xxviij die Aprilis (1286).

XXVI.—AN AGREEMENT BETWEEN ARCHBISHOP ROMANUS AND THE PRIOR AND CONVENT OF HEXHAM ABOUT DIVERS LANDS AND PRIVILEGES. [MSS. Lansd., ccccii., 14 *a*, *b*.]

Omnibus Christi fidelibus hoc scriptum visuris vel audituris, Johannes, permissione Divina Ebor. archiepiscopus, Angliæ primas, salutem in Domino. Noverit universitas vestra nos dedisse, concessisse, et hoc præsenti scripto nostro confirmasse Deo et ecclesiæ Sancti Andreæ de Hextildesham, et Priori et Canonicis ibidem Deo servientibus, xxxv acras et unam rodam terræ jacentes juxta terram suam in campo de Dottelande, et duas de wasto nostro versus parcariam suam, ad includendum, et in suo seperali omnibus diebus anni retinendum; reddendo nobis et successoribus nostris annuatim pro prædictis triginta quinque acris et una roda terræ firmam inde debitam et consuetam, videlicet xjs. et ix denarios; et pro prædictis duabus acris de wasto viijd., scilicet medietatem ad Pentecosten, et aliam medietatem ad festum Sancti Martini in hyeme, pro omni alio servitio et demanda: videlicet, quod pro qualibet acra quatuor denarios, sicut aliæ terræ ibidem censuales, reddunt. Dedimus etiam eisdem Priori et Canonicis xv acras et tres rodas de vasto nostro, quæ jacent circa grangias suas de Dotteland, in escambium pro quindecim acris et tribus rodis terræ suæ arabilis, quas nobis et successoribus nostris dederunt: quæ quidem quindecim acræ et tres rodæ terræ jacent in orientali parte terræ suæ in eadem villa de Dotteland, propinquiores terræ nostræ de Wardelake. Concessimus autem eidem Priori et Canonicis quod ipsi includant et includere possint quandam partem terræ suæ in Dotteland, et prædictas xxxv acras et unam rodam terræ, simul cum prædictis xv acris et tribus rodis vasti, et eas in soli *(sic)* seperali omnibus temporibus anni teneant, per divisas subscriptas: videlicet, incipiendo a superiori parte culturæ Prioris quæ vocatur Erdeley, versus orientem, usque ad terram nostram de Ewardes-lawe; et sic, descen(den)do versus aquilonem, per sykettum ex orientali parte ejusdem, usque in Thrysteley-burn; et de Thristeley-burn, ascendendo ex parte boriali, versus occidentem usque ad parcum ipsius Prioris ex occidentali parte; et sic, ex transverso, versus austrum ex occidentali parte grangiarum ejusdem Prioris, usque ad superiorem partem culturæ de Erdeley prænominata. Præterea concedimus, pro nobis et successoribus nostris, quod prædicti Prior et Canonici includant grangias suas in Prioratu suo et tofta vasta juxta easdem, circuiendo culturam suam quæ vocatur le Seel; et sequendo rivulum a porta sua australi usque ad torrellum suum prædicti Prioratus; reddendo nobis et successoribus nostris annuatim pro prædictis toftis quatuor solidos, ijd. et ob. argenti ad prædictos terminos pro aliis servitiis omnibus, operatiônibus, auxiliis, tallagiis, et demandis. Et quia accepimus per sollempnem inquisitionem, quam fieri fecimus per sacramentum quatuor hominum de libertate nostra de Hextildesham, quod prædicti Prior et Canonici habere debent, et prædecessores sui habere consueverunt tres gurgites in stagno molendini sui de Extildesham, a tempore quo non exstat memoria, concedimus eis quod habeant de cætero duos gurgites in stagno prædicto; ita tamen quod non exaltant prædictum per quod molendina nostra in aliquo disturbentur vel deteriorentur. Et iidem Prior et Canonici concesserunt quod plures gurgites quam duos de cætero ibidem non habebunt nec clamabunt. Volumus etiam et concedimus quod libere possint piscari in aqua de Tyne, ubicunque piscatores nostri piscari possunt, prout in cartis prædecessorum nostrorum plenius continetur; et quod habeant quoddam molendinum suum le Hame-burn, et quandam placeam juxta molendinum suum de Hextildesham, quæ vocatur le Staneres, prout per prædictam inquisitionem invenimus quod habuerunt et habere consueverunt, sine impedimento nostri, aut successorum nostrorum. Præterea concedimus, pro nobis et successoribus nostris, et præsenti scripto confirmavimus eisdem Priori et Canonicis omnes alias terras, tenementa et possessiones suas, quas habuerunt die confectionis hujus scripti, de dono prædecessorum nostrorum, seu aliorum quorumcunque in Hextildescham-schire, in perpetuam elemosinam, sicut cartæ suæ et feoffamenta sua rationabiliter testantur; salvis tamen nobis et successoribus nostris servitiis inde debitis et consuetis. Et pro hac donatione, concessione, et confirmatione, prædicti Prior et Canonici dederunt nobis duo tofta jacentia juxta manerium suum de Hextildesham, ad dilatationem ejusdem manerii nostri; ita tamen quod habeant quandam viam sufficientem in prædictis toftis ad ducendum blada et alia necessaria sua per summagia ad molendinum suum de Tyne, quandocunque voluerint. Reddent etiam prædicti Prior et Canonici, et eorum successores de cætero, nobis et successoribus nostris annuatim, xij marcas argenti, ad terminos prædictos, pro molendino de Hameburn et terra adjacente; pro quo prius reddere solebant x marcas tantum. In cujus rei testimonium parti hujus scripti cyrographati penes prædictos Priorem et Canonicos residenti sigillum nostrum apposuimus; altera parte sigillo prædictorum Prioris et Canonicorum signata penes nos remanente. Hiis testibus dominis Johanne de Haulton, Thoma de Dyvelleston militibus, magistris Willelmo et Roberto de Pykering, Roberto de la Forda, Johanne de Lythegraynes, Waltero de Stokes, Johanne Sampson, Willelmo de Kelhou, Thoma de Fycheburn, Johanne de Insula, Roberto de Skypton ballivo, Johanne de Vallibus, Johanne de Eryngeton, et multis aliis. Datum apud Burton, quinto ydus Aprilis, anno gratiæ m° cc° lxxx° vij°, et pontificatus nostri anno secundo.

XXVII.—CITATION OF THE PRIOR AND CONVENT OF HEXHAM FOR NOT HAVING VICARS INSTITUTED IN THEIR CHURCHES. [Reg. archiep. Romani, 98 *a*.]

Officiali libertatis de Hextildesham salutem, gratiam, et benedictionem.[c] Cum non(n)ulli ecclesias, quæ per proprios consueverunt gubernari rectores, in usus eorum concessas, ut omnia quæ ex appropriatis sibi ecclesiis provenerunt absorbeant et consumant, dimittant vicariis destitutas; nos, et animarum saluti, et ecclesiarum statui diligentia, qua possumus, ex officii nostri debito prospicere cupientes, vobis injungimus, quod citetis peremptorie Priorem et Conventum de Hextildesham, quod sufficienter et legitime compareant coram nobis, vel commissionariis nostris, in nostra Ebor. ecclesia, die, etc., jura sufficientia, si quæ pro se habent, quare in ecclesiis de Hextildesham et Alwenton, nostræ jurisdictioni subjectis, curam habentibus animarum annexam, quas iidem religiosi in usus

[c] A citation issued in 1294 to require the Prior and Convent to answer for their conduct in not having vicars regularly instituted in their livings of Hexham and Alwenton. There are other documents on the same subject.

proprios optinent, non habent vicarios juxta juris exigentiam canonice institutos, præposituri, ac super præmissis, et aliis sibi objiciendis, ex officio responsuri, facturi, et recepturi quod justitia suadebit. Et nos super, etc., data, etc., supra.

XXVIII.—LICENCE FROM ARCHBISHOP CORBRIDGE FOR THE PRIOR AND CONVENT TO USE HIS QUARRY AT AKEWOOD FOR THE MILL-DAM AT HEXHAM. [Reg. archiep. Corbridge, 92 *a*.]

Suo ballivo de Hextildesham salutem, gratiam, et benedictionem. Si dilecti filii, Prior et Conventus de Hextildesham, prædecessorum nostrorum temporibus, de gratia eorumdem, aisiamentum quarreræ nostræ de Acwod, ad sustentationem stangni molendini sui de Hextildesham, habuerint, placet nobis quod, absque impedimento, aisiamentum hujusmodi habeant de gratia ista vice; proviso quod gratia hujusmodi non pro debito, sed pro gratia aliis innotescat. Vale. Data apud Cawod, iiij kalendas Novembris, pontificatus nostri anno secundo.

XXIX.—THE GREAT CHARTER OF INSPEXIMUS GRANTED BY EDWARD I. TO THE PRIOR AND CONVENT OF HEXHAM, CONFIRMING TO THEM THEIR LANDS AND POSSESSIONS IN NORTHUMBERLAND. [From the original in the possession of W. B. Beaumont, M.P.][d]

Edwardus, Dei gratia rex Angliæ, dominus Hiberniæ, et dux Aquitaniæ, archiepiscopis, episcopis, abbatibus, prioribus, comitibus, baronibus, justitiariis, vicecomitibus, præpositis, ministris, et omnibus ballivis et fidelibus suis salutem. Inspeximus quandam inquisitionem quam per dilectos et fideles nostros Guichardum de Charrun et Adam de Crokedayk nuper fieri fecimus in hæc verba.

Inquisitio facta apud Novum-Castrum-super-Tynam coram Guichardo de Charron et Adam de Crokedayke, die Veneris proxima ante festum Exaltationis S. Crucis, anno regni regis Edwardi filii regis Henrici vicesimo quinto, per Willelmum de

[d] Next to the Black Book, this is the most valuable document in this volume. The former gives the extent of the estates of the Convent; this shews how they came into its possession. It appears that the muniments of the Priory were destroyed by the Scots in 1296-7, and, to keep the canons of Hexham safe, the king issued a commission to ascertain what the lands were to which they were really entitled, and by whom they were given. This is the result of the enquiry. The document has been printed by Mr. Hodgson (vol. ii., part iii., 156-170) from a very incorrect copy, which is full of blunders.

Halton, Nicholaum de Yatteham, Willelmum de Swethop, Willelmum de Tyndal, Ricardum de Boceland, Ricardum Turpyn, Ricardum filium Alani, Willelmum de Echewyk, Thomam Fetherstanhalgh patrem, Thomam filium ejus, Robertum Mangevileyn, et Willelmum Bataillie, per breve domini regis in hæc verba.

Edwardus, Dei gratia rex Angliæ, dominus Hiberniæ, et dux Aquitaniæ, dilectis et fidelibus suis Guichardo de Charrom et Adæ de Crokedayk salutem. Quia ex querela dilectorum nobis in Christo Prioris et Conventus de Hextildesham accepimus, quod omnes cartæ et munimenta sua, per quæ ipsi et prædecessores sui terras, redditus, et tenementa ecclesiæ suæ de Hextildesham tenuerunt, nuper in invasione Prioratus illius, et diversis incendiis per Scotos ibidem nequiter perpetratis, combusta fuerunt, et consumpta; per quod eisdem Priori et Conventui, et ecclesiæ suæ prædictæ, exhæreditationis periculum de facili poterit im(m)inere: nos, statui eorundem Prioris et Conventus, ac ecclesiæ suæ prædictæ pio compatientes affectu, et eidem providere volentes in hac parte, assignavimus vos ad inquirendum per sacramentum proborum et legalium hominum de comitatibus Northumbr', Cumbr', et Ebor., per quos rei veritas melius sciri poterit, quas terras, quos redditus, et quæ tenementa idem Prior et Conventus tenuerunt tempore invasionis prædictæ, et a quo tempore, et de quibus, et per quæ servitia; et quas terras, redditus, et quæ tenementa iidem Prior et Conventus tempore prædicto tenuerunt per cartas et munimenta, et per quas cartas et quæ munimenta; et quas terras, quos redditus, et quæ tenementa tenuerunt sine cartis et munimentis; et qualiter, et quomodo, et in quibus locis terræ illæ et tenementa existunt. Et ideo vobis mandamus, quod ad certos diem et locum, quos ad hoc provideritis, inquisitionem illam faciatis, et eam distincte et aperte factam nobis sub sigillis vestris, et sigillis eorum per quos facta fuerit, sine dilatione mittatis, et hoc breve. Mandavimus enim vicecomitibus nostris comitatuum prædictorum, quod ad certos diem et locum, quos eis scire facietis, venire facient coram vobis tot et tales probos et legales homines de comitatibus prædictis, per quos rei veritas in præmissis melius sciri poterit et inquiri. In cujus rei testimonium has literas nostras fieri fecimus patentes. Teste meipso apud Westmonasterium, duodecimo die Julii, anno regni nostri vicesimo quinto.

Qui dicunt super sacramentum suum quod prædicti Prior et Conventus tenent ecclesiam de Hextildesham in proprios usus, et Prioratum suum de Hextildesham, cum omnibus suis pertinentiis, in liberam, puram, et perpetuam elemosinam, de dono domini Thome Secundi, Eboracensis archiepiscopi; et inde habuerunt cartam dicti domini Thomæ, et confirmationem capituli Eboracensis; et tenuerunt a tempore quo non extat memoria. Dicunt etiam quod tenent manerium et villam de Aynewyk, cum omnibus suis pertinentiis, et villas de Sandhou et Yaru-rigg, cum suis pertinentiis, in campis, silvis, boscis, aquis, viis, semitis, et molendino de Tyne, cum stagno ejusdem, et cum tota secta quæ ad illud pertinet, vel pertinere debet; et decimam omnium rerum tam episcopi quam aliorum infra libertatem de Hextildesham existentium, in liberam, puram, et perpetuam elemosinam, de dono domini Thomæ Secundi, Eboracensis archiepiscopi; et inde habuerunt cartam, et confirmationem capituli Eboracensis. Habent etiam, de dono prædicti domini Thomæ archiepiscopi, sok et sak, et alias libertates, videlicet emend' assissæ panis et cervisiæ; et servientes suos virgam portantes ad faciendum districtiones, summonitiones, et attachiamenta; et omnium transgressionum emendationes de tenentibus suis in curia ipsius Prioris. Tenent etiam quasdam terras in villa de Hextildesham, scilicet totum vicum integrum qui vocatur Cokeshou. Tenent etiam in eadem villa viginti et quatuor mesuagia, cum pertinentis suis, in vico qui vocatur Prestpoffel. Tenent etiam quatuordecim messuagia in vico qui dicitur Vicus Fori, cum pertinentiis. Tenent etiam in eadem villa sexdecim mesuagia, cum pertinentiis, in vico qui dicitur Hennecotes. Tenent etiam totam villam de Dotteland, cum pertinentiis, et Knitelhesell, et utramque Grotinton, cum omnibus suis pertinentiis; et decimam omnium animalium infra libertatem de Hextildesham; in liberam, puram, et perpetuam elemosinam, ex dono domini Thurstini, quondam Eborancensis archiepiscopi; et tenuerunt a tempore quo non extat memoria, sine aliquo sæculari servitio faciendo. Tenent etiam medietatem villæ de Byngefeld, cum suis pertinentiis, in liberam, puram, et perpetuam elemosinam, de dono Ger(mundi), a tempore quo non extat memoria, sine aliquo servitio sæculari faciendo; et inde habuerunt cartam. Tenent etiam sex marcatas redditus in villa prædicta de Byngefeld, in liberam, puram, et perpetuam elemosinam, ex dono Roberti de Skipton;[e] et eas tenuerunt per decem annos et amplius per feoffamentum ipsius Roberti; et inde habuerunt confirmationem domini regis nunc. Tenent etiam duo molendina aquatica, cum suis pertinentiis, in Hamburne et Neubiging, et quater-viginti acras terræ in eisdem

[e] York, 6, 27th Dec., 1289, licence for Robert, bailiff of Hexham, to give "septem mercatas terræ" to the Priory, if he can get the royal licence (Reg. archiep. Romani, 94 *b*). Skipton, for such was the donor's name, died a year or two afterwards.

villis, cum secta omnium terrarum novarum assartarum, et assartandarum, ad illa duo molendina prædicta, ex dono domini Walteri le Gray quondam Eborancencis archiepiscopi, per servitium duodecim marcarum per annum; et tenuerunt per cartam; et tenuerunt tenementa prædicta a tempore H. regis, patris domini regis nunc. Tenent etiam unam placiam, quæ continet unam rodam terræ, in villa de Akum; et unam placiam continentem unam rodam in villa de Walle; et unam placiam continentem unam rodam terræ in villa de Haliden; et unam placiam continentem unam rodam terræ in Kepwyk; et unam rodam terræ in villa de Catteden; et unam rodam terræ in villa de Ninebenk; et unam rodam terræ in villa de Rouley pro grangia decimali ædificanda, de dono dominorum Walteri Gray et Walteri Giffard, episcoporum Eboracensium, unamquamque per se, per servitium quatuor denariorum per annum tantum, a tempore regis H., patris domini regis nunc; de quibus habuerunt cartas. Tenent etiam manerium integrum de Wardon, cum omnibus suis pertinentiis, et ecclesiam ejusdem loci in proprios usus, una cum capellis suis de Stayncroft, Hayden, et Langley, in liberam, puram, et perpetuam elemosinam, de dono domini Adæ de Tyndal; de quibus ipsi habuerunt cartam, et confirmationem domini episcopi Dunelmensis; et tenuerunt a tempore quo non extat memoria. Tenent etiam quadraginta acras terræ, et sex acras prati, et duo messuagia, in Sadelingstanes, de dono Adæ de Sadeling-stan, in liberam, puram, et perpetuam elemosinam; et inde habuerunt cartam; et tenuerunt a tempore quo non extat memoria. Tenent etiam in Qwyneteley duo mesuagia, et quadraginta acras terræ, cum pertinentiis, et decem solidatas redditus, de dono Adæ de Thorngraffton, in liberam, puram, et perpetuam elemosinam; et inde habuerunt cartam; et tenuerunt a tempore quo non extat memoria. Tenent etiam totam terram del Byres, per suas rectas divisas, et etiam communam pasturæ extra divisas terræ prædictæ, cum pertinentiis, de dono domini Adæ de Tyndal, in liberam, puram, et perpetuam elemosinam; et inde habuerunt cartam; et tenuerunt a tempore quo non extat memoria. Tenent etiam molendinum de Alrewess, cum pertinentiis, de dono Uctredi de Alrewes, in liberam, puram, et perpetuam elemosinam; et inde habuerunt cartam; et tenuerunt a tempore quo non extat memoria. Tenent etiam unam carucatam terræ in Alrewes, cum suis pertinentiis, in quodam loco qui vocatur Oulemers, de dono Ricardi[f] quondam ballivi Hextildesham, in liberam, puram, et perpetuam elemosinam; et inde habuerunt

[f] Probably Richard, son of Alexander, who was bailiff of Hexham in the thirteenth century.

cartam; et tenuerunt a tempore quo non extat memoria. Tenent ecclesiam de Cholverton cum suis capellis, scilicet, Birteley, Chipchesse, Gonewarton, Est-Swyneburne, Parva Heton, et Colewelle, cum suis pertinentiis, in proprios usus; et octo bovatas terræ, cum pertinentiis, in villa de Cholverton, de dote ipsius ecclesiæ; una cum quinque acris terræ, quæ vocantur le Michel-croft, ex boreali parte illius ecclesiæ, in liberam, puram, et perpetuam elemosinam, de dono Odenelli de Umframvill; et inde habuerunt cartam et confirmationem; et tenuerunt a tempore quo non extat memoria. Tenent etiam totum hamlettum de Beumond, cum suis pertinentiis, per suas rectas divisas, in liberam, puram, et perpetuam elemosinam, de dono Gilberti de Umframvill; et inde habuerunt cartam; et tenuerunt a tempore regis H., patris domini regis nunc. Tenent etiam unum toftum et septem acras terræ cum suis pertinentiis in Birteley, in liberam, puram, et perpetuam elemosinam, de dono Ricardi de Umframvill; et inde habuerunt cartam; et tenuerunt a tempore quo non extat memoria. Tenent etiam totam terram et pasturam de Colden, cum suis pertinentiis, per suas rectas divisas, in liberam, puram, et perpetuam elemosinam, de dono Ricardi de Umframvill; et tenuerunt a tempore quo non extat memoria; et inde habuerunt cartam. Habent etiam communam pasturæ in mora de Gonewarton ad quinquies viginti averia exeuntia de scalinga de Colden, tam tempore clauso, quam tempore aperto, de dono Radulfi de Gonewarton; et inde habuerunt cartam; in liberam, puram, et perpetuam elemosinam; et tenuerunt a tempore quo non extat memoria. Tenent etiam duo tofta et triginta acras terræ, cum suis pertinentiis, in villa de Barweforde, in liberam, puram, et perpetuam elemosinam; et inde habuerunt cartam; de dono Margeriæ de Umframvill; et tenuerunt a tempore regis nunc. Tenent etiam duo tofta, et duas bovatas terræ cum pertinentiis, in villa de Chestrehorp, in liberam, puram, et perpetuam elemosinam, de dono Radulfi de Gonewarton; et inde habuerunt cartam; et tenuerunt a tempore quo non extat memoria. Tenent etiam unam carucatam terræ, cum suis pertinentiis, in Neuton-in-Cokedal, in liberam, puram, et perpetuam elemosinam, de dono Walteri de Insula; et inde habuerunt cartam; et tenuerunt a tempore quo non extat memoria. Tenent etiam communam pasturæ ad triginta et duos boves, decem vaccas, et ad ducentas et quadraginta oves, in Colewell, in liberam, puram, et perpetuam elemosinam, de dono Walteri Corbet; et inde habuerunt cartam; et tenuerunt a tempore H. regis, patris regis nunc. Tenent etiam manerium de Parva Heton et de Calde-strother, cum pertinentiis, in liberam, puram, et perpetuam elemosinam, de dono Alinæ de Bolum, et Jacobi de Caus et Alisiæ uxoris suæ; et inde habuerunt cartam; et tenuerunt a tempore quo non extat memoria. Tenent etiam unum toftum et sex acras terræ in Parva Babington, de dono Stephani Bataillie; et tenent in eadem villa duo tofta et tres acras et dimidiam, cum pertinentiis, cum communa pasturæ ad quindecim averia, sexaginta oves, et ad duos equos, de dono Gilberti de Wircestre, in liberam, puram, et perpetuam elemosinam; et inde habuerunt cartam; et tenuerunt a tempore quo non extat memoria. Tenent etiam tria tofta cum grangia decimali, et duas bovatas et duodecim acras terræ, cum pertinentiis, in villa de Gonewarton, de dono Radulfi de Gonewarton et Thurkilly de Cadeiou; et inde habuerunt cartam; in liberam, puram, et perpetuam elemosinam; et tenuerunt a tempore quo non extat memoria. Tenent etiam ecclesiam de Slaveley[g] in proprios usus, et unam carucatam terræ, cum pertinentiis, de dote ejusdem ecclesiæ; et communam pasturæ in eadem villa ad ducentas et sexaginta oves; et communam pasturæ in le Stele ad ducentas et sexaginta oves, in liberam, puram, et perpetuam elemosinam, de dono Gilberti de Slaveley; et inde habuerunt cartam, et confirmationem domini episcopi et capituli Dunelmensis; et tenuerunt a tempore regis H., patris domini regis nunc. Tenent etiam unam domum et unam acram terræ, cum pertinentiis, in villa de Chipches, in liberam, puram, et perpetuam elemosinam, de dono Roberti de Insula; et inde habuerunt cartam; et tenuerunt a tempore domini regis H.; et, etiam, quadraginta et tres solidatas, et quatuor denariatas redditus, exeuntes de octo mesuagiis in villa Novi-Castri-super-Tynam, in liberam, puram, et perpetuam elemosinam, de dono diversorum; et inde habuerunt cartas; et tenuerunt a tempore quo non extat memoria. Tenent etiam quadraginta et tres solidatas et duas denariatas redditus, exeuntes de quindecim mesuagiis in villa de Corbrigg, de dono diversorum; et inde habuerunt cartas; et tenuerunt a tempore quo non extat memoria. Tenent etiam unum mesuagium, septem acras terræ cum pertinentiis in Hayden, et communam pasturæ ad ducentas et sexaginta bidentes, in liberam, puram, et perpetuam elemosinam, de dono domini Adæ de Tindal; et inde habuerunt cartam; et tenuerunt a tempore quo non extat memoria. Tenent etiam unam acram terræ in campo de West-Swyneburne, in liberam, puram, et perpetuam elemosinam, de dono Johannis

[g] Memorandum quod xxiij die Novembris, anno Domini millesimo ccc° xij°, concessit dominus xl dies indulgentiæ omnibus conferentibus de bonis suis ad fabricam ecclesiæ de Slaveley, Dunelmensis diocesios (Reg. Kellawe at Durham, 67).

de Wirecestre; et inde habuerunt cartam; et tenuerunt a tempore regis H., patris domini regis nunc. Tenent etiam totum manerium de North-Milneburne cum pertinentiis, et cum communa pasturæ in mora de Crekelagh, ex dono domini Thomæ de Dyveleston, in liberam, puram, et perpetuam elemosinam; et inde habuerunt cartam, et licentiam domini regis nunc ingrediendi, non obstante statuto domini regis inde edito; et tenuerunt a tempore domini regis nunc. Tenent etiam totam terram de Stelden, per certas suas divisas, in excambium pro servitio viginti et trium solidorum per annum, ex concessione Abbatis Novi Monasterii; et inde habuerunt cartam; et tenuerunt a tempore quo non extat memoria. Tenent etiam et habent dominium totius villæ de Whitefeld, et sexdecim solidatas et quatuor denariatas redditus, in liberam, puram, et perpetuam elemosinam, de dono Willelmi regis Scotiæ; et inde habuerunt cartam; et tenuerunt a tempore quo non extat memoria. Habent etiam quandam moram, quæ vocatur Karraue-sid, in suo seperali, in liberam, puram, et perpetuam elemosinam, de dono prædicti Willelmi regis Scotiæ; et inde habuerunt cartam; et tenuerunt a tempore quo non extat memoria. Tenent etiam quoddam hamelettum, quod vocatur Carrawer, in suo seperali, cum suis pertinentiis, in liberam, puram, et perpetuam elemosinam, de dono Ricardi Comyn; et habent de dono ejusdem Ricardi unam carucatam terræ cum pertinentiis in Rischeles, per suas rectas divisas, una cum communa pasturæ de Hethenes-halgh, in liberam, puram, et perpetuam elemosinam; et inde habuerunt cartam; et tenuerunt a tempore quo non extat memoria. Tenent etiam unum toftum et triginta acras terræ, cum pertinentiis, in Stayncroft, in liberam, puram, et perpetuam elemosinam, de dono prædicti Ricardi Comyn; et inde habuerunt cartam; et tenuerunt a tempore quo non extat memoria. Tenent etiam sex tofta et unam carucatam terræ, cum pertinentiis, in Thirlewall; et communam pasturæ ad quaterviginti averia, quaterviginti jumenta cum secta, et ad quadraginta porcos, et ad quaterviginti capras, in liberam, puram, et perpetuam elemosinam, de dono Bricii de Thirlewall et Rogeri filii ejus; et inde habuerunt cartas; et tenuerunt a tempore quo non extat memoria. Tenent etiam quandam pasturam quæ vocatur Presdale, cum suis pertinentiis, per suas rectas divisas, in suo seperali, in liberam, puram, et perpetuam elemosinam, de dono Ivonis de Veteri-Ponte; et inde habuerunt cartam, et confirmationem domini regis H., patris domini regis nunc; et tenuerunt a tempore quo non extat memoria. Tenent etiam octo mesuagia et unam carucatam terræ cum pertinentiis in Aldeneston, in liberam, puram, et perpetuam elemosinam, de dono Ivonis de Veteri-Ponte; et inde habuerunt cartam; et tenuerunt a tempore quo non extat memoria. Habent etiam octo solidatas redditus, cum pertinentiis, in Teket, in liberam, puram, et perpetuam elemosinam, de dono Laurentii de Teket; et inde habuerunt cartam; et tenuerunt a tempore quo non extat memoria. Habent etiam tresdecim solidatas et quatuor denariatas redditus in molendino de Elrington, in liberam, puram, et perpetuam elemosinam, de dono Ivonis de Veteri-Ponte; et inde habuerunt cartam; et tenuerunt a tempore quo non extat memoria. Habent etiam octo solidatas redditus in Ald-schel, in liberam, puram, et perpetuam elemosinam, de dono Henrici de Graham; et inde habuerunt cartam; et tenuerunt a tempore quo non extat memoria. Tenent etiam medietatem manerii de Echewyk, in liberam, puram, et perpetuam elemosinam, de dono Roberti filii Huberti de la Vale, et Richoldæ, matris ejus; et inde habuerunt cartam; et tenuerunt a tempore quo non extat memoria. Et tenent in eadem villa, de dono Thomæ de Echewyk, decem acras terræ cum pertinentiis, in liberam, puram, et perpetuam elemosinam; et septem acras terræ in eadem villa, ex dono Petri de Faudon, in liberam, puram, et perpetuam elemosinam, a tempore domini regis H., patris domini regis nunc; et inde habuerunt cartam. Tenent etiam tresdecim solidatas et octo denariatas redditus in villa de Stokesfeld, de dono Willelmi filii Bosonis, reddendo inde per annum ad wardam castri septem solidos; et inde habuerunt cartam; et tenuerunt a tempore quo non extat memoria. Tenent etiam et habent tres solidatas redditus in villa de Stokesfeld, in liberam, puram, et perpetuam elemosinam, de dono Johannis filii Heliæ de eadem; et inde habuerunt cartam; et tenuerunt a tempore H. regis, patris domini regis nunc. Tenent etiam quinque tofta et decem bovatas terræ, tres acras prati, cum pertinentiis, in Thornton, in liberam, puram, et perpetuam elemosinam, de dono Willelmi de Insula; et inde habuerunt cartam, et confirmationem domini Walteri de Bolbek; et tenuerunt a tempore quo non extat memoria. Tenent etiam unum manerium et tres acras terræ, cum pertinentibus, per suas rectas divisas, de Hugone de la Vale, in Benewell, in liberam, puram, et perpetuam elemosinam; et inde habuerunt cartam; et tenuerunt a tempore regis H., patris domini regis nunc. Habent etiam in villa de Throkelagh duas acras terræ, et sexdecim solidatas redditus, cum pertinentiis, in eadem, de dono Roberti de Ivestanes et Cristianæ de Throkelagh, in liberam, puram, et perpetuam elemosinam; et inde habuerunt cartam; et tenuerunt a tempore quo non extat memoria. Habent etiam in Est-Mathfen unum manerium, sex mesuagia, et tres carucatas terræ, cum pertinentiis, in eadem, in liberam, puram, et perpetuam elemosinam, de dono Thomæ de Fenewyke; et inde habuerunt cartam, et confirmationem domini Roberti de Insula; et tenuerunt a tempore regis H., patris domini regis nunc. Habent etiam in villa de Stani(n)gton unum toftum et duas bovatas terræ, cum suis pertinentibus, in liberam, puram, et perpetuam elemosinam, de dono Rogeri de Merley, et inde habuerunt cartam; et tenuerunt a tempore quo non extat memoria.[h] Habent etiam in eadem villa decem et octo denariatas redditus, de dono ejusdem Rogeri; et inde habuerunt cartam; et tenuerunt a tempore quo non extat memoria. Habent etiam in molendino de Brinkelagh unam marcatam redditus, in liberam, puram, et perpetuam elemosinam, de dono Henrici de Ferlington; et inde habuerunt cartam; et tenuerunt a tempore regis H., patris domini regis nunc. Tenent etiam in villa de Whalton unum toftum et croftum, et quadraginta et duas acras et dimidiam terræ, cum pertinentiis, et communam pasturæ ad quadringentas oves matrices et ad agnos earumdem, in liberam, puram, et perpetuam elemosinam, de dono Walteri filii Willelmi et Isabellæ uxoris ejus; et inde habuerunt cartam; et tenuerunt a tempore quo non extat memoria. Habent etiam in villa de Riplengton octo solidatas redditus, cum pertinentiis, de dono eorundem Walteri et Isabellæ uxoris ejus, in liberam, puram, et perpetuam elemosinam; et inde habuerunt cartam; et tenuerunt a tempore quo non extat memoria. Habent etiam duas piscarias in aqua de Tyne, et unam placiam ad sic(c)andum retia sua; quarum piscaria una vocatur Dripinttell, altera Foul; in liberam, puram, et perpetuam elemosinam, de dono Rogeri Bertram; et inde habuerunt cartam; et tenuerunt a tempore quo non extat memoria. Habent etiam et tenent in villa de Stanfordeham unum toftum et duas carucatas terræ, cum pertinentiis, in liberam, puram, et perpetuam elemosinam, de dono Johannis de Normanvill; et inde habuerunt cartam; et tenuerunt a tempore quo non extat memoria. Tenent etiam manerium de Cheseburgh, et de Nesebith, cum pertinentiis, scilicet, in dominicis, servitiis, bondis, et omnibus aliis suis pertinentiis, in liberam, puram, et perpetuam elemosinam, de dono Johannis de Normanvill; et inde habuerunt cartam, et confirmationem domini de Balliolo; et tenuerunt a tempore quo non extat memoria. Habent etiam quandam portionem in ecclesia de Staneferdeham, videlicet, decimas garbarum quinque villarum,

[h] Roger de Merley, the Third, made an endowment for a chaplain to celebrate at the altar of the Virgin in the church of Stannington. A part of the endowment was "decem acras terræ cum pertinentiis in villa de Clifton, quas habui de dono Prioris et Conventus Haugustaldensis." The chaplain was to pay 18d. to the Prior and Convent, annually. The charter of endowment is printed in Hodgson's Northumberland, vol. ii., part iii., 71-6.

scilicet, Mathfen, Est-Nesebith, Ulkeston, Haukwell, et Bechefeld, ex concessione et ordinatione domini Nicholai Dunelmensis episcopi; et inde habuerunt cartam, et confirmationem capituli Dunelmensis; in liberam, puram, et perpetuam elemosinam; et tenuerunt a tempore quo non extat memoria. Habent etiam et tenent manerium de Stelling, cum suis pertinentiis; et in villa de Newbiging-super-mare unum toftum et duas acras terræ, cum suis libertatibus, et omnibus aliis pertinentiis suis, in liberam, puram, et perpetuam elemosinam, de dono Bernardi de Balliolo; et inde habuerunt cartam; et tenuerunt a tempore quo non extat memoria. Habent etiam, de dono ejusdem Bernardi, quadraginta solidatas redditus in villa de Seton, in liberam, puram, et perpetuam elemosinam; et inde habuerunt cartam; et tenuerunt a tempore quo non extat memoria. Tenent etiam tertiam partem villæ de Dalton, cum pertinentiis, in liberam, puram, et perpetuam elemosinam, de dono Radulfi de Gonewarton; et tenent, etiam, in eadem quatuor bovatas terræ, et quinque solidatas et sex denariatas redditus, provenientes de molendino ejusdem villæ, de dono Willelmi de Dalton, in liberam, puram, et perpetuam elemosinam; et inde habuerunt cartam; et tenuerunt a tempore quo non extat memoria. Tenent etiam in villa de Prodehou unum toftum et octo acras terræ, cum pertinentiis, in liberam, puram, et perpetuam elemosinam, de dono Richardi de Umframvill; et inde habuerunt cartam; et tenuerunt a tempore quo non extat memoria. Habent etiam homagium Johannis de Swyneburne-Est, et hæredum suorum, et servitium duodecim denariorum annui redditus pro capitali messuagio suo de Est-Swyneburne, de dono Hugonis de Balliolo, in liberam, puram, et perpetuam elemosinam; et tenuerunt a tempore quo non extat memoria; et inde habuerunt cartam. Habent etiam homagium hæred' Nicholai de West-Swyneburne, et servitium trium solidorum per annum pro cantaria capellæ de West-Swyneburne, ex concessione Johannis de Wircestre, in liberam, puram, et perpetuam elemosinam; et inde habuerunt cartam; et tenuerunt a tempore regis H., patris domini regis nunc. Habent etiam homagium Johannis de Cambhou, pro terris et tenementis quæ tenet in Parva Heton et Caldestrother, de dono Alinæ de Bolom, Jacobi de Cauz, et Alesiæ uxoris suæ, in liberam, puram, et perpetuam elemosinam; et inde habuerunt cartas; et tenuerunt a tempore quo non extat memoria. Habent etiam homagium Richardi de Thirlewall, et tres solidatas annui redditus pro terra quam tenet de eis in Thirlewall, in liberam, puram, et perpetuam elemosinam, de dono Bricii de Thirlewall et Rogeri filii ejus; et inde habuerunt cartas; et tenuerunt a tempore quo non extat memoria. Habent etiam homagium Adæ de Whitelagh, et servitium quatuor solidorum annui redditus de eodem, in liberam, puram, et perpetuam elemosinam, de dono Adæ de Tindale; et inde habuerunt cartam; et tenuerunt a tempore quo non extat memoria. Habent etiam homagium Thomæ filii Ricardi filii Bricii de Thirlewall, pro terra quam tenet de eis in Thirlewall, in liberam, puram, et perpetuam elemosinam, de dono Adæ de Tindale; et inde habuerunt cartam; et tenuerunt a tempore quo non extat memoria. Habent etiam homagium Johannis de Normanvill pro terra de Stokesfeld et Apetre-ley, per servitium tresdecim solidorum et octo denariorum, in liberam, puram, et perpetuam elemosinam annuatim, de dono Willelmi filii Bosonis; et inde habuerunt cartam; et tenuerunt a tempore quo non extat memoria. Habent etiam homagium Roberti de Ribil, et servitium decem solidorum annui redditus, et tres sectas ad curiam Prioris per annum, in liberam, puram, et perpetuam elemosinam, de dono Theophaniæ de la Bataillie; et inde habuerunt cartam; et tenuerunt a tempore quo non extat memoria. Habent etiam homagium Mathei de Whitefeld, pro terra et tenementis in Whitefeld, cum pertinentiis, quæ de eis tenet in eadem, in liberam, puram, et in perpetuam elemosinam; et inde habuerunt cartam Willelmi regis Scotiæ a tempore quo non extat memoria. Habent etiam homagium Roberti de Throkelagh pro terris et tenementis quæ de eis tenet in eadem, in liberam, puram, et perpetuam elemosinam; et inde habuerunt cartam; de dono Roberti de Ivestanes et Christianæ de Throkelagh; et tenuerunt a tempore quo non extat memoria. Tenent etiam quandam grangiam decimalem cum gardino in villa de Est-Swyneburne, in liberam, puram, et perpetuam elemosinam, de dono Hugonis de Balliolo; et inde habuerunt cartam; et tenuerunt a tempore quo non extat memoria. Nos autem præmissa testificari, et veritati volentes testimonium perhibere, ne prædicti Prior et Conventus, aut successores sui, vel ecclesia sua prædicta, per defectum cartarum et munimentorum suorum prædictorum, sic combustorum, dampnum aut exhæreditationis periculum futuris temporibus incurrant, inquisitionem prædictam sub sigillo nostro duximus exemplandam. Hiis testibus venerabili patre W. Covent' et Lichefeld' episcopo, Gilberto de Umframvill comite de Anegos, Johanne Tregoz, Waltero de Bello-Campo senescallo hospitii nostri, Willelmo de Rither, Waltero de Huntercumbe, Eustachio de Hacche, Waltero de Teye, Johanne de Merk', et aliis. Data per manum nostram, apud Novum-Castrum-super-Tynam, vicesimo tertio die Novembris, anno regni nostri vicesimo septimo. Per ipsum regem. Et dupplicatur.

[The great seal, in white wax, slightly damaged, is appended.]

XXX.—A GRANT OF THE ADVOWSON OF THE LIVING OF STAMFORDHAM FROM EDWARD I. TO THE PRIOR AND CONVENT OF HEXHAM. [Rot. Chart., 33rd Edward I., No. 20.]

Rex archiepiscopis, etc., salutem. Sciatis quod cum nuper in curia nostra, per considerationem ejusdem curiæ, recuperaverimus advocationem ecclesiæ de Staunfordham,[i] Dunelm. diocesios, versus venerabilem patrem Antonium episcopum ejusdem loci; et dilecti nobis in Christo Prior et Conventus de Hextildesham postmodum asseruerint coram nobis prædecessores suos aliquo tempore veros patronos ejusdem ecclesiæ, et in possessione advocationis ejusdem, ut de jure ecclesiæ suæ de Hextildesham, fuisse; et advocationem illam super prædictos prædecessores per Nicholaum,[j] quondam episcopum Dunelmensem, prædecessorem prædicti episcopi, fuisse occupatam voluntarie et detentam; nos, visis et examinatis coram consilio nostro cartis, quas dictus Prior coram eodem consilio ad declarationem juris sui protulit in hac parte, per finem quem idem Prior fecit nobiscum coram thesaurario et baronibus nostris de scaccario, dedimus et concessimus præfatis Priori et Conventui advocationem prædictam; habendam et tenendam sibi et successoribus suis imperpetuum. Quare volumus, et firmiter præcipimus, pro nobis et hæredibus nostris, quod Prior et Con-

[i] There had been a struggle between the king and Anthony Bek, bishop of Durham, for the advowson of this church, and the bishop had lost his cause. The Prior and Convent now claim it as their own in right of a grant from Nicholas, bishop of Durham, and their plea is allowed.

In the Registry of the Dean and Chapter of Durham there are some uninteresting details of the suit with bishop Bek. It appears, moreover, from a charter now lost, that that prelate himself appropriated Stamfordham to Hexham to repair "lamentabilem statum ecclesiæ et monasterii eorumdem, per repentinam incendii voraginem jam consumpti." Dated at Somerton, Oct. 2, 1307 (MSS. Dodsworth, xlv., 33 *a*. MSS. Lansd., cccxxvj., 108, taken from Sir John Fenwick's deeds). The bishop, it appears from this, was determined not to give in, and makes a present of what the law had deprived him.

Edward II., as the following deed will shew, followed up what his father had done:—"*Pro Priore de Hextildesham.* Rex, omnibus ad quos, etc., salutem. Sciatis quod de gratia nostra speciali concessimus, et licentiam dedimus, pro nobis et hæredibus nostris, quantum in nobis est, dilectis nobis in Christo Priori et Conventui de Hextildesham, quod ipsi ecclesiam de Staunfordham, cum pertinentiis, cujus advocationem habent de dono et concessione domini E., quondam regis Angliæ, patris nostri, appropriare, et in usus proprios tenere possint, sibi et successoribus suis imperpetuum, sine occasione vel impedimento nostri vel hæredum nostrorum, justitiariorum, escaetorum, vicecomitum, aut aliorum ballivorum seu ministrorum nostrorum quorumcumque; statuto de terris et tenementis ad manum-mortuam non ponendis edito non obstante. In cujus, etc. Teste rege apud Mortelak, xxij die Maii. Per breve de privato sigillo." (Rot. Pat., 2nd Edward II., part ii., membr. 6.)

[j] The deed of this bishop, appropriating the living of Stamfordham to Hexham, is printed in Hodgson's Northumberland, vol. ii., part iii., 105-7. It was executed in 1245.

ventus, et successores sui, habeant et teneant advocationem prædictam imperpetuum, sicut prædictum est. Hiis testibus, venerabilibus patribus R. Cantuar. archiepiscopo, totius Angliæ primate, W. Coventr' et Lych', J. Karliol' episcopis, Henrico de Lacy comite Linc., Humfrido de Bohun comite Hereford et Essex, Adomaro de Valencia, Johanne de Britannia juniore, Hugone le Despenser, Roberto de Clyfford, Johanne Buteturte, Roberto de la Warde senescallo hospitii nostri, et aliis. Data per manum nostram, apud Shene, vij die Octobris. Dupplicatur.

XXXI.—A GRANT OF THE ADVOWSON OF THE CHURCH OF ALSTON BY EDWARD I. TO THE PRIOR AND CONVENT OF HEXHAM. [Rot. Chart., 34th Edward I., No. 13.]

Rex archiepiscopis, etc., salutem. Sciatis quod cum nos nuper in curia nostra, coram Hugone de Cressingham et sociis suis, justitiariis nostris, ultimo itinerantibus in comitatu Cumbriæ, per considerationem ejusdem curiæ recuperaremus versus Priorem de Hextildesham advocationem ecclesiæ de Aldenyston,[k] Dunelm. diocesios, ut jus nostrum; nos, ad honorem Dei et Sancti Andreæ, ac ob devotionem quam erga eundem Sanctum Andream, in cujus honore ecclesia dicti Prioratus dedicatur, gerimus et habemus, volentes præfato Priori et Conventui ejusdem loci gratiam in hac parte specialem, dedimus et concessimus eisdem Priori et Conventui pro nobis et hæredibus nostris, advocationem prædictam, et eam eis reddidimus; habendam et tenendam sibi et successoribus suis imperpetuum, sine occasione vel impe(dimento) nostri vel hæredum nostrorum, aut ministrorum nostrorum quorumcumque. Quare volumus, et firmiter præcipimus, pro nobis et hæredibus nostris, quod prædicti Prior et Conventus, et successores sui, habeant et teneant advocationem prædictam imperpetuum ——. Hiis testibus venerabili patre W. Coventr. et Lych. episcopo, Henrico de Lacy comite Linc', Adomaro de Walencia, Hugone le Despenser, Roberto filio Rogeri, Willelmo le Latimer, Roberto de la Warde senescallo hospitii nostri, et aliis. Data per manum nostram, apud Lanrecost, viij die Octobris. Per breve de privato sigillo. Dupplicatur.

[k] See Hodgson's Northumberland, iii., part ii., 36-7, 57. This is but one of many cases which shew what a precarious possession an advowson was. The church was not securely appropriated to Hexham until the time of bishop Hatfield in 1378. The deed is printed in Hodgson, vol. ii., part iii., 82-7. An ordination of the stipend for the vicar was not made until 1420 (Ibid.)

XXXII.—AN INSPEXIMUS OF THE CHARTER OF IVO DE VETERI-PONTE, GRANTING LANDS AT ALSTON TO THE PRIOR AND CONVENT OF HEXHAM. [Rot. Chart., 35th Edward I., No. 22.]

Rex archiepiscopis, etc., salutem. Inspeximus cartam Ivonis de Veteri-Ponte, quam fecit Deo et ecclesiæ Sancti Andreæ Haugustaldensis, et canonicis ibidem Deo servientibus, in hæc verba.

Omnibus sanctæ matris ecclesiæ filiis hanc cartam visuris vel audituris, Ivo de Veteri-Ponte[1] salutem in Domino. Noverit universitas vestra me, caritatis intuitu, et pro salute animæ meæ, et antecessorum et successorum meorum, dedisse, concessisse, et hac præsenti carta mea confirmasse Deo et ecclesiæ Sancti Andreæ Haugustaldensis, et canonicis ibidem Deo servientibus, in liberam, puram, et perpetuam elemosinam, totam terram illam de dominico meo in villa de Aldeniston per has divisas; scilicet, sicut rivulus de Nateres-gile cadit in Tyne versus austrum; et ita, descendendo ex parte occidentali, usque ad pontem; et, ita a ponte, ascendendo per antiquum fossatum, usque ad terram Sancti Johannis ex parte aquilonari; et per terram Sancti Johannis directe usque ad longum fossatum versus orientem; et sic, sequendo longum fossatum, usque ad rivulum de Nateris-gile prius nominatum: et communem pasturam ad quadraginta vaccas, et ad decem equas, et ad centum oves, cum omnium prædictorum sequela duorum annorum: et totam terram illam ex parte occidentali de Tyne infra has divisas; scilicet, incipiendo ad occidentale caput superioris pontis de Aldeneston; et ita, circumdando et ascendendo per viam et fossatum, usque ad rivulum proximum juxta crucem ligneam versus austrum; et ita, descendendo per rivulum, usque in aquam de Tyne; et sic, in descendendo per Tyne ex parte orientali, usque ad pontem prius dictum: ita quod libere faciant et disponant sine impedimento de omnibus infra prædictas divisas contentis, in omnibus, et per omnia, ad commodum et ad aisiamentum illorum, sicut melius sibi viderint expedire. Habendum et tenendum prædictis canonicis de me et hæredibus meis libere, quiete, pacifice, honorifice, et solute, cum omnibus libertatibus, et communibus, et liberis aisiamentis in omnibus locis ad prædictam villam de Aldeneston pertinentibus, sicut aliqua elemosina ab aliquo liberius, purius, et honorificentius dari possit vel teneri; cum libero ingressu, et transitu, et exitu per totum feodum meum de Aldeneston, sine impedimento, ad homines

[1] This deed was made early in the thirteenth century.

prædictorum canonicorum; et ad omnia genera animalium suorum. Et molent bladum suum, quod super prædictas terras crescet, ad molendinum de Aldeneston, libere, et sine multura danda. Et habebunt prædicti canonici, et homines eorum in prædicta terra manentes, in bosco nostro de Aldeneston, per visum servientis mei, ad ædificandum, et ad domos et ad sepes suas sustinendas, sine contradictione; et ad alia necessaria, sine vasto, quantum opus habuerint. Ego vero, et hæredes mei, omnes prædictas terras, cum omnibus prædictis pertinentiis suis, et integris libertatibus, et aisiamentis prænominatis, prædictis canonicis in liberam, puram, et perpetuam elemosinam, contra omnes homines imperpetuum warantizabimus et defendemus: et ad perpetuam hujus rei securitatem præsentem cartam sigillo meo attentico corroboravi. Hiis testibus domino W. Karl. episcopo, domino B. priore Karl., magistro G. archidiacono Karl., Waltero Cumyn, Roberto de Castel-Kayroc, Roberto persona de Whitefeld, Johanne Prat, Ranulpho de Haltton, Nicholao de Wylmotewyk, Ricardo filio Alexandri, Adam de Thirlewall, Johanne de Whitefeld, Laurentio de Veteri-Ponte, Willelmo de Kirkehalch, Hugone de Buckecastre, Alano filio Joelis, Adam de Elrington, Johanne de Rideleye, Ricardo filio Thurstani, Roberto de Elrington, Johanne de Hayton, Roberto Maresca . . , Uctredo de Chereburn, Johanne de Stivelyngton clerico, et aliis.

Nos autem donationem et concessionem prædictas ratas habentes et gratas, eas pro nobis et hæredibus nostris, quantum in nobis est, concedimus et confirmamus, sicut carta prædicta rationabiliter testatur. Hiis testibus venerabilibus patribus W. archiepiscopo Ebor. Angliæ primate, W. Coventrensi et Lichefeldensi, J. Cicestrensi, J. Karl., R. Lond. episcopis, Henrico de Lacy comite Linc', Guidone de Bello-campo comite Warr., Hugone le Despenser, Roberto filio Rogeri, Rogero de Mortuo-mari seniore, Hugone de Curtenay, et aliis. Data per manum nostram, apud Karliolum, xx die Martii.

XXXIII.—THREE DOCUMENTS RELATING TO THE APPROPRIATION OF THE CHURCH OF HEXHAM AND ITS DEPENDENT CHAPELS TO THE PRIOR AND CONVENT OF HEXHAM. [Reg. archiep. Greenfield, pars i., 36 *a*, 50 *b*.]

I.

Willelmus, permissione Divina, etc., dilectis filiis custodi spiritualitatis nostræ de Hextildesham, et domino Thomæ de

Erington, vicario ecclesiæ de Herteburn, salutem, etc. Dudum vobis in negotio contra Priorem et Conventum de Hextildesham,[m] nostræ diocesios, super appropriatione quarumdam ecclesiarum, in quibus non sunt perpetui vicarii instituti, ex officio nostro moto, testium examinationem ex parte dictorum religiosorum coram vobis productorum monuimus commisisse; quorum attestationibus nobis per vos transmissis seriatius intellectis, invenimus dictos testes examinatos fuisse super quibusdam articulis minus plene. Nos, itaque, volentes in eodem negotio plenius informari, vobis ad recipiendum iterato in forma juris eosdem testes, prius in eodem per vos examinatos negotio; et alios quos dicti religiosi, certis die et loco ad hoc per vos sibi legitime assignatis, duxerint producendos; ipsosque super articulis in cedula contentis præsentibus interclusa ex nostro plenius examinandum officio; et ad compellendum eosdem, si se gratia, odio, vel timore subtraxerint, veritati testimonium perhibere; vobis conjunctim committimus vices nostras cum cohercionis canonicæ potestate. Proviso quod dicta eorumdem testium in scriptis distincte redacta, et sub vestris sigillis inclusa, nobis citra festum Sancti Martini proximo sequens, una cum vestris literis certificatoriis, harum seriem continentibus, fideliter transmittatis. Valete. Data apud Otteleye, decimo kalendas Novembris, pontificatus nostri anno quinto.

II.

Alexander, papa Quartus, servus servorum Dei, dilectis filiis Priori et Conventui de Hextildesham, ordinis Sancti Augustini, Ebor. diocesios, salutem et Apostolicam benedictionem. Devotionis vestræ sinceritas promeretur ut vestris petitionibus, quantum cum Deo possumus, favorabiliter annuamus. Hinc est quod vestris precibus inclinati, ut in ecclesia vestra de Hextildesham, curam habente, in qua personaliter residentes Domino deservitis, nullus, auctoritate ordinaria, vel litterarum Apostolicæ sedis, vicarium de novo instituere sæcularem, aut vos ad

[m] These documents are all that have been preserved out of a long series. The Prior and Convent of Hexham were in possession of the parish church of Hexham and its dependent chapels, holding them in their own hands, and appointing no vicars or clergy, but performing the necessary offices and duties through their own canons or some of the clergy attached to the monastery. The archbishop, with wise precaution, wishes to have vicars formally appointed, but the canons produce a bull from Alexander IV., sanctioning the state of things then existing. To this the archbishop was obliged to submit. Hence the poverty of the livings and chapelries in the neighbourhood of Hexham. The Reformation came, and the tithes, etc., which should have been devoted to the endowment of the livings, went away from the monastery into lay hands. The system, too prevalent among the religious houses, of preventing endowments being made, is much to be reprehended.

ipsum instituendum ibidem compellere valeat; dummodo ibidem nec animarum cura, nec Divini obsequii celebritas negligatur; nisi eædem litteræ specialem et plenam fecerint de hac indulgentia mentionem, auctoritate vobis præsentium indulgemus. Nulli igitur omnino hominum liceat hanc paginam nostræ concessionis infringere, vel ei ausu temerario contra-ire. Si quis autem hoc attemptare præsumpserit indignationem Omnipotentis Dei, et Beatorum Petri et Pauli Apostolorum Ejus, se noverit incursurum. Data Anagniæ, id. Julii, pontificatus nostri anno primo.

III.

In Dei nomine, amen. Olim nos, Willelmus, permissione Divina Ebor. archiepiscopus, Angliæ primas, ex officii nostri debito monasterium Sancti Andreæ de Hextildesham, nobis pleno jure subjectum tam in capite quam in membris, visitantes,[n] comperimus quod religiosi viri, Prior et Conventus monasterii prædicti, ecclesiam parochialem de Hextildesham, cum capellis Sancti Johannis de Lega, Sanctæ Mariæ de Hextildesham, Sancti Oswaldi, Byngefeld, et Alwenton, in quibus ecclesia et capellis non sunt vicariæ perpetuæ ordinatæ, aut vicarii instituti infra jurisdictionem nostram de Hextildesham, contra jus commune possident atque tenent. Nos, itaque, super præmissis volentes procedere contra eos, mandavimus et fecimus ipsos coram nobis ad judicium evocari, ad proponendum et ostendendum jus speciale, si quod super præmissis habebant. Parte vero ipsorum religiosorum coram nobis in judicio comparente, objectis et expositis capitulis, liteque legitime contestata; necnon de calumpnia et de veritate dicenda præstito juramento; productis per partem eandem testibus, et eis in forma juris admissis, juratis, et examinatis, eorumque attestationibus pupplicatis; nonnullis etiam literis tam Apostolicis quam prædecessorum nostrorum et capituli ecclesiæ nostræ Ebor., ac quamplurimis aliis autenticis et pupplicis instrumentis exhibitis seu productis; præfixo quoque termino competente ad proponendum

[n] On April 1st, 1307, the archbishop ordered the official of the liberty of Hexham to summon all the clergy of the churches and chapels within the liberty, together with eight trustworthy persons from the town of Hexham, and two or three from each village within the jurisdiction, according to its size, to appear at a visitation in the church of Hexham before the archbishop or his clerks, on the Thursday after the Sunday on which *Quali Modo* was sung (Reg. Greenfield, i., 35 *a*).

On Dec. 15, 1310, the archbishop ordered Roger de Folkton, keeper of the spirituality of Hexham, to visit the chapels of St. Mary at Hexham, Alwenton, St. John Lee, St. Oswald, and Bingfield, the roofs, books, vestments, and ornaments of which were defective, and to compel the parishioners to amend and supply what was wanting or wrong (Ibid., i., 51 *a*).

et introducendum omnia quibus uti volebat pars prædicta; et demum in facto concluso, ac ad diffinitivam sententiam audiendam certo termino assignato; nos processum prædictum, et omnia exhibita et producta examinavimus, et examinari fecimus diligenter. Auditis igitur et plenius intellectis meritis negotii supradicti, de juris-peritorum nobis assidentium consilio, Christi nomine invocato, dictam ecclesiam de Hextildesham, cum supradictis capellis et omnibus pertinentiis ejusdem, præfatis religiosis, et eorum monasterio fuisse et esse canonice concessam et assignatam in usus proprios possidendam; eosque religiosos ipsam, ut præmissum est, licite atque juste tenere, et in præfata ecclesia de Hextildesham omni prædictis capellis posse et debere per presbiteros stipendiarios, absque alia taxatione seu ordinatione vicariæ, congrue deservire; ac super præmissis omnibus sufficienter munitos esse; et super eis in posterum imp . . . non debere pronuntiamus et declaramus; eosdem religiosos et eorum monasterium super præmissis omnibus et singulis sententialiter absolventes. Lecta, lata, et in scriptis pronuntiata fuit ista sententia per nos archiepiscopum supradictum, præsente parte religiosorum prædictorum apud Scroby, decimo quarto die mensis Novembris, anno gratiæ millesimo trescentesimo decimo, et pontificatus nostri quinto.

XXXIV.—DECREE OF ARCHBISHOP GREENFIELD AGAINST THE LEGALITY OF THE STIPEND ALLOTTED TO THE OFFICIATING MINISTER AT ST. JOHN LEE, NEAR HEXHAM, BY THE PRIOR AND CONVENT OF HEXHAM. [Reg. Greenfield, pars i., 51 *b*.]

In Dei nomine, amen. Nos Willelmus, permissione Divina Ebor. archiepiscopus, Angliæ primas, dudum visitationis nostræ officium in monasterio Sancti Andreæ de Hextildesham, nobis pleno jure subjecto tam in capite quam in membris, canonice exercentes, comperimus quod Johannes del Clay, presbiter, portiones aliquas in capella Beati Johannis de Lega, quæ ecclesiæ parochiali de Hextildesham est annexa, et ab eadem dependens, tamquam vicarius percepit, ac etiam occupavit, absque aliqua ordinatione vicariæ, seu institutione canonica in eadem. Nos, itaque, archiepiscopus supradictus, super præmissis volentes ex officii nostri debito procedere, contra ipsum, eundem Johannem, fecimus coram nobis ad judicium legitime evocari, ad exhibendum et ostendendum pro termino præciso et peremptorio quicquid pro se haberet canonicum super dictarum portionum retentionem et occupationem; ac ad faciendum ulterius et recipiendum quod justitia suaderet. Ipsoque presbitero coram nobis personaliter comparente, objectoque sibi articulo, et facta responsione ad eundem; nichilque ex parte dicti presbiteri proposito vel ostenso, per quod dictas portiones, tamquam vicarius perpetuus, valeat occupare; sed quadam litera Prioris et Conventus monasterii prædicti per eundem exhibita, per quam apparuit dictos Priorem et Conventum præfato Johanni certas portiones ejusdem capellæ percipiendas, quoad vixerit, absque cujuslibet ordinarii auctoritate vel consensu, contra statuta canonica assignasse; habitoque postmodum processu legitime, et juris ordine qui requiritur in hac parte, juxta qualitatem negotii, in omnibus observato; ac demum ad diffinitivam sententiam seu pronuntiationem nostram audiendam in eodem negotio dicto presbitero competenti termino assignato; nos processum supradictum examinari fecimus diligenter. Auditis igitur, et plenius ipsius negotii meritis intellectis, Christi nomine invocato, pronuntiamus et declaramus prædictum Johannem presbiterum jus in dictis portionibus non habere, vicariumque perpetuum præfatæ capellæ non esse, nec fuisse; sed eosdem religiosos prædictæ capellæ per presbiteros stipendiarios posse et debere, absque taxatione vicariæ in eadem, futuris temporibus congrue deservire; assignationem portionum prædictarum, quatenus per præfatos religiosos perpetuo facta fuerat presbitero memorato, irritam et inanem penitus decernentes. Lecta, lata et in scriptis nuntiata fuit ista sententia per nos, archiepiscopum supradictum, apud Cawod, præsente procuratore dictorum religiosorum, et Johanne del Clay, xiiij kalendas Februarii, anno gratiæ m° ccc^{mo} x°, et pontificatus nostri quinto.

XXXV.—AN ORDINATION OF THE VICARAGE OF THE CHURCH OF EDSTON. [Reg. archiep. Greenfield, pars i., 99-100.]

Universis sanctæ matris ecclesiæ filiis, ad quorum notitiam præsentes litteræ pervenerint, Willelmus, permissione Divina Ebor. archiepiscopus, Angliæ primas, salutem in Domino sempiternam.[o] Ut in subjectis nobis ecclesiis, quibus animarum cura

[o] This ordination of the vicarage of Edston in Yorkshire was forced upon the Prior and Convent of Hexham by the vigilance of archbishop Greenfield. He had a dispute with the Convent about it, the canons being represented in the contest by two members of their body, William de Alwenton and Nicholas de Misterton. The following document shews the grounds of the archbishop's complaint:—"Septimo die Octobris, anno eodem (1308), apud Lanum, coram nobis W., etc., in negotio ex officio moto, contra Priorem et Conventum de Hextildesham, Willelmum de Poynton, olim vicarium ecclesiæ de Edeston, et Simonem de Saulton, nunc tenentem vicariam prædictam, super quibusdam articulis in visitatione nostra compertis, qui hic inferius sunt conscripti.

"Willelmus de Poynton, presbiter, olim vicarius ecclesiæ de Edeston, anno

im(m)inet, religiosis personis in usus proprios concessis, ordinandi per nos et instituendi vicarii, pro sustentatione sua perpetua, congruam de ipsarum ecclesiarum proventibus assignatam sibi habeant portionem; eo nos convenit studiosiorem operam adhibere quo in ipsis ecclesiis assidue servituri, et facturi continue residentiam personalem, de commissa sibi per nos animarum cura, nedum pro se-ipsis, verum etiam pro nobis, et successoribus nostris, teneantur in districto venturi Judicis examine respondere. Sane dudum ex officii nostri debito in diocesi nostra visitationis officium exercentes, comperimus, quod religiosi viri, Prior et Conventus monasterii Sancti Andreæ de Hextildesham, ecclesiam parochialem de Edeston tanquam sibi appropriatam per nonnulla tempora tenuerunt; in qua non est perpetuus vicarius institutus, nec quivis alius ad animarum curam in parochia dictæ ecclesiæ exercendam per loci ordinarium deputatus; sicque dicta ecclesia, non absque nostro et animarum parochianorum ejusdem ecclesiæ periculo, ... regimine hactenus extitit desolata. Cupientes igitur tam periculoso defectui congruum remedium adhibere, felicis recordationis domini Octoboni, quondam legati in Angliam, vestigiis inhærentes; qui super ecclesiis religiosis domibus in usus proprios concessis pie et provide inter cætera noscitur statuisse, ut in eisdem per loci ordinarios perpetui instituantur vicarii, ordinata eis de ipsarum ecclesiarum proventibus sufficienti et congrua portione, ex qua honeste sustentari valeant, et incumbentia sibi onera supportare; perpetuam vicariam in dicta ecclesia parochiali de Edeston, vocatis legitime religiosis prædictis, invocato Christi nomine, in

elapso et amplius, admisit ecclesiam de Aldeston, in archidiaconatu Northumbriæ, spectantem ad præsentationem Prioris de Hextildesham, per cujus receptionem vacavit vicaria prædicta; a quo tempore hucusque idem Willelmus de facto tenuit vicariam illam, et fructus percepit.

"Item dominus Simo de Salton tenet nunc vicariam illam ex assignatione Prioris de Hextildesham, absque alia institutione canonica; nec ipse, nec prædecessores sui fuerunt instituti per archiepiscopum.

"Item Prior de Hextildesham, rector ecclesiæ de Edeston prædicta, per multa tempora, sciens prædictam vicariam vacantem, fraudulenter omisit personam idoneam domino archiepiscopo præsentare; et posuit ibi vicarios, auctoritate propria, pro libito voluntatis, in elusionem et contemptum domini archiepiscopi." (Reg. Dec. et Capit. Ebor., sede vacante, 122 *b*.)

The result of this contest was the present ordination of the vicarage.

The Prior and Convent, as will be seen from the Black Book, had a considerable estate in Edston. The following is the notice of the place in an early copy of Kirkby's Inquest in the possession of the Dean and Chapter of York (fol. 37 *b*):—"*Ediston.* In Ediston sunt viij carucatæ terræ de feodo Rogeri Bygod: unde Prior de Hexthid tenet v carucatas terræ et j bovatam non geld de libertate Beati Petri. Et Priorissa tenet v bovatas terræ non geld. Et Waterus Romayn tenet ij carucatas terræ geld de Ricardo de Bronhue; et Ricardus de comite Albem', et comes de comite de Bygod, et Bygod de rege in capite; unde ix carucatæ terræ faciunt feodum militis et reddunt ad finem wapp. ijs."

forma quæ sequitur duximus ordinandam. In primis statuimus, decernimus, et etiam ordinamus, quod vicarius perpetuus in dicta ecclesia de Edeston, per nos et successores nostros qui pro tempore fuerint, ad præsentationem dictorum religiosorum institutionem habeat; et percipiat omnes minutas decimas, videlicet lanæ, agnorum, pullanorum, vitulorum, porcellorum, aucarum, ovorum, columbarum, lini, canabi, et aliorum quorumcumque fructuum in ortis et virgultis crescentium ubicumque infra parochiam antedictam; necnon omnes oblationes, ac mortuaria quæcumque, et alias quascumque minutas decimas ad dictam ecclesiam quandocumque obvenientes, seu quomodolibet pertinentes; decimis de quibuslibet animalibus dictorum religiosorum existentibus seu commorantibus, infra prædictam parochiam provenientibus, duntaxat exceptis; de quorum animalium suorum incrementis iidem religiosi vicariis, qui pro tempore fuerint in eadem ecclesia, decimas solvere nullatenus teneantur. Decimas vero garbarum et fœni totius parochiæ ipsis religiosis integraliter volumus remanere. Ordinamus insuper quod præfati religiosi illud toftum, jacens prope ecclesiam prædictam ex parte australi, inter toftum Henrici filii Rogeri ex parte occidentali, et aliud toftum dictorum Prioris et Conventus ex parte orientali; continens, ut dicitur, decem perticas in longitudine, et tres perticas cum dimidia in latitudine; quod toftum, una cum crofto eidem contiguo, ex parte australi adjacente, et duabus bovatis terræ, quæ et quas Willelmus Freman in eadem villa de dictis religiosis quondam tenuit, eidem vicariæ, et vicariis qui pro tempore fuerint in eadem, deputamus perpetuo ac etiam assignamus, juxta ordinationem cujuslibet vicarii, in eadem instituendi[p] infra annum a data præsentium, competenter ædificare, et claudere propriis eorum sumptibus teneantur. De oneribus insuper ecclesiæ prædictæ incumbentibus sic duximus ordinandum; videlicet, quod dicti religiosi cancellum dictæ ecclesiæ, quotiens opus fuerit, reficere, ac etiam, si necessitas immineat, de novo construere teneantur. Vicarius vero, qui pro tempore fuerit, libros, vestimenta, et cætera ipsius ecclesiæ ornamenta, quatenus de consuetudine patriæ ad rectores ecclesiarum pertinet, invenire; procurationemque archidiacono loci pro visitatione sua debitam solvere; cæteraque quoque onera ordinaria subire et agnoscere annis singulis teneatur. Extraordinaria vero onera dicti religiosi, quotienscumque emerserint, solvere teneantur: institutione et destitutione vicarii in ecclesia memorata, ac etiam omni jure et jurisdictione episcopali, tam in ipsam ecclesiam quam in quoslibet ejus ministros ac paro-

[p] On Feb. 2, 1310-11, John de Salton was instituted to the vicarage at the presentation of the Prior and Convent of Hexham (Reg. Greenfield, i., 100).

chianos, nobis et ecclesiæ nostræ Ebor. nostrisque successoribus in perpetuum reservata. Hanc autem ordinationem nostram, in omnibus et singulis suis articulis, ratam, firmam, et illibatam futuris perpetuis temporibus statuimus et decernimus permanere. In quorum omnium testimonium huic ordinationi sigillum nostrum duximus apponendum. Data apud Cawod, xiij kalendas Februarii, anno gratiæ millesimo trescentesimo decimo, et pontificatus nostri quinto.

XXXVI.—AN ORDINATION OF THE VICARAGE OF SALTON BY ROBERT DE WHELPINGTON, PRIOR OF HEXHAM. [Ex libro vocato Domesday book, penes Dec. et Capit. Ebor., 94 *b*.]

Universis pateat per præsentes quod die Dominica, proxima post festum Sancti Bartholomei Apostoli, anno Domini millesimo ccc^{mo} duodecimo, ordinatum fuit per nos R., Priorem de Hextildesham, præbendarium de Salton, quod dominus Johannes de Tweng,[q] perpetuus vicarius in ecclesia nostra de Salton, per nos secundum consuetudinem et statutum ecclesiæ et capituli Ebor. admissus ac noviter ordinatus, habeat et percipiat totum alteragium ejusdem ecclesiæ in minutis decimis, oblationibus, et mortuariis quibuscumque, ac etiam decimam fœni de Salton et de Brauby; salvis nobis et successoribus nostris decimis subscriptis; videlicet, decima lanæ et agnorum, necnon omnimodis decimis garbarum cujuscumque bladi, sive in campis sive in ortis crescentis, per totam parochiam; una cum decimis de omnimodis dominicis rebus et animalibus nostris quibuscumque; et denariis Sancti Petri. Ordinatum est, insuper, per nos, quod idem vicarius solvat pensionem annuam decem solidorum, debitam ecclesiæ de Normanby; et quod inveniat ornamenta summi altaris dictæ ecclesiæ de Salton per nos consueta et debita inveniri: item luminaria in choro, et stipendia clericorum, una cum vino, hostiis, et cæteris Divino officio op(p)ortunis; ita quod ab omnibus aliis oneribus, ordinariis et extraordinariis, dictus vicarius penitus sit quietus. In cujus rei testimonium huic ordinationi nostræ indentatæ sigillum nostrum sub alternatione duximus apponendum. Data apud Salton, die et anno prænominatis.

[q] Tweng, or Thweng, was admitted to the vicarage *in crastino festi S. Barnabæ*, 1311 (Liber intitulat. T. penes Dec. et Capit. Ebor., 20 *a*). This is a quiet little arrangement between the prebendary of Salton and his vicar.

XXXVII.—AN ORDER FROM ARCHBISHOP GREENFIELD FOR MARMADUKE, CALLED THE SERJEANT, TO BE ADMITTED INTO THE HOSPITAL OF ST. GILES AT HEXHAM. [Reg. archiep. Greenfield, pars ii., 37 *a*.]

W., etc., dilecto filio ballivo nostro de Hextildesham salutem, gratiam, et benedictionem. Quia intelleximus a fidedignis nostris quod Marmaducus, dictus Serjaunt,[r] nobis et prædecessoribus nostris in officiis sibi commissis fideliter et laudabiliter diutius deservivit; qui jam senio adeo est confractus, et sui ipsius impotens, ac paupertate depressus, quod victum sibi quærere jam non valet; volumus, et mandamus, quatinus eundem Marmaducum in hospitali nostro Sancti Egidii de Hextildesham ponatis; et, juxta facultates ejusdem hospitalis, faciatis, quoad vixerit, vitæ necessaria ministrari. Valete. Data apud Munketon, ij idus Septembris, pontificatus nostri anno septimo.

XXXVIII.—LICENCE FROM EDWARD II. FOR THE PRIOR AND CONVENT OF HEXHAM TO ACQUIRE HALF OF THE MANOR OF HETON PARVA. [Rot. Pat., 7th Edward II., membr. 14.]

Rex omnibus ad quos, etc., salutem. Licet de communi consilio, etc.; per finem tamen, quem dilectus nobis in Christo . . . Prior de Hextildesham, fecit nobiscum, concessimus, et licentiam dedimus, pro nobis et hæredibus nostris, quantum in nobis est, Johanni de Cambhou, quod ipse medietatem manerii de Parva Heton, cum pertinentiis, dare possit et assignare præfato Priori et Conventui ejusdem loci: habendam et tenendam sibi et successoribus suis imperpetuum: et eisdem Priori et Conventui, quod ipsi dictam medietatem manerii illius, cum pertinentiis, a præfato Johanne recipere possint et tenere, sibi et successoribus suis imperpetuum, sicut prædictum est, tenore præsentium similiter licentiam dedimus specialem: nolentes

[r] Several documents connected with the hospital of St. Giles occur subsequently; and, elsewhere in this volume, I propose to give a short account of the foundation and a list of its masters. The old servant, for whom the archbishop finds a resting-place, had probably been one of the serjeants of the town. I give another mandate of the same character:—"Willelmus, etc., dilectis nobis in Christo ballivo nostro de Hextildesham, et fratri Thomæ de Appelton, custodi spiritualitatis nostræ ibidem, salutem, gratiam, et benedictionem. Quia Ricardo Felawe de Acum, harum bajulo, intuitu caritatis concessimus, quod ut unus leprosus in hospitali nostro de Hextildesham percipere valeat; et in eodem suo perpetuo immorari; vobis mandamus quatinus ipsum Ricardum in dicto hospitali, vice nostra, in statu hujusmodi collocetis. Valete. Data apud Cawod, octavo idus Martii, anno gratiæ m° ccc^{mo} xxij°, et pontificatus nostri sexto." (Reg. Melton, 414 *a*.)

quod prædictus Johannes, vel hæredes sui, aut præfati Prior et Conventus, vel successores sui, ratione statuti prædicti, per nos vel hæredes nostros inde occasionentur, molestentur in aliquo, seu graventur: salvis tamen, etc. In cujus, etc. Teste rege apud Beverlacum, xxix die Aprilis. Per finem xx marcarum.

XXXIX.—AN ENQUIRY BY ORDER OF ARCHBISHOP MELTON INTO THE STATE OF THE HOSPITAL OF ST. GILES AT HEXHAM. [Reg. archiep. Melton, 399.]

Venerabili in Christo patri et domino, domino W., Dei gratia Ebor. archiepiscopo, Angliæ primati, suus Radulphus de Empingham,[s] canonicus monasterii de Hextildesham, custos spiritualitatis suæ inde, salutem, . . . reverentiam, et honorem. Mandatum vestrum vij idus Octobris recepi, tenorem continens infrascriptum.

Willelmus, permissione Divina Ebor. archiepiscopus, Angliæ primas, dilecto filio custodi spiritualitatis nostræ de Hextildesham, salutem, gratiam, et benedictionem. Super statu hospitalis de Hextildesham volentes effici certiores, vobis committimus, firmiter injungentes quatinus super fundatione, rebus etiam, redditibus et possessionibus ejusdem; quis, videlicet, et quo zelo; quorum auctoritatibus intervenientibus; et ad quos usus illud primitus fundavit; quot etiam et quæ personæ recipi potuerint, consueverint, et debuerint in eodem, ac jam habeantur in ipso; et quæ bona ac facultates jam exstant ibidem pro sustentatione præsentium personarum; et ad quot ultra sufficere potuerit admittendos, per viros fidedignos, non suspectos, per quos hujus rei veritas melius sciri poterit et inquiri, juratos, et diligentius examinatos, plenam veritatem exactius inquiratis. Et nos de tota continentia dicti hospitalis, tam in personis, quam rebus, ac aliis circumstantiis singulis, in præmissis, vel circa ea, quomodolibet attendendis; ac omni eo quod inveneritis et

[s] A document of the greatest possible interest, the only one, in fact, which gives us any insight into the history of the old hospital of St. Giles at Hexham. I shall speak of it elsewhere. This is the original return made by Empingham, and addressed to the archbishop. It is inserted between two leaves of the register. The following document relates, also, slightly to the hospital:—" Willelmus, etc., dilectis filiis officialibus curiæ nostræ Ebor., et ejus commissario generali, salutem, gratiam, et benedictionem. Ex parte Prioris et Conventus de Hextildesham nobis extitit supplicatum, quod contra quosdam husbondes de eadem Priori et Conventui fieri faceremus justitiæ complementum; quod renuere nolumus, nec etiam hiis negare; proviso tamen quod status et jura hospitalis nostri de Hextildesham, ad se defendendum, ut accepimus, impotentes, in nostra absentia non decidant quovis modo. Valete. Data apud Westmonasterium, x kalendas Maii, pontificatus nostri anno nono." (Reg. Melton, 570 *a*.)

feceritis in præmissis, ad singulos respondendo articulos certificetis per vestras literas, quæ harum seriem repræsentent. Valete. Data apud Crathorn, ij kalendas Octobris, anno gratiæ millesimo ccc^{mo} vicesimo, et pontificatus nostri quarto.

Hujus igitur auctoritate mandati, ij idus Octobris, anno domini supradicto, apud Hextild', in pleno loci capitulo tunc ibidem celebrato, per viros fidedignos infrascriptos, juratos, et non suspectos, super præmissis et ea contingentibus inquisitionem feci fieri diligentem : videlicet, per Antonium de Erington, Robertum de Vauz, Johannem de Falufeld, Henricum filium Radulfi, Thomam Crane, Johannem piscatorem, Willelmum del Burn, Thomam de Coquina, Adam Co . . . , Thomam de Gosseden, Laurentium sutorem, Willelmum de Ewarde-lawe, et Ricardum de Falufeld : qui dicunt, per sacramentum suum, quod quidam archiepiscopus Ebor. ab antiquo fundavit prædictum hospitale, cujus nomen ignorant; de cujus fundatione habuerunt factum ejusdem archiepiscopi, et confirmationem capituli Ebor., ac quædam alia privilegia a curia Romana; quæ quidem munimenta, una cum omnibus aliis cartis et scriptis dictum hospitale tangentibus, a quodam fratre domus prædictæ, per Scottos in principio guerræ fugiente et interfecto hostiliter, fuerant asportata. Dicunt etiam quod totam terram arabilem, quam habent ubique, de una caruca de facili possunt colere, et eo amplius si haberent. Item dicunt quod habuerunt in villis de Hextildesham, Falufeld, et Porteyate quemdam annuum redditum xjs. ijd. de dono diversorum; de quibus nichil nunc percipiunt, eo quod loca hujusmodi jacent vasta. Item dicunt quod solebant percipere et habere, ante guerram Scotiæ, singulis diebus per annum, quatuor panes nigros et quatuor lagenas cervisiæ secundariæ de Prioratu de Hextild'; ac etiam unam lagenam cervisiæ de quolibet braciante super terram Prioris in Hextild', quotiens braciaverit; de quibus nunc non percipiunt nisi sex nigros panes et duas lagenas cervisiæ secundariæ singulis septimanis. Dicunt etiam quod caritatis intuitu fuerat prædictum hospitale fundatum, auctoritatibus domini archiepiscopi et Prioris tunc temporis intervenientibus, maxime pro pauperibus husbandis, infirmis, et leprosis, per inopiam depressis, videlicet, de libertate prædicta oriundis; ita quod dominus archiepiscopus, qui pro tempore fuerit, possit ponere duos de hujusmodi tenentibus suis infirmis ibidem, et Prior alios duos de suis, et non plures, existentibus ipsis vivis. Item dicunt quod bona et facultates domus, quoad præsens, vix sufficiunt pro sustentatione trium personarum, nunc in dicta domo existentium, et non propter eos, nisi quilibet eorum fortius laboraret; nec debent ibi esse nisi quatuor fratres ex assignatione seu ordinatione domini archiepiscopi et Prioris, una vice; sed si aliquis alius de libertate, vel extra, qui bona sua dictis fratribus et hospitali, pro sustentatione vitæ suæ in eadem optinenda, conferre voluerit, liceat magistro et fratribus dictæ domus ipsum pro utilitate domus suæ sic admittere, consulto super hoc tantummodo custode suo per dominum archiepiscopum deputato. Dicunt etiam quod solebant esse in dicta domo aliquando septem, aliquando octo fratres, secundum majus et minus, prout facultates domus tunc temporis habundabant; sed, diebus et rebus se habentibus ut nunc, plures nondum bene admitti poterunt in eodem, nisi conferendo dictis fratribus de bonis suis, ut superius est expressum. Item dicunt quod non habent in præsenti nisi quatuor equos affros, et quatuor boves pro eorum caruca, et unam vaccam tantum; de quibus duo equi et duo boves sunt ex commodato cujusdam Willelmi le Walde, pro voluntate sua revocandi. Bladum ibidem nunc inventum vix sufficiet pro semine hujus anni et sustentatione eorumdem. De aliis circumstanciis nesciunt plus deponere requisiti. Et sic mandatum vestrum reverendum juxta vim, formam et officium ejusdem reverenter sum, prout condecet, executus. Conservet Altissimus vitam vestram diu prosperam, ad honorem et regimen ecclesiæ suæ sanctæ. Data apud Hextild', die et anno prænominatis.

XL.—LICENCE FROM EDWARD II. FOR THE PRIOR AND CONVENT OF HEXHAM TO ACQUIRE DIVERS LANDS IN KIRK-HETON, NESBIT, EAST-MATFEN, EACHWICK, AND DALTON. [Rot. Pat., 16th Edward II., membr. 4.]

Rex omnibus ad quos, etc., salutem. Sciatis quod cum per literas nostras patentes de gratia nostra speciali, in subsidium relevandi statum domus de Hexteldesham, concesserimus, et licentiam dederimus, pro nobis et hæredibus nostris, quantum in nobis est, dilectis nobis in Christo Priori et Conventui loci prædicti, quod ipsi viginti libratas terræ et redditus, cum pertinentiis, tam de feodo suo proprio quam alieno, (exceptis terris, tenementis, et redditibus, quæ de nobis tenentur in capite) adquirere possint; habendas et tenendas sibi et successoribus suis imperpetuum, statuto de terris et tenementis ad manummortuam non ponendis edito non obstante, prout in literis nostris prædictis plenius continetur; nos, volentes concessionem nostram prædictam debito effectui mancipari, concessimus, et licentiam dedimus, pro nobis et hæredibus nostris, quantum in nobis est, Willelmo Hecson, quod ipse duo tofta et novem acras terræ cum pertinentiis in Kyrk-heton; Gilberto de Babynton, quod ipse unum toftum et novem acras terræ, cum pertinentiis, in eadem villa; Roberto filio Hugonis de Cambhowe, quod ipse duo mesuagia et decem et octo acras terræ, cum pertinentiis, in eadem villa; Willelmo de Shafthowe, quod ipse duo tofta et quinquaginta et quinque acras terræ, cum pertinentiis, in Nesbyt; Henrico Derlyng, quod ipse tres acras prati, cum pertinentiis, in Est-Matfen; Willelmo de Belyncham, quod ipse unum mesuagium et decem et octo acras terræ, cum pertinentiis, in Echewyk; et Roberto de Appelton et Johanni Fissher, quod ipsi medietatem villæ de Dalton juxta Stanfordham, cum pertinentiis, quæ de nobis non tenentur in capite; et quæ quidem mesuagia, tofta, terra, et pratum, valent per annum in omnibus exitibus, juxta verum valorem eorumdem, quadraginta et duos solidos et octo denarios; et prædicta medietas tempore pacis valere consuevit per annum, juxta verum valorem ejusdem, centum solidos, et nunc non valet per annum nisi viginti solidos, sicut per inquisitiones de mandato nostro inde factas et in cancellaria nostra retornatas plenius est compertum; dare possint et assignare præfatis Priori et Conventui: habendum et tenenendum sibi et successoribus suis imperpetuum, in partem satisfactionis viginti libratarum terræ et redditus prædictorum. Et eisdem Priori et Conventui, quod ipsi prædicta mesuagia, tofta, terram, pratum, et medietatem, cum pertinentiis, a præfato Willelmo ——, etc.,—recipere possint et tenere, tenore præsentium licentiam dedimus specialem ——. Teste rege apud Pontem-fractum, xij die Februarii.

XLI.—A LIST OF THE LANDS, ETC., BELONGING TO THE PRIOR AND CONVENT OF HEXHAM BY THE GIFT, ETC., OF THE ARCHBISHOPS OF YORK. [Reg. archiep. Melton, 426 *b*.]

Tenemus in liberam, puram, et perpetuam elemosinam ecclesiam de Hextildesham, et Prioratum ejusdem, cum omnibus pertinentiis suis, de dono domini Thomæ Secundi, Ebor. archepiscopi; et inde habuimus cartam dicti domini Thomæ; et tenuimus a tempore quo non extat memoria.[t]

Tenemus, etiam, duas villas de Aynewik, cum omnibus suis pertinentiis, et Sandhou et Yerurige, et quicquid ad eas pertinet in campis, silvis, et aquis, et molendinis de Tyne cum stagno ejusdem; et cum tota secta quæ ad illud pertinet, vel pertinere debet; et decimam omnium rerum, tam domini archiepiscopi,

[t] This rental is undated, but it occurs among the documents of the year 1328. It is a singular mixture of French and Latin.

quam aliorum infra libertatem de Hext' existentium, de dono dicti domini Thomæ; et inde habuimus cartam ejusdem, et confirmationem capituli Ebor., et tenuimus a tempore quo non extat memoria.

Habuimus, etiam, de dono ejusdem domini Thomæ archiepiscopi, a tempore quo non extat memoria usque tempus guerræ ultimo ortæ inter dominum regem et Scotos, sok, et sak, et alias libertates, videlicet, emendas assisæ panis et cervisiæ.

Tenemus, etiam, in villa de Hext' quasdam partes terræ: videlicet, totum vicum integrum qui vocatur Koxhou; xxiiij mesuagia, cum pertinentiis, in vico qui vocatur Prestpoffil; xiiij mesuagia, cum pertinentiis, in vico qui dicitur Vicus Fori; xvj mesuagia, cum pertinentiis, in vico qui dicitur Hencotes; et illam terram ubi constructum fuit hospitale peregrinorum,[u] cum pertinentiis; et totam villam de Dotlond cum pertinentiis de Knytelhesil; et utramque Grotyngton, cum omnibus suis pertinentiis; et quendam agrum (juxta) Tyne flumen; et quietum pastum propriis porcis nostris et porcis villicorum hominum nostrorum in terra Sancti Andreæ manentium, de dono domini Thurstini, quondam Ebor. archiepiscopi; et tenuimus a tempore quo non extat memoria, sine aliquo sæculari servitio faciendo.

Tenemus, etiam, vij acras et dimidiam terræ in quadam cultura quæ dicitur le Sele, libere et quiete, sine aliquo servitio faciendo; de dono domini Galfridi, quondam Ebor. archiepiscopi; et inde habuimus cartam ejusdem et confirmationem capituli Ebor.: et tenuimus a tempore quo non extat memoria.

Tenemus, etiam, medietatem villæ de Byngfeld, cum suis pertinentiis, in liberam, puram, et perpetuam elemosinam, de dono cujusdam Germundi; et inde habuimus cartam ejusdem, et confirmationem domini Thurstini et capituli Ebor.; et tenuimus a tempore quo non extat memoria.

Nous tenoms, du doun l'ercevesque Wauter, vij^{xx} v acres et demye de terre, c'est asaver, xl acres entre Aynewyk et Akwod devers le north; et iiij^{xx} x acres desous Dotland vers le suth; et xv acres de terre et di. desouz Dotlond devers le north; par feaute et les services de iiij marcs par an p^{r} touz services, de qui nous ne proismes profist de gaigneurye ces xxx anns passez.

Estre ce nous tenoms les molins de Hamburn et de Neubigyng, oue la sente que a eux apertiegnent, par feaute et les services de x marcs par an p^{r} touz services: lez queux molins ne valent nul, an communement xxxs.

Estre ce nous tenoms lx acres de terre, que nous feurent

[u] This is the only place in which this hospital is mentioned, for it seems to be distinct from that dedicated to St. Giles.

donez en fraunche et perpetuele aumosne, en amendement de la ferme des molins avantditz; pour quele terre nous sumes chargez de deux marcs par an: de quei nous ne proismes nul profist ces xxx auns.

Estre ce nos tenoms xxvij acres de terre j rode, enclos deniz notre park de Dotland, par les services de ixs. jd. par an p^{r} touz services; et un Estiephne del Hill et sa soer, et Johan le fuiz Hawyse tenent viij acres de terre: les queles nous feurent grantez par l'ercevesque Johan, d'avoir encloz deniz le dit park: p^{r} quey nos avoms paye la fyn iiijd. pour l'acre, tantque en cea; et les autres gentz avantdites tenent la terre avantdite, et paient la ferme due a ce que nous entendoms auxi come nous fesoms; par qui nos prioms au seigneur que de ces ijs. viijd. nous ne soioms mye charges deficome autres gentz tenent la terre, et paient la ferme a ce que nous entendoms.

Estre ce nous tenoms deux acres de terre wast devers le comune petere, par les services de viijd. par an pour touz services.

Estre ce nous tenoms divers toftes deniz le Sele enclos, par les services de iiijs. ijd. o. par an pour touz services.

Estre ce nous tenoms une terre q'est appellez Whetewang; pour quele nous solioms payer iijs. par an: de qui nous ne proismes nul profist ces xxx auns; par qui nous la rendoms au seigneur par c'este lettre: et prioms a sa seigneurye qil ce ne veoille a mal prendre.

Estre ce nous tenoms vij graunges pour noz dismes en vij villes, par feaute et les services de ijs. iiijd. per an, pour touz services.

Estre ce nous tenoms la terre, qui feust a Robert de Skipton en Byngfeld, par foialte et les servi de di. marc par ane, pour touz services.

Estre ce nous tenoms ascunes menues parceles de terres et toftes en Hext', appendantes et assignez as officers; des queux nous ne pooms uncore savoir la verite combien yad, ne queux services de ceux sont duz; car nous n'entremedlasmes unques de cels offices mes a plus cost; que nous pourroms avoir la verite, nous serroms la conoissance auxint volentres du petit come nous avoms fait du remeraunt.

Estre ce nous tenoms xxxiiij acres de terre entre la ville de Dotland et l'assart que adonque feust de Thornleye, par foialte et les services de xjs. iiijd. par an, pour touz services, du doun l'ercevesque Wauter: le quele terre adgiene waste ces xxx anns passez.

Præterea concessimus eisdem canonicis unam viam ab exitu villæ suæ de Aynewyk per mediam hayæ nostræ de Acwode a bercaria sua directe versus aquilonem, usque ad communem pasturam suam ultra Birke-burge; quæ continet in latitudine decem perticatas: pro hac autem donatione, et concessione remiserunt nobis et successoribus nostris prædicti canonici, pro se et successoribus suis, et hominibus suis, imperpetuum, totum jus et clameum quod habuerunt, vel habere potuerunt, in haya nostra de Akwode; scilicet, ad exitum villæ de Sandhou, per divisas Petri de Vallibus usque Birkeburne, et de Birkeburne descendendo usque ad molendinum de Akum.

XLII.—AN AGREEMENT BETWEEN ARCHBISHOP MELTON AND THE PRIOR AND CONVENT OF HEXHAM ABOUT THE TITHE OF HAY IN THE FORESTS BELONGING TO THE ARCHBISHOP IN HEXHAMSHIRE. [Reg. Melton, 432 *a.*]

Hæc indentura testatur quod cum inter religiosos viros, Priorem et Conventum de Hextildesham, petentes, ex una parte, et venerabilem patrem, dominum Willelmum de Melton, Dei gratia Ebor. archiepiscopum, Angliæ primatem, suosque tenentes in forestis suis infra libertatem de Hextildesham, defendentes, ex parte altera; super decima fœni in eisdem forestis mota fuisset materia quæstionis; ita inter dictas partes convenit, quod præfatus dominus archiepiscopus, et successores sui, a præstatione hujus decimæ fœni de pratis, seu clausis, infra forestas suas infra libertatem prædictam provenientis, pro tempore quo dicta prata seu clausa in manibus suis tenuerint, liberi sint et immunes, sicut prædecessores sui Ebor. archiepiscopi liberi et immunes esse consueverant in hac parte; et pro tempore quo idem venerabilis pater et successores sui dicta prata seu clausa aliis ad firmam dimiserint, tenentes ipsi decimas suas fœni, sicut et alias decimas suas, ecclesiæ suæ parochiali de Hextildesham integraliter solvere teneantur. In cujus rei testimonium tam dictus venerabilis pater, et tenentes sui prædicti, quam dicti Prior et Conventus, huic indenturæ alternatim sua sigilla apposuerunt. Data apud Ripon, decimo kalendas Aprilis, anno gratiæ millesimo ccc^{mo} xxxj^{o}.

XLIII.—RELEASE FROM RICHARD DE BURY, BISHOP OF DURHAM, TO THE PRIOR AND CONVENT OF HEXHAM OF A PART OF THE PENSION DUE TO HIM OUT OF THE CHURCH OF STAMFORDHAM. [Reg. Bury at Durham, 331 *b.*]

Ricardus, permissione Divina Dunolm. episcopus, dilectis nobis in Christo Priori et Conventui de Hextildesham salutem in Auctore salutis. Cum fructus, et redditus, et proventus ecclesiæ de Standfordham,[v] nostræ diocesios, de qua annua pensio quinquaginta marcarum sterlingorum nobis et ecclesiæ nostræ debetur, sint propter frequentes Scotorum incursus, (et) varia exactionum onera, quæ hiis diebus plus solito invalescunt, et alia incom(m)oda, ita tenues et exiles, quod supportatis ipsius ecclesiæ, quam in usus proprios detinetis, oneribus, hospitalitate debita et consueta servata, dictaque pensione soluta, nichil aut parum vobis supererit in usus illos convertendum pro quibus vobis appropriatur ipsa ecclesia; sicut fida et frequens nobis relatio patefecit. Nos ad præmissa considerationis nostræ aciem provide convertentes, vobis et ecclesiæ vestræ de Hextildesham de dicta pensione, ex causis præmissis, et de gratia nostra speciali, decem marcas annis singulis, quamdiu regimini ecclesiæ nostræ Dunolm. præfuerimus, condonamus, et remittimus per præsentes, sigilli nostri appensione munitas. Data apud Novum-Castrum-super-Tynam, nono decimo die Julii, anno Domini millesimo trescentesimo quadragesimo, et consecrationis nostræ septimo.

[v] In consequence of the misery caused by the Scottish invasions, and the other troubles of the times, Richard de Bury, the scholar-bishop of Durham, reduces the annual pension due to him out of the church of Stamfordham, during his tenure of the see of Durham, from fifty marks to forty. The following extract from the Roll of the Repairs made on the bishop of Durham's estates, etc., from the 5th to the 6th of Edward VI., thus alludes to Stamfordham :—

"*The chaunsell of Stannerden.* Payd to one glaser by Arthure Shaftowe for comyng to tayke mesure of the wyndois, and for maykyng of xij foytte of new glasse; and for wirkynge ix dayes in mendynge of old wyndois, booith for his bord-wages and his daye-waigis, payd to Arthure Shaftow by Mr. Chaunseler comaundment, xxiijs. vjd. Paid for th'one half of the Paraffrases of Erasmus vjs. Payd for th'one half of the Bybyll vijs. *Summa,* xxxvs. vjd." [From the original roll in the Auditor's office at Durham.]

Among the miscellaneous documents in the possession of the Dean and Chapter of Durham, No. 4305, is the following undated letter (written in the fifteenth century) from the collector of some tax on several of the livings belonging to the Prior and Convent of Hexham. The writer seems to have been a brother of the house :—"Seipsum totum in Domino Salutari. Juxta discretum et circumspectum consilium vestrum, computato per nos juxta æstimationem nostram vero valore ecclesiarum nostrarum, videlicet, Cholverton xxxli; cujus præstatio hac vice xxxs.: Wardon xxliijli; cujus præstatio xxiiijs.. Slaveley lxxs.; cujus præstatio iijs. vjd.: Stanfordham nil, quia dominus episcopus et vicarius omne percipiunt emolumentum. Quibus computatis, sic mittimus vobis per præsentem bajulum lvijs. vjd., per vos, si placet, vel per procuratorem vestrum, secundum ordinationem vestram dominis collectoribus persolvendos; sub spe gratiæ et remedii per vos excogitati, si clerus, Deo volente, circa ipsa duxerit insistendum. Et, si opus fuerit, in animas nostras jurare poterit quod ad valorem, vel prope, se habent, omnibus computatis. Pro expensis in hac parte contribuendis, bursarii domi respondebunt, prout viderit expedire. Valete." [Sigillum deest.]

XLIV.—A WRIT FROM EDWARD III. AUTHORIZING THE TAXING AFRESH OF THE CHURCH OF SALTON, ON ACCOUNT OF THE INJURIES DONE TO IT BY THE SCOTS, ETC. [Reg. archiep. Zouche, 156 *a*.]

Edwardus, Dei gratia rex Angliæ et Franciæ et dominus Hiberniæ, venerabili in Christo patri, W., eadem gratia archiepiscopo Ebor., Angliæ primati, salutem. Supplicarunt nobis dilecti nobis in Christo Prior et Conventus de Hextildesham quod cum parochia ecclesiæ præbendalis de Salton, vestræ diocesios, quam tenent in usus suos proprios, fuerit et sit per invasiones Scottorum et incendia plurimum destructa, miserabiliter et collapsa; et licet aliæ ecclesiæ dictarum partium, sic destructæ, fuerint taxatæ de novo; et primæ taxationes eorum mitigatæ, juxta valorem tunc currentem; dicta tamen ecclesia de Salton, per negligentiam tunc Prioris loci prædicti agentis in remotis, taxata non extitit, nec ejus taxatio mitigata, in grave dampnum dictorum Prioris et Conventus; cum juxta antiquam taxam (licet dicta ecclesia propter destructionem hujusmodi tantum non valeat), in singulis præstationibus et impositionibus decimæ clero dictæ vestræ diocesios factis, solvere sit compulsa; velimus eis super hoc de remedio congruo providere. Nos, compatientes depressioni dicti Prioratus, cui per guerram Scotiæ noscitur subjacere, et provide volentes cum ipsis Priore et Conventu in hac parte agere gratiose, vobis mandamus, quod super vero valore dictæ ecclesiæ de Salton, quantum, videlicet, valeat hiis diebus, diligentem faciatis inquisitionem; et, juxta comperta per inquisitionem illam, præfatam ecclesiam de Salton taxetis moderate, prout prius factum est in aliis beneficiis ecclesiasticis dictarum partium sic destructis: taxationem inde per vos de novo faciendam nobis in cancellaria nostra sub sigillo vestro remittentes cum hoc brevi. Teste meipso apud Westmonasterium, xxviij° die Augusti, anno regni nostri Angliæ decimo octavo, regni vero nostri Franciæ quinto.

Certificatio ejusdem.

Excellentissimo principi et domino suo reverendissimo, domino Edwardo Dei gratia regi Angliæ et Franciæ illustri, et domino Hiberniæ, Willelmus, permissione, etc., salutem in Eo per Quem reges regnant et principes dominantur. Breve vestrum nuper recepimus hiis annexum, cujus auctoritate super vero valore ecclesiæ præbendalis de Salton, et aliis articulis omnibus et singulis in dicto brevi contentis, juxta vim, formam, et effectum ejusdem, per rectores, vicarios, capellanos, et circumvicinos, ac parochianos ecclesiæ de Saulton prædicta, tam clericos quam laicos fidedignos, in hac parte juratos, et distincte examinatos, hujus rei habentes notitiam pleniorem, inquiri fecimus diligenter. Et quia per inquisitionem hujusmodi comperimus, quod dicta ecclesia de Saulton, per invasiones Scotorum, et incendia, sicut aliæ ecclesiæ circumvicinæ, plurimum jam destructa; cujus taxatio, sicut aliarum ecclesiarum circumvicinarum, ob negligentiam Prioris de Hextildesham, rectoris dictæ ecclesiæ, qui tunc fuerit in remotis agens, nullatenus fuerat alias mitigata, vix valet xxli[w] hiis diebus; ipsam ecclesiam de Saulton, ad viginti libras sterling duntaxat taxavimus; quam quidem taxam excellentiæ vestræ regiæ innotescimus per præsentes, sigilli nostri appensione munitas; ut ulterius, quæ in hac parte requirentur, vestra exequetur si placet, regia celsitudo; quam ad regimen ecclesiæ populi sui Altissimus diu dirigat et conservet. Data apud Cawode, octavo die mensis Octobris, anno Domini millesimo trescentesimo quadragesimo quarto.

XLV.—A RECOGNITION BY THE PRIOR OF HEXHAM OF THE SERVICES DUE BY HIM TO THE ARCHBISHOP OF YORK FOR LANDS WHICH HE HOLDS WITHIN THE LIBERTY OF HEXHAM. [Reg. archiep. Zouche, 297 *a*.]

Recognitio Prioris de Hextildesham de servitiis suis debitis domino archiepiscopo Eboracensi pro terris et tenementis, quæ de ipso tenet infra libertatem de Hextildesham.[x]

In primis, pro quibusdam toftis inclusis infra Prioratum suum, in loco qui dicitur le Seele, reddendo per annum quatuor solidos, duos denarios, ob. pro omnibus servitiis. Item reddendo pro vij^{xx} v acris terræ di., videlicet, xl acris terræ inter boscum de Akewode et villam de Aynewyk, et iiij^{xx} x acris sub Dotland versus austrum, et xv acris et dimidia subtus Dotland versus aquilonem, liijs. iiijd., pro omnibus. Item pro xxvij acris et una roda terræ inclusæ infra parcum suum de Dotland, ixs. jd., pro omnibus. Item pro xxxiiij acris terræ inter villam de Dotland et Thornley xjs. iiijd., pro omnibus. Item pro duabus acris vasti juxta petrariam viijd. Item pro aqua vertenda ad molendinum de Whiteley xijd. Item pro vij placeis terræ in vij villulis pro grangiis decimalibus, ijs. iiijd., pro omnibus. Item pro terris et tenementis, quæ fuerunt Roberti de Skipton in Byngford, reddendo per annum vjs. viijd. pro

[w] By an earlier taxation, without date, the church was valued at 80 marks per ann., and taxed at 46s. 8d. (Ex libro intitulato T. penes Dec. et Capit. Ebor., 78.)

[x] The same register contains two other copies of this recognition.

omnibus servitiis. Item pro molendinis de Hamburne et Neubigging, cum secta pertinente, x marcas per annum, pro omnibus. Item pro tribus toftis, quæ sunt in manibus Sacristæ et Elemosinarii, quæ jacent in vico Sancti Egidii, et quodam tofto in Hencotes, cum una roda terræ adjacente, reddendo per annum xiijd. di. qu. Item pro duabus acris terræ in campis de Hencotes, quæ vocantur Haynyng-croft, in manu Elemosinarii; et pro duabus acris terræ quæ vocantur Cou-croft; et pro quodam loco, qui vocatur Dudmans-knoll; et quadam placea terræ quæ dicitur Beaumond, in manu ejusdem Elemosinarii, reddendo per annum ijs. ijd., pro omnibus. Et protestatur dictus Prior, quod, si in posterum constare sibi poterit ab aliqua firma ulterius debita, quæ a retro fuerit propter munimenta sua combusta, vel ex quavis alia causa, fideliter in eventu dictum dominum suum reddet certiorem, et eam cognoscet fideliter, ut tenetur. Exhibita apud Cawode, xxviij° die Maii, anno pontificatus domini Willelmi la Zouche octavo.

XLVI.—LICENCE FROM ARCHBISHOP THORESBY FOR THE PRIOR AND CONVENT OF HEXHAM TO ENCLOSE DOTLAND PARK. [Reg. Thoresby, 299 *b*.]

Johannes, etc., dominus libertatis de Hextildesham, ad quos præsentes literæ pervenerint salutem. Sciatis quod concessimus et licentiam dedimus, pro nobis et successoribus nostris, dilectis nobis in Christo Priori et Conventui de Hextildesham quod ipsi quendam boscum suum, vocatum Dodland park, infra libertatem nostram prædictam, jam muratum, altiori muro includere;[y] et parcum inde facere; et boscum illum, sic inclusum, et parcum inde factum, tenere possint sibi et successoribus suis imperpetuum; sine occasione, vel impedimento nostri, vel successorum nostrorum, seu ballivorum, aut ministrorum quorumcunque: dum tamen boscus ille infra metas alicujus forestæ non existat. In cujus, etc., has literas nostras fieri fecimus patentes. Data in manerio nostro juxta Westmonasterium, sexto die Octobris, anno, etc., ut supra.

[y] The Dean and Chapter of York confirmed this grant on July 6th, 1355. The archbishop made it in the previous year (Acta Cap. Ebor., G^cy, 15 *b*).

XLVII.—PERMISSION FROM THOMAS HATFIELD, BISHOP OF DURHAM FOR THE PRIOR AND CONVENT OF HEXHAM TO ACQUIRE TEN MARKS' WORTH OF LAND AT LANCHESTER, CO. DURHAM. [Ex Rot. A. Tho. Hatfield, episc. Dunelm., in Cur. Canc. Dunelm asservato; sch. 2, no. 13, in dorso.]

Thomas, Dei gratia episcopus Dunelmensis, omnibus, etc. Sciatis quod de gratia nostra speciali, et per finem, quem Adam de Bowes fecit nobiscum, concessimus, et licentiam dedimus, pro nobis et successoribus nostris, quantum in nobis est, eidem Adæ, quod ipse unum mesuagium, sexaginta acras terræ, quatuor acras prati, et sexdecim acras bosci, cum pertinentiis, in Langcestre, quæ de nobis tenentur in capite, dare possit et assignare dilectis nobis in Christo Priori et Conventui de Hexaldesham, in liberam, puram, et perpetuam elemosinam; habendum et tenendum eisdem Priori et Conventui, et successoribus suis, in liberam, puram, et perpetuam elemosinam imperpetuum: et eisdem Priori et Conventui quod ipsi mesuagium, terram, pratum et boscum a præfato Ada recipere possint et tenere, sibi et successoribus suis prædictis, in liberam, puram, et perpetuam elemosinam imperpetuum, sicut prædictum est, tenore præsentium scilicet, licentiam dedimus specialem statuto de terris et tenementis ad manum-mortuam non ponendis edito non obstante. Nolentes quod præfatus Adam, vel hæredes sui, aut præfati Prior et Conventus, seu successores sui, ratione statuti prædicti, per nos, vel successores nostros, etc., occasionentur, molestentur in aliquo, seu graventur. In cujus rei testimonium, etc., — pat. Data per manum Johannis de Sculthorp, primo die Maii, anno supradicto (1347). Per ipsum dominum episcopum.

XLVIII.—LICENCE FROM EDWARD III. FOR THE PRIOR AND CONVENT OF HEXHAM TO ACQUIRE LANDS IN EACHWICK, WHITCHESTER, ETC. [Rot. Pat. 21st Edward III., part ii., memb. 29.]

Rex, omnibus ad quos, etc., salutem. Sciatis quod cum dominus E., nuper rex Angliæ, pater noster, per literas suas patentes concessisset, et licentiam dedisset, pro se et hæredibus suis, quantum in ipso fuit, dilectis nobis in Christo Priori et Conventui domus de Hextildesham, quod ipsi viginti libratas terræ et redditus, cum pertinentiis, tam de feodo suo proprio quam alieno, (exceptis terris et redditibus quæ (ab) ipso patre nostro tenebantur in capite) adquirere possent — statuto, etc.,

— non obstante — concessimus — Gilberto le Milnestonacres, capellano, quod ipse novem mesuagia, centum et sexaginta et unam acras terræ, quinque acras prati, et quadraginta solidatas redditus, cum pertinentiis in Echewyk, Whightchestre, Hirlawe, et Dalton, quæ de nobis non tenentur, et quæ ad sexaginta et sex solidos et octo denarios extenduntur per annum, sicut per inquisitionem inde per dilectum et fidelem nostrum Robertum Bertram, escaetorem nostrum in comitatu Northumbriæ, captam, et in cancellaria nostra retornatam, est compertum, dare possit et assignare præfatis Priori et Conventui — in valorem octo marcarum, in partem satisfactionis viginti libratarum terræ, etc. Teste custode prædicto apud Redyng, xx die Junii (1347).

XLIX.—THE PRIOR AND CONVENT OF HEXHAM ESTABLISH THEIR TITLE TO THE LIVINGS OF ISELL AND RENWICK, BEFORE THE BISHOP OF CARLISLE. [From the register of bishop Welton at Carlisle, 27 *a*.][z]

Universis, etc., Gilbertus, permissione Divina Karliolensis episcopus, salutem in Domino sempiternam. Cum nos, diocesin nostram jure nostro diocesano nuper visitantes, invenimus religiosos viros Priorem et Conventum monasterii de Hextildesham ecclesias parochiales de Isale et Ravenwyk, diocesios nostræ, tanquam sibi appropriatas habere et tenere, cum omnibus suis juribus et pertinentiis; ac de fructibus et proventibus earumdem ecclesiarum disponere; et eos percipere et possidere, tanquam veros rectores et possessores earumdem: volentes, prout ad nos pertinet, certiorari de jure et titulo ipsorum religiosorum, quibus ecclesias ipsas fuerint et sint assecuti, eosdem religiosos ad certos dies et loca, ea occasione, ad proponendum, ostendendum, et exhibendum causas rationabiles, jus, et titulum; et quicquid aliud pro se haberent super occupatione, retentione, assecutione, possessione dictarum ecclesiarum, fecimus coram nobis ad judicium legitime evocari. Quibus diebus et locis, dictis religiosis per procuratorem eorumdem sufficienter comparentibus, fuit ex parte eorumdem per ipsum procuratorem, nomine procuratorio, allegatum, propositum, et sufficienter probatum, quod iidem religiosi hujusmodi ecclesias justis et sufficientibus titulis, eisdem religiosis et eorum monasterio canonice appropriatas, cum omnibus suis juribus et pertinentiis obtinuerunt,

[z] The Prior and Convent of Hexham maintain their title before the bishop of Carlisle to the livings of Isell and Renwick in Cumberland. At the same time the bishop excuses William de Kendal, the Prior, from appearing at synods in his diocese.

retinuerunt, et adhuc obtinent et retinent in præsenti; ac ipsas ecclesias, sicut eis appropriatas, canonice possederunt, a tempore, et per tempus, cujus contrarii memoria hominum non existit, pacifice et inconcusse, et adhuc possident; scientibus, permittentibus, et non contradicentibus, sed expresse approbantibus episcopis, loci diocesanis, omnibus et singulis qui per dictum tempus successive extiterant in ecclesia Karl. — Super quibus occupatione — dictarum eccl. — dictus procurator quamplurima instrumenta publica et munimenta loco probationis coram nobis judicialiter ostenderit et exhibuerit; et, nichilominus, ex habundanti testes quamplures super possessione ipsorum religiosorum, quam per totum tempus supradictum habuerunt in ecclesiis prænominatis et adhuc habent, produxerit: quibus in forma juris admissis — ac etiam vocatis omnibus et singulis, qui fuerunt evocandi, nulloque contradictore in die comparente, demum — ipsas ecclesias, cum omnibus suis juribus et pertinentiis, eis legitime appropriatas, juste habere, et retinere — judicialiter pronuntiamus et declaramus. In cujus, etc. Data apud manerium nostrum de Rosa, quinto die mensis Aprilis, anno, etc., lix.

L.—AN AGREEMENT BETWEEN THE PREBENDARY OF SALTON AND SOME OF HIS TENANTS AS TO CUSTOMS AND PRIVILEGES.

[MSS. Cotton, Claudius, B, iii., 203 *a*, *b*.]

A toutz ceaux q^{i} cestes lettres verront ou orront, William, Prior de Hextildesham, et Covent de mesme le lieu, salutz en Dieu. Com debate estoit mue parentre nos et noz tenanntz de Brawby de notre prevendre de Salton, sur divers articles et poyntez tochantz la droit de notre dite proveyndre: la quel debate par divers tretise parentre noz chiers sirez Richard de Morland, et Thomas de Cave, noz con-chanonis, et altres de notre consaile, en notre noune, d'une parte, et noz ditz tenauntz d'altre part, est accorde et fynee en manere q'ensuyte.

Hæc indentura testatur, quod cum quædam dissensiones et discordiæ ante hæc tempora exortæ et motæ fuerint, inter Willelmum de Kendale, Priorem de Hextildesham, præbendarium præbendæ de Salton in Ridale, in ecclesia Beati Petri Ebor., et ejusdem loci Conventum, et quosdam tenentes ipsius præbendæ, secundum consuetudinem præbendæ prædictæ; jam die Martis, proximo post festum Circumcisionis Domini, anno Domini millesimo ccc^{mo} sexagesimo, facta est concordia subscripta inter prædictos Priorem et Conventum, et tenentes suos de Brawby in præbenda prædicta. Videlicet, quod quandocunque aliquis

Prior dicti loci obierit, et post ejus decessum aliquis Prior electus fuerit, ipse Prior electus capiet in primo adventu suo apud Salton de tenentibus de Brawby et Bergh, in præbenda prædicta, ad quemdam palefridum, quatuor marcas argenti tantum, nomine cognitionis. Cessante vero aliquo Priore dicti loci, alioque Priore loco ejusdem cessantis electo, prædicti tenentes de Brawby et Bergh nichil solvent eidem Priori tunc electo pro cognitione dominii. Item concordatum est quod omnes et singuli tenentes de Brawby in præbenda prædicta debent molere blada sua ad molendinum ipsius Prioris de Salton, solvendo multuram, prout alii tenentes præbendæ prædictæ solvunt; absque cariatione lapidum molarium, seu reparatione stagni dicti molendini, vel coopertura dicti molendini facienda. Item concordatum est quod prædicti tenentes de Brawby de cætero exonerentur a mundatione fossati circa clausum, vocatum Frense-holme, facienda. Item concordatum est quod de cætero erunt duo collectores denariorum ipsius Prioris in Brawby, tamen absque hoc quod aliqui eorumdem tenentium de cætero eligantur, cessend' *(sic)* milnegraves lathegraves, vel aliqui alii servientes pro compoto reddendo. Item concordatum est quod prædicti tenentes de Brauby possint facere blada sua et avenas in propriis terris suis crescentia in brasium, absque tolneto solvendo, vocato kyln-mulntre. Et si aliquis tenentium prædictorum emerit ordium vel avenas ad faciendum in brasium, vel ad ulterius mercandizandum, ipsi tenentes solvent multuram, prout pertinet ad xx^{m} vas. Item concordatum est, quod cum prædicti tenentes de Brawby metierint blada sua, et ea adunaverint, prædicti tenentes præmuniri facient prædictum Priorem, vel ministros suos, per unum diem antequam blada sua cariare debeant, pro salvatione decimæ ejusdem Prioris; et, post prædictum diem elapsum, iidem tenentes cariabunt blada sua absque aliqua perturbatione facienda. Item concordatum est quod si prædictus Prior, qui nunc est, vel aliquis successorum suorum apud Brawby, de novo construxerit, vel ædificaverit molendinum aquaticum seu ventriticum, ipsi tenentes de Brawby facient sectam ad molendinum ipsius Prioris ibidem, et alia opera ad eundem molendinum pertinentia, prout temporibus retroactis dicti tenentes, quando molendinum fuerit ibidem situatum, facere consuerunt: et quod extunc omnino exonerentur de aliqua secta ad prædictum molendinum de Salton facienda. Item concordatum est inter dictos Priorem et Conventum et tenentes prædictos, quod prædicti tenentes de Brawby, simul cum aliis tenentibus dictæ præbendæ, cariabunt meremium domini ad domos construendas, et ædificia reparanda tantum, ubicunque fuerit emptum; et cariabunt cibum domini tantum, simul cum tenentibus præbendæ prædictæ apud Ebor. et alibi, quotienscunque fuerint requisiti; prout ante confectionem hujus concordiæ facere consuerunt; et prout in quodam libro de tenuris libertatis Beati Petri Ebor., vocato Domesday,[a] plenius continetur.

Sachez nos avoir assigne et ordeine noz chiers, les ditz Richard et Thomas, noz conchanoignez, ou l'un d'eux, noz procurators et attornez, a conoistre la dite accorde en la chapitre del eglise Seint Pier d'Euewyk, devant les chanoignez de ycele: et la dite acorde par noz et noz successours finier et establer a touz jours: et, ultre ceo, de requer les ditz chanoignes que la dite acorde en perpetuele memorie puys estre registre devant eaux, eaunt ferme et estable ceo que nos ditz conchanoignez, noz procuratours et attornez, ou l'un d'eaux, serra ou serront en les chosez susditz. En testmoignanntz de quel chosez, a cestez noz lettres patentez avoms mys notre comune seale. Escript a Hextildesham, le vyntesyme primer jour de May, l'ane de grace mille treicent sexaunt et primer.

Et sciendum, quod octavo die mensis Junii, anno Domini millesimo ccc^{mo} sexagesimo primo, comparuerunt coram capitulo Thomas de Cave, canonicus supradictus, ex parte dictorum Prioris et Conventus, exhibens omnia et singula suprascripta in quadam litera, sigillo communi dictorum Prioris et Conventus sigillata; in præsentia plurimorum tenentium prædictorum dictum capitulum humiliter requisivit, quatinus prædictam concordiam, sive compositionem, in registro ipsius capituli, ad perpetuam rei memoriam, registrari et conscribi mandare et facere dignarentur. Quæ quidem concordia, ad instantem rogatum dicti fratris Thomæ procuratoris, et tenentium prædictorum, hic extitit, et est ad perpetuam memoriam de mandato ipsius capituli plenarie registrata.

LI.—THE APPROPRIATION OF THE HOSPITAL OF ST. GILES AT HEXHAM TO THE PRIOR AND CONVENT OF THAT PLACE BY ARCHBISHOP NEVILLE. [Ex registro appropriationum eccles., etc., penes Dec. et Capit. Ebor,, cui titulus T^{c}y., 92.]

Alexander, permissione Divina Ebor. archiepiscopus,[b] Angliæ primas, et Apostolicæ sedis legatus, dilectis filiis Priori et Conventui monasterii sive Prioratus Sancti Andreæ de Hextildesham,

[a] This is the agreement in No 1.

[b] The hospital of St. Giles is so much out of order that archbishop Neville despairs of being able to mend it. He gives it up to the Prior and Convent in the hope that they may be able to do something with it. The chapter of York confirm this deed of appropriation on Jan 14th, 1377-8.

ordinis Sancti Augustini, nostræ diocesios, salutem, gratiam, et benedictionem. Nuper, fama publica referente, recepimus quod hospitale Sancti Egidii juxta Hextildisham, nostrarum collationis et jurisdictionis, per unum magistrum sive custodem solitum gubernari, certis terris et tenementis et redditibus pro sustentatione ipsius magistri sive custodis, ac quorumdam pauperum et miserabilium personarum in eodem hospitali degentium abolim fundatum et dotatum, per hostiles incursus Scottorum, partibus ipsis vicinorum, ac diversarum mortalitatum pestilentias, adeo in suis facultatibus miserabiliter est collapsum, quod ex ipsius possessionibus, fructibus, redditibus, et proventibus, ultra sustentationem necessariam unius custodis, vix aliqui pauperes et miserabiles parte hujusmodi jam poterunt sustentari: nec aliquis idoneus, qui ipsius hospitalis curam gerere velit et custodiam, ejusque onera supportare modernis temporibus poterit inveniri; sicque a sustentatione pauperum hujusmodi, ac aliis piis operibus in eodem hospitali fieri consuetis, totaliter necessario cessari oportebit, nisi celerius eidem de op(p)ortuno remedio succurratur. Unde nos, Alexander, archiepiscopus supradictus, desolationi dicti hospitalis paterno compatientes affectu, dum ad debitæ considerationis examen reduximus qualiter mederi possit, ne pia fundatorum ipsius hospitalis intentio suo frustretur effectu; nobis pium et expediens videbatur ipsum hospitale, cum suis possessionibus, redditibus et proventibus universis, vobis et vestro monasterio, ad supportationem onerum eidem hospitali incumbentium, an(n)ectere et unire; attendentes quod ipsum hospitale est vestro monasterio satis propinquum, et quod vos absque sumptibus magnis possitis fructus et proventus ejusdem in usum personarum miserabilium dispensare; et alia onera eidem hospitali incumbentia supportare. Et propterea, subsequenter, super sic nobis per famam publicam delatis, ac omnibus aliis et singulis suprascriptis, per viros fidedignos, juratos, examinatos, rei hujus notitiam pleniorem habentes, vocatis omnibus quorum intererat, inquiri fecimus diligenter; ac plena causæ cognitione perhibita, ipsisque veris inventis, et per nos approbatis, decreto insuper per nos interposito, ac aliis solempnitatibus subsecutis quæ in concessionibus hujusmodi et alienationibus rerum ecclesiasticarum in hoc canonice juxta juris exigentiam in qualitatem negotii requiruntur, et adhiberi debent de jure vel de consuetudine in omnibus observatis; habitoque super præmissis per nos cum dilectis filiis capitulo ecclesiæ nostræ Ebor., decano ejusdem in remotis agente, solemni tractatu et diligenti juxta qualitatem negotii et naturam; ac submissione vestra ordinationi, arbitrio, laudo, decreto, pronunciationi, et diffinitioni nostris in hac parte factis; invocata

Spiritus Sancti gratia: quia invenimus quod evidens utilitas et urgens necessitas unionem hujusmodi fieri exposcunt, de consensu expresso dicti capituli nostri, prædictum hospitale Sancti Egidii juxta Hextildesham, cum suis juribus, pertinentiis, et dependitiis, ac commoditatibus et libertatibus universis, vobis, Priori et Conventui, ac monasterio sive Prioratui vestro prædicto, vestrisque successoribus, auctoritate nostra ordinaria et pontificali, concedimus, annectimus, et unimus. Volumus etiam et ordinamus quod exnunc, vigore præsentis concessionis, unionis, et annectionis nostrarum prædictis, fructus, redditus et proventus, jura, libertates et commoditates ad prædictum hospitale spectantes, (salvis nobis et successoribus nostris Ebor. archiepiscopis mineris plumbi, ferri, et carbonum infra terras et tenementa ipsius hospitalis existentibus,) libere percipere et habere possitis; nostra, vel successorum nostrorum Ebor. archiepiscopum, aut alterius cujuscunque, ulteriori licentia per vos petita minime vel optenta. Ita tamen quod onera eidem hospitali incumbentia, in quantum ipsius hospitalis sufficere poterunt facultates, supportare et subire teneamini in futurum. Et ne de hujusmodi oneribus per vos inveniendis in futurum dubitationem exoriri contingat, volumus et ordinamus quod unum capellanum idoneum, singulis septimanis uno die in capella dicti hospitalis missas celebrantem, ac duos pauperes et miserabiles personas infra septa Prioratus vestri, seu in eodem hospitali, in esculentis, et poculentis, ac vestitu, et cæteris suis necessariis de redditibus et proventibus ad dictum hospitale spectantibus invenire teneamini in perpetuum; absque aliquali onere ulteriori, ratione reddituum, fructuum, vel proventuum ipsius hospitalis, a vobis vel successoribus vestris exigendo. In quorum omnium et singulorum fidem et testimonium, præsentes nostras literas patentes eisdem Priori et Conventui fieri fecimus testimoniales, sigillo nostro consignatas. Data apud Cawod, nono die mensis Januarii, anno Domini millesimo ccc^mo^ septuagesimo septimo, et nostræ consecrationis quarto.

LII.—COMMISSION TO TREAT WITH THE DEAN AND CHAPTER OF YORK FOR THE APPROPRIATION OF THE CHURCH OF ILKLEY TO THE PRIOR AND CONVENT OF HEXHAM. [Reg. archiep. Neville, pars i., 92 *b*.]

Alexander, etc., dilectis filiis, magistris Thomæ Salkeld, commissario curiæ nostræ Ebor., et Johanni de Houden, jurisperito, salutem, etc. Exhibita nobis dilectorum filiorum Prioris et Conventus de Hextildesham, nostræ jurisdictionis, petitio continebat, quod possessiones, redditus, et proventus monasterii sui in loco non multum fertili, non longe a marchia Scotiæ situati, per frequentes invasiones Scotorum, et guerrarum discrimina ibidem quasi continua, ac mortalitatum pestes quæ in partibus illis notorie viguerunt, sunt adeo notabiliter et enormiter diminuti, quod iidem Prior et Conventus non possunt ex eis com(m)ode sustentari; nec in dicto monasterio, ad quod inibi hospites, tam nobiles quam alii, juxta morem illarum partium, indies confluunt, hospitalitatem tenere, et onera eis necessario incumbentia supportare : quare nobis humiliter supplicarunt ut ecclesiam parochialem de Ilklay, nostræ diocesios, in qua dicti Prior et Conventus jus optinent patronatus, ipsis Priori et Conventui et eorum successoribus, ac eorum monasterio, ex causis præmissis, perpetuo unire, appropriare, et annectere dignaremur. Nos autem, variis et arduis negotiis impediti, quominus ad tractandum cum dilectis filiis capitulo ecclesiæ nostræ cathedralis Ebor., decano ejusdem in remotis agente, ad præsens intendere valeamus; nec ad dictam Ebor. ecclesiam personaliter declinare, ad eorum solempnem et diligentem tractatum cum eisdem, hac instanti die Sabbati, proxima post festum Sanctæ Luciæ Virginis, cum continuatione et prorogatione dierum subsequentium, si necesse fuerit, ineundum, tenendum et habendum, super appropriatione sua hujusmodi, si licuerit, in eventu facienda; necnon ad examinandum et discutiendum, prout justum fuerit et approbandum, causas in suggestione superius expressas, de quibus per dominum Johannem Porter, capellanum, inquiri fecimus, prout per merita inquisitionis hujusmodi et attestationis inde habitarum vobis liquere videbitur; ac in casu quo causas hujusmodi veras et legitimas dicti capituli approbaveritis, ad consentiendum pro nobis et vice nostra appropriationi hujusmodi per nos faciendæ, indempnitate ecclesiæ nostræ Ebor. in omnibus semper salva; necnon consensum dicti capituli ad præmissa requirendum, consequendum et admittendum; cæteraque omnia, etc.: vobis, tenore præsentium committimus vices nostras : proviso quod nos de omni eo quod feceritis et inveneritis in præmissis, ac de toto processu vestro in hac parte habendo, expedito negotio, distincte et aperte certificetis per literas vestras patentes harum seriem continentes; inquisitionem, et attestationes prædictas nobis similiter remittentes. Valete. Data apud Cawode, primo die mensis Decembris, anno Domini millesimo ccc^{mo} lxxviij^{mo}, et nostræ consecrationis quinto.

LIII.—THE APPROPRIATION OF THE CHURCH OF ILKLEY TO THE PRIOR AND CONVENT OF HEXHAM BY ARCHBISHOP NEVILLE. [Ex reg. appropr. eccl., etc., penes Dec. et Capit. Ebor., cui titulus T^cy., 98 *b*.]

Alexander permissione Divina Ebor. archiepiscopus,[c] Angliæ primas, et Apostolicæ sedis legatus, dilectis filiis Priori et Conventui monasterii de Hextildesham, nostræ jurisdictionis, salutem, gratiam, et benedictionem. Suadet Divina pietas, et pastoralis officii debitum nos ammonet et inducit, ut depressionibus, et facultatum defectui Christi-fidelium, et præcipue religiosarum personarum Divino cultui jugiter insistentium provisione paterna misericorditer occurrentes, eorum necessitatibus relevationis subsidio, prout cum Deo possumus, consulamus. Sane vestra nuper nobis exhibita petitio continebat quod possessiones, redditus, et proventus monasterii vestri in loco non multum fertili, nec longe a marchia Scotiæ, in transitu publico situati, per frequentes Scottorum invasiones, et incursus hostiles, qui domos vestras interdum comburunt, vestros homines, et tenentes, et animalia, res, et cætera bona vestra sæpius more prædonio capiunt, abigunt, et consumunt; et quasi per continua guerrarum discrimina, necnon pestilentiam et epidemiam hominum, et animalium vestrorum mortalitatem, quæ nuper in vestris partibus contigerunt; ac per grave æs alienum, quod ex præmissis et aliis urgentibus causis vos contrahere oportebat, sunt adeo diminuti notabiliter et exhausti, quod vos ex eis com(m)ode sustentari; nec in dicto monasterio, ad quod hospites tam nobiles quam alii divites et pauperes, juxta morem illarum partium, hospitalitatis et recreationis causa, indies confluunt multitudine copiosa, hospitalitatem, et alia pia opera caritatis ibidem per vos fieri consueta, non potestis quomodolibet sustinere; nec onera vobis necessario incumbentia supportare, nisi aliunde vobis de alicujus subventionis uberioris remedio succurratur. Unde nobis humiliter supplicastis quatinus ecclesiam parochialem de Ilklay, nostræ diocesios, in qua ex collatione nobilis et potentis viri, domini Henrici de Percy, comitis Northumbriæ, canonice vobis et monasterio vestro facta, jus patronatus optinetis, ad aliquale relevamen vestrum, et onerum vobis incumbentium, vobis et monasterio vestro annectere et unire; ac vobis in usus vestros proprios perpetuo possidendam concedere paterna benivolentia dignaremur. Nos, igitur, qui monasteriorum et aliorum locorum religiosorum conservationem, et statum prosperum appetimus, vestris supplicationibus in-

[c] Confirmed by the chapter of York on Feb. 25th.

clinati, super causis prædictis appropriationis ecclesiæ de Ilklay faciendæ per vos allegatis, per viros fidedignos, juratos, et singillatim examinatos; vocatis omnibus quorum intererat in forma juris; inquiri fecimus diligenter; et, subsequenter, super appropriatione hujusmodi facienda, ac causis prædictis, necnon depositionibus hujusmodi juratorum, cum dilectis filiis capitulo ecclesiæ nostræ Ebor., decano ejusdem in remotis agente, diligentem tractatum habuimus et solemnem. Et quia, præmissis solemnitatibus, et aliis quæ in hujusmodi concessionibus et appropriationibus faciendis adhiberi debent de consuetudine vel de jure in omnibus observatis, per deducta allegata, perducta et probata coram nobis et dicto capitulo, invenimus causas prædictas veras, legitimas, et canonicas, ac sufficientes, et plene fore probatas; quodque evidens utilitas et urgens necessitas appropriationem dictæ ecclesiæ de Ilklay fieri exigant et exposcant; de voluntate et consensu expresso capituli nostri Ebor. prædicti, ac de consilio peritorum nobis assidentium, invocata Sancti Spiritus gratia, dictam ecclesiam parochialem de Ilkelay, cum suis juribus et pertinentiis universis, ex causis prædictis, et propter eas, auctoritate nostra ordinaria annectimus, unimus, et incorporamus per decretum, vobis, et monasterio vestro, et successoribus vestris, in usus vestros proprios perpetuo possidendam. Volentes et indulgentes quod, cedente vel decedente rectore dictæ ecclesiæ de Ilklay, qui nunc est, liceat vobis auctoritate vestra propria corporalem possessionem dictæ ecclesiæ apprehendere; ac fructus, redditus, et proventus ejusdem percipere, et in usus vestros et monasterii vestri convertere; nostra, vel successorum nostrorum Ebor. archiepiscoporum, archidiaconi loci, seu cujuscunque alterius licentia vel assensu minime acquisitis: reservata ordinationi nostræ de ipsius ecclesiæ fructibus, proventibus, et redditibus pro perpetuo vicario in ipsa ecclesia perpetuo servituro, et in vicaria hujusmodi canonice intitulando, portione congrua, ex qua idem vicarius congrue sustentari valeat, et onera sibi incumbentia debite supportare. In recompensationem vero læsionis ecclesiæ nostræ Ebor. prædictæ; et propter indempnitatem ejusdem; ac in signum subjectionis ecclesiæ de Ilklay antedictæ, quæ amplius non vacabit, annuum censum sive pensionem viginti solidorum argenti de fructibus dictæ ecclesiæ de Ilklay; (quorum tresdecim solidi et quatuor denarii nobis et successoribus nostris Ebor. archiepiscopis, qui pro tempore fuerint, plena sede; et, ea vacante, decano et capitulo dictæ ecclesiæ nostræ Ebor.; vel ipsi capitulo, decano in remotis agente, ut custodibus prædictæ sedis, futuro archiepiscopo Ebor. liberandi: ac sex solidi et octo denarii dictis decano et capitulo ecclesiæ nostræ Ebor.; vel ipsi capitulo, decano in remotis agente, per vos Priorem et Conventum monasterii de Hextildesham præfatos, ac successores vestros, ad festa Pentecostes et Sancti Martini in yeme per æquales portiones perpetuo persolvantur,) de vestro consensu expresso specialiter reservamus. Quem quidem censum seu portionem annuam ecclesiæ de Ilklay prædictæ, postquam ipsius possessionem habueritis, ac fructus et proventus libere perceperitis de eadem, de consensu vestro expresso adjicimus, et imponimus, ac decernimus futuris perpetuis temporibus, per vos et successores vestros in forma præmissa præstandum fideliter et solvendum. Quod si præsens appropriatio ecclesiæ de Ilklay prædicta aliquo modo cassata, revocata fuerit, vel annullata; vel vos in aliquo canonice eam amittere contigerit in futuris; volumus quod a præstatione et solutione dictæ portionis, in eventu amissionis, cassationis, anullationis, vel revocationis appropriationis prædictæ, sitis extunc liberi totaliter et immunes: juribus, libertatibus, statu bonorum, et dignitate dictæ ecclesiæ nostræ Ebor., in omnibus, et per omnia, semper salvis. In quorum omnium testimonium præsentes literas per Henricum de Axiholm, clericum, publicum auctoritate Apostolica notarium, subscribi; ac signo et subscriptione ejusdem, ac nostri sigilli appensione fecimus communiri. Data et acta in manerio nostro de Cawode, duodecimo die mensis Januarii, anno ab Incarnatione Domini, secundum cursum et computationem ecclesiæ Anglicanæ, millesimo tricentesimo septuagesimo octavo; indictione secunda; pontificatus sanctissimi in Christo patris et domini nostri domini Urbani Divina providentia papæ Sexti anno primo; et consecrationis nostræ quinto. Præsentibus dilectis filiis magistris Johanne de Clifford thesaurario ecclesiæ nostræ Ebor., Johanne de Waltham canonico ejusdem ecclesiæ, Johanne de Scardburgh, et Roberto de Manfeld clericis nostris, testibus ad præmissa vocatis specialiter et rogatis.

LIV.—LICENCE FROM ARCHBISHOP BOWET TO THE PRIOR AND CONVENT OF HEXHAM TO ACQUIRE CERTAIN LANDS BELONGING TO HIS FEE, ETC. [Reg. Bowet, pars i., 276 *b*.]

Henricus, permissione Divina Ebor. archiepiscopus, Angliæ primas, et Apostolicæ sedis legatus, dominus libertatis de Hextildesham, omnibus ad quos præsentes literæ pervenerint salutem. Sciatis quod de gratia nostra speciali, et in subsidium relevandi statum domus de Hextildesham, concessimus, et licentiam dedimus, pro nobis et successoribus nostris, quantum in nobis est, dilectis in Christo Priori et Conventui ejusdem loci, quod ipsi decem libratas terræ et redditus, cum pertinentiis, tam de feodo nostro proprio quam alieno, infra libertatem nostram de Hextildesham (exceptis tantum terris, tenementis, et redditibus, quæ de nobis tenentur in capite per servitium militare), adquirere possint: habendum et tenendum, sibi et successoribus suis, in liberam, puram, et perpetuam elemosinam imperpetuum, statuto de terris et tenementis ad manummortuam non ponendis non obstante. Ita tamen quod per inquisitionem, inde in forma debita faciendam, et in cancellaria nostra et successorum nostrorum rite retornandam, compertum sit, quod id fieri poterit sine præjudicio nostro, vel alterius cujuscumque. In cujus rei testimonium has literas nostras fieri fecimus patentes. Data in castro nostro de Cawod, undecimo die mensis Januarii, anno Domini millesimo cccc^{mo} duodecimo, et nostræ translationis anno sexto.

LV.—A LEASE OF THE PREBENDAL HOUSE IN YORK BELONGING TO THE STALL OF SALTON. [Ex Reg. Confirm., etc., penes Dec. et Capit. Ebor., 252.]

Sciant —— quod ego, Thomas Farrour,[d] Prior monasterii sive Prioratus Sancti Andreæ de Hextildesham, canonicus ecclesiæ cath. Ebor., ac præbendarius præbendæ de Salton in eadem ecclesia, et ejusdem monasterii, sive prioratus, Conventus, licentia domini nostri regis præhabita et obtenta; de consensu et assensu reverendissimi in Christo patris et domini, domini Willelmi Eboracensis archiepiscopi, Angliæ primatis, et Apostolicæ sedis legati; necnon de consensu et assensu venerabilium virorum decani et capituli dictæ ecclesiæ cath. Ebor.; unanimi assensu et consensu dedimus et hac præsenti carta nostra indentata confirmavimus supervisori et sacerdotibus cantarias in prædicta ecclesia cath. habentibus, vocatis *persones in ye kyrk of York*, collegii Sancti Willelmi in dicta ecclesia noviter fundati, totum illud tenementum, domum, placeam, sive habitationem ad prædictam nostram præbendam pertinentem sive spectantem, et dictæ præbendæ annexam, appropriatam; cum gardinis, ædificiis, et pertinentiis universis et singulis —— situatam inter domos præbendales de Langtoft ex parte occi-

[d] It appears from this deed that the college of St. William occupies the site, or nearly so, of the house formerly appropriated to the prebendary of Salton. This deed was confirmed by the archbishop on Jan. 31st, and by the chapter of York on Feb. 4th. From the same MS., p. 277, it appears that Prior Welles and his Convent renewed the lease upon the same terms on May 18th, 1461. It was confirmed by archbishop Neville on May 20th, 1466, and by the chapter on March 14th, 1466-7.

dentali, et de Husthwaite et tenementa vicariorum in choro eccl. cath. prædictæ ex parte orientali; et in longitudine a venella quæ ducit a dicta ecclesia cathedrali versus regiam stratam de Gotheromgate ex parte australi, ante usque ad regiam stratam de Uggleford ex parte boriali a retro —— reddendo inde prædicto Priori et Conventui, et successoribus suis, quadraginta solidos per annum ——. Data apud Hextildesham, in domo nostra capitulari, Jan. 26, 1456-7.

LVI. AN ORDER FROM ARCHBISHOP NEVILLE FOR THE EXCOMMUNICATION OF THOSE WHO HAVE BURNED THE VILLAGE OF ACOMB, NEAR HEXHAM. [Reg. Geo. Neville, 46 *b*.]

Georgius, etc., venerabili et religioso viro, Priori Prioratus de Hexham,[e] cancellario nostro, ac omnibus et singulis rectoribus, vicariis, curatis, et capellanis quibuscumque per jurisdictionem nostram in Hexham et Hexhamshire constitutis, salutem, gratiam, et benedictionem. Fama publica et facti notorietate referentibus, ad nostrum nuper pervenit auditum, quod quidam iniquitatis filii, quorum nomina ignorantur pariter et personæ, Deum præ eorum oculis non habentes, Dei timore postposito, quamdam villam, vulgariter Acom nuncupatam, in Hexhamshire prædicta situatam, ad nos et ecclesiam nostram cath. Ebor. pertinentem, maliciose ac nequiter incenderunt; ac ipsam comburi et destrui crudeliter nempe fecerunt; nonnullaque bona ibidem inventa abstulerunt; sententiam excommunicationis ipso facto dampnabiliter incurrendo; in suarum interitum animarum, libertatis ecclesiasticæ violationem manifestam, atque plurimorum perniciosum exemplum. Vobis, igitur, communiter et divisim, in virtute sanctæ obedientiæ firmiter injungendo mandamus, quatinus in singulis ecclesiis vestris, diebus dominicis et festivis, intra missarum solempnia, dum major affuerit populi multitudo in eisdem, omnes et singulos hujusmodi incendiores, malefactores, eorumque autores et fautores; eisque auxilium et consilium in præmissis dantes; in dictam excommunicationis majoris sententiam incidisse; et occasione præmissa sic excommunicatos fuisse et esse, diebus, horis, et locis antedictis, pulsatis campanis, candelis accensis et extinctis, ac in eorum vituperium in terram projectis, cruceque in manibus reverenter erecta, ut moris est; publice et solempniter denuncietis; et sic denunciet quilibet vestrum, quotiens et

[e] An outrage by which the archbishop was the greatest sufferer. A marauding party had burned the village of Acomb, near Hexham.

quando super hoc fueritis requisiti, sub pœna contemptus; quorum absolutionem nobis specialiter reservamus. Data nostro, etc., in manerio nostro de Scroby, nono die Martii, anno Domini millesimo cccc^{mo} lxvij^{o}, et nostræ translationis anno tertio.

LVII.—A SHORT SURVEY OF THE LANDS, ETC., BELONGING TO THE PREBEND OF SALTON. [Ex libro intit. per Jac. Torre G^{h}y, penes Dec. et Capit. Ebor., 34.]

PRÆBENDA DE SAULTON.[f] Prior de Hexsam, præbendarius de Saulton, est rector ecclesiæ de Saulton, et dominus totius villæ. Et habet manerium suum ibidem, et jurisdictionem totius familiæ suæ commorantis in eodem. Et habet jurisdictionem vicariæ et vicarii ejusdem, et totius familiæ ipsius vicarii commorantis in eadem vicaria. Habet etiam dominium et jurisdictionem utramque totius villæ de Saulton, et omnium et singulorum commorantium in eadem villa.

BRAUBY. Item præbendarius præbendæ de Saulton est rector et dominus totius villæ de Brauby, et habet utramque jurisdictionem in eadem, et in omnibus et singulis commorantibus et inhabitantibus in eadem villa de Brauby.

MIKKIL-BERGH. Item præbendarius præbendæ de Saulton habet in Mikil-bergh plura tenementa tam vasta, (quæ solebant ædificari et inhabitari,) quam ædificata; et omnia illa tenementa tam vasta (quæ solebant ædificari et inhabitari), quam ædificata; et omnes et singuli morantes et inhabitantes in eisdem sunt de jurisdictione dicti præbendarii de Saulton; et idem præbendarius habet in eisdem merum et mixtum imperpetuum: quorum tenentium nomina sequuntur.

Alicia Shephird tenet j ten. et ij bovatas terræ. Willelmus Nightgall tenet j ten. vastum et ij bovatas terræ, et solebat ædificari et inhabitari. Ricardus Faber tenet j ten. et ij bovatas terræ juxta, ex parte orientali. Sunt ibidem j ten. vastum et ij bovatæ terræ, quæ Johannes Smythe dudum tenuit, et solebat ædificari et inhabitari; de eadem jurisdictione. Willelmus Baystan tenet j ten. et vj bovatas terræ, juxta. Sunt ibidem j ten. vastum et ij bovatæ terræ, quondam Willelmi Waud, et solebat ædificari et inhabitari, etc. Willelmus de Kepwike tenet j ten. et iiij bovatas terræ, juxta. Janinus tenet j ten. cum gardino adjacente, et buttat super exitum villæ prædictæ.

[f] This survey is undated, but it seems to have been made in the latter part of the fifteenth century. A similar description is given of the possessions of all the stalls at York.

Walterus de Borgh tenet ij ten. ibidem, quæ Willelmus Nightgall tenet de eo.

NEWTON IN PAROCHIA DE STANEGRAVE. Item præbendarius de Saulton habet dominium et jurisdictionem totius villæ de Newton in parochia de Stanegrave, et omnium et singulorum morantium et inhabitantium in eadem villa; qui percipit annuatim ls. vjd. de Roberto de Newton pro toto dominio ejusdem villæ.

FLAXTON. Præbendarius de Saulton habet in Flaxton in mora ij ten. et vj bovatas terræ; de quibus Johannes Plaice tenet ibidem j ten. et ij bovatas terræ ex parte orientali villæ, ad finem australem ejusdem; et Willelmus Watson tenet. j ten. et iiij bovatas terræ juxta eum ex parte boriali; et habet jurisdictionem eorumdem, et omnium et singulorum commorantium in eisdem.

GEVELDALL. Item præbendarius de Saulton habet in Geveldall juxta Millyngton j ten. et vj bovatas terræ, quæ Willelmus de Geveldall tenet ibidem: qui tenentes, et omnes morantes, et inhabitantes in eisdem, sunt de jurisdictione dicti præbendarii de Saulton.

Johannes Forster mortuus est, et decanus probavit testamentum.

Akyson de Flaxton.

LVIII.—THREE VISITATIONS OF THE PARISH OF SALTON. [Ex Libro Visitat. penes Dec. et Capit. Ebor., 17, 57, 187 *b*.]

MCCCCLXXIII.

Frater Johannes Welles, Prior domus de Hextildesham, præbendarius præbendæ de Salton, nullo modo comparuit.

Willelmus Smyth, firmarius ibidem, nullo modo comparuit, quia in longinquis partibus moratur.

Dominus Laurentius Pacok, vicarius ibidem, præstitit obedientiam in forma usitata; et titulum suæ incumbentiæ ac literas ordinum suorum exhibuit.

Robertus Spenlove, clericus parochialis, præstitit obedientiam.

Thomas Katerynson, Thomas Browne, Willelmus Luderyngton, Johannes Talyor de Salton, Robertus Hare, Robertus Luderyngton de Brawby, Robertus Frank de Mikil-bergh, Willelmus Salton de Litil-bergh, Willelmus Thornton de Newton generosus, Petrus Clerk de Colton, Willelmus Thomson de Nawton, Robertus Thomson de Wymbleton, et Willelmus Est de Grymmeston.

Detecta. Mansum præbendale est maxime ruinosum in omni sui parte. Item cancellus ecclesiæ de Salton est ruinosus in muris et tecturis, ac stalla in choro deficiunt. Item navis ecclesiæ est defectivus in tectura plumbea. Moniti sunt parochiani quod reparari faciant navem ecclesiæ citra festum Michaelis sub pœna iijs. iiijd. Item dicunt parochiani quod præbendarius tenetur sternere ecclesiam cum stramine bis annuatim, viz., in festis Natalis Domini et Paschæ; quod non factum erat per duos annos ultimo præteritos.

Item Johannes Wartre de Fryton et Ricardus Carter de eadem, servientes domini Radulphi Ashton, vice-comitis comitatus Ebor., intrarunt libertatem Sancti Petri infra villam de Salton vi et armis, et quendam Johannem Bolland, de Salton, juniorem, per eosdem ibidem violenter captum, in cippis ibidem posuerunt; et eum sic in cippis sedentem dimiserunt; libertatem Sancti Petri notorie infringendo, et sententiam majoris excommunicationis dampnabiliter incurrendo.

Item cimiterium non est sufficienter clausum. Igitur moniti sunt parochiani quod competenter claudere faciant cimiterium citra festum Pentecostis sub pœna cujuslibet non facientis partem suam xijd. fabricæ ecclesiæ Ebor. applicandorum.

Item ordinatum est de consensu parochianorum, quod nullus de cætero utetur ludis inhonestis et inhibitis infra cimiterium, ut puta, pilo pedali vel manuali, aut luctatione; sub pœna forisfacturæ ijd. de quolibet ludente, vel de magistris, aut parentibus eorumdem levandorum; et per eosdem fideliter et absque mora fabricæ ecclesiæ de Salton persolvendorum.

Item ordinatum est quod nullus pretendat litigare, aut cultellum, gestrum, vel aliud defensibile trahere infra ecclesiam aut cimiterium de Salton, ad aliquem percussiendum; sub pœna cujuslibet sic facientis iijs. iiijd. fabricis ecclesiarum cath. Ebor. et de Salton æqualiter applicandorum.

MCCCCLXXXI.

Jacobus Hird de Shirefhoton, cum complicibus suis, intravit libertatem Sancti Petri in Salton in profesto Exalt. S. Crucis, et fregit domum habitationis Thomæ Brown ibidem, ac vi et annis cepit Willelmum Brown; et ab eadem eum duxit ad castrum de Hoton, libertatem S. Petri violando, et sententiam excommunicationis majoris dampnabiliter incurrendo. Item cancellus ibidem est defectivus in muris et tectura plumbea.

MDXIX.

Ornamenta ecclesiæ sunt defectiva; viz unum superpellicium; quod habet de novo fieri.

Item fenestræ vitreæ in navi ecclesiæ sunt defectivæ, fractæ per ventum.

Item fons baptismalis caret sera. Emendentur præmissa citra festum Michaelis sub pœna xiijs. iiijd.

Fenestræ vitreæ in choro emendentur citra festum Michaelis proximum sub pœna vs.

Porci, sues, veniunt in cimiterium et dehonestant illud. Emendetur citra festum Ascensionis Domini sub pœna iijs. iiijd.

Item usi sunt infra cimiterium ludi inhonesti, prout pililudus pedalis, et manualis, viz tuttes, et handball ac Pennyston. Desistant quoad hujusmodi ludos, sub pœna excommunicationis.

Item parvi infantes, portati ad ecclesiam, in eadem clamant, et turbant Divinum officium, et alios orantes. Porticus ecclesiæ ibidem emendetur citra festum Michaelis proximum sub pœna xiijs. iiijd.

Johanna Cattall, uxor Thomæ Catall, de Brawby usualiter in ecclesia communicat cum eis qui has communicationes non audire *(sic)*.

Johanna Mason, soluta, de Salton, concepit proles tres per diversos presbyteros.

Johanna Barkar de Salton suspicatur super fornicatione cum Willelmo Boz, nuper capellano parochiali de Salton.

LIX.—PORTIONS OF THE SURVEY OF THE ESTATES OF THE PRIORY OF HEXHAM, TAKEN AT ITS DISSOLUTION IN 1536. [Ex Misc. libr. in cur. Augment. cccxix, 210; ccclxxxii, 8, 19.]

Com. Northumbriæ.

In libro supervisoris diversorum monasteriorum ibidem, mense Julii, anno regni regis H. octavi xxviij°, inter alia continetur prout inferius patet.

Monasterium de Hexham. Exitus terrarum, tenementorum. et possessionum, tam spiritualium quam temporalium.

Terræ dominicæ in manu monasterii occupatæ. Scitus monasterii ibidem, cum j columbari et divers graing' sive orrers, j pomarium, et j gardinum infra præcinctum dicti monasterii, cont' per æstimationem ij acras terræ. Et valet per annum iiijs. Item habent prope Hexham unum hospitale Sancti Egidii continens j mesuagium, cum j clauso et certis terris; et valet per annum xiijs. iiijd.—xvijs. iiijd.

Item habent ad firmam de archiepiscopo Ebor. certas terras juxta Hexham, videlicet j clausum vocatum Cow-feld, j clausum vocatum Cote-feld, j clausum vocatum Dotelande parke; et reddunt per annum . . . . xxiiij*l.* et, ultra, de incremento per annum nihil. *Summa* xvijs. iiijd.

Temporales possessiones in diversis comitatibus. Et habent in Hexham villa diversa burgagia, quæ reddunt per annum xijli. xiiijs. vd. Item habent in villa de Sandowe diversa tenementa, quæ r. per a. cvjs. viijd. Item habent in villa de Anyk diversa tenementa, quæ reddunt per ann. viijli. xiijs. jd. Item in villa de Yarwithe j ten., quod valet p. a. xlvjs. viijd. Item in villa de Dotlande, etc.

Ovyngeham, cella de Hexham. Scitus mancionis et decim' gran' ibidem vjli. xiiijs. viijd. Fœno decimali xs. Agnell' et lan' liiijs. Vittul' ijs. Gallin' xs. Auc., vjs.; Decim' salmonum viijs. Oblationes minutæ, privatæ, et cætera decim', ut in libro Paschali, xls. in toto.——xiijli. iiijs. viijd. *Summa* xiijli. iiijs. viijd.

In penc' soluta episcopo Dunolm. xxs. Priori Dunolm. xs. Archidiacono Dunolm. pro sinod' et procur' xijs.——xlijs. *Summa* xlijs.

Et valet clare xjli. ijs. viijd. [Ex^r cum tenore record', et concordat, per Jacobum Rokeby aud.]

per Willelmum Grene rec.

Salton. Præbenda in comitatu Ebor. Spiritualia. Rectoria de Salton, videlicet, in decimatione granorum villat' de Salton iiijli. xiijs. iiijd.; Edston iiijli. xiijs. iiijd.; et Brawby lxs.: ac in decimatione agnellorum et lanæ totius parochiæ de Salton prædicta xxjs. iiijd. Valet in toto per annum, ultra reprisas, xiijli. viijs.

Temporalia. Manerium de Salton cum terris dominicalibus, pratis, pascuis et pasturis ordin' manerio pertinentibus, modo in tenura Jacobi Rideley. Valet per annum, ultra reprisas, xixli. xvjs. Terræ et tenementa, cum pertinentiis, in tenura diversorum tenentium in villatis de Edston et Brawby, valent per annum, ultra reprisas, iiijli. iiijs.——xxiiijli. *Summa* xxxvijli. viijs. [Ex^r cum record. per me Jacobum Rokeby, auditorem.]

The rent of Hexham, besydes, ccxxviijli. xvijs. ijd.——cclxvjli. vs. ijd.

LX.—A SURVEY OF THE ESTATES OF THE PRIORY OF HEXHAM, MADE AT THE DISSOLUTION. [From a transcript of the original in the possession of W. B. Beaumont, M.P.]

THE DEMANEZ OF LATE MONASTERYE OF HEXHAM. The scite of the saide monasterye, w^t all maner of edificez, one dofe coote, one grannge, one orceyerd, and one garthing, conteyning in all ij acres of grounde; and is worthe by yere, iiijs.

The hospitall of Saynct Gyles adjoning the sayde monasterye; that is to saye, j mes., wythe a cloose conteyning ij acrez pasture; and in the feldes of Hexham in diverse places xxx[ti] acræ terræ arrabilis: and is worthe by yere xiijs. iiijd.

The profettes of diverse landes belonging the archebyshope of Yorke, late in the handes of the sayde monasterye; that is to saye, dyverse landes arrable, in the feldes of Hexham; j cloose callyd Cou-felde, one cloose callyd Dotland parke; whyche in all renttes unto the sayde archebisshope xxiijli. by yere; and is worthe unto the sayde monasterye yerely of increase, nil. *Summa* xvijs. iiijd.

Hexham: burgagia. The wyfe of Wylliam Herryson holdythe a cotage ther withe a garth cont. j rode, and common upon the mores and pastures, and renttes by the yere at Martyn and Penthecost, equally, iiijs. Alexaundre Leisman holdyth a cotage there w[t] one garth cont. j rode, and comon, etc., by yere vs. Thomas Nicholson holdyth a tenement ther, w[t] j garthe cont. j rode di., ij acre land in the felde, w[t] common and pasturs therunto belongyng, and renttes by yere xs. iijd. Thomas Smythe holdyth a cotage ther w[t] j garthe., cont. di. rode, and comon there, by yere ijs. viijd. Richarde Leisman holdyth a tenement ther w[t] edificez, j cloose cont. j acre, iij acrez land arrable in the feldes, and comon of pasture there, etc., xjs. vd. Hughe Iryngton holdyth a tenement ther, wythe j garth cont. di. rode and renttes by yere, etc., ijs. John Armestronge holdyth a tenement ther, w[t] a garthe cont. j rode, and renttes by yere iiijs. The wyfe of John Levenwood holdith a tenement there wythe edificez, a garth conteining one rode in the feld, and x acre, w[t] comon and pastur ther, and renttes viijs. The wyfe of Richarde Milner holdithe a cotage there, w[t] a litell garthe ther, iiijs. Rowland Swan holdythe a cotage ther w[t] a litell garthe, and rentes by yere iijs. William Browne holdithe a house w[t] a littell garthe there, and renttes by yere iijs. iiijd. Edmund Gibson holdithe a cotage there wythe one lytell garthe, and renttes, etc., iijs. iiijd. Edward Hirste holdithe a tenement ther w[t] edificez, one croft cont. one rode, ij acrez lande in the feldis, w[t] comon and pasture there, viijs. William Elleson holdithe a cotage there, w[t] a litell garth, and rentes by yere, etc., ijs. Richard Davyson holdith a cotage ther w[t] a litell garth, and rentes by yere ijs. John Stevenson holdithe a cotage ther, w[t] a garth cont. one rode, and rentes by yere, etc., ijs. ixd. John Yarroo holdith a cotage there w[t] a litell garthe, and rentes by yere, etc., xvjd. John Laveroke holdith a shopp there, viijd. Thomas Laveroke holdith a cotage there, w^t a garthe cont. j rode, and rentes by yere ijs. viijd. Robert Stevynson holdith a cotage there w^t a garthe, and rentes by yere iijs. John Grene holdith a cotage there wyth a garth, and rentes by yere iijs. iiijd. Robert Wanles holdith a cotage there w^t a litell garthe, and rentes by yere, etc., viijd. The wyfe of Rowland Grene holdithe a cotage there w^t j lyne garthe cont. j rode, and rentyth by yere, etc., iijs. Thomas Robson holdithe a cotage ther, w^t a litell garthe, conteyning di. rode, and rentes by yere xijd. Jeffray Bell holdith a cotage there, wythe a litell garthe, and rentithe by yere, etc., ijs. Thomas Wallis holdith a cotage there, w^t a crofte cont. j rode, and ij acres land in the feldes, w^t comon and pasture there, vjs. viijd. Cooke wyfe holdithe a cotage ther, w^t a crofte cont. j rode, and rentes by yere, etc., ijs. Henry Levenwood holdithe a cotage ther, w^t a litell garth, and rentes by yere, etc., iijs. Richard Corbye holdith a cotage w^t a letill garthe, and rentithe by yere, etc., xijd. John Whichelles holdith a tenement there wythe a litell garth, and rentes by yere, etc., iiijs. Thomas Robson holdith a tenement there w^t the edificez, j cloose cont. j acre, et iij acrez land arrable, w^t pasture and comon there, and rentythe by yere, etc., viijs. viijd. The wyfe of Rowland Crayne holdith a tenement there, j cloose cont. ij acrez, and iiij acres lands arrable, pasture in the Weste-moore, and comon, xxs. John Wilkynson holdithe a tenement there, w^t j cloose cont. di. acre, and iij acrez lande arr., w^t comon and pasture in the Weste-moore, xs. Roger Pigges holdith a ten. there, w^t a cloose cont. j acre medoo, ij acres land arr., wythe comon and pasture, and rentes by yere viijs. iiijd. Thomas Bedell holdithe a cotage ther, w^t a lyne garthe, and rentes by yere, etc., xijd. Christofer Leighton holdith a tenement there, j cloose cont. di. acre, ij acrez land arrable, and rentes by yere vjs. viijd. Edward Litle holdith a ten., w^t j garthe cont. di. acre, and rentes by yere iiijs. Alexaundre Armestrong holdithe a ten. there, j cloose cont. di. acre, ij acrez land arrable, wythe comon and pasture in the Weste-more, vjs. viijd. William Robynson holdith a ten. ther, j cloose cont. di. acre, ij acres land wyth comon there, vjs. Robert Lighton holdithe a ten. there, j cloose cont. iij rode, et *(blank)* acrez land arrable, wythe comon and pasture, and rentes by yere, etc., vjs. viijd. John Patenson holdithe a ten. withe a litell garthe, and renteth by yere, etc., xxd. Thomas Laveroke holdith a ten. ther, w^t a litell garthe, and rentes by yere, etc., xxd. Robert Johnson holdithe a ten. there w^t edificez, j cloose, di. acre and ij acrez land arrable, w^t comon and pasture, and rentithe by yere, viijs. ixd. Alexaundre Armestronge holdithe a cotage ther w^{t} a litell garth, and rentes by yere ijs. vjd. Edward Ridley holdithe a ten. with edifices, j litle garthe cont. di. acre, ij acres lond arr. in the feldes, w^{t} comon of pasture there, and rentes by yere vijs. Hugh Johnson holdithe a ten. there, wythe j garthe cont. j rode, and comon of pasture in the Westmoore, and rentes iiijs. The wyfe of Edmonnd Stokeall holdithe a cotage ther, w^{t} a litell garthe, and rentes by yere iiijs. William Elleson holdithe a ten. there, w^{t} a cloose cont. di. acre in the feldis, ij acrez lond arrable, and rentes by yere vijs. Nicholas Patenson holdithe a ten. there w^{t} edifices, j cloose cont. j acre, and ij acrez land arrable, w^{t} comon, and rentes vjs. Miles Lesheman holdithe a ten. ther, j litell lyne garthe, and comon, by yere iijs. iiijd. Anthonye Johnson holdithe a ten. there, w^{t} a litell garthe, and rentes by yere xviijd. William Johnson holdithe a ten. there w^{t} a little garthe, and rentes by yere, etc., iijs. ijd. The wyfe of Anthony Hudson holdithe a cotage there, w^{t} a little garth, by yere ijs. viijd. Robert Hirde holdithe a cotage there w^{t} a litle garthe, and rentes by yere, etc., ijs. Robert Pigge holdith a cotage there, wyth a litell garth, and rentyth by yere, etc., ijs. viijd. John Symond holdithe a cotage there w^{t} a litell garthe conteyning one rodde, and renttes by yere ijs. viijd. Item there is ij cotagis late in the holdyng of *(blank)*, and rentes by the yere vs. ixd. *Summa burgagiorum et tenementorum ibidem* xij*l*. xiiijs. vd.

HEXHAMSHIRE.

SANDHOW. John Errington holdith a ten. there w^{t} edifices, j cloose cont. j acre in the Law Inges, iiij acres medoo; and in the Towne-feldis xxiiij acre land arr., w^{t} comon there, and renttes by yere, etc., xxvjs. viijd. Richard Hudchonson holdith a ten. there, w^{t} j cloose cont. j acre in the Law Inges, iiij acre medoo; and in the Toune feldis xxiiij acres land arrable, w^{t} comon ther, and rentes by yere, etc., xxvjs. viijd. Robert Buteland holdith a ten. there, j cloose cont. j rode in the Law Inges, iij acrez medoo, xviij acrez land arrable, and comon there, etc., xxs. Robert Sowreby holdithe a ten. there, j litle cloose; and in the Law Inges iij acre; in the Toune feldis xviij acre, and comon there by yere, etc., xxs. John Stevynson holdithe a ten. ther, w^{t} bithe *(sic)* vj acres land arrable, and ij acres in ye Law Inges, w^{t} comon there, and rentes by yere, etc., xiijs. iiijd. *Summa* cvjs. viijd.

ANEWYKE VILLATA. Thomas Spayne holdithe a ten. there w^{t} edifices, ij acres medoo in Est-myres, xiiij acres land arrable in the feldis, w^{t} comon in Cotland moore, and rentes by yere xvijs. xd. William Huchynson holdith j ten. ther w^{t} edifices, xj acres land arr. and comon of pasture in Cotland moore, and rentes by yere xvs. ijd. John Smythe holdithe a ten. there w^{t} edifices, xiiij acres land arr. and comon, by yere xvjs. ijd. William Greene holdith a ten. there w^{t} edifices, ij acres medoo, and xv acres land arr. w^{t} comon there, by yere xviijs. iijd. Robert Sowerby holdith a ten. ther wythe edifices, ij acrez medoo, and xiiij acres land arr., withe comon, and rentes by yere, etc., xvs. ijd. John Thomson holdithe a ten. ther callyd Belles leez, conteyning vj acres land arrable, and rentes by yere. etc., xs. Roger Robinson holdith a ten. ther wyth edifices, ij acres medoo, and xviij acrez lande arrable in the feldis, and rentes by yer, w^{t} comon, xxvijs. John Sowreby holdithe a ten. there withe edifices, j acre medow, and xv acrez land arrable in the iij feldes, with comon ther, and rentythe by yere xvs. iijd. John Spayne holdith a ten. there w^{t} edifices, ij acrez medoo, and xviij acrez land arrable, withe comon, and rentes by yere, etc., xxvijs. Thomas Soureby holdith a ten. there, withe vj acrez land arrable and comon of pasture there, by yere, etc., xjs. iiijd. *Summa* viijli. xiijs. jd.

Yarwith villata. Cuthbert Stokehall holdith a ten. there, withe ij acres medoo, v acrez land arrable, and comon ther, by yere, etc., xs. George Tayllor holdithe a ten., j acre medoo, v acrez land arrable, with comon of pasture, and rentes by yere, etc., xs. William Wilber holdithe a ten. there with edifices, j acre medoo, vj acres land arr., and comon there, and rentes by yere, etc., xs. George Bell holdith a ten. there, with j acre medoo, v acrez land arr., and comon of pasture there, and rentes xs. Item there is certen landes in the holdinge of the tennantes there, by yere, etc., vjs. viijd. *Summa* xlvjs. viijd.

Dottland villata. Richard Cokeman holdithe a ten. there w^{t} edifices, on acre medoo in the Small Inges, v acrez land arrable, and comon in Depestone more, and rentes by yere, etc., viiijs. iiijd. Thomas Greene holdithe a ten. there w^{t} edifices, ij acrez medoo, vij acrez lond arr., and comon of pasture, and rentes by yere, etc., xvjs. viijd. George Robson holdith a ten. ther w^{t} j acre medoo, v acrez land arrable, and comon ther, and rentes by yere viijs. iiijd. Alexandre Rowlle holdithe a ten. ther, ij acrez medoo, vij acrez land arr., and comon of pasture ther, by yere, etc., xvjs. viijd. Alexanndre Leddell holdithe a ten. there, j acre medoo, and v acre land arr., w^{t} comon, and rentes by yere, etc., viijs. iiijd. Hughe Donne holdithe a ten. there, j acre of medoo, and v acres land arrable by yere, etc., viijs. iiijd. *Summa* lxvjs. viijd.

Beyngfelde. Nicholas Herrington holdith by indenture

the capitall meese withe demanes ther, cont. iiij^{xx}. x acrez, at liijs. iiijd. by yere; and also iiij ten. there withe iiij frontes, v acrez medoo, and iiij^{xx}. j acres lande arrable, withe comon of pasture in the Feldis, Longe-moore and Downez-moore, at iiijli. vjs. viijd. by yere, in all, vijli.

BEAUFRONTE. Edward Hirste holdith a ten. there, with ij acres medoo, v acres land arrable, withe common of pasture in Birke-borne morez, and rentes by yere xs. William Leegh holdith a ten. ther, ij acrez medoo in the Myll-fall, viij acrez land arrable, withe comon of pasture, and rentes by the yere xs. *Summa* iijli.

GROTTINGTON. The wyfe of Thomas Harryngton holdith a ten. ther, withe x acres medo in the Moore-flate, xxx acrez lande arrable and comon in Dounes moore, and rentith by yere, xls.

MILBURNE GRANNGE. Edmund Horseley holdith a ten. there callid Mylborne grannge by indenture under Convent seale, w^{t} a cloose callid Hye-cloose, cont. v acrez in the Est-inges, x acres medoo, and in the feldes xxx acrez land arr., w^{t} comon of pasture in the Longe-bankes, and rentes by yere cvjs. viijd.

KIRKHETON VILLATA. William Musgrave holdith viij ten. there, xv acrez medoo callyd the Law Inges, and xlv acrez land arr., withe comon in Hyndes-fell, and rentes by yere vijli. *Summa* (of the three) xiiijli. vjs. viijd.

ALESTON MOORE. William Lawson holdith a ten. there withe edifices, iiij acrez medoo in the Wrange cloose, and x acrez in the Long-medoo, w^{t} comon in Aleste moore, and rentes by yere xxiijs. iiijd. Henry Teysdalle holdith a ten. w^{t} edifices, j cloose cont. v acre, and in the Long Inges xv acrez, w^{t} comon there, and rentes by yere, etc., xxs. viijd. William Walton holdith a ten. there, with j cloose callid Drye cloose cont. v acrez, and xij acrez in the Longe Inges, w^{t} comon there, and rentes by yere, etc., xxiiijs. viijd. William Milner holdith a ten. there, w^{t} a cloose callyd the Calfe-cloose, and xv acrez medoo in the Longe Inges, withe comon there, by yere xxiiijs. viijd. *Summa* iiijli. xiijs. iiijd.

DALTON VILLATA. John Bonnton holdith a ten. there w^{t} edifices, iij acrez medoo, x acres lande arrable, and comon there, by yere xxs. William Wallis holdithe a ten. ther with ij acrez medoo, and x acrez land arrable, w^{t} comon in Rowle-borne, by yere, etc., xviijs. Robert Atkinson holdith a ten. there, w^{t} ij acrez medoo, and ix acres land arrable, w^{t} comon there, and rentes by yere, etc., xvjs. John Smyth holdith a ten. ther, with ij acres medoo, and x acrez land arrable, w^{t}

comon ther, and rentes by yere xviijs. The wyfe of Edwarde Wayles holdith a ten. ther, ij acres medoo, ix acres land arrable, and comon of pasture in Roulle-borne, and rentes by yere xvs. John Wallis holdith a ten. there withe edifices, ij acres medoo, and xij acres land arrable, withe comon there, and rentes by yere, etc., xxs. Robert Wallis holdithe a ten. there, iij acrez medoo, and xij acres lond arrable, withe comon of pasture in Rolle-borne, and rentes, etc., xxs. The vicare ther holdith a water corne myll ther, and rentes yerely, over and bysides all charges, xls. There is certeyn landes in the holdyng of the same tennantes, and rentes by yere, etc., vjs. viijd. *Summa* viijli. xiijs. iiijd.

NEYSEBY. John Akinside holdith a ten. there, iiij acres medoo, xv acres lond arrable, and comon of pasture in Matfen-morre, and rentes by yere xxijs. jd. William Butler holdith a ten. there, withe iij acres medoo, xij acres land arr., and comon there, etc., xxs. jd. Mathew Richerson holdith a ten. there, iij acrez medoo, and xiij acres land arr., withe comon there, and rentes by yere, etc., xxjs. jd. John Okenwood holdith a ten. there, w^{t} iij acres medoo, and xiij acres land arrable, w^{t} comon of pasture there, by yere xxijs. jd. John Collyng-wood sen. holdith a ten. ther, w^{t} iij acres medoo, xiij acres land arrable, withe comon ther, and rentes by yere, etc., xxjs. *Summa* cvjs. viijd.

CHESBORNE-GRANNGE. Gawyn Swyneborne holdithe a ten. callid Chesborne grainge, v acres medoo, lv acres land arrable, w^{t} comon of pasture of Stonefell by indenture under Covent seale; and rentes by yere at Martyn and Pent. cvjs. viijd., and by the first survey but iiijli.

LEEZ STELLYNG. Thomas Swyneborne holdithe a ten ther, ij cloosis cont. iij acres medoo, x acrez land arr., xviij acres, w^{t} comon of Welling-moore, and rentes by yere xxxiijs. iiijd. *Summa* (of both) cxiijs. iiijd.

ECHEWYKE VILLATA. Richard Walters holdith a ten. there with edificies, one close conteyning di. acre medow in the Lawe West feld, v acre arrable lande, xij acrez, w^{t} comon of pasture in the West-more, and rentes by yere (at Martyn and Pente-cost) xvjs. iiijd. The wyfe of Nycholas Clerke holdithe a ten. there, j cloose cont. j rode in the Weste-felde, iij acrez medoo, and x acres land arrable, w^{t} comon of pasture, by yere xiijs. iiijd. The wyfe of Robert Bowre holdith a ten. there, j cloose cont. di. acre in the feldes, iij acres medoo, and xiij acres land arr.; and rentithe by yere, w^{t} comon there, xxjs. viijd. Robert Walles holdith a ten. there, wyth j garth cont. j rode in the feldes, iiij acres medoo, and x acres land arrable, wythe comon there, and rentes by yere xxjs. vjd. Thomas Elleson holdith a ten. there, j crofte. cont. j rode in the West-felde, ij acres medo, and viij acres land arr., w^{t} comon in the moore ther, and rentes by yere, etc., xijs. vjd. William Boure holdithe a ten. there w^{t} edifices, ij acres medoo in the West-felde, and iiij acres land arrable, w^{t} comon, and rentes by yere, etc., viijs. *Summa* lxvjs. viijd.

INGOO-MILLNE. William Story holdith the mylle there, and rentes by yere xiijs. iiijd.

PORDOO. Edward Bell holdith j ten. there, j crooft cont. j rode, ij acres medoo in the mylle-stede, vij acres land arr., withe comon in Pordoo moore, and rentes by yere viijs.

QUALTON. Robert Tolland holdithe a ten. there withe edifices, j crofte cont. di. acre, viij acrez land arrable, and ij acres medoo, w^{t} comon in Qualton morez, and rentez by yere xs. *Summa* (of the three) xxxjs. iiijd.

NEWCASTELL. Thomas Atkinson holdithe a ten. there, w^{t} edifices, and rentes by yere, etc., xijs. The wyfe of Richard Milner holdith a ten. ther, and rentes by yere, etc., viijs. John Watson holdithe a ten. there, and rentith by yere vijs. Thomas Benyke holdithe a ten. there, and rentes by yere iiijd. John Almere holdith a cotage ther, and rentith by yere iiijd. *Summa* xxvijs. viijd.

EST MATFEN. Gererd Fenwyke holdithe a ten. there, j close cont. di. acre in Morton-syde, iiij acres medoo in the feldes, xv acres land arr., w^{t} comon there, and rentes by yere, etc., xxvjs. viijd. Thomas Rutter holdithe a ten. ther, with ij acres medoo, iiij acres land arr., and comon there, and rentith by yere vjs. viijd. Thomas Archer holdith a ten. ther, ij acrez medoo, viij acres land arrable, wythe comon there, and rentes by yere xiijs. iiijd. The wyfe of William Rutter holdith a ten. there, wythe j acre medoo, and v acres land arrabilis, and rentyth by yere, etc., vjs. viijd. *Summa* liijs. iiijd.

WESTE MATFEN. John Thomson holdithe a cotage ther, w^{t} j litell garthe, and rentes by yere, etc., xvjd.

STAVELLE. George Hirde holdithe a ten. there, w^{t} ij acres medoo, and v acre land arr., and rentes by yere vs.

STOXEFELD HALL. John Newton holdithe a ten. ther, with edifices, ij acres medoo, v acres pasture and lond arrable, w^{t} comon in Slevally more, and rentes by yere xiijs. iiijd.

BIRTELEY. Thomas Lee holdithe a ten. there, j acre medoo, iij acrez land arrable, w^{t} comon of past' in Birtley moore, by yere, etc., iijs. iiijd.; and now lettyn unto the same for vs. xd.

NEWBORNE. John Dalton holdithe a fisshinge ther, and rentes by yere, over all charges, vs. *Summa* (of all) xxviijs.

STANNYNGTON. Thomas Robson holdith a ten. ther, with ij acrez land arr., and common of Stainyngton-moorez, and rentes by yere vs.

GUNNERTON. William Cooke holdeth a ten. ther, j acre medoo, and iij acres land arr., w^t^ comon in the West-more, and rentes by yere, etc., vjs. viijd. John Cooke holdithe a ten. there, j acre medoo, and iij acres land arrab., w^t^ comon, and rentes by yere, etc., vjs. viijd. *Summa* xviijs. iiijd.

WARDON. The vicar of Wardon holdith a ten. ther, w^t^ j cloose conteyning ij acrez, x acrez land arrable, withe comon upon the morez ther, and rentes xvjs. viijd. Rolland Stokeall holdith a ten. ther, w^t^ one cloose conteyning one acre, x acrez land arrable, withe comon there, and rentes xvjs. viijd. Thomas Kirsop holdith a ten. there, w^t^ iij acrez medoo, xj acres land arr., w^t^ comon there, and rentes by yere, etc., xixs. iiijd. Robert Kirsope holdith a ten. withe the edifices, one crofte, iiij acrez medoo, x acrez lond arrable, w^t^ comon upon the mores there, and rentith by yere xvjs. viijd. Thomas Pikeryng holdith a ten. there, iij acres medoo, and x acres lond arr., wythe comon there, and rentes by yere xvs. John Crake holdith a ten. there, iij acrez medoo, and x acrez lond arrable, w^t^ comon ther, and paith yerely xvs. Nicholes Ledbitter holdith a ten. there, iij acrez medoo, and x acrez lond arr., and comon there, and rentes by yere, etc., xvs. William Ledbitter holdith a ten. ther, iij acrez medoo, and x acrez land arrable, w^t^ comon, and by yere xvs. Robert Hesley holdith a ten. ther, one acre medoo, ij acrez lond arrable, withe comon ther, and rentes by yere iiijs. iiijd. *Summa* vjli. xiijs. viijd.

BYRES PARKE. William lorde Dacre holdith a ten. ther, w^t^ certeyn landes medoo and pasture therunto appertenyng, and rentes by yere xxxiijs. iiijd.

COLLERTON. The vicar of the churche of Collerton holdith a ten. ther, w^t^ appurtenances, and rentes by yere xlvs.

TEMPLE THORNETON. Richard Cowper holdith a ten. there, iiij acrez medoo, and viij acres land arrable, w^t^ comon ther, by yere, xiijs. iiijd. Robert Helpell holdith a ten. ther, iiij acrez, and viij acres land arr., w^t^ comon of past', and rentes, etc., xiijs. iiijd.——xxvjs. viijd.

KARESLEY. William Shaftow holdith a ten. ther, with certen grounde and comon therunto belonging, and rentyth by yere vjs. viijd., and now lettyn unto the same Will. for xviijs. *Summa* cvjs. viijd.

EPISCOPATUS DUNOLLMENSIS.

FARNEDALLE HALLE. William Blakeston holdith by indenture under Covent seale diverse ten. and landes thereunto belonging, and rentith by yere cvjs. viijd.

STAYNETON. John Dubbye holdith a ten. there, w[t] edifices, and certen landes therunto belonging, and rentes by yere xxvjs. viijd.

LAUNCHESTER. John Smerte holdith a ten. there w[t] edifices and certen landes therto belonging, and rentes by yere, etc., xiijs. iiijd. William Smert holdith a ten. ther, w[t] appurtenances, and rentes by yere, etc., xiijs. iiijd.——xxvjs. viijd. Thomas Forster holdith a ten. there, w[t] certeyn landes therto belonging, called the Manested hall, and rentes by yere, etc., viijs.

COMITATUS EBOR.

LITELL BROUGHTON. William Warden holdith diverse ten. ther by indenture under Covent seale, w[t] certen landes therunto belonging, and rentithe by yere xijli. xviijs. iijd. ob.

EYKELEY RECTORIA. The personage of Eykeley lettyn by indenture by Covent seale unto Thomas Meryng, and is worthe by the yere, over all reprises, cs. *Summa* xxvj*l.* vjs. iijd. ob.

[*A line or two torn.*]

Item the tithe cornez of Anewyke x*l.* Item the tithe cornez in Sanndehowe is worthe by the yere xiijs. iiijd. Item the tythe cornez in Acome, liijs. iiijd. Item the tythe cornez in the towne of Walle is worthe by the yere xlvjs. viijd. Item the tythe of cornez in the towne of Cokeley is worthe by the yere xs. Item the tithez of the towne of Kepike xiijs. iiijd. Item the tithez of Irryngton by yere xxs. *Summa* xviij*l.* iiijs. viijd.

Item the tithez and offiringes belonging the chappell of Alwendalle, lettyn by Covent seale unto diverse persons ther, and is worthe by yere, xvli. *Summa patet.*

HEXHAM AND HEXHAM SHIRE.

Item the tithez of agnell commyng of all the parishinges within Hexhamshere is worthe by yere lxvjs. viijd. Item the tithez of woll of all the parishinges aforesayde is worthe by yere, over all charges, xxvijs. vjd. Item the personall tythez, oblacons, Lentyn tithez, w[t] other profectes in the parishinges afforesayde, is worthe by yere ix*l.* Item the tithez and offeringes w[t]in ye chapell of Sancte John, by yere, xliijs. *(a line or two gone).* The offeringes and tithez within the chapell of our Ladye in

Brengfelde is worthe by the yere lxvjs. viijd. *Summa* xxijli. vs. ixd.

COMITATUS NORTHUMBRIÆ.

Item the personage in tithe cornez belonging the churche in Aldstone-moore is worthe yerely lxvjs. viijd. Item the tithe cornez of Newburghe, late in t'handes of the lorde, is worthe yerly xxvjs. viijd. Item the tithe cornez of the towne of Alerwithe, late in the handes of the sayd house, and is worthe by yere xxs. Item the tithe cornez of the towne of Fourstones in t'handes of lorde, and is worth by yere, over all charges, xiijs. iiijd. Item the tithez of the towne of Slavelle, w[t] the chapell ther, lettyn by Covent seale unto John Swynborne for the yerely ferme of iiijli. Item the tithez cornez of Chollerton, late in t'hand of the lorde, and is worthe by yere xxvjs. viijd. Item the tithez cornez of Bareforth, late in t'handes of the lorde, and is worthe by yere xxxiijs. iiijd. Item the tithez of cornes of Chipchesse, Stewden, and Birtle, lettyn by Covent seale unto John Heron by yere, iiijli. vjs. viijd. Item the tithe cornez of Gunnerton is worthe by the yere xls. Item the tithez of cornez in the towne of Colnewell, lettyn unto Sir John Witrington, wythout Covent sealle, and is worthe by yere xls. Item the tithe cornez of Heyden brigges, w[t] diverse parcelles of tithe cornez within the lordship of Langley and the parishe of Heidon, lettyn unto Sir Raynolde Carnaby, knyght, by indenture under Covent sealle, and is worthe by yere xvijli. xiijs. iiijd. *Summa* xxxix*l*. vjs. viijd.

COMITATUS CUMBRIÆ.

Item the tithe cornez of the parishe churche of Isell within the diocez of Carlesle is worthe by yere cs. *Summa* cs.

Summa totatis rentalis de Hexham cum pertinentiis ccxxix*l*. xiiijs. vjd.—*De quibus*.

RESOLUTIO REDDITUS CUM PENTIONIBUS ANNUALIBUS.

Idem computat in redditu resoluto Domino regi pro ward castri exeunte annuatim de terris in Salton, per annum xiijs. iiijd. Et in annuali pencione exeunte de præbenda de Salton, ad manus capituli Ebor., per annum xls. Et in annuali pencione soluta ad manus choristarum ecclesiæ metropoliticæ Ebor., exeunte de præbenda de Salton prædicta, per annum iiijs. Et in annuali pencione soluta episcopo Dunollm., exeunte de ecclesiis de Wardon, Chollerton, and Aldston, per ann. xxxiijs. iiijd. Et in annuali pencione soluta Priori de Dunollm., exeunte de ecclesia de Aldstane, cum iijs. iiijd., et Ovingham ad xs. p. a., xiijs. iiijd. Et in pencione annuali exeunte de capella de Slevele soluta abbati et conv. de Albyland, p. a. xxiijs.

Summa vj*l.* vijs. Disallocatur quousque ostenderit — . . . a cancellario et consilio curiæ Augmentationum.

Salaria capellanorum. Et in salario curati capellæ sive ecclesiæ de Hexham dicto monasterio pertinentis ibidem iiijli. Et in salario unius capellani servientis curam animarum infra capellam S. Johannis ibidem, p. a. iiijli. Et in salaria unius capellani servientis curam animarum infra ecclesiam de Bengfeld, dicto monasterio pertinentem, p. a. iiijli. Et in salario unius capellani servientis curam animarum infra capellam de Slavele, p. a. iiijli. Et in salario unius capellani servientis curam animarum infra parochialem ecclesiam de Alandall, p. a. iiijli. *Summa* xxli.

Summa allocationum xxli. *Et respondere debet ultra clare de* ccix*l.* xiiijs. vjd.

Concordat cum rentali facto super dissolutione dicti nuper Prioratus, etc.

R. Hochonson, auditor.

GENERAL INDEX TO THE PREFACE,

VOLUME I.

C

D

E

T

Z

INDEX OF NAMES,

VOLUME II.

A

B

C

D

E

W

Y

Z

INDEX OF PLACES,

VOLUME II.

A

B

C

D

E

S

T

U

V

W

Y

ADDENDA ET CORRIGENDA.

VOL. I.

Preface, p. xxxi. Bede, iii., 13, mentions Acca being with Wilfrid when he was visiting Willibrord, and records a miracle of St. Oswald which Acca described. There is a short account of Acca in Batavia Sacra, p. 47.

Preface, p. xxxvi, note *e*. There is some farther information on this point in Mr. Mac Lauchlan's memoir of his Survey of the Roman Wall.

Preface, p. xlix. A recent examination of the MS. of Simeon in the library of the University of Cambridge has shewn me that the word is *Hefresham,* not *Hexesham.* My conjecture, therefore, about Tilred falls to the ground.

Preface, p. lxxviii, line 1. Dele "*And a few years after Gray's decease, we find the same monarch making an annual present to the canons of two casks of red wine.*"

Preface, p. cxx. The reviewer of Vol. I. in The Churchman has added another name to my list of Augustinian scholars,—Walter Hilton, of Thurgarton.

Preface, p. clvii, line 21. Dele "*He tells us that pope Eugenius would as soon have become an Arian as disobey St. Bernard.*"

Preface, p. clx. Henry, Prior of Hexham, witnesses a deed between archbishop Giffard and William Swinburn about common of pasture at Staworth, etc., circa 1275 (Hodgson's Northumberland, iii., part ii., 374, 443-4).

Preface, p. clxiv. The following document has been omitted :—"Willelmus, etc. Inter discretum virum magistrum Guillelmum dictum Comyn de Buchan, cancellarium ecclesiæ Glasguensis, ex parte una, et dominos Henricum de Bellomonte, Thomam Grahi et Johannem de Kyngeston, milites, Ricardum de Insula et Martinum de Candelis, laicos Dunelmensis et Sancti Andreæ diocesios, ex altera, judex unicus a sede Apostolica delegatus, venerabili patri domino. . . . Dei gratia Sancti Andreæ episcopo, dilectis filiis. . . . Priori de Hextildesham ordinis Sancti Augustini, et . . . archidiacono Cliveland in ecclesia nostra Ebor. salutem in Domino sempiternam. De vestræ providæ circumspectionis industria plenius confidentes, in causa quæ movetur seu moveri speratur inter partes memoratas, nobis a sede Apostolica, ut præmittitur, delegata, et cuilibet vestrum in solidum, cum canonicæ cohercionis potestate, vobis committimus vices nostras, donec eas duxerimus revocandas. In cujus rei testimonium sigillum nostrum præsentibus est appensum. Data apud Sanctum Symphorianum juxta Viennam, xv kalendas Februarii anno Domini, secundum cursum curiæ Romanæ, m° ccc° xij°, et pontificatus nostri sexto." (Reg. archiep. Greenfield, ii., 229 *a*.)

On April 26, 1318, Prior Whelpington was made warden or master of the hospital of St. Giles at Hexham (Reg. archiep. Melton, 400 *b*).

Preface, p. clxiv. In 1326, during the vacancy of the see of Whitherne, Thomas de Appleton, canon of Hexham, was made keeper of the spirituality of that see by the archbishop of York (Reg. Melton, 467 *b*).

Preface, p. clxxii. On Nov. 6, 1423, the king granted the custody of the see of York, on the death of archbishop Bowet, to Ralph Cromwell, Wm. Haryngton, Thomas Chaworth, and Walter Beauchamp, knights, the Prior of Hexham, Robert Rolleston, clerk, Roger Rolleston, Thomas Mayn, and Wm. Carnaby, bailiff of Hexham; Roger Rolleston and Mayn to be answerable (Acts and Ord. of the Privy Council, iii., 121).

Preface, p. clxxvii, line 20. For "Leschman's Priorate," read "Bywell's Priorate."

Preface, p. clxxviii. On March 30, 1499, John, bishop of Ross, suffragan of the bishop of Durham, ordained Edward Jay, acolyte, in a chapel on the south side of the nave in Durham cathedral (Reg. Fox, at Durham).

p. 13, note. I believe that the *atrium* is really the site of the church, or all within the enclosing wall.

p. 15, note. I am wrong in speaking of St. Mary's as the parish church of the town. *It* was in the monastery, and St. Mary's was only a chapel. See Preface to Vol. II., p. viii.

p. 35, note *o*. I have to thank Mr. W. Skene for a copy of a paper by him which is published among the Transactions of the Society of Antiquaries of Scotland, in which he tries to shew that Acca, during his retirement, was founding the see of St. Andrew's in Scotland. Mr. Skene makes out a very fair case, but of course positive proof is impossible. Curiously enough, there is a place called Herneshow close to St. Andrew's.

p. 60, note *a*. Strike out what is said about Henry III.

p. 91. Dele note *r*.

p. 151, line 4. Read "*quasi peccatum arriolandi reputavit repugnare, et quasi scelus idolatriæ nolle acquiescere,*" striking out note *f*. These words are taken from 1 Kings xv. 23. I am indebted to the reviewer in the Saturday Review for pointing out this absurd mistake.

Appendix, pp. ix, x. In charter No. VI. the following alterations must be made. For "*barononibus,*" read "*bareronibus.*" For *te*, read *tē*. For *portam*, read *portum*. After *menbra* insert T. It is quite possible that there are other inaccuracies in my version, as the charter is much defaced, and cannot easily be read. I am much indebted to Mr. Beamont, of Warrington, for the interest he has kindly taken in it.

Appendix, p. xiv, charter No. X. I believe that this deed refers not to Newbigging-by-the-Sea, but to Alnmouth, near Alnwick, which was called St. Waleric's, and which was in the Vescy fee. Mr. Tate has shewn this satisfactorily in his History of Alnwick, and I thank him for directing my attention to the subject.

Appendix, p. xvi, deed No. XII. The erroneous endorsement of the Inspeximus induced me to ascribe this grant to Henry III.; it should be Henry VI. I am obliged to Mr. C. H. Cooper, of Cambridge, for pointing this out to me. Strange to say, the date exactly corresponds with the year of the restoration of Henry III. The Inspeximus, dated May 22nd, "anno regni nostri septimo," may have been granted either by Henry VII. or Henry VIII., probably the latter monarch. It may be fairly assumed that this is the document shewn by the sub-prior at the rebellion of the canons in 1536 (Appendix, cxxix). It is merely a copy of that of Edward I. which is printed in Vol. II.

Appendix, p. cx, note *k*. Dele *Shakespere*.

VOL. II.

Preface, p. liii, note. For *one* annulet, read *three annulets*.

Preface, p. lxvii. Mr. Fairless has kindly given me some additional information about the "Ogle shrine." It did not stand upon a stone base, but was panelled with oak to the floor. The height was 7 feet 8 inches; the breadth 10 feet. From back to front 6 feet 6 inches, independent of a canopy above.

"Mr. Fairless had in his possession a massive gold ring, weighing 168 grains, which was found in a field near Corbridge. The hoop was divided into eight compartments, chased with interlaced and foliated ornament, resembling in character the sculptured decoration of the ancient crosses in the North. Some traces of enamel remained in the cavities of the work." It is now in the museum at Alnwick.

The most valuable account of the architecture of Hexham hitherto in print is that drawn up by Mr. Longstaffe, and printed in the Arch. Æl., *n. s.*, xvii, 150-9. I may also mention—

A Guide to the Abbey Church, etc., at Hexham. By Joseph Fairless. 8vo. Hexham: 1853.

Recollections of Recent Alterations in the Abbey Church of Hexham. By James Reed. 8vo. Bishopwearmouth: 1852.

Hexham Abbey Church. By F. R. Wilson. A valuable paper printed in the Ecclesiologist for December, 1862.

I have also been favoured with the loan of some beautiful drawings of the Priory church by Mr. Johnson.

In 1429, Roger Thornton, the wealthy Newcastle merchant, says in his will, "Item I wylle yat cccc marc whilk ye Priour and Covent Hexham awe me bee dispendet upon bygging of yeir kyrk, if yei wol make greable seurtez yat it shal soo be deuly doon." (Durham Wills, i., 79.) It is not easy now to say to what purpose this money, if used, was applied. Perhaps it was devoted to the woodwork.

In 1421, archbishop Bowet says in his will, "Item lego monasterio de Hexteldesham pro uno vestimento eidem monasterio emendo xli." (Test. Ebor., i., 399.) When that prelate died, his tenants in Hexhamshire owed him the large sum of £483 13s. 10d., the recovery of which was considered to be hopeless (ibid., iii., 81).

p. 6, line 28. For *appronata*, read *approuata*.

p. 42. On the Monday before the feast of St. Hilary, 1362, William de Kendale, the Prior, and the Convent of Hexham lease to Sir Wm. de Tyndale, knight, their lands and tenements in Heigham "quex jadys fuerent a Andr' de Tyndale, cosin mesme celuy mons[r] William, du terme de quarrant annes," paying 3s. 4d. per ann. Defaced seal of convent. (Misc. Doc. penes Dec. et Capit. Dunelm.)

p. 47, line 8 from foot. For iiijd., read iiijs. Line 7. For xxxiiij, read xxiiij.

p. 48, line 18. For *ville*, read *villa*.

p. 87, line 13. For fratre meo comite, read fratre meo, comite.

p. 116, line 1. For Mathfen, Est Nesebith, read Mathfen Est, Nesbith.

www.ingramcontent.com/pod-product-compliance
Lightning Source LLC
LaVergne TN
LVHW020230110826
845151LV00003B/875

* 9 7 8 1 4 2 5 5 3 1 1 3 3 *